# Contents

· · ·

Part Two: *a Career*

Part Three: *a Mom*

M y *whole life flashed before my eyes.* I've always been intrigued by this concept. Biologists explain this phenomenon as a byproduct of vision. They explain that how we see the world is really a series of still pictures produced by a process called persistence of vision. The brain takes a picture with each eye, stores the picture in the hippocampus and then compares the two pictures to create depth and peripheral vision. The process then begins again, repeating several times per second. Even more intriguing, while the brain is comparing these images, we are in a state of temporary blindness. Scientists believe that, as the brain begins to shut down, it is interrupted by one last surge of adrenaline that may cause these stored images to replay in rapid succession.

I've often wondered: If I were to recount my life visually, what would I see? What would my brain have stored for my life's review?

Through this book Joy took me closer to this experience than I cared to be. Her amazing ability to recount the order of events and to capture the sights, sounds and emotions of each breath made this part of my life flash before my eyes. I was back there, reliving every moment, and each word became more difficult to read. It was painful. Joy was telling *our* story. She had captured our emotions, and I wasn't sure I was ready to see it—and feel it— all over again.

We were two, young urban professionals—soon-to-be-parents— who had no clue how life was about to radically change.

While reading I found that Joy's relentless push for direct, honest expression made each successive chapter more difficult. I did not want to relive a past that had almost destroyed us. However, as I read on, I felt Joy's journey become different from mine, starting a path that was uniquely her own. And I discovered how she had survived our shared experiences by taking a path that only she could travel. And I learned from it.

I have always admired Joy's quest for justice and her search for truth. And I continue to admire her willingness to question everything and then bravely deliver a story exactly how she sees it. I have found during our 21 years of marriage that this relentless expression of truth both attracts and infuriates me—sometimes simultaneously. And yet I am thankful for every moment I've been privileged to experience life with her. She is my true soul mate.

Because of Joy this self-righteous choirboy has found sight through blindness. Without her influence I would have missed some of the most important pictures of life, and my life would have been much less without them.

Perhaps her boldness in telling our story will cause images of your life to interrupt your vision the way Stross' life interrupted mine that early Sunday morning in May of 1991. And if that happens, may you—like me—discover that persistence of vision can draw all that is important into sharper focus.

• • •

# Happy Birthday, Stross

• • •

Each May our neighbors emerge from their homes to groom flower beds. I stare at my previous year's attempt to connect with nature and reject any notion that pulling weeds is a spiritual endeavor.

If the weather is even remotely warm (to an Iowan, 50 degrees after a string of subfreezing days is hot) my husband, Mark, bounds outside like a puppy left near the door too long. He begins his outdoor adventures by sweeping out the garage and organizing its contents. The highlight of this activity is his inventory of the pretreated lumber and wood decking. If he finds enough, he will launch a campaign to justify adding on—for the fifth time—to the tree house in our backyard. For some reason, we manage to begin each year with a fresh supply of leftover decking.

The tree house is already a wonder. With 48 feet of ramps; a patio deck that's bordered by benches that seat 50 people; a climbing tower; and a caged, second-story loft that's attached to the tower by a bridge, the tree house dominates and defines our family's time outside. The tree house is decidedly more than a tree house. It symbolizes social equality and freedom for Stross, our oldest son, who can tear up and down its ramps at a speed that makes his wheelchair shake.

• • •

So when May arrives Stross and his brother, Skye, four years his junior, invent reasons to stay outside regardless if school is the next day. The countdown to summer has begun.

Something entirely more important happens each May, though. Stross turns another year older. After 16 years of his birthdays, I know what to expect. I know sometime that morning, amid the normal festivities of opening presents, dressing for school and discussing birthday treats, I'll find time to be alone to cry.

I look forward to these tears. Through them I relive my son's entire lifetime beginning with the traumatic day of his birth when I learned I'd be the mother of a child born with birth defects. Once the tears start, I'm ready for my annual motherhood performance review. With vulnerabilities exposed and raw emotions at the surface, I test my faith by inviting God to sweep in and meet me intimately just as he did on the first May 5th of Stross' life.

During our birthday time together, God and I review promises made and how they have been fulfilled. Together we cry about the realities of a life that seems overwhelming at times.

Stross has had 16 birthdays now. But it is his fifth birthday I recall best, for on that day I learned how subjective reality can be.

•  •  •

May 5, 1996, started as a hectic day, like many had since Skye arrived nine months before. My standard morning routine involved securing my youngest son into his infant seat and buckling my oldest son into position. After I picked up Stross' friend Anthony, the back seat of our blue Honda station wagon was full of boys—as it was every Monday, Wednesday and Friday. Yet this day wasn't like any other preschool day. This day was Stross' birthday, his golden birthday, according to my Grandma Delma, because he had become 5 on the 5th.

Stross knew he would get to wear a birthday crown with his

• • •

name and age on it. According to Happy Time Preschool tradition, Stross—the Birthday Boy—would be first in line for everything. He would choose the game at playtime and be the center of attention when "Happy Birthday" was sung just for him. Then after the song he would blow out five candles on the classroom's dinosaur-shaped, all-purpose cake; and every boy and girl would eat the sprinkle cupcakes he had helped me decorate the night before.

What more could a 5-year-old ask for?

Stross could barely contain his excitement as our station wagon moved into position behind the other mom and dad drivers in Happy Time's drop-off line. While two positions from the front, Stross began to call out to the teacher whose task it was to greet the children and insure each safely hopped out of the cars, pickups, or mini-vans that had brought them.

"It's my birthday," he chirped to her through the closed window. Anthony, Skye and I had heard this refrain three times during the last quarter mile of our morning drive.

"Today's my birthday."

When our car finally stopped in front of the long sidewalk that led to Happy Time's little red school building, Stross' body language told me in no uncertain terms to hurry up. He sat rigidly at attention wearing a smile that turned his cheeks into hard, plump mounds. Stross' arms bent at the elbows, his hands pointing forward while each fully extended finger individually wiggled in a fluctuating pattern. His shoulders pushed down making his neck appear longer and his jaw tight. Stross could not get out of the car fast enough; and since he could not physically get out of the car without my help, I worked quickly to match his animated state.

Fortunately for Stross our disembarking procedures were well rehearsed. Anthony quickly unbuckled himself, climbed out from his spot behind me, and headed for Happy Time's door. Stross had already unbuckled himself and nearly fell out as I opened his door. His legs caught on the seat in front of him, holding him in position.

Full-length leg braces and a walker were part of his regular school attire. They enabled my short-statured son to proudly stand eye-to-chin with his peers. Using them he could independently maneuver throughout his two and one-half hour school day. But with his mobility came a sense of confinement. Braces prevented Stross' legs from being in any position other than proper alignment. When he sat, Stross' feet had to be directly in front with his toes pointed at a rigid 90 degrees. His ankles, thighs and knees always formed parallel lines. The plastic, Velcro®, leather and metal braces that held his lower limbs were visible from the base of his shorts to the top of his shoes.

Stross grabbed his Aladdin school bag while I lifted him out of the car. He handed me the bag, then I set him in his walker and on a course for the door. A quick glance at Skye assured me he would wait cooperatively in his car seat until I returned for the treats.

Happy Time's sidewalk presented its usual hassles. Because it was constructed at the exact width of Stross' front walker wheels, any variance left or right meant a drop off into the soft grass. He had become adept at regaining his footing, and most days I only needed to help lift his front wheels back into place two or three times. Some days—depending on the weather, my mood and Stross' concentration level—the sidewalk seemed incredibly long. This day was one of those. Birthday eagerness caused a record number of side trips.

I hated the sidewalk more than ever this day.

Happy Time's doors also presented logistical nightmares. There was one step up to the first door. Stross could lift his front walker wheels, hike himself up into the entry and then pull his back wheels up to the same level. Simultaneously I needed to reach over his head to hold open the inside door, only four feet away, allowing the first door to fall shut on my backside. Sometimes either a teacher or another child, usually Anthony, acted as a door stop for us; but the hectic activities of morning drop-off often left Stross and me fending for ourselves.

A ledge at the threshold of the second door also required another lift-and-step combination. Once inside, both Stross and I relaxed a little with a familiar feeling of accomplishment.

After placing his school bag on his octopus-labeled hook, I left Stross propped inside his walker, wrestling with the task of hanging

...

up his coat. The rest of the 4- and 5-year-olds were either hanging their coats or busily playing with toys. The teachers clearly intended to occupy early arrivers while draining as much energy as possible before the school day officially began.

I also noticed the teachers had set their most popular indoor toy, a portable plastic slide with four rungs on its ladder, in the center of the room. I hated this colorful nuisance for an admittedly biased reason, the same reason I hated the room's elevated reading loft. These extra-special play areas were physically off-limits for my physically disabled son. If either Mark or I could spend the day assisting Stross, I was certain I'd hate them less. We often served as our son's legs and feet, especially Mark. We'd carted him on many pieces of playground equipment, taking pleasure in his obvious enjoyment. His laughter never failed to reward our efforts, and introducing new experiences assured us the opportunity to see his face brighten with a new awareness of the world we shared.

Of all the playground items he'd tried, slides were Stross' clear favorite. That's probably why I had such a visceral reaction to this one. We couldn't hang out at school with him to take him up and down this slide. He was growing up, and our goal to help him learn independence had crashed into our desire to help him fully experience the world. He could not independently slide down the Happy Time slide.

Ever since Stross began attending Happy Time, I had struggled to come to terms with that slide, an object that only 15 of the 16 kids in this class could use. I fought against the hurt I felt knowing that the left-out child was my son. The prospect that I'd ever successfully overcome my hurt and anger was dim. The school year was nearly over, and today I had more pressing matters. The sprinkle cupcakes and chocolate milk needed to be delivered.

As I jogged back up the sidewalk, I decided to shift into survival mode and protect the knot in my stomach with subdued, righteous anger. With goodies in hand, I cooed some mother-speak to Skye, hit a switch to lock all the car's doors and then shut the hatch.

The Happy Time doors were easier to negotiate now, even

with my left arm balancing a tray of cupcakes and my right hand clutching a gallon of milk and a grocery bag of Batman napkins, plates and paper cups. Mrs. Leland took the goodies off my hands, and I turned to locate Stross for our quick good-bye. After disposing of his coat, Stross maneuvered his walker over to stand at the base of Happy Time's portable, indoor slide to watch six other children frantically engaged in an activity he could not do. One after another, children were sliding down and then clambering into position for their next trip up the slide's ladder.

The instant I saw him, the reality of my life slammed into divine focus. I was ill-prepared for what I saw; I needed time to emotionally catch up—time to sort through what was true. I felt uneasy because what I saw did not conform to my perceptions about the world and how people in the world should be. I had emotionally protected myself from something I perceived as a threat to my son. Because the slide's existence hurt me, I assumed it hurt him as well. Because I preferred to avoid feelings and experiences that might hurt me, I assumed Stross reacted that way as well.

Swoosh. Down came Anders. Swoosh. There went Holly. Swoosh. There went Scott with Nate fast behind. Again and again they passed by while Stross, legs planted firmly and willingly in place, stood at the bottom and laughed his wonderful, infectious laugh. With each child's ride, Stross' laugh got a little louder, a little sillier and a little more joy-filled. If the emotion of joy had a face, it was his.

My son, who was unable to fully use his lower limbs because of life circumstances, was in the thick of it, face-to-face with an inanimate object I'd nearly allowed to consume me. Not only that, he had found a way to participate, experiencing the activity to its fullest.

I couldn't deny what I saw. Joy radiated from his face, undeniable joy. Stross' whole body emitted joy in its purest form while I held inside me a mix of rage and despair.

My stomach emptied into my heart, then lodged in my throat.

Going over to Stross, I leaned down to kiss him good-bye and forced out words that would assure him his dad and I would be back

• • •

in time to watch him blow out the candles and share his cupcakes. He was too busy laughing and enjoying the children's antics to acknowledge my departure.

By now Stross was nearly doubled over in laughter, tightly gripping the red handles of his shiny, metal walker so he wouldn't fall. The children, caught in the wake of his exuberance, began to slide faster and with greater drama. Stross rewarded their performances by accentuating his own mirth. His face, with eyes squinted and tears dancing in the rim, couldn't have worn a larger smile.

Tears brimmed my eyes as well. They threatened to fall even as the Happy Time doors closed behind me. The sidewalk blurred, and I struggled to get my keys in the car's door lock. Skye's head turned to follow me into my seat. He was safe and sound and content.

I was a mess.

I wasn't certain I could drive safely but decided I had to leave before being spotted by another mother or father. I'd risk my life before risking embarrassment or pity. Driving away while crying seemed a more rational act than sitting in a car to cry about a slide, especially since I wasn't fully certain why I was crying anyway.

My oldest son had turned 5 years old. He had lived to celebrate his fifth birthday. In spite of nine surgeries, a few hospitalizations unrelated to surgery, countless childhood illnesses, one broken bone and hundreds of trips to doctors and therapists, Stross had done it. He attained the magic age of kindergarten readiness.

Somehow that slide undermined all we'd accomplished together, boldly reminding me my son wasn't normal. No matter what therapy goals we'd achieved or medical milestones we'd crossed, my son could not do the simple, everyday things his peers could do.

My rage built with every house I drove past. It fought to get out of my body through my throat. I didn't want to scare Skye with audible sounds of anguish, so I silently screamed about what the slide represented while streams of tears cascaded down my cheeks.

Injustice, inequity, ignorance, contempt, apathy, insensitivity.

Damn that slide. That stupid, stupid slide. Banishment from Happy Time or destruction, that's what that slide deserved.

I was beyond angry, and to my horror, a portion of my anger was directed at Stross. Why didn't he hate that slide? Of all people, didn't he care? Couldn't he see the injustice? Didn't he feel as trapped by his life as I did? Didn't he hate the fact life was anything but fair?

If he didn't—if he couldn't—he should. What happened to him wasn't right.

Stross should have the right to slide down that stupid slide. He should be able to walk to the ladder, climb each rung, fling his legs out in front of him and throw himself haphazardly down it. A 5-year-old should be able to experience the thrill of sliding down a slide on his own, especially on his birthday.

The drive home from Happy Time Preschool took less than three minutes. My rage only lasted two. At some point I acknowledged my rage as renewed grief; and by the time I pulled into our driveway, anger had been replaced with something else, something inexplicably tied to Stross' face. I could not shake the image of Stross' face. It told me he had gone down the slide. In fact, he had gone down more than anyone else.

Stross, as only he could, had vicariously experienced the thrill of the slide. With every child that zoomed to the bottom, Stross had been there for the ride. He felt it, and if possible, enjoyed it even more than they had. He had not avoided the obstacle. Instead, he had stood at its base, taken in all the experience offered, and been rewarded with joy.

Stross' joy was undeniable, inescapable and transforming.

I had attempted to mask fresh grief with anger, and Stross, once again, had led me through the grief and anger to joy. He helped me process my pain.

Explaining how the transformation took place may never be possible. I believe I was unable to forget Stross' face that morning because its fullness was singed into my soul. Somehow his face, as it had thousands of times before, pointed me to the beauty that existed in that moment in spite of everything. Stross' face was my invitation to rid myself of emotions that threatened to consume me.

I was led to pure joy instead.

Manifested in Stross, joy became a unique combination of awe, elation and glee. The awe I felt was for a Creator who could fashion such an incredible human being. The elation I felt was for the taste of pure joy my son had served in celebration of his fifth birthday. The glee I felt was for the privilege of accompanying Stross on his life's journey. On that morning my tears, first shed in anger, frustration and self-pity, transformed into tears of silent gratitude.

And then I acknowledged a voice that seemed to speak directly to me, in tones that reverberated from deep within.

"Your son turned 5 years old today, Joy. I can help you be like him when you grow up."

I first encountered Stross' link to spiritual insights on May 5, 1991, the day he was born. Now each of his birthdays gives me a reason to keep the appointment I've made for my annual reality check.

As I've learned during the balance of each year, my most intense periods of learning are not reserved for birthdays alone. They have also come in doctors' offices, hospital rooms, classrooms, grocery stores, office hallways, shopping malls, church aisles and at my children's bedsides. I've also discovered the lessons arrive unannounced and usually are not welcome. They have uprooted my family, magnified the dynamics of my marriage and challenged my sense of self. But they have always resulted in joy—involuntarily so, but authentically real.

As I've grown, I've learned to appreciate others whose lives have given them "God vision" and "God ears." I've even grown to understand how my way of relating to the world through a prism of faith isn't a prerequisite for others' spiritual insights. And the way my life finds focus may not be how it happens for someone else, for I've witnessed others celebrating moments of enlightenment that have occurred outside my lens of faith. Therefore, the God of my faith might not be someone else's process to spiritual growth.

I understand that now.

But while my manner of interpreting life may differ from someone else's, I believe we share a multitude of things in common. In particular a human condition that has inherent processes for discovery such as understanding wrought by pain, renewal shaped by acceptance and rebirth born of tested faith.

Regardless of who we are or how we got where we are going, it seems we are each invited to follow a path of love that points to life.

I'm just deeply grateful for a love that connected me to the power I regard as my Creator—God—in a way I could never have comprehended before becoming a mother, especially Stross' mother. Welcoming him into my life has brought me insights I did not know I wanted and joy I did not know possible.

How I got to this point is my story, my *Involuntary Joy*.

After 16 years of life with Stross, I can hardly remember who I was before his birth except for what I captured in writing.

My last memory of life BS (before Stross) reflects innocence. The scene could have easily been taken from a family television drama. Mark is dressed in surgical scrubs and standing over my swollen belly. His eyebrows are raised in anticipation with the corners of his mouth barely containing his excitement. I peer over my burgeoning waistline and look at a fetal monitor racing in time to the rhythm of our baby's heartbeat. Our first child is about to be born.

I remember saying a silent prayer for strength and letting a private thought slip out.

"Sunday is a good day to be born," I said, proud of a hidden person who displayed an uncanny sense of timing. My pride grew more intense after he drew his first breath, after we learned the full scope of the gift we'd been given.

Until then I had not known, in any rational way, that the child who'd formed in my womb was mis-formed. I had no idea his life would be full of medicines, surgeries, daily therapies, insurance battles and anguish over inaccessible places. Neither could I have imagined the joy in which he'd live every moment of his waking life or how he'd be able to impact someone else's life simply by living out his.

Maybe if I had known, my more naive self would not have wanted to be his mother. If so, I'm glad I didn't know.

While I had already established a relationship with the God who created me, I had not fully comprehended how pervasive this relationship could be until Stross arrived and entwined my life with his. After he arrived, I sensed his soul was already more open to God's leading than mine. Many believe children arrive with a spiritual homing device unclogged by signals of a mortal world. By 26 years of age and without fully realizing it, I'd allowed a considerable amount of static to disrupt my own spiritual interface. So when life sent me a baby with special features, one with an undeniably pure connection to God, I latched on for dear life.

The succeeding years have been full of images and feelings—such a wide range of feelings. They arrive unannounced and are followed in rapid succession by things I can't speak of or explain. Yet on each of Stross' birthdays, I've come to the same conclusion: God continues to break into my life in countless ways offering to make sense out of all of it.

It's incredibly beautiful.

It's life—my life's story enhanced by my son's. And the best parts began the day of his birth.

• • •

*Part One*

## a Son

# Chapter 1

# Insidious Surprise

• • •

When I awoke the clock on my night table displayed 5:18 a.m. I tried to decide if I should pull myself out of bed to go to the bathroom for the fourth time that night or if I should push my bladder to capacity and attempt to sleep until the alarm sounded at 6 a.m. Our baby's sleep position—sprawled as if my abdomen were a hammock—had altered mine; and for several weeks, Mark had helped me prop my body with pillows so I could sleep—or at least attempt a soothing state of rest—while in a sitting position. My nocturnal perch left me tired, not refreshed.

As I headed to the bathroom I realized that although my due date remained two weeks away, it appeared my body—or perhaps the child inside my body—had decided I'd be a mother by the end of the day. I was uncommonly relieved. For eight months I'd been fighting back irrational, private fears—an insidious realization that something was wrong with my pregnancy. Today, it seemed, I would get to find out.

My hasty exit from bed had awakened Mark, who now rolled over to acknowledge my return to our bedroom.

"Morning," he said, offering a cautious, tired smile. His eyelids looked heavy. "Everything okay?"

"Umm," I hedged. "I think my water broke. At least, my body

seems to still be going to the bathroom even though I've quit."

I nervously smiled now. Mark's eyelids instantly lightened.

"What do you mean you think your water broke?" he asked, rising to sit at attention. "Are you sure?"

His questions sounded hopeful, yet I couldn't tell if he hoped my answer would affirm the imminent birth of our first child or cast doubt that anything life-changing might occur.

"Well, yes," I said, making the last word sound more decisive than the first. He didn't respond, so I continued.

"I've never had my water break before, but either it just broke or I can't stop peeing." Lying down or even sitting on the bed was no longer practical. My day had begun.

While I called my doctor's answering service, Mark threw some clothes on and began filling a suitcase we'd located the night before. Lamaze class had intended to enlighten and desensitize us to the rigors of labor and a vaginal birth. I had intended my previous night's reading on cesarean birth to accomplish a similar purpose. Our bedtime conversation still played in my head.

"Why did we think this was a good idea nine months ago?" I had asked Mark, feeling trapped by the tiny human inside and not enjoying the thought of delivery, regardless of the method. My question had been a veiled invitation to commiserate.

"I think because we wanted to have a baby, a little human that was part you and part me," he had responded, offering a patient look framed by kind eyes and a gentle smile.

"Yeah." I felt a little patronized. "But I don't think I like how it happens."

"Are you scared?" he had asked, not revealing whether or not he was.

"Not really. Just very willing to stay pregnant the rest of my life."

Mark laughed.

"I'm serious about that. That's exactly how I feel."

"I'm pretty sure you wouldn't like being pregnant forever, and I'm fairly certain the baby will come one way or another."

"I know. That's what scares me."

Now that labor had officially begun my emotional state was better defined. Our lazy Saturday night had given me a chance to reflect on my feelings and acknowledge that I was scared, but mostly about having a c-section. Our baby's transverse breech presentation had made it—basically—a foregone conclusion. Fortunately my fear of surgery was now tempered by a sense of comfort that had come from reconnecting with my husband hours before someone derived from a mixture of our genetic codes would redefine our lives.

Looking back, nothing else we could have done that night would have better prepared us for our child's birth. Most helpful was a full night of sleep that had begun shortly after our conversation ended. We had both felt uncommonly at ease.

In the morning, however, life intensified.

When we got to the hospital shortly after 6:15 a.m., the resident on call confirmed I had indeed broken my water—not only that, I had begun to dilate and was fully effaced. The nurse who had hooked me up to a fetal monitor then handed me a button with instructions to push it when I felt a contraction.

"It will help us determine how you are progressing," she said.

As soon as she left, I turned to Mark in confession.

"I can't tell when I'm having them, Mark. I can't."

"Well just hit the button when you think you are having them," he advised.

"Okay," I said, turning my attention inward and concentrating on what I felt. For several minutes I lay quiet, listening to our baby's steady heartbeat amplified by the monitor and pushing the button anytime I felt a twinge.

When our doctor returned, he attempted to feel the position of our baby, then ordered an X-ray to confirm our child's breech presentation and the subsequent need for a cesarean. The results told him what we already knew, so preparations for surgery began in earnest.

Occasionally a nurse entered the room to ask questions about my pregnancy and record the answers. She also took my blood pressure and marked it down. Mark, now covered by a white paper jumpsuit with a blue hair cap and blue shoe covers, studied the video camera we'd borrowed two days earlier. Since I wouldn't need his skills as a breathing coach, he gravitated to another task at which he excelled.

Mark quickly acquainted himself with the camera and began taping. He recorded me in the bed wearing my own special gown and blue cap. I nervously smiled for him and for posterity. Next he held the camera out to record a smiling image of himself.

Because shooting video was part of his job as a video producer for Younkers, an Iowa-based clothing retailer, holding the camera helped Mark calm his nerves. I watched him move through the room taking cutaway shots of things like signs on the door, the wall clock and the readings on the fetal monitor. Obviously Mark was producing a documentary about our soon-to-be-born.

"How many contractions do you think you've had?" he asked, setting the camera down and inspecting a long strip of paper that had steadily rolled from the monitor.

"I don't know. A few, I guess."

"This says you are having them every three minutes, and I don't think you've been pushing the button," he informed me.

"I have too. What do you mean?"

Somehow my husband, the same man who'd been a better Lamaze breather than me during our birthing classes, seemed to know more about contractions than I did. I looked to the clock and made mental calculations, certain I'd hit the button more than enough times. Mark studied the paper a few more seconds.

"Honey, you've had a bunch of contractions. You're just not marking them. Well, you are making marks, but not necessarily during the contractions."

He showed me the line of tiny mountains my body had created on the monitor's paper as proof and pointed to my misplaced indicators. For months I had worried about my ability to give birth and had wondered if I lacked a full measure of mothering inclinations. Now, it seemed, the fetal monitor provided clear evidence: My maternal instincts truly were lacking.

I grilled the next nurse who entered the room with questions about what contractions felt like. She offered her description and then assured me it didn't matter in my instance, because I would be in surgery soon anyway.

"Your cesarean will stop the contractions soon," she said.

I wasn't consoled. This was my opportunity to experience what millions of women had and would for generations to come. I could not be incompetent at this, not at tuning in to the most specialized function of the female anatomy. If I couldn't do that how well would I do at discerning all the other instinctive things expected of mothers?

Because Mark seemed more attuned to the task, I enlisted his assistance. I asked him to watch the monitor and then tell me when a contraction occurred. "Just until I catch on," I promised. And so when Mark said I was having one, I hit the button.

He and I noticed simultaneously how the skin on my belly tightened as a contraction began, outlining the form of my uterus and the baby it held.

"You can feel that," Mark said, stating the obvious.

"I've been having those for months," I said, brushing off his observation as inconsequential. "I don't think they count. My belly just gets really tight. I get them when I walk too fast at work too."

"Well, they correspond to the marks on this paper," he said with his own growing authority. "They must count now. When one of them starts, hit the button and we'll see."

Within seconds I realized biology had cheated Mark out of an experience at which he could have excelled. Embarrassed by my lack of feminine common sense, I began mentally reviewing what I'd read in my *What to Expect When You Are Expecting* book and soon became comfortable enough to release Mark from his post near the fetal monitor. He used the opportunity to leave the room in search of a snack to substitute for breakfast.

Sometime in the next half hour, Mark called my parents and his from the phone next to my bed. He informed each set of impending grandparents that we were headed for surgery and would call again soon to inform them about the gender and name of their newest grandchild. Both factors remained a surprise to them—and us.

A nurse came to insert a urinary catheter and talk me through what I could expect in the operating room. I assured her Mark and I were well prepared. Somehow I believed she would be impressed that we'd read about cesarean surgery the night before.

"Well, I'm sure that will come in handy," she politely intoned.

My doctor stopped by for another check. He seemed more awake now and anxious to deliver our baby, not because there was an urgent need—simply to get on with the rest of his day. As soon as the neonatologist arrived, he said, we would begin.

"A neonatologist?" I asked. "Is there something wrong?"

"No," he assured us. "It's standard procedure. Cesarean babies don't get the benefit of the birth canal to help clear their lungs, so sometimes they need a little help opening their airway to breathe.

"One good thing about cesarean babies, though," he said, sounding as though he was offering a consolation prize, "they come out with beautiful round heads that haven't been squeezed through the birth canal. I guess that lets them look cuter, sooner."

That sounded good to us. But we'd soon learn there were other things that could make a baby's head extremely round, and it had nothing to do with the mode of delivery.

We entered the operating room at 7:35 a.m. Mark entered the room with me, walking behind my gurney. Before he could get oriented, the anesthesiologist ushered him into a small room just off the operating room and pointed to a chair.

"Have a seat here while we get your wife situated," he said. "Sometimes we lose dads when they look at the needle."

"Oh, Mark will be okay," I called to them.

"Trust me on this," the anesthesiologist called back. "I think you want Dad with you later on for sure. It's best if he stayed here just in case."

I craned my neck and squinted my eyes in Mark's direction. He wore a resigned—even relieved—look and began fiddling with the video camera. I finally noticed how nervous he was. Self-consumed, I'd believed our pregnancy had only happened to me. In spite of biology, Mark would experience birth and in a way, it was worse for him. He hated feeling helpless, and on this day it was unavoidable. I didn't need a breathing coach, and he couldn't take video right now. Plus there was absolutely nothing he could do to free our child from my body. His role was to wait and watch.

"I'll see you soon, honey," I called out. The anesthesiologist shut the door to Mark's private waiting room and came to administer the anesthetic into my spine.

"He'll be back in here soon," the anesthesiologist said. "Let's get you going so you can meet your baby."

I liked this man. I wanted someone authoritative in charge of my breathing.

By the time Mark came back, I had lost feeling in my lower torso; a drape was positioned so only my head was visible. Because of my blue cap, Mark could only see me from my eyebrows to my chin. My arms lay strapped to the operating table, perpendicular to my body in a crucifixion-like pose. Such an open position shouldn't leave you feeling vulnerable, I thought.

Oh, but it does, I imagined Christ saying. It does. Your life jeopardized in turn for another's—what could be more vulnerable?

This unanticipated spiritual exchange seemed to heighten all my senses. I listened as the anesthesiologist placed his equipment about two feet from my right cheek. Periodically I felt him reach over to adjust medication levels in response to a monitor's beep.

"Do you need me to adjust your glasses?" Mark asked. I shook my head "no."

A flurry of nurses set out trays of instruments, and I noticed Mark avoided looking over the drape as he sat on a chair to the left of my head.

"Are you feeling any contractions?" asked the anesthesiologist.

"No," I said, and then added a confession. "You know, I couldn't really feel them before."

My doctor came close to the table as if to start.

"Well, can you feel that?" my doctor asked.

"A little," I said, trying not to think about whether he had just prodded me with his finger or poked me with a scalpel.

"Are you sure?" asked the anesthesiologist?

I wasn't. Part of me still believed I could find some way to hold back time. My whole body had become one huge sensory receptor. I had felt something but not a tactile sensation, more of a vague awareness that I had been touched. Because I couldn't sort through all I was feeling, this simple question had me stymied.

"Well, we can wait," he said, and stepped out of my view.

"How do you feel?" the anesthesiologist asked. "Are you warm enough?"

"Yes, but it feels like I'm going to roll off the table."

Only minutes earlier I had learned it's standard practice for cesarean patients to have their bodies slightly lifted on one side to aid their breathing. I had not liked the tilting sensation from the beginning and even less now that my senses were magnified.

"Am I sliding off?"

"I don't think so," the anesthesiologist said. My doctor, overhearing my comment, came back into view and glanced toward my torso. He shook his head side to side.

"Well, it feels like it," I gently retorted.

"Sometimes patients have that sensation," said the anesthesiologist, who stood from his stool just enough to reach over the drape and apparently do something literally behind my back. When he returned to his sitting position at the crown of my head, he asked, "How's that? Better?"

"I guess so." I couldn't tell if he had really adjusted anything or simply pretended to so I'd be appeased.

"It'll be okay." My statement was an attempt to convince myself.

Metaphorically, the off-balance sensation matched my mood. Someone was breathing for me; someone else had strapped me to a table so yet another someone else could cut open my body. The one person I considered my best friend, the man I trusted more than anyone in the world, stood helplessly by looking very scared.

I didn't like that either.

After another check for sensation, my doctor began. I comforted myself by thinking the worst would be over soon.

Mark remembered he'd brought the video camera into the operating room and wondered aloud why he had. He wanted to sit with me, not act like he was at work. My primary nurse volunteered to tape the birth for him—for us. I jumped at her offer. Mark wasn't as certain, unsure he'd want to watch what she would preserve on tape.

"I can tape it, then you can decide if you want to watch it later," she said. "You'll be surprised how fast things go."

I doubtfully hoped she was right.

Within minutes my doctor had informed us of the first incision then began a steady play-by-play of the surgery.

"I'll make certain you know when I start to pull the baby out, Dad," he said. "So you can look over the drape. "These breech babies like to show us their feet and backsides first, making us guess at their gender longer," he said as he moved various parts of my insides.

I could hear my doctor's voice above the messy sounds of body fluids being suctioned. He worked swiftly, with an air of confidence.

"You'll know if it's a boy or girl soon enough."

Every once in a while, I'd catch a glimpse of someone's eyes— bright and attentive, with corners lifted expectantly—peering from between his surgical mask and cap. The air grew thick. Obviously, the birth experience never got old for even the oldest medical veteran.

When my doctor called out a request, the response came quickly. Everyone appeared as eager to meet our child as we were.

"Here's a foot. Does Dad want to look?"

I turned my head toward Mark. He shook his head "no."

"Are you sure?" I asked. Mark nodded that he was sure.

I would have pulled down the drape if they had let me. While I felt no pain, I did feel my body jostling on the table in response to the doctor's effort to free our child. Mark, too, noticed the table move in response to the doctor's tugging and pulling.

"Here's the other foot," he called out. Mark couldn't help himself this time. He rose slightly to glance over the drape, then suddenly dropped back into place.

I searched Mark's face. Like the others, all I could see were his eyes. While the skin around them was pale, his pupils were dancing. I could tell he'd seen something remarkable. Mark didn't speak. It appeared he couldn't.

"It won't be long now," I said. Mark's eyes smiled back.

"So what do you think? Boy or girl?" the doctor asked.

"Girl," Mark said. He'd found his voice.

"Boy," I said, making our decision balanced.

Our doctor wasn't paying attention to our answers. I was vaguely aware, however, that the anesthesiologist—who couldn't help but overhear—was listening.

The hustle and bustle of the operating room gradually quieted even though the collective work pace increased. People's actions became more intense and deliberate. Our doctor hadn't announced the arrival of a body part in more than a minute. Surely, I thought, the baby must be out now. My body didn't feel as packed. Certainly someone must know the gender of our child.

"There we go," said the nurse with the video camera. She sounded like a mother telling her toddler the food was all gone.

". . . and the time is 8:08," she announced.

Mark and I looked at each other and smiled. We both had tears in our eyes.

"You're a mom," he said. "I love you."

He didn't rise to look over the curtain. His gazed stayed on me.

"I love you, too," I said. "You're a dad."

All sensations suspended in an awkward pause. Something didn't feel right. Two primary characters in this surgical room drama—Mark and I—were being ignored, and no one had talked directly about our baby yet. I kept looking at Mark.

"So is it a boy or girl?" I asked him, hoping he'd peer over the drape. Before Mark could summon the courage, the video nurse handed him the camera.

"I'd better give this back to you, Dad. It's time for me to help." She still sounded cheery, but more intentional.

Then someone I believed to be the neonatologist walked away from the operating table carrying his gloved arms extended. In his hands he held the body of our child. Using peripheral vision, I watched him set our baby on a table under a warming light. He worked swiftly, suctioning our baby's mouth and nose. Mark walked to the table to personally inspect our child.

"Boy or girl?" I asked again to anyone who would respond. The pinnacle of action seemed to have come and gone with less fanfare than I'd anticipated.

I heard someone ask my doctor, "It was a boy, right?"

"I think so. I believe it was a boy, yes."

My doctor's earlier excited banter about learning the gender of our child contributed to my confusion about his confusion. How could a doctor miss something that basic?

"A boy," he called over to the neonatologist, seeking clarification. "Right, doctor?"

"Yes, a boy," the neonatologist hastily yelled back as he continued to work. Mark confirmed his answer.

"Joy, it's a boy. We have a son," Mark sounded surprised, but extremely proud. "He's beautiful."

Faint squeaky sounds came from the table. I couldn't tell if they were artificial or human.

"A boy," said the video nurse with the pleasant voice. "I hope you have a boy's name picked out."

Mark sensed how alone I felt and came over.

"It's a boy, Joy, and he's beautiful," he said again. Mark sounded like a dad. He also sounded anxious. He brought the camera to his shoulder, walked back to our son and began shooting video.

"Is he breathing, Mark?"

I had not heard a cry yet. I wanted to hear one—and soon. I wanted it loud and lusty.

Mark partially blocked my view as he instinctively switched into the role of a videographer and began to watch events unfold through a lens.

"He's blue. He's not breathing, Joy." I heard concern in his voice.

"I know. I can tell."

"He is breathing," asserted the neonatologist, still suctioning our son's mouth and nose. "He's breathing." The last statement sounded like an afterthought. The neonatologist worked with distracted urgency.

In seconds the squeaks got louder, then became cries from the throat. Finally our son wailed from deep within. He sounded angry, and I was thrilled.

Mark began going back and forth between our son and me. He kept telling me how beautiful our son was and repeating things he'd told me before.

He'd say, "He was really blue, but he's breathing now."

And I'd say, "I know. I saw. That's supposed to be normal."

After a few more minutes of inspection, Mark would walk back to me to repeat more sentences.

"He's beautiful, Joy. He's beautiful."

"Of course," I'd say, wanting to draw those conclusions firsthand.

I found Mark's odd behavior unsettling, even annoying. I tried to discount it considering he'd never experienced becoming a father before. Plus I trusted that if he'd seen something I should know about, he would tell me, especially since I'd heard about the blue skin tone even after our son looked more fleshy pink.

I didn't take into account Mark's inability to process all that he had seen.

After the neonatologist wrapped our son in a warm, cotton blanket and a soft, cotton hat, he brought him to me. Our son was quiet now, peaceful, and his head was round, just like my doctor predicted.

"Look at your son," said the neonatologist. I tried to turn my head so I could see him even better. The neonatologist thought I was straining to touch him with my face because I wasn't free to use my hands. To help me, he pressed our son's cheek next to mine. It felt wonderful. It felt alive.

"Can I look again?" I asked, prompting the neonatologist to bring him into my line of sight.

My son was adorable. He held his tiny hands under his chin,

allowing me to see each finger. The cap and blanket hid everything but his face and hands, so I counted his fingers knowing I'd have to wait for the chance to count his toes. Each hand had five perfectly formed digits, 10 total—a perfect score.

The doctor lingered. He tolerated my examination, much longer than I'd imagined he would. During Lamaze we'd been told that babies were whisked off to the nursery where moms could meet them later. Because he was lingering I changed my mind about waiting for the toe count.

"He has 10 fingers. Does he have 10 toes?"

"Yes, yes," said the neonatologist, sounding kind yet distracted. His next words were a soft command. "Look at your baby."

His behavior caused apprehension. Why was he so insistent? Why did I need to look more? And, why must I examine him right then? Wouldn't I have a better opportunity later?

He held our son close to me for what felt like five minutes when it was actually less than one. My eyes scanned our son's face. Mark moved the blanket down so I had more baby to inspect. I could see our son's wrists.

"His fingers are blue," I said, sounding like Mark. I hoped my statement would lead to some sort of explanation. I wanted an answer, but I wasn't certain of the question.

"That's fine," he said, "That's normal. They'll be pink soon."

He'd said normal. Did that mean something wasn't normal?

I began to look for characteristics of Down syndrome then realized I had no idea what to look for. Our son appeared beautiful to me, but no one other than Mark acted like he agreed. I was worried. I needed to know more.

"Is he all right?" I probed, wanting to sound like the worried mom of a normal baby.

"No," he said, without hedging. "We must take him now, and your husband can go with him. We'll talk to you later."

"How much later?"

No one answered. Mark looked torn. He'd just heard he needed to go with our son, but he wanted to stay with me.

My doctor, still completing my surgery, spoke first.

"Go ahead and go with him," he told Mark. "We'll help you find Joy when she's out of surgery."

"Before you go," called out the kind nurse, "do you have a name for your son?"

Mark and I looked at each other, and together said, "Stross David." The name had recently gone to the top position on our list. We had not been certain about giving our child such a unique name until this moment. In this moment Stross David seemed perfect.

I offered its spelling while my nurse punched it into a small machine. Within minutes of Stross' birth this label maker had printed dozens of stickers used to identify all the gadgets and medicines that had become his. The labels acknowledged his status as one of this world's unique inhabitants.

Only minutes before I had hoped that the sense of foreboding I'd felt could be attributed to private speculation about my lack of maternal abilities. Instead my intuition proved prophetic, and only I had known. Now I even had evidence. Something had been wrong. My private mystery was now public.

With Mark and our son gone, a new sensation filled the space. In the silence of the operating room, I felt others worrying about how I was reacting or, perhaps, how I would react. In desperate need of direction, I looked to the one most skilled at alleviating pain—the kind anesthesiologist who had thoughtfully and gently placed warm blankets near my face to combat a wicked case of the shivers.

"Can you tell me what's going on?" I asked him.

He didn't answer immediately. I imagined him looking to my doctor for a nod of approval that signaled permission for him to answer. Perhaps the silence signified how difficult it was for him to find the right words.

"Have you ever heard of myelomeningocele?"

A random memory of the word "meninges" came to me from some type of science class. I remembered its definition had something to do with the nervous system or spine.

"No," I answered.

"Your son's spine has grown outside of his body, and he will probably be paralyzed from the waist down."

Paralyzed. I knew what that meant. People who are paralyzed cannot walk.

"Will it grow correctly after birth?" I asked him, choosing to focus on the first part of what I'd heard. My child had been born during an era of medical miracles. Premature babies matured outside the womb all the time. While not classified as premature, my son needed a miracle.

"No. They treat this by closing the spine surgically, and then he'll have a lifetime of therapy. He will need surgery as soon as possible," said the anesthesiologist.

"How soon?" I asked.

"They will probably try to schedule it today, don't you think so, doctor?" My surgeon responded with a distracted "yes."

I fell silent, hoping to absorb all I'd heard. The silence lasted only a moment. I desperately needed to know at least one more thing.

"What causes it?"

I knew I might not like the answer. I also knew my question might not have an answer. The anesthesiologist's response spoke directly to my deepest fear.

"They're not exactly sure what causes myelomeningocele," he said. "It happens during the very first weeks of pregnancy, probably before you knew you were pregnant. It was nothing you did."

Nothing I did—nothing I had done had caused this to my son. For now I would believe the information this man offered. He knew how to deaden pain.

I hoped someone as thoughtful was caring for Mark. I wanted to see him—to be with him. I wanted to touch him and feel he was real—that this moment was really happening to both of us. And I wanted to have Mark look at me again. I needed to verify something I thought I'd learned: that Mark's eyes looked like my son's.

• • •

# Chapter 2

# Becoming a Mom

• • •

M y surgery ended. As I left the operating room I realized that I had no idea when I would see either Mark or Stross—let alone together.

Instead of being taken into the multi-bed recovery area, attendants moved me into a private recovery room. Those attending me moved quickly, yet my mind operated on another frequency. While I was able to confidently reply to their questions in real-time, the confidential responses to my private thoughts felt sluggish.

The world simultaneously moved at two speeds: everyone else's and mine.

It wasn't that I mentally checked out. In fact the opposite was true. I had mentally checked in to a multitude of topics I had no business addressing—yet. It was as if the trickle of data my brain regularly processed had been increased to a torrent of information. Incredibly, my ability to comprehend remained the same even though my information processing system was overloaded, bogged by the volume of my thoughts.

One of the first thoughts I addressed: freaking out. I reassured myself that I felt no need for such a reaction. Fearing how selfish I'd feel if I allowed myself to become that kind of victim, I moved on. Next topic: making certain no one believed I was freaking out. I classified this goal as decidedly more difficult.

I was certain Mark wasn't freaking out. The last I'd seen him, he looked worried and anxious but not spooked. Confident we had made a parallel shift into parenthood, I addressed the topic of how to be supportive of Mark. Before he had left me in the operating room, he had turned to say a quick good-bye. The look on his face conveyed how he felt—torn by an emotional need to be in two places at the same time.

I wanted to tell him not to worry about me, that I would be fine physically and emotionally as long as I knew he was looking after the best interests of our son. Because I was sidelined, Mark's undivided attention was the best I could offer Stross. If Mark felt guilty or worried about me, then he—and therefore I—could not help my son.

Everyone else seemed to want Mark to be with me.

The nurse who took me into recovery promised—unsolicited—to let Mark know where I was. When the anesthesiologist came to check on me, he too volunteered to help Mark find me. Minutes later my doctor came bearing news that he'd been with Mark and our son. He said Mark was talking to our pediatrician and would be in as soon as he could.

When Mark and I finally saw each other again, about 30 minutes later, so much had changed. He looked scared, and I wanted to reassure him.

"How is Stross? He looked beautiful," I said, reiterating the content of our last conversation.

"Yes."

Mark did not immediately look at me. His movements were slow. Tentatively, he found my eyes. "He has an opening on his back."

"I know," I returned. "They told me. It will be okay."

My efforts to reassure him seemed to make him nervous; and his reaction shook my confidence. Perhaps I was confident only because I did not have the whole picture. I did not know everything the neonatologist had discovered. Mark struggled to tell me all the devastating information he'd learned.

He started with what I already knew: that the opening on Stross' back meant our son may never use his legs to stand, walk or run. Permanent paralysis, they had called it. I also knew he needed surgery and that performing surgery on a tiny baby born only hours earlier was risky. No one had told me it was risky before. I had just known.

Before Mark could choose the words for his next sentence, a nurse came to tell him our pediatrician wanted to talk to him again. I assumed this consultation would be related to the conversation I'd overheard in recovery. The words "surgery," "transfer" and "arrangements" had been used, and I thought I'd heard a nurse use our pediatrician's name.

"Our son needs you more than I do. Don't worry," I told Mark, assuring him I was fine and would be fine. "Really."

My recovery room nurse appeared to notice Mark's frustration over his conflicting loyalties for she promised to take "extra good care" of me. Mark then looked slightly released from his guilt. He had been with Stross. He had stood nearby while our son cried in angry confusion at people poking his body with sharp objects to test for sensation and shining bright lights into dark spaces to learn what may or may not have formed correctly. Mark had bonded with our son; with our son is where Mark most wanted to be.

"Just let me know what's going on after you talk," I said.

My nurse, attentive and thorough, provided a full explanation about my morphine drip and suggested guidelines for self-administering the medication. She peppered our conversation with phrases like "so much has happened" and "try to help you know what to expect about your recovery" and "not certain where your doctor wants us to move you."

This nurse seemed to know more than I did about "plans" and "arrangements." Unlike me, she'd left the room several times and had walked through the hubbub outside my door.

I decided to seek answers myself and began a line of questioning that—by intention—sounded innocent. I made certain my voice was soft and that my questions appeared curious, not clinical.

In response she told me that the surgery Stross needed had to be done at another hospital only a few blocks away. Plus, after our pediatrician got signed release forms from Mark, Stross would be transferred. Stross was to have his own ambulance, and a special team of caregivers from the other hospital was on their way to travel with him. She thought they'd arrange for the surgery to happen as soon as possible.

"I think your doctor is attempting to have you transferred as well," she finished.

Poor Mark. If Stross transferred and I didn't, he'd be even more torn. As things were, only a walk down a hallway separated the two most important people in his life. If I were to remain at this hospital while Stross received specialized care down the street, Mark would have even more internal conflict, and I'd feel even more detached. I was beginning to want a chance to test my maternal instincts, to see if I'd bonded with our son at all. But, I told myself, bonding was probably overrated anyway—it would happen—sometime soon. That's what I hoped to be true.

Even though I had not held my son, we shared an undeniable connection. Perhaps that was bonding. I understood the weight of my responsibility as his mother: to see he received the best care possible. Unfortunately my ability to do so had been circumvented. So had other things.

From the moment he breathed life, Stross became an overwhelming presence. Not only had my pregnancy ended, my illusions of motherhood had turned upside down. For all the uneasiness I'd felt during pregnancy, I'd never gone so far as to speculate about the kind of mother I'd be for a less-than-normal child; I'd never imagined being unable to hold the baby I bore.

Stross had not only modified my maternal function, he had usurped my position medically. I may have had a cesarean, but for everyone except my doctor and assigned nurses, Stross was our family's primary patient.

The upheaval arrived with a quirky familiarity, and I was lulled by a strange sense of calmness. Unlike Mark, an entire pregnancy had prepared me for this moment. For nearly nine months I had wondered what was wrong inside my body. Pregnancy itself had been

• • •

wonderful, but I had regularly stifled fears about the pregnancy's conclusion. I had not known what the fears related to—my own health or the baby's—I just knew I'd been afraid about something.

As a result of my uneasiness I goofed off during birthing class, refusing to practice breathing for labor. I'd told Mark I wouldn't need it since our baby wouldn't be born vaginally. My conclusion that I would need a cesarean had come months before our doctor presented the option. "You can't be so sure about that, Joy," Mark had cautioned me. But something had told me I could be sure.

I'd also refused a procedure called external version when my doctor offered it as a way to coax our baby into position. Instinct or intuition told me it wasn't a good idea for us. But when our baby appeared to disappear during a flurry of activity one night, I (and the labor nurse who witnessed the movement) took it as a sign our child was hunting for the birth canal. So at 34 weeks I reluctantly agreed to the procedure then secretly celebrated when it didn't work. Instinct or intuition told me our breech baby knew a cesarean delivery would be best.

Finally I'd spent hours wondering why our child was so quiet in my womb. Hiccups were often my only reassurance that a life lay hidden inside. Our child's lack of prenatal movement had been, perhaps, his greatest attempt to help prepare us for what was to come. His life had been so calm in utero that the events that had unfolded after his birth seemed to belong to an otherworldly existence.

But a sense of assurance lived at the center of the upheaval, for I had been right. Stross' birth marked my emancipation from my most central fear—that I'd been irrationally fearful while pregnant. His uncommon condition validated my feelings.

During pregnancy it had been easy to rationalize why I had fear: My first pregnancy had ended in miscarriage. That experience 10 months before Stross' birth had caused me to doubt my body's ability to carry a child. Yet after Stross' birth it seemed clear that my uneasiness foreshadowed his arrival. I heard myself thinking, "Ah, ha. But of course," and the thought re-instilled a confidence I'd not realized as lacking.

Stross would forever be my first child but not my first pregnancy. I'd come of maternal age nearly one year earlier. Something had not felt right then either. No matter how hard I'd tried, I could not imagine having that child. I had wanted to believe a baby—*that* baby—would be, but I had been apprehensive then too—mostly that I would never have a baby—especially *that* baby.

The opening sentence of a journal I kept while pregnant the first time reads: "I have a difficult time believing I'm pregnant." And the last journal entry foreshadowed that pregnancy's outcome: "I can't help but be anxious about the health of this little 'critter.'"

I'd attributed those feelings to watching a coworker and his wife experience a miscarriage. Their loss had justified my fears. But when I'd mentioned my fears to other women—especially women who were mothers—they had brushed my feelings aside as the jitters of a first-time mom. I had never mentioned those fears to Mark, deciding it was in his best interest to sit out my private dance of fear.

It was bad enough he'd had to endure my hormonally induced mood swings. One day I'd be thrilled about becoming a mother and nearly ready to believe I had a life growing inside. The next day I was an anxious, emotional mess. Nothing was as I dreamed it would be. There had been no inner glow, no thoughts of nursery patterns and baby names and no sense of oneness with my child. I had wanted to believe in the promise of life, but believing I'd be a mother someday seemed the most difficult thing of all.

A few weeks after my coworker's miscarriage, I walked down the street with a friend from work, a new mother herself. We talked about the other couple's loss, and I cautiously confessed my feeling of emptiness, of my inability to believe that life—that anything really—was growing inside.

"That's normal," she assured me with the authority of a veteran. "You'll know it's real soon enough when that baby is keeping you awake at night kicking."

It won't be long now, she assured me.

Eleven weeks into my first pregnancy things did start to feel almost normal. I was resigned to the fact that pregnancy wasn't

• • •

going to be the same as I'd vicariously lived it before. So I wore my uneasiness proudly and comfortably since "that must be how pregnant women feel."

My body had acted pregnant. Mornings were spent near the toilet, my breasts ached, my pants were snug, and I had cravings—mainly for Wisconsin cheese curds. For a brief time parenthood looked promising. I had believed if anything were to happen, it would have happened before I'd attained this level of comfort. I could see the second trimester on my desk calendar, yet one nagging fact remained. The doctor had not heard a heartbeat.

Then on July 11, 1990, I became a woman who'd had a miscarriage.

That day I'd left work in a hurry in order to get to church early. Typically a Wednesday night meant directing the youth choir in rehearsal and leading a Bible study on a topic like dating or friendship or God's grace. Mark and I worked as a team in this part-time job that helped us afford our urban professional lifestyle.

This Wednesday, no youth activities were scheduled, only the church's monthly business meeting, which meant I had a report to type. So I slid my tiny, but growing tummy under the secretary's desk feeling, for the first time, like I might have a glow.

I wore no maternity clothes yet—just an outfit that was loose enough for strangers to wonder. Only one pair of summer slacks fit comfortably, white ones that always showed any speck of food or dirt accumulated during the day. Mark was working late shooting video on location somewhere, so I indulged in baby conversations with anyone who asked how I was feeling. I welcomed every diversion.

"Yes. My clothes are getting tighter."

"Well, the morning sickness disappeared last week."

"Yeah, it's beginning to sink in. I guess. I've never been pregnant before."

"Yes, Mark will be an incredible dad."

Ten minutes into my typing-talking phase, I felt a warm gush. My first thoughts were of embarrassment about stained white pants, not of loss of life. I had not worried like a protective mother-to-be.

Instead I tingled with raw anticipation. Something had gone wrong just as I'd known it would.

Miscarriage.

It was real. I could believe it, and as it began to happen, I felt myself relax into it even as my heart began to beat faster. I felt my breaths coming slow and deep as parts of my body began to contradict themselves.

A quick trip to the bathroom confirmed my diagnosis, and I shook uncontrollably, feeling very alone as I sat in the dark bathroom stall. Questions raced in my mind, but only questions about me, not about any baby who may or may not be fighting for life.

How was I to act now that my body had betrayed me? Should I just wipe everything away and walk into the hall as if nothing life-changing was happening?

One, maybe two full minutes went by as I held my forehead on my knees thinking. I had felt fine moments before, but I wasn't fine. I'd thought I wanted someone to come find me, the right someone—a woman who would notice what was wrong just by looking at my face. She could then assure me that I had overreacted. I needed a woman who had been where I was headed and knew what to say. But as busy as our church was that evening, no one came in. So I breathed a prayer for guidance, lifted my forehead, straightened my clothes, took a deep breath and stepped beyond the bathroom door.

This, without a doubt, had been the beginning of some end. Only years later would I reinterpret that day as the preface to a greater beginning, for I'd faintly acknowledged a voice I recognized as God—not as coherently as I would in years to come—but clearly and directly: "Get down the road. There is much in store for you, so let's be on with it."

My crying waited for rushed good-byes to the church staff and reassurances to them that: Yes, I could drive home. Yes, I could locate Mark. Yes, I would keep them posted. Yes, I knew spotting could be a normal part of pregnancy. Then I'd headed out the door and toward the reality I'd unconsciously expected.

What I'd neglected to tell them was something I felt deep

within, deeper than I'd ever felt before. I didn't tell them what I, in fact, knew: I was a woman having a miscarriage.

The next day I stared at an ultrasound screen realizing what the technician couldn't—wouldn't—tell me. My amniotic sac contained nothing of importance. No embryo, no fetus, no baby—just a tiny spot, a speck really, where I'd assumed a baby should have been.

I glanced at Mark to make a quick assessment of his emotional state and realized that he, too, had made a similar diagnosis.

"What is that?" I asked the technician pointing to a dark watery sac the size of a quarter. I'd wanted to hear her say "an empty amniotic sac."

"That is your amniotic sac," she dutifully replied, offering no information about its contents, lacking or otherwise.

I didn't ask the next obvious question: Where was the baby? Instead I let my inquiry float, unspoken. I needed no official verification.

As the technician finished, she swiped her gooey wand across my abdomen, wiped up her trail with a handful of tissues and then left Mark and me to our private thoughts.

I looked to Mark.

"There's nothing in there," I said.

I'd spoken about my body as if it belonged to somebody else. In a sense, it had. The only problem was, the person who'd inhabited it was no longer there. She, or he, had stopped growing a few days after conception. A blighted ovum, we'd been told, a condition that sounded more like a plague than a pregnancy gone wrong.

"Mark. I'm having a miscarriage."

My spoken thoughts broke the silence. My words acknowledged that what had begun remained incomplete. The end of that pregnancy would fully come hours later—only after a doctor surgically scraped away something that had hardly been there in the first place.

"I know," Mark said and touched my hand. His smile conveyed love mixed with pain, and his eyes betrayed his heart. I felt stunned by his ability to look at me and express empathy without speaking. He managed to say "I love you" and "I hurt for you" through softened eyelids and the down-turned corners of his mouth.

"I'm a woman who has had a miscarriage," I blurted in a matter-of-fact tone. "That's who I am now."

My announcement sounded almost like a warning. It was as if I felt the need to reintroduce myself to Mark. Sort of, "Hey, I'm your wife, but there is something you really need to know about me. I have had a miscarriage, and I'm not sure what that means about me or our future."

In that instance I'd redefined who I was. I was human, which meant I was susceptible to human afflictions, human pain. I had a body that could betray me. Until then I had not realized how superhuman I believed myself to be.

That was the first day Mark's and my future became different than what I had imagined it to be. The miscarriage made all coming moments unpredictable. In the darkened ultrasound room, there was only Mark and me and my empty womb.

"We are a long way from Carvers," I told him.

He offered a half smile and squeezed my hand.

"A long way," he agreed.

Carvers Restaurant had been our Camelot, the magical location of our first meeting and subsequent courtship. Every Friday and Saturday night during our junior year of college, we donned tuxedo aprons and sang our way into each others' hearts as singing waiters. No matter how many dined in the restaurant's Chalet Room those glorious evenings, I could always count on one pair of eyes to lock on mine across a finely laden sea of glassware and candlelight. Mark and I had not cared that our infatuation was obvious. We were intrigued with each other and excited about our newfound friendship.

At Carvers I'd never seen pain in Mark's eyes. But sitting in the exam room where we learned of our miscarriage, I could see his pain—feel it even. Had it been possible, I'd have transported us back to the place where our dreams had essentially begun—back to a time when he was the tenor with a huge smile, and I was the flirtatious alto who always managed to be near him when a song required a male partner.

Had we been able to go back then, perhaps we could have navigated away from the place we found ourselves on the day of Stross' birth. For if a miscarriage could turn Carvers into a faraway land of distant memories, perhaps Stross' birth would cloak all our happy times in a fog dense enough to obscure a lifetime of happiness.

But our earliest connections couldn't be so easily dismissed. As friends and then as a dating couple, we had wrestled with big topics, drawing energy from impassioned conversations that bordered on debates. Day after day we'd offered important topics to each other for full examination: our families—his spiritually conservative, mine politically active; our manner of addressing conflict—his silent avoidance, mine loud confrontation; and our concept of spirituality—his an exclusive relationship that defined a means to an end, mine an open relationship that invited definition.

When our dating turned into an engagement, we also discussed career aspirations—his connected to the music and audio industries, mine on a path to a corporate vice presidency; our desire for children—his a family of four, mine a family of two; and our regard for marriage—for us both, a partnership.

Our courtship had laid the groundwork for our relationship, just as our miscarriage had prepared us for the extraordinary circumstances of Stross' birth. I could tell we remained partners and that Mark's pain and fear were catching up to mine.

I'd written off my earlier fears as oddities of pregnancy—like a baby who rarely kicked in utero. In fact, our baby—Stross—had been unresponsive even when Mark or I attempted to jostle him into a reaction. His unresponsiveness while in my womb had haunted me—and now I knew why.

Now I knew why my baby—Stross—had laid quietly in my womb for hours at a time, never moving or shifting positions. A paralyzed baby cannot kick against its mother's womb.

I'd learned one more important thing: I could carry a baby to term. I had given birth to a living, breathing son.

• • •

# Chapter 3

# Hold On

• • •

Nurses buzzed around checking my vital signs and bringing warm towels for my shivers. The violent, uncontrollable shaking had subsided but no matter how many thermal blankets the nurses packed around my chest and arms, my body trembled. Fighting my cold sensations became a team effort. Anything I asked for or about was met with an immediate, kind response.

When I wondered aloud about the number of nurses assigned to help Stross and me, the nurse closest to my bed said no other babies had been born at this hospital this particular Sunday morning. She said word had filtered through the ward, and everyone who had been moved by our family's situation came to help as he or she could. Only after my own discharge would I learn that myelomeningocele babies are born about once in every 1,000 births. Our son was a rarity in these nurses' careers, and they, too, wondered what would come next.

After an attempt to call our insurance company, my doctor decided to transfer me along with my son even though it was not medically necessary. Had it been a weekday, the insurance company would have answered its phone and, most likely, denied my doctor's request. The hospital we'd chosen for Stross' birth could care for me—just not accommodate his surgical needs.

My doctor seemed pleased he could play the Well-I-Tried-to-Call-for-Authorization game on our behalf. He, as well as Mark and I, understood our new family needed to stay together. The nurses were pleased, too, and hurried to prepare me for transfer. One nurse taped a sheet together as a pillow so I could hold it against my incision on the short ride to the other hospital.

"We don't want that ride to be any more uncomfortable than necessary," she said.

I'd watched her take extra care making my custom cushion and could tell she was genuinely worried. Whether her concern was for my physical pain or my emotional pain, I couldn't tell.

"We don't normally transfer moms this early," she said, sort of distracted, then added, "but I'm glad you'll get to be near your baby."

While Mark was out of the room, one of the nurses came to take my fingerprints for Stross' birth certificate. I had unknowingly swiped my forehead and cheek with dark ink, and Mark, back from his conversation with the pediatrician, stared at me with grave concern.

"Are you all right?" he asked, apparently trying to make sense of my blotchy coloring. "You don't look so good."

Actually I was surprisingly fine considering I had just become the mother of a child with birth defects and a series of life changing decisions had been made minutes apart.

I couldn't bring myself to use the term "handicapped" even in my mind. "Birth defects," "paralysis," "abnormalities"—surprisingly those terms held no stigma for me. This day I keenly disliked the term "handicapped," and no one had even used it in my presence. I wondered how I had regarded the word only a day earlier.

"I'm okay. Really," I told Mark and held out my hand to squeeze his. "How are you?"

He didn't answer directly.

"There's a bunch of stuff to tell you," he said.

Mark had been a constant presence at Stross' side as the neonatologist looked for evidence that helped make sense of our son's birth condition. Telling me what he had learned was the most difficult assignment he'd ever taken on. The first details he offered

· · ·

were a review for me, but Mark authenticated the information I'd been told by the anesthesiologist. He laboriously spoke, referring to a piece of paper with scribbles and a diagram written in someone else's handwriting. Because Mark began talking about Stross' spine, as the anesthesiologist had, I determined the gaping lesion on Stross' back was our son's most defining medical characteristic. The doctors had made it clear to Mark, as they had to me, this opening must be closed as soon as possible.

Mark's haltering voice spoke of his uneasiness about what he'd learned. In tentative tones, he continued to fill in my mental blanks. I had learned a surgery was needed; Mark was telling me why. But there was more to learn.

Stross had no anal opening—at least nothing workable. They called it an imperforate anus and scheduled an additional surgery to create a passage for waste. Mark said they wanted to create something called a colostomy. He understood that even this condition alone—no anus—was life threatening. Stross needed a way to get waste, or stool, out of his body as soon as possible. The longer we waited, the higher his chances of becoming toxic.

This was new information to me—another problem requiring another surgery.

"They are sure? About his anus, I mean. He really doesn't have one?" I asked. I had never heard of such a thing, and I was uncomfortable thinking about how we would share that information with family and friends.

"Yes. They have called surgeons," Mark said. "They are coming here. We'll get to meet them."

We both talked in short sentences that betrayed our staccato thinking. Our challenge was to deal with raw emotion while piecing together facts and accepting the information as it came.

Mark continued: Stross' head seemed relatively normal in size, but doctors worried its rounded shape may indicate hydrocephalus. They wanted to check to see if he'd need a surgery—sometime in the near future—for his brain. Later in the day we'd learn that hydrocephalus meant "fluid on the brain." We'd also learn hydrocephalus is a companion defect for 85 to 90 percent of those born with an open spine and, if left untreated, causes severe mental retardation and even death.

Doctors' names had been said aloud in the operating room along with instructions for them to be paged. I had listened, not realizing their connection to my son until now. My son, little more than one hour old, was scheduled for two surgeries, both to be performed the afternoon of his birth. The first would allow him to go to the bathroom; the second would close the opening in his spine. Unfortunately, fixing his anus was not a possibility at this time; fixing his spine would never be possible. The surgeries scheduled for that afternoon were necessary to simply keep him alive and give his body an opportunity to function relatively normal.

Already the word "normal" had taken on new meaning. The Stross I had met while he nestled in a blanket looked very normal, but evidently many things had been wrong. Mark said no part of Stross' body had gone unchecked. He told me how our pediatrician had joined the neonatologist on a quest to discover even more about our son. Mark, afraid they would withhold information, said he had stayed nearby during the examination even though they'd asked him to wait in another room. Mark had listened for both of us.

One discovery heightened Mark's interest: Stross' soft palate was high, but seemingly intact. Days later, during a hushed conversation in my hospital room, Mark shared his interpretation of this as good news. From what he'd learned in a college vocal pedagogy class, Mark believed this would allow our son more room to resonate as a vocalist. Yet something else abnormal inside our son's mouth Mark could not reason away. His uvula was split. Instead of one small piece of soft tissue hanging down at the top of his throat, our son had two.

The list of oddities continued. Mark told how they had noticed Stross' ears were slightly misshapen, at least one was, and his eyes seemed too slanty. I believed his eyes looked like Mark's. This trait—I believed—worked in our son's favor, not against him.

I pressed Mark for more details: Had he looked in and seen the palate also? What was the exact shape of the ear? (I had not noticed

• • •

it.) And which ear? Why was the shape of Stross' eyes a concern? And what about the tone of their voices? How had they delivered the information? I pushed Mark for content and context he did not have.

"Joy, I asked for brochures or something for you to read," he offered apologetically. "I knew you would want more information. He just wouldn't give me any. He said we weren't ready for it."

The "he" Mark referred to was our pediatrician. According to Mark, when he'd requested more information from our pediatrician, he'd told him that "in his experience, parents were too overwhelmed to fully comprehend the information they received," and that Mark and I "couldn't absorb it now."

Mark now smiled at me.

"I told him, he didn't know you."

Mark didn't mean his comment to sound like the understatement it was; however, I was intensely aware that Mark and I had only met our pediatrician once when we had interviewed him two weeks previous, and that I was not very good at first impressions.

Time and again I'd learn that someone I regarded as a friend or even a friendly acquaintance had needed time to make sense of a poor first impression. In a business situation I fared far better, but in a social situation—I had been told—I could come off as unnecessarily assertive, uncomfortably forthright and arrogantly self-confident.

Perhaps the pediatrician was still processing our prior meeting. I wished that he knew I tackled complications as an information processor.

As friends explained it, I had (and truthfully still have) a way of embracing a moment that can feel rather suffocating and self-consuming. I want to know so much, so fast that I disregard the fact that friendships and conversations thrive on reciprocity. It's not that I don't want to hear what others have to say. It's that I want to hear it so much that I want them to let down their barriers and get on with it. I'm more than ready to let them in and can't fully understand how such openness could ever be threatening or unappealing.

I could tell that Mark had attempted to become my bridge to our pediatrician, our primary source of information. Mark had managed to coax the doctor into scrawling an ink drawing of a hole in a spine, and he offered it to me now in lieu of a brochure.

Mark's tone of voice told me how desperately he wanted to appease my need for knowledge, and how disappointed he was to not have more to offer. The information he brought had come from a variety of sources, much of it gathered while eavesdropping on doctors' conversations.

"I'm sorry, honey," I said, feeling guilty about adding to Mark's obvious sense of inadequacy.

"I think they are looking for more things wrong," he said, continuing the report of all he had learned.

Evidently the crease lines in Stross' hands were different. Most people have two parallel lines in their palms and Stross, Mark said, only had one. According to the doctors, that characteristic alone wasn't earth shaking, but combined with the ears, the eyes, the palate and the more obvious birth defects, our son's doctors believed Stross' palms indicated even larger problems.

While listening to the surgeons confer with our pediatrician and the neonatologist, Mark said he had heard them mention probable chromosome abnormalities or some sort of rare syndrome. He paused, I assumed, to gauge how I well I had received this news. Until then I had been making appropriate verbal responses.

"They said if we were lucky, it would only be Downs."

Lucky? I thought. They used the word "lucky" in reference to Down syndrome?

"How do they know?" I asked, "I mean, for sure."

"I don't know," Mark said. We were both quiet for a while.

Stross' life condition had become unfathomable. I could not grasp the idea my child might be both mentally and physically disabled. I closed my eyes and produced silent groans deep inside my being. They formed a message to the Creator of the Universe that articulated unspoken desires. I could not pray in sentences. Instead pieces of thoughts and fragments of fears shaped what I wanted to say: God, not that. I can take one disabling condition but not both. Only one. Either one. Take away either the mental disability or the physical one.

I cannot be the mother of a child who has both. God, you take the rest. At least one. Change my son or transform me this instant.

Mark had been silent for several minutes. He looked exhausted, as if relaying the information had drained his life force.

Even though Stross' physical characteristics pointed to the probability of a chromosome abnormality, we learned a blood test was needed to verify it. Already blood had been drawn from our son's umbilical cord and sent to the Mayo Clinic in Rochester, Minnesota, a medical facility that would become comfortably familiar during his life. Unfortunately the information gleaned from this chromosome analysis would not come for more than a week.

Mark asked how I was feeling again. I interpreted his question as an inquiry about both my emotional and physical health. Before I answered, I reviewed all I'd learned: My baby had physical disabilities that could be seen. I understood their reality and even accepted them—just them.

I was fine, I assured him.

Had the anesthetic worn off? he asked.

Not yet, I returned.

My shivers were gone but, like Stross, I couldn't feel my feet. My mind entertained morbid thoughts. Perhaps the anesthesiologist had caused major damage to my spine when he'd inserted the needle and I, too, would be paralyzed.

My horrific thoughts were—oddly—a good sign. I was coping as I typically did by preparing for the worst things I could imagine. In spite of all the awful things Mark had told me, I could think of even worse.

Mark and I were now alone in the crowded room that was my holding pen. There was no clock, but a phone hung on the wall offering contact with the outside world.

"We should probably call our folks," I said. "Can you do that?"

Both my parents and Mark's knew I was having a cesarean. So did our pastor. We had called each prior to surgery, giddy with the knowledge we would become parents. Now we needed to call to let them know what kind of parents we were and what kind of grandparents they had become.

Mark looked at his watch. "My parents are probably in church," he said. "I'll try to catch yours "

He took our calling card from his wallet and the list of names and numbers I had prepared weeks earlier. Fumbling with the card and paper, he paused then closed his eyes. I was silent. Finally he opened his eyes, dialed and waited for an answer. Nothing.

"Joy, do you think they are already on the way?"

My parents' church service didn't begin for another hour, and Mom had sounded like she planned to stay near the phone. My mother was so excited about her first grandchild's impending birth that, if she had been home, I was certain the phone would have only rung once.

"Uhgh," I sighed an inhuman sound, unwilling to think about the consequences of my parents' spontaneous decision. I estimated their arrival time as less than four hours. "What should we do?"

"There is nothing we can do," he said. Mark actually looked relieved. "They'll find out when they get here."

"But they'll go to the wrong hospital."

"They'll find us."

"Well, please try your folks," I begged, knowing it was easier for him not to call.

"I'm certain they'll be in church, Joy."

"Try anyway," I insisted. I did not want two sets of unsuspecting grandparents arriving within hours of each other. I needed others to begin living through this with us, and I preferred to have them begin at a distance.

Mark took more slow, deep breaths then dialed again. This time he got an answer. It was his 17-year-old brother, Jason, his sleep disturbed by Mark's call.

"Hey, Jay, are Mom and Dad there?" I listened. It was my turn to breathe slowly.

"Yeah, I thought they might be at church...you sleeping in today?...You and Paul must have been out late last night."

I knew Mark hated small talk. Now he was using it to avoid

• • •

something he hated even more. Maybe Mark would just hang up. His mom and dad could tell Jason later, once we had located and then told them.

"Well, we had a little boy," Mark said with an unnatural lift in his voice.

"Yeah, thanks." Mark offered an uncomfortable chuckle in response to his brother's congratulations. "His name is Stross David, and he's 5 pounds and 10 ounces."

I had a lump in my throat and tears started to fill my eyes. Mark faced the phone as it hung on the wall, his sagging shoulders shaped a brave profile. I wanted to take the phone from him and finish the conversation myself.

"There are some problems," Mark continued, his voice faltering and cracking. I wondered if Jason could detect the anguish in his big brother's voice.

"He has an opening in his back and his legs are paralyzed. He needs surgery, but he won't be able to walk. He doesn't have an anus either. He needs surgery for that and his back."

Mark's explanation of what was wrong was confusing, even to me. He pressed on.

"Uh, well, he won't be able to go to the bathroom without the surgery. And, and he'll need a wheelchair when he gets older. He won't be able to walk or run or play baseball."

Baseball? The word constricted my heart. What did baseball have to do with anything? Had that really been part of Mark's dreams for fatherhood? He'd never told me. I wondered what else Mark longed to do as a father.

While Mark talked my thoughts wandered. His words had ignited old memories, and I reflected back on my days of T-ball and softball. I'd grown up on a ball field playing the sport with my father as my varsity coach. Of course Mark wanted to play ball with his child too. I began to envision ways he might refashion his baseball fantasy. I could see our son, an adorable little baby, wrapped in Mark's arms while his grandfather, the coach, tossed him a ball. Mark and my dad would help him learn to catch a ball then when he entered elementary, they could show him how to hit a ball off a batting tee from his wheelchair. Of course our son would play baseball. If it was important to Mark, it needed to happen.

I was too busy imagining Stross at play to listen to the rest of Mark's conversation. Instead my mind drifted into the future, speculating about life—his, mine, ours. I didn't get very far until I acknowledged something—or someone—affirming my dream of a full life for my son.

"Hang on," it told me. "It's gonna be one wild ride."

I recognized the message as God—present in the midst of upheaval—reassuring me that Mark and Stross and I were not alone. The encouragement brought hope for our family's future.

Mark hung up the phone and turned to me with silent man-tears streaming down his face. I cried, too.

"Mark," my voice was barely audible. He came to my side and took my hand in his. I wanted to tell him everything, to relay the promise I'd heard. Instead, like Mark, I spoke of baseball.

"There are a lot of ways to play baseball," I said. My throat muscles tightened as I fought through tears. I needed him to hear what I was really saying. I groped for words that would give him the hope he desperately needed. "So what if he won't be able to run the bases. He can hit a ball off a batting tee. He will play baseball, Mark, if we help him to. There are all kinds of ways to play baseball."

"I know," he said, head bowed and voice halting. "I really don't know why I said that. It just came out."

"Honey, I'm so sorry," I whispered. "I'm sorry."

"I know. Me, too," Mark said. We fell silent—tears becoming our means of communication.

A nurse entered the room to check my IV and soon left.

We didn't speak for several minutes, uncertain of what we were sorry about, but certain that we were sorry, very sorry. Perhaps our sorry—rather our sorrowfulness—was for our son and all the unknown obstacles he would face each day of his life. Perhaps we were sorry we did not fully understand what those were. Maybe we were just sorry for ourselves.

• • •

When our tears diminished I spoke first.

"I'm very glad we had a name ready when he was born. Have you noticed it is already written on everything?" Mark nodded. "And I'm very glad we named him Stross David."

Stross was the name of Mark's grandfather, his dad's dad, and David was Mark's dad. No question about it. He belonged to a family well equipped to love him and guide him through life, and it was a unique name for a child who already had shown how unique he was.

"It is a strong name with a heritage," I said. I wanted Mark to believe this ability to name our son was a hopeful sign for us. Mark smiled.

"Dad will be surprised," he said.

Surprised, yes, by so many things.

Mark wiped his face and cleared his throat.

"You know, I should probably call our church," he said. "Sunday school is about ready to start, and they will be wondering about us."

I agreed, thankful that Stross' surgeries would not start until afternoon making it possible for the members of our church to pray for him. I tried to imagine how the news would be received but couldn't. I had no idea what people would say or do or think, mainly because I wasn't sure how I would have reacted to news that a baby born to one of our friend's had arrived with birth defects. Now I'd never know that kind of innocence again.

Feeling still had not returned to the lower half of my body, but I was not as concerned as I had been. Surely, I thought, I'll be able to feel everything soon enough.

I rested and listened to Mark talk to our pastor on the phone. He sounded more in control this time, speaking in measured tones. A pair of nurses came into the room busy with tasks that let me know the ambulances would soon arrive. They told me about arrangements for Stross to be brought to my bedside before he left the hospital. After the medical team had him ready for transfer, one nurse said, I would be able to hold him. She was enthusiastic and the other woman seemed equally eager for this event to take place.

I wasn't certain how I felt. Stross' need for surgery had been explained with urgency, and surgical preparations had quickly been made. Why was there time for me to hold him? I assumed the nurses' collective insistence stemmed from the morbid reality Stross could die in surgery. Should he die, I imagined, they believed I might regret never having held my baby while he was alive.

It was a risk I was willing to take.

Thankfully those nurses matter-of-factly insisted I have the opportunity to meet my son face-to-face. Not holding him wasn't an option. Unfortunately the same opportunity was not offered to Mark.

After calling the church, Mark had returned to our son's bedside, now an isolette. Both of us felt Stross shouldn't be alone. We knew little about this child of ours, but our instinct to protect him was strong. Every few minutes Mark would leave to check on Stross then pop back into my private and dimly-lit recovery room to give me updates.

Mark said Stross slept comfortably when left alone but he let out loud cries, clearly irritated, whenever poked or repositioned. To calm him, Mark said, he would hold one of his tiny hands and stroke his dark hair—that is all he could reach through the isolette's portholes.

Having met Mark and Stross in intensive care, both the neurosurgeon and pediatric surgeon made separate visits to meet me in the close quarters of my recovery room. They were awkward meetings. I wanted to make a positive first impression but, lying flat on my back, I felt at a disadvantage.

I listened to their names and shook their hands but could not grasp the significant role each was to play in my son's life. I understood they were Stross' surgeons. I also understood why they were needed. Yet I could only focus on impressions, gleaning as much information as I could simply by assessing what they looked like, how they acted and what they said.

The neurosurgeon introduced himself first. He wore a colorful, knitted sweater—ornate in its design—and vaguely smelled of expensive cologne. He was short and emitted an air of high energy. He also acted slightly aloof which added validity to his chosen profession for he seemed like the kind of man who would only enjoy operating on important parts of the human body.

In the span of two minutes, he explained how Stross' exposed spine would be tucked into his body then protected by as much tissue and skin as he could pull over it. The risk of infection was high for this microscopic procedure, he said, and grew higher with each passing minute. It was good Stross would be in surgery soon.

The neurosurgeon left allowing us undivided time with the pediatric surgeon. He filled the door frame as he entered the room then came near my bed. I immediately noticed that he had kind eyes that shone from behind his eyeglasses. As he talked he regularly offered us a relaxed, wide smile. After shaking his hand, I could not believe that someone with such long fingers and large palms could operate on tiny babies.

He explained how he would create a colostomy for Stross by pulling out his large intestine and stitching it open on his abdomen. He told us that solid stool would be able to leave Stross' body through this opening and be caught in a pouch he'd wear tucked into his diaper. Because meconium, or excrement produced in utero, was already inside Stross, it was imperative the colostomy be created as soon as possible, he said. The goal was to keep him from becoming toxic from the waste products trapped in his body.

I asked how long the surgeries would take, and the pediatric surgeon estimated that Stross would be under anesthetic approximately five to six hours total. They would locate my room, he assured us, and either he or our pediatrician would keep Mark and me posted on how things were going.

Just then a small parade of nurses came to the door, escorts for Stross in his isolette. There was one to look after his IVs, one to push his special bed and its associated monitors and another to assist me with the awkward task of holding a baby while my body lay flat. Mark brought up the rear. Another nurse stuck her head in long enough to report that the ambulance crew was making its way to the maternity ward. We needed to be quick, she said, because Stross would leave soon. My ambulance had not arrived.

The pediatric surgeon stepped aside as Stross' motorcade parked at my bedside but he remained close enough to watch.

Our son had a network of IV lines and monitor leads attached to his small body. A mainline IV had been threaded through the stump of his umbilical cord, an effective entry point for medications and fluids. The lesion on his back was now covered with a special type of gauze coated in Vaseline, small protection against further damage or infections.

As the nurse lifted Stross out the mainline tubing caught and pulled on his tummy. He let out a yell. Suddenly awake Stross cried out in loud sounds of complaint and began to pull at the oxygen tube inserted into his nostrils. Instinctively Mark and I reached to pull his little hand down, scolding him simultaneously.

"Hey, little guy," Mark cooed, "You've got to leave that alone."

"No, no," I said gently, already proud of his coordinated efforts. "Don't pull that out."

The pediatric surgeon smiled and spoke some words I would reflect on the rest of the day.

"Boy, he is a tough little guy. He sure is making it known that he does not like all the things we are doing to him. He's a fighter."

With that our son's surgeon said good-bye and slipped out of the room.

A fighter—my son's doctor had admired his spirit. He had called Stross a fighter and he was. I had noticed that characteristic and believed Mark had too. We just had not used that word. I liked it: fighter.

Stross soon quieted in my arms, nestling between my breast and upper arm, seemingly oblivious to all that was about to happen. Someone offered to take our first family photo with the maternity ward's Polaroid. Mark leaned in close, and I attempted to position myself and Stross a little higher. We smiled for the camera and everyone in the room. We were a family.

In an instant the glow of his new life radiated into my being and his innocence communicated wisdom. We were surrounded by people and machines, yet Stross commanded an unearthly focus. It was as if he were inviting me to revel in the world as he knew it, fresh from the one who'd designed it. He reminded me that God holds up as perfection a newborn son awaiting surgery for a broken and imperfect body.

I wanted to find a way to tell him what I felt: How amazed I was about everything that had turned out so beautifully—tiny fingernails and tiny toenails, a little bitty nose set above adorably petite lips. I wanted him to know that I loved how the corners of his mouth expressed contentment at being held.

But so many were watching us. People who couldn't fully appreciate his beautiful hands—small yet strong like my Grandpa Fred's—or his tiny fingers, powerfully wrapped around mine while carrying part of me and part of Mark inside every cell that had formed them.

My heart called out to his: "Hold on, little baby. Hold on, my Stross."

I began to fear what I'd miss if he died. I wanted to see him fully grown and to learn what kind of mother—what kind of woman—he could help me become.

A nurse took Stross out of my arms and placed him into the artificial warmth of an incubator. He let out a cry of protest. Mark and I kissed, exchanged "I love yous" and said a hurried good-bye. Our son was being wheeled to the elevators and Mark had to go. Stross needed his father with him as he faced the first surgeries of his life.

•   •   •

# Chapter 4

# Helplessness

...

While I waited for my ambulance, Mark gathered our belongings, repacked them in our car and drove to the new hospital. He arrived through the emergency room entrance, and so would I only minutes after him. Stross and I had the benefit of medical escorts. Mark was on his own.

Because it was Sunday, Mark had to find his way to us through the emergency room, a difficult task because—according to the hospital's computers—neither Stross nor I had been admitted. While arguing with the woman at the admission desk about Stross' existence, Mark watched me being wheeled by on a gurney about 50 feet from where he stood. Stross had, unbeknownst to Mark, been taken to the neonatal intensive care unit (NICU) on the hospital's fourth floor.

My field of vision was limited to the ceiling tiles and wall hangings that outlined long corridors, so I didn't see Mark as I wheeled past. I was oblivious to everything except the conversation of the two men and one woman who were my attendants. One man carried our diaper bag, a gift from the previous hospital, which now doubled as a piece of luggage. Inside were Stross' birth certificate, a supply of free baby samples, postpartum medical supplies and items thought to be keepsakes that nurses from the first hospital had sent along.

One nurse had tucked in a slip of paper with a phone number I was to use if, as she said, "your new nurses don't treat you as well as you think they should." It was from my admitting nurse, the same woman who had taken the video of Stross' birth for us. As I'd left her care she promised to call me the next day to see how our family was doing. I appreciated her genuine concern and also the light humor of the ambulance crew. They made concerted efforts to include me in conversations about parenthood. Each had asked about Stross' name then shared stories of his or her own children in infancy. Burpings, dirty diapers, sleepless nights—all were ready diversions from the reality of my day. By engaging me in small talk, they unwittingly bridged my life to the standard version of parenthood. And because they shared stories about typical newborn experiences, I assumed they didn't know about the overwhelming obstacles my child would face.

In time I'd learn that they had no other way to include me in conversations about children other than talking to me as if my child were normal. Also in time I'd learn that even my coming normal experiences would make my contributions during future parenthood conversations feel counterfeit. It wouldn't be long before I'd learn that fitting in to conversations with parents of children without disabilities would require leaving out things I considered valuable or that daring to share the experiences I most treasured could stop a conversation cold and set me uncomfortably apart. I would forever be a different kind of parent because the child who had made me a parent was different.

Things were beginning to sink in, however. Twice during the half-mile ambulance ride, the crew had received instructions via radio to take me into NICU before going to my room. Stross was there, the message said, and they—whoever was sending the messages— wanted me to see Stross again before he went into surgery.

He really might die, I thought. That had to be the reason so many were concerned I see him before surgery. Where was Mark? I wondered. He needed to be with Stross too.

The elevator ride caused me to lose any orientation I might have had. A sign on the wall read "The Birthing Center." After a few tight

•••

turns, I was in a strangely lit area with windowed walls covered with bright blue mini-blinds and baby decorations. The room felt very warm but dark.

I noticed Stross, alone and asleep on one of the unit's open beds. Two nurses were nearby looking through a clipboard of papers—his chart, I assumed. The neonatologist had come to this hospital as well; so had our pediatrician. They stood near Stross engaged in what appeared to be a polite argument about his likely genetic prognosis.

I marveled at how many adults it took to care for one so small and helpless.

The man pushing my gurney figured out who Stross was and pushed me as close to his bed as possible. We weren't at the same height so I couldn't really see him, and the IV tubing kept me from freely using my right hand to reach over and touch him. After a little maneuvering by my driver, I reached over with my left hand and awkwardly touched his thigh, as he lay propped on his side. Stross jerked in surprise and scrunched his closed eyes.

"Leave me alone," he seemed to say. "If I just shut my eyes tight, you will all go away."

I wasn't sure where I wanted to be. I did not want Stross to be alone, but I was uncomfortable here. We were on display, being watched by the ambulance crew and the nurses in the unit. I was keenly aware that my facial expressions, how I touched him and the interest I showed in him as my son were all under scrutiny and open to interpretation by those now responsible for his care.

"Where is Mark?" I asked, keeping my hand on Stross' thigh.

"They just called from downstairs and said he was headed to the surgical waiting area. We are taking Stross there soon," said a nurse. She seemed seasoned and experienced. I wondered how many babies like Stross she had seen before.

"You will make sure Mark sees him?" I asked.

She assured me, and I knew Mark—determined and persistent—would find him even without her help. I was beginning to feel weary and very hot. The heater on Stross' bed added to the warmth of the room and soon became too much for me.

"Well, let's get you settled in your room," said my gurney driver.

I was glad he initiated my departure lest my desire to leave was misinterpreted.

As soon as I arrived in my room, the space crowded with nurses. They transferred me into bed, attached my IV to a monitor, examined my incision and took my vitals. I lay there, the consummate post-operative patient.

No one talked directly about Stross. Instead these nurses made general comments about the rough day I'd had, and "so sorry to hear what brought you to us." There were many references to my son's doctors, reassuring me that, "They'll take good care of your son."

It was time to cry now. Not the little tears I had allowed myself off and on in my little recovery room at the first hospital. It was time for big tears, tears that shook my aching abdomen and spoke of my sense of helplessness. Someone placed a box of tissues on my pillow, and I quietly wept.

I would learn later from Mark where he had found Stross: Our son had been the sole occupant of the pre-surgical holding area located on the lowest level of the hospital. The pre-surgical area was actually one large room sectioned into a dozen 8-foot by 10-foot white, curtained cubicles. After being escorted into Stross' cubicle, Mark and he were left alone while the pediatric surgeon, the neurosurgeon and the rest of the surgical team readied themselves.

Mark said he had watched Stross as he slept and stroked his hair, noticing how our son's serenity warmed an otherwise sterile environment. And Mark described looking at the curtained aisle, feeling as if the room spoke to his loneliness. Cubicle after cubicle was empty, and rows of white curtains slowly billowed with the changing currents of the hospital's cooling system. The vacant spaces moved as apparitions, Mark said, calling to him, and he took solace in their company.

Shortly after noon physical bodies dressed in white arrived to take Stross into surgery. A few words were exchanged, then Mark watched these attendants escort our sleeping son through a large set of double doors where the doctors we'd met earlier would correct what they could of Stross' congenital imperfections. One nurse had stayed behind to point Mark to the exit, and then she too passed through the doors leaving Mark to find his way to my room alone.

Stross was in surgery until 5:45 p.m. Mark and I spent the time in my room doing whatever seemed appropriate. He joined the nurses in attending to my needs; I joined with him in attempting to play host to those who came into my room.

My parents arrived first. As they entered the door I looked at their faces, unable to tell what, if anything, they knew. My father came to my bed, leaned down next to my face and kissed my cheek.

"We love you, Kiddo," he said. As he raised, I saw sadness in his eyes and knew that someone had told him. My mother began to cry as she, too, bent down to kiss my cheek and take my hand. She didn't speak. I was her firstborn child—the baby who had first ushered her into motherhood. She must feel as helpless as I do, I thought.

I wanted to speak, but I wasn't sure what to say. What I wanted was assurance of their solidarity. They were my parents—the people most responsible for shaping how I had learned to relate to others and for defining my earliest perceptions of life. On this day their definition of parenthood had been redefined as swiftly as my own. And while their love for me was not in question, I was aware their regard for me was being reformed. I needed to know who I was to them now. And regardless of who I had become or how I had transformed their concepts of parenthood, I wanted them to be proud.

"Did they tell you everything?" I asked.

My mother nodded in response to my question, and I began to cry, sorry that my parents had been cheated of experiencing the fullness of joy that should come with the birth of their first grandchild. Somehow I had failed them.

"I'm sorry," I said.

My mother cried more, still unable to speak, then sat in a chair keeping vigil.

Months later I'd learn that she sat at my bedside that day thankful that my life had not been jeopardized. That day she could not tell me of the horror she and my father had experienced at the first hospital when a nurse in the maternity ward had unknowingly misled them to believe I was the one whose life was in peril.

It felt good to have my parents near, but an indescribable chasm existed between us. I had ventured farther away from them, into uncharted territory. Their helplessness mimicked my own, yet inconceivable differences hampered our ability to relate. Conversation eluded us, and eventually crying subsided for us all.

My parents found common ground with others who began to arrive. As visitors entered my room, my parents rose to greet each one and began awkward conversations about the day's events. Our pastor arrived next followed by Mark's parents who were accompanied by his younger sister, Iris, and her husband, Joe.

After learning the size of our families and of our role as youth ministers at our church, hospital staff moved me to a larger, private room at the end of the hall. Room 403 was farther away from the NICU, the place that would become Stross' home. It was also farther from the Well Baby Nursery and the rooms that housed the moms of other babies.

Periodically the neonatologist or our pediatrician would come to give us updates on Stross. We learned which surgical procedures were underway and how he was doing. He was always "fine" or "stable." I wondered how quickly they would report back if that ever wasn't the case.

Every once in a while I'd look around the room, attempting to take in the magnitude of the scene. My thoughts came as torrents. I attempted to hold them back, yet my new reality was undeniable. I was in a room full of people trying to make sense out of life as they knew it—Mark and me included—and we, I believed, had the toughest jobs.

It was as if the assembled puzzle of our interlocking lives had been knocked off a table, and it was our job to piece it back together. Only now the puzzle's dimensions had radically changed and the image of the finished piece was unknown. In fact some of the pieces were even fully different than before.

Mark and I, it seemed, needed to start sorting through our

personal needs and desires; our spiritual assertions; our professional aspirations; our families' expectations; and our understanding of parental responsibilities so that everyone could better understand what to say and do. Basically we needed to reconstruct our identities as soon as possible. No one was telling us that. It was simply clear that the sooner we redefined who we were, the easier life would be for all of us.

I only wish I hadn't liked the previous puzzle so much. And I wish I could have better realized how cumbersome a well-developed ego can be when it's forced to begin a personal reconstruction.

Merely hours before I'd known exactly what I wanted out of life with fairly solid plans that defined ways to achieve them. Identity reformation had not been part of the picture. And maybe it didn't need to be now. Maybe I was getting ahead of myself. For now it was enough to realize I'd just given birth to my first child—a son named Stross who had some birth defects—and he was in surgery fighting for his life. Surely I couldn't be expected to do anything other than exist now anyway. This wasn't a good time to be defining or redefining anything.

Fresh tears formed and quietly spilled into nearly imperceptible streams. Mark's and my parents attempted small talk to pass the time. Mark's mom and dad had been to Des Moines to visit us the day before, and they joked that I should have had the courtesy to let them know I was about to go into labor so they could have stayed. I laughed in spite of the tears. We all laughed.

When conversation dwindled, my parents compared notes on who should be called on our side of the family and when. The decisions hinged on what should be said. Until the surgeries were over, no one was certain.

My parents then began making frequent trips out of the room, partly to make these numerous phone calls. I learned later that these trips had also been my mother's opportunities to sob. Outside the door of my room she would break down, releasing her grief—my nurses becoming my mother's caregivers as well.

At one point Mark's parents disappeared also. They left without much notice and were gone for over an hour. No one knew where they went, nor did anyone feel it appropriate to ask upon their return.

Joe and Iris took turns sitting by the window and helped each other stay occupied. Iris, a new mother herself, helped me sort through the contents of our diaper bag offering commentary on the quality of the baby samples and advice on postpartum care.

Our pastor, looking uncomfortable, remained with us regardless of who took a turn coming or going. He never led us in prayer, yet his physical presence provided a visible link to a community of friends we already counted on for support. Once during a lull in conversation he had told us about how he had led the congregation in prayer for us during worship that morning. We believed many in the congregation continued to think of us, awaiting news of Stross' surgical outcome.

About three hours after we'd been informed of the surgery's start, Stross' pediatric surgeon came to see us with news that the colostomy was complete. He reported that all had gone well and that the neurosurgeon had begun the procedure to close Stross' spine. Someone offered him a chair. He sat down and leaned back against the wall looking relaxed and relieved that his assignment was over.

The surgeon's calm demeanor wore off on Mark and me, leaving us hopeful. He told us our son was doing well under anesthesia. He also said that many babies are born in need of a colostomy each year, and our little fighter would be just fine. The doctor explained the decision he'd made to secure the lower half of Stross' colon in such a way that we could elect to undergo a repair someday and create an anus for him. That decision could not be made for many years, he told us. First we had to learn the extent of Stross' disabilities and how they might affect his sensation and ability to care for himself. Those conversations, he reminded us, were for another day.

We thanked him and asked how much longer it would be until Stross would be back in the NICU for recovery. He said Stross was probably halfway there. I looked at the clock on the wall and did some quick math. I calculated that, by the time Stross got out of surgery, he would have spent more than half of his life in an operating room.

Then it would only get better for him, I thought. It had to.

Our periodic updates increased with other doctors or nurses stopping in with news from Stross' surgical suite. Many of the updates supplied identical information. I sensed that some who had met our new family only that morning simply wanted an opportunity to commiserate with us. Their collective concern felt oddly reassuring.

On one of his visits with Mark and me, the neonatologist, the man who had met our son the same time we had that morning, paused after his report to take my hand in his. He started to say something and stopped with a catch in his throat. Instead of attempting again, he leaned down and gave me a quick hug. I heard his whispered, "Sorry, I'm so sorry," and then felt a tear hit my cheek. He grabbed a tissue from the box near my head and turned away, leaving the room.

One of my son's doctors was crying, I realized. Surely it took dire circumstances to make a neonatologist cry. Perhaps Stross was not doing as well as reported. Perhaps the updates had been bogus.

I started to cry again. No one else in the room had seen the doctor break down, yet there was no doubt he had. I had felt his tear on my dry cheek and watched him carry the tissue away. I attempted to release grief through more tears. There was nothing left to do now, it seemed, but to cry and wait.

Time wore slowly the rest of that afternoon except for the few eye-opening minutes of a visit from a family in our congregation. With our parents and Joe and Iris somewhere in the hospital and our pastor keeping vigil, Mark and I expected no one else, so when our pastor responded to a knock on my door, I thought it would be another nurse wanting my vitals or a doctor bringing a report on Stross. Instead I heard our pastor talking to Deb and Steve Davis. I was shocked that someone from church was here so soon, but of course, the Davises had a special reason for wanting to see us today. I knew them as The Family of the Handicapped Boy. They probably wanted to welcome us into their realm of life circumstances.

Our pastor asked permission on their behalf to visit with Mark and me. He told us that after learning about Stross at church that

• • •

morning, they felt compelled to come and see us in person. We certainly were not going to be rude and say no. After all, we had become like them. We were parents of a special son too. Of course our circumstances must be wildly different, I thought.

After two years of being in the same, small congregation, I had no idea why their son, Austin, wore leg braces or used a walker. Thinking he resembled a child from a telethon, I had decided 3-year-old Austin must have muscular dystrophy—at least he looked like the children on the telethon. I certainly had never asked Deb about it during small talk at church. That, I believed, would not have been appropriate.

Now here she was visiting me in the hospital, because I had a son born with some condition the doctors had called both myelomeningocele and meningomyelocele. Perhaps the doctors weren't even fully sure which he had. Some of them had even shortened the term to myelo. I had been able to remember that because it sounded like "my-low." Unfortunately no one had given me any brochures or books to read yet, and I wanted to be able to tell Deb what was wrong with my son. I hardly knew her, but it seemed my son's myelo meninges problem and her son's MD might be a little similar. Conversing about medical abnormalities was something to do other than think about Stross surviving surgery. I could certainly have a conversation with her—parent to parent.

Our pastor escorted Deb in first without Steve or Austin. She entered slowly and unassumingly. As she entered I heard her soft-spoken voice before I could see her face.

"Congratulations," she said. I could now see her wide smile and soft eyes behind large glasses. "You have a baby boy. How wonderful."

I had not expected that. In fact, no one had said that to either Mark or me yet. Her cheeriness was extremely welcome. I had given birth to a son. She acknowledged that, and it was wonderful.

"Uh, yes. Thank you," I said, too astonished to say anything else.

"I heard your son has spina bifida," she said.

Spina bifida? Of all the words the doctors had used to describe

Stross' medical condition, not one of them had said that. I had heard of that term before, but what we were told our son had sounded much worse.

"No," I told her. "That's not what they said."

Deb looked puzzled. "Oh?"

"They said it was my lo meninges or meninge my lo seal. Something like that. I think they are the same thing, though. He needed surgery to close his spine in. It was open."

My explanation of my own son's condition was as awkward as my understanding. In no way did I fully comprehend what he had or even know how the terms describing it were spelled. I did my best to repeat the pronunciations as I had heard them. I knew no one had said anything about spina bifida though.

I looked to Mark to see if he had a better grasp of the situation, hoping he would come to my rescue. He simply nodded in agreement and slightly shrugged one shoulder. Mark then resumed his role as host to Steve and young Austin who, after entering my room, had gone to sit in the windowsill. While Mark and Steve talked, Austin quietly looked through a stack of his favorite books. I wished our parents back into the room but to no avail. I wanted them to see Austin.

"Yes, myelomeningocele," Deb said. She spoke with quiet authority. How did she know?

Deb then smiled at me and, like a kind elementary school teacher, positively affirmed my knowledge while correcting my response. "Myelomeningocele is the medical description of spina bifida."

I was stunned. Why had no one said that to us in the past eight hours? Why had no one used the term "spina bifida"? I was slightly relieved because spina bifida somehow sounded a lot better.

"Really?" I asked, a little skeptical that she could know more about my son than I did. Maybe I was finally ready to hear it.

"Yes. That is what Austin has."

"Oh, really?" I was embarrassed now. "I guess I never knew that. I always assumed it was muscular dystrophy or something like that."

Something like that. I could hear how ignorant I sounded. Here was a woman who actually did know more about my son than I did, at least the technical stuff. Deb transformed before my eyes. She was a messenger from the side I was now on. She could fill me in on everything I needed to know, everything the doctors wouldn't tell me.

I stared at Austin now, content and patient as he sat looking through his books. Occasionally he asked a nearby grown up for help describing what was on the pages. What a great kid. I had always thought this brown-haired boy with big brown eyes was cute. Now he was adorable and outright amazing.

In a brief conversation only minutes long, Deb had told me more than the doctors had. She explained things we'd been told and foreshadowed things we might face in the near future. She cautioned us not to be discouraged by doctors' predictions and told about others in the Des Moines area who had children with spina bifida. There was even a state spina bifida group we could join. She offered more words of support and then left her phone number with a promise to call for updates on Stross' progress.

I was too busy watching Austin to hear everything she said. I would have a boy like him someday. How amazing.

Steve spoke a few encouraging words to me and Mark, and then told Deb it was probably time to go. Mark and I watched intently as Austin placed his hands on either side of his bottom, pivoted to align his feet with the floor, and plopped his braced legs down into his walker. He maneuvered around a hospital recliner and joined his mom and dad as they left our room together. Amazing. Austin had spina bifida: Austin from our church.

As they left the room, I expressed a silent note of thanks for the gift we had just been given.

• • •

# Chapter 5

# Identity

...

T he Davis' visit left hope in the room. However, my mother's noticeable anxiety kept her from feeling buoyed by the atmosphere. She had briefly met the Davises as they were leaving, only long enough to learn of their significance: They could serve as a point of reference for Mark and me in the days to come.

Unfortunately my mother—who had announced in previous months that she was to be called Nana and not Grandma Fran—had no such reference. I imagined she must be struggling with unfamiliar feelings related to her new role as Stross' Nana—and even with her redefined role as my mom.

I was only vaguely aware of my own emerging identity struggles.

Off and on during pregnancy I had wondered if I could analytically look at my mom as a way of forecasting the type of mother I'd become. I had decided it was impossible, for other factors seemed equally important, in particular: my father's impact, my idiosyncratic ambitions and Mark's growing influence. Still I couldn't deny that a woman's primary role model for motherhood was the woman who had mothered her. So what, if anything, did that mean for me?

My mother had become a mom when she was a 20-year-old college student, one month after her first wedding anniversary. Despite my unplanned existence both Mom and Dad completed

· · ·

their college degrees with honors—Dad on schedule; Mom a few years later. Both had studied to become teachers. Dad began his first teaching position shortly after my first birthday while Mom waited until my younger sister, Jill, and me had both entered school.

Based on what I had observed growing up, my mother's identity, I believed, was as a working mother—more specifically, a teacher. I knew she had looked forward to becoming a grandma; however, I was certain she had not imagined a grandmotherhood like this.

I know I had not imagined becoming the mother of a disabled child. And even though my mother had modeled becoming a stay-at-home mom, I had not chosen that identity for myself.

Would Stross' life circumstances demand that of me now?

I knew Deb Davis had continued to work full time after Austin's birth; I'd been led to believe it was for financial reasons. Mark and I had just bought our first home four months before in a nice West Des Moines neighborhood. We were probably facing financial difficulties now too. I wondered when we would know for certain.

Financial hardship or not, I wasn't prepared to contemplate leaving my job. I liked the work I did, the lifestyle it afforded us and colleagues who shared my sense of purpose. Besides I had only ever seen myself as a career woman, a working mom. And for a variety of reasons I was ill-prepared to think of myself any other way. Primarily because I had to feed the beast that was my ego.

My self-awareness required brutal honesty, and I knew I needed large quantities of affirmation to get through my days. Not only that, I wasn't afraid to go looking for it even if it meant wandering into a colleague's office in search of a compliment. Fortunately one good session of affirmation could keep me going for days; and because my tactics were fairly transparent, I believed my methods were easily tolerated. However, I often wondered if coworkers ever felt the need to coordinate their efforts: "Is it your day to tell Joy she's doing a good job or mine?"

Motherhood, as I understood it, was too solitary a job to meet my personal daily requirements. Becoming a mom had seemed manageable only because of Mark's implicit promise of support and our joint plan to secure day care. As I awaited the outcome of Stross' surgery I wondered if he would demand far more of me than I would be able to give.

Spoken conversation remained an activity for others in my room. I continued a silent vigil, quietly contemplating my future. I would need a safer place to express my angry grief and more time to sort through the implications of all that had happened.

Around six o'clock in the evening, a nurse came to tell us Stross was back in the NICU to begin his recovery. His surgeries were over, and we could go see him. Only 10 hours old, he had already survived so much. I wasn't certain I was ready to see a post-surgical Stross, but I knew I had to.

Both my parents and Mark's were eager to meet their new grandchild, a five-pound heavyweight who shared their collective genetic heritages, and Mark and I were to be their escorts. Joe and Iris joined our entourage as we headed en masse to the NICU entrance. Everyone washed his or her hands according to the ward's policy, and then Mark wheeled me to Stross' bedside. The grandparents politely followed.

There was Stross, asleep in a drugged stupor. A ventilator and suction tube came out of his mouth, now gaping open to accommodate the intrusion. A large amount of tape held his ventilation tube in position, covering both his cheeks and hiding the middle part of his face. His face itself was puffed from anesthetic and IV fluids, and no fewer than three electrodes were attached to various points of his midsection to monitor his respirations, heart rate and body temperature. Another line, attached with Velcro® to his tiny foot, kept track of the oxygen content in his blood.

The mainline IV they'd inserted into his belly button immediately after birth was still doing its work. A huge tongue depressor was now attached to it holding a fluid-filled syringe taped in an upright position. I assumed this was how the nurses administered his medication. I pondered the amount of pain medication a five-pound-ten-ounce baby could receive and how a nurse could determine if or when a baby needed such a dose.

Stross didn't really look in pain, but he looked far from comfortable. Mark started stroking Stross' hair. I reached out to touch my index finger in the palm of Stross' hand, wondering if he even knew I was there. Tiny fingers gently wrapped around mine as they had earlier that day. I started to cry. I loved how he felt.

"Hey, baby. Hi, Stross," I whispered, tears rolling down my cheeks. "How are you?"

The grandparents all drew closer, quietly inspecting our firstborn son. Joe and Iris remained farther back. Stross made an awkward yet dramatic first impression.

"Hey, little guy. Hey, buddy," said Mark, so tender and soft-spoken. "You've had a pretty tough day."

Leads and lines aside, the most noticeable change for us was the ostomy—a large, clear plastic pouch secured to his tiny abdomen. This would become our way to care for our son's bowel movements, at least until he was in grade school, if not for the rest of his life. It was difficult to know what to think.

After a while I asked Mark to help me stand. I wanted to lean over as close as I could. Since Stross recovered on his side, the incision that repaired his spinal outbreak was clearly visible. I peered over and saw a neat row of black stitches nearly five inches long lining his back. The lesion had been covered in gauze the first time I had seen him. Only Mark had viewed the bulging, bluish portion of spine that had protruded from the center of our son's back prior to surgery. The length of the incision told me how severe the outbreak had been.

Mark helped me to sit again. I felt warm and a little faint. Stross' nurse commented that the extreme warmth of the NICU was often too much for recovering moms, especially on the same day as their own surgery. She encouraged me to head back to my room without guilt. There was no need to worry about Stross tonight, she said. He was her only charge for the evening and, as such, would get her undivided attention. Besides he'd probably sleep all night, she said, then promised that I would get to see him with his eyes open the next morning.

As she talked I wiped a steady stream of tears from my puffy eyes.

There were other wet eyes, but no one else was noticeably crying.

I didn't want to leave just yet, so Mark compromised with the nurse by rolling my wheelchair back from the warmth of Stross' specialized bed. I fanned myself with the edge of my robe and took in the sterile details of Stross' surroundings. The room looked a lot different sitting up, not like it had when I'd lain on the ambulance's transfer gurney that morning.

My crying slowed. I noticed the grandmas had taken my position at Stross' side and each was stroking one of his tiny, motionless legs. My mother looked at me and smiled.

"I think I saw him move his leg, Joy," she said.

God, please spare me from this, I thought. What is she thinking? They said he wouldn't walk; we told her that. I can't deal with my mother's wishful delusions. She is the grandmother of a disabled child. Doesn't she know that?

Carolyn, Mark's mother, turned to me as well and joined her counterpart in subdued optimism.

"We're just going to keep praying that he'll be made whole, won't we Fran?"

Now Carolyn too. God, please make them stop.

Anger started to build inside me. I couldn't form thoughts that weren't bathed in anger. I wasn't angry with Stross or even about all the things related to him that I couldn't change. I was angry with them—it was much easier. Simpleton grandmas, I thought. This is their grandchild, my beautiful son. You better love him just as he is, future wheelchair and all.

I stopped crying.

"Mark, I need to go back to the room."

As we left the NICU, all four grandparents gathered even closer to Stross, quietly conversing and musing about their tiny offspring.

Mark and I entered Room 403 once again, and a radical thought came to mind. Perhaps Stross came into this world already whole, and we were the ones lacking. I wasn't about to wait or even ask for a miracle of physical healing. Prayers for acceptance seemed far more appropriate. My son already was perfect, and if I could arrive at such a conclusion, perhaps the grandmas could too. Maybe if we all held the same belief, I'd have no use for this brand of anger.

Ten hours had passed since Stross' birth. It felt like 10 years.

Earlier in the day I'd acknowledged receiving the promise of a wild ride, but I had not known what it meant. Now it was becoming clearer. I could imagine a life of chaos, struggle and uncertainty and how that kind of life could be tinged with a mixture of joy, pride and tested faith—certainly a wild way to live.

I believed the communication had included no prophetic message about healing. I'd been promised a lifetime that would be "one wild ride." Perhaps that meant my miracles would come in smaller moments—like receiving the ability to commune with the Creator through my son. I couldn't explain this to the grandmas. I couldn't even describe what I was experiencing or thinking to my husband—not yet.

Mark helped me back into bed and collapsed on a sofa against the far wall.

"Mark, they don't get it," I said. His body was slumped with the nape of his neck resting against the top edge of the sofa. His eyes were closed, even as he spoke.

"I know."

"They'd better love him just as he is." I sounded protective—even threatening.

"I know," said Mark, with a long, exasperated sigh. I could tell he held similar feelings about our mothers and I was relieved. I could also tell Mark didn't want to talk anymore.

I watched him as he rested and allowed myself to grieve over what we had lost: innocence, freedom and blissful ignorance about how difficult life can be. We no longer courted fast track dreams. We didn't even really know who we were anymore. But we—most certainly—were headed down a wild course with no opportunity to turn back.

• • •

# Chapter 6

# Rebound Pain

...

R ebound pain—that's what Mark and I felt knowing our family hurt for us—rebound pain. There is no way to comprehend the pain someone else feels for you, and it hurts to know that what has happened to you is incredibly hard on them. Without intention, without any direct cause or effect, circumstances that Mark and I had set in motion hurt each member of our family and shook each one's faith to the core. It was a pain that began with us, shot straight into them and then reflected back to us through facial expressions and silences.

We hurt, and they hurt for us—and they worried about what our pain would do to our marriage.

So did we.

Before Stross nothing had threatened our marriage. In fact a marital strife chart I'd once consulted in a woman's magazine had predicted our greatest known "stressors"—other than having a baby—still lay two years in the future when we would celebrate our seventh wedding anniversary (a stressor) two weeks after Mark turned 30 (a stressor for him, I'd still be the real 29). But that was before Stross. In the days immediately following Stross' birth, I kept an eye on my still-20-something husband for any sign he'd arrived at a crisis point two years ahead of schedule. He had every right to.

Life had just handed us a complete package of things that potentially cause divorce, and they all hinged on parenting a child born with disabilities. Financial strain, chronic medical issues and job upheaval had arrived without warning. Stress-related illnesses, insurance battles and relocation to a more accessible and affordable home conceivably loomed in our future. This was no time to ignore each other.

But we did.

The day after Stross' birth Mark maintained a vigil at Stross' bedside, spending hours at a time there. While Stross slept, Mark watched him. If Stross appeared to be in pain, Mark would ask the nurse when the next dose of pain medication was due. If it were too early for Stross to get medication, Mark would massage his arms and legs and stroke his hair to soothe him. Mark would also alert me if Stross had a wakeful period, and then help me navigate the long hallway to NICU for a visit.

While Mark dealt with our new life by becoming our son's primary caregiver, I began to take on the role of Stross' primary medical advocate and spent time reading the brochures and booklets about spina bifida and hydrocephalus that had finally arrived in my room. Nurses and visitors who were polite enough to listen became my private audience for monologues on these issues. Thinking aloud helped me deal with the day-to-day intrusions that altered our family's version of reality.

Our personal identity was no longer as Mark and Joy "The Couple" but Mark and Joy "The Couple with the Disabled Son." We spent our energy attempting to prepare for emotional intrusions and naturally fell into a divide-and-conquer collaborative relationship: Mark, the nurturer, and I, the nuts-and-bolts specialist. We recognized it happening, for it was how we had symbiotically functioned countless times before. There was no need to acknowledge our roles formally. We simply fell into them. And while we spent much of our time mentally separated even though physically together, each day brought opportunities to simultaneously surface from our escape methods in order to conquer what came next.

···

There were simple things like hearing a doctor's update or listening to a nurse instruct us how to care for our son. And there were more difficult things, such as signing treatment waivers and understanding what life would be like if our son did have something far worse than Down syndrome. The suspected genetic disorders were Trisomy 13 and Trisomy 17. If Stross had one of these his life could end before his first birthday.

The little maternity leave planning we'd done prior to Stross' birth involved Mark resuming work two days after our child's birth. Now he resented the need to return to a job that seemed meaningless in comparison to the life issues we were facing. His job didn't fundamentally change the world. Making videos to train sales associates so a company could earn more money selling clothes had little impact on our lives let alone anyone else's. The only value Mark found in his job now—only a day after our son's arrival—was the paycheck it generated to offset our mounting bills.

Not wanting to lose that security Mark called his boss and, based on the extenuating circumstances of Stross' birth, successfully obtained an indefinite unpaid leave. He didn't want to be at work if he didn't have to. His identity, he was learning, was no longer tied to his means of employment. He was a dad now, and he wanted to spend his days with our son. For Mark being a dad was less about supporting his son financially, and more about being his son's support. While Mark's boss had responded positively to his leave request, she had also issued a firm warning. Mark, she reminded, would need to return to work "soon" if he wanted to remain employed. Therein lay Mark's problem: if he wanted to return.

Mark had always perceived his job as a stepping-stone to something bigger, not an end in itself. Now it was unclear what might happen if he lost the job he didn't want anyway. The Friday before Stross' birth, he had been intent on biding time until he discovered a better way to change the world. Now he indicated suspicion that the world planned to change him instead.

All family members but my mom had gone back to their own homes. When she was at the hospital, she floated in and out of my room, dividing her time between my bedside and Stross'. My mom recognized—maybe even facilitated—Mark's and my need to be together. When we were alone in my hospital room, Mark and I simply existed together, and often we were sleeping or attempting sleep. Nurses kept reminding me that sleep would aid my recovery. But I didn't feel tired, not a normal kind of tired. So when they encouraged me to nap, Mark coaxed me into it by agreeing to nap also. I'd gladly do anything with Mark. Even though we couldn't be on the same bed or sofa, we could be together—almost like we had days earlier. If we both slept, we could suspend time. But if only one of us slept, the other was abandoned, forced to deal with our new life alone.

To help me sleep the nurses positioned my sore body so I could face Mark. Then they shut the shades, switched off the lights and left. Mark drifted to sleep swiftly. It took longer for me. Inactivity mixed with anxiety caused my mind to spin. In so many ways sleep represented a waste of time. It kept me from thinking about what my life had become, and there was a great deal to think about. Plus I disliked the mental ritual of waking up. Because I had not fully incorporated my son's life into my own, Stross did not exist in my dreams—not the first few days. Waking up meant reliving the revelation of Stross' birth.

The Monday after Stross' Sunday birth, a volunteer accidentally disturbed my afternoon nap by entering my room behind a pushcart jammed with balloons and floral arrangements. In the fuzzy first minutes of consciousness, I filled my lungs with an incredible aroma and believed I was in a flower shop. As I opened my eyes, she offered an apology about disturbing my nap. I fought to remember why I was in a hospital bed.

"You must be very popular," she said cheerily. "These are all for you. I just had to count them. There are 18!"

Mark rose to his feet and began assisting her with the task of finding space to unload her deliveries.

Eighteen? Why so many? Why was I getting flowers at all?

Balloons with blue bears and babies in blue blankets bore the news I needed to hear again: Congratulations! It's a Boy.

I'd given birth to a son. I was a mom. The bittersweet truth

...

came crashing back.

Naps continued to contradict the reality of my days, so I reluctantly slumbered, beginning each nap time the same. I'd stare at Mark, his tall frame extending the full length of the sofa. He slept like a little boy, with a blue and gray striped afghan he'd brought from home stretched from chin to toes. Mark's mother had knitted it for him as a child, and even though he had not used it during the first years of our marriage, he'd searched through our home specifically to bring it to the hospital. As he slept under it, I realized how different we were. Mark invited opportunities to escape; I avoided them. He escaped back to carefree times because life hurt too much now. I chose to stay in present reality because it hurt too much to consider the things life had taken away.

Sometimes I successfully avoided sleep altogether. I simply watched my husband and wondered what our future held. I wasn't the kind of woman who was supposed to bear babies with birth defects. I was the kind who believed I'd been gifted with the ability to make a significant difference in the world—a difference that had nothing to do with motherhood. Better still I'd found a talented husband who believed he could make an impact with me. So what were we supposed to do now that life had handed us a child that others might view as deformed?

"I love you," Mark told me one afternoon, fresh from a brief nap. "Don't ever leave me."

"Don't you leave me," I said, nearly pleading, "because I love you. I need you, Mark."

We both recognized how high the stakes had become. The value of our marriage—our life together and the team we had become—had increased exponentially. We couldn't accomplish anything we'd dreamed if we didn't stay together. Yet I had routinely taken our marriage for granted; Mark understood how naive my approach could be. A series of doomed dating relationships had left him scarred, and until he'd proposed marriage to me, he'd harbored a fear of abandonment and even divorce.

Prior to Stross' birth, Mark's fear had seemed irrational. His parents and grandparents enjoyed long, seemingly healthy marriages, and my own parents and grandparents had done the same. Divorce had not splintered either of our family trees. Still Mark had hesitated to propose marriage fearing the emotional upheaval of yet another ill-fated relationship.

Oddly enough, the fact that I wasn't the type Mark thought he would marry (a quiet, soft-spoken, Southern conservative female who could play the piano) worked in my favor. I—who could play no musical instrument—was loud, argumentative and passionately articulate about my differing (and comparatively liberal) beliefs. Mark sensed I had been placed in his life for a reason and believed God had provided signs that I was soul mate material. In particular, he reported regularly conversing with God about me in early morning hours—typically after lingering in my dorm room following a weekend dinner show at Carvers.

"Are you sure, God?" he'd ask into the darkness of his car. "This is the woman I'll marry? She's opinionated and incredibly assertive, and she's not what I thought my wife would be."

Mark claimed the answers to his questions had arrived in pieces—through lyrics of songs playing through his car's speakers and in free-flowing thoughts that arrived through prayer. Sometimes, he said, I had unwittingly provided answers in more abstract ways—like reluctantly agreeing to take cocktail orders for him so he could avoid feeling as if he'd facilitated sin.

On some level Mark was aware that if he were to change the world, he would need a partner capable of helping him accomplish his goals. He found me intelligent and adventuresome with a drive to succeed. He liked how I didn't shy away from conflict but confronted it head on. And, from somewhere deep within, I recognized that I needed a partner who could balance me too. Someone who could help me learn how to focus my drive for justice by transforming confrontational tactics into something productive. Mark excelled at that, and he happily took on the role as my life tutor in exchange for his own lessons.

A few weeks before Mark proposed, after he'd purchased my engagement ring but before he'd generated the nerve to present it, Mark sought a heart-to-heart conversation with his dad.

• • •

"How do you know you have found the right person to marry?" he'd asked.

Mark said his father had paused to think, then offered a response that sounds prophetic today: "When you think you've found a person who can take on anything that happens in life and still be with you—a person you can count on to work things out together."

Five years after our marriage began—on the first Sunday in May, "anything" had happened. We were no longer a couple, we were a family of three; the newest member of our family promised us a lifetime of "anythings." There was a great deal we three needed to work out together. Our families could only stand by—hurting—as they watched us deal with the "anythings" that had come our way. I wondered what both sets of parents felt about (or feared for) us, but I wasn't curious enough or ready to begin those conversations. They would have only brought more pain.

I was also reluctant to help others sort through their individual perceptions, spiritual references and life philosophies. The upheaval caused by Stross' arrival largely related to Mark and me and how we would deal with having a son like Stross. Where Stross was concerned, even family members were outsiders. Only Mark and I could fully understand our altered existence. In fact dealing with other people's reactions made me angry. I had no time for idiosyncrasies, misconceptions and stereotypes about disabilities. Others could waste time questioning God and praying for miracles. I had other things to figure out. I needed to decide what kind of mother I'd be.

Years of playing house and baby-sitting had given me rudimentary maternal skills. Yet I had become a different kind of mother and didn't want anyone in my way as I became the mom Stross needed me to be—no questioning my decisions, no analyzing my responses, no advising on issues—unless, of course, the questions, analysis and advice came from Mark. He was well acquainted with my emotional warfare having survived battles before. He understood that I dealt with pain by turning it into righteous anger, and that I wasn't good at identifying anger as pain.

My pattern—to turn pain into righteous anger—couldn't be

circumvented, it seemed. But perhaps what I did with it could be productive. Perhaps recognizing anger as pain, and even pain as grief, could be the first step. The process might enable me to transform grief into purpose, and I could share that with Mark. However, I was not open to sharing the process with anyone other than him and God.

Mark and God knew one other thing about me. I could now cry whenever and wherever the mood struck; I'd never been a crier before. Depending on the time or reason for the tears, others might catch a glimpse of my visible expression of sorrow. But I never vocalized the emotions. To do that risked breaking down my dam of resolve, threatening my ability to cope. My tears were my pain—my anger—on display. And, instead of sharing my feelings in words, I spoke proudly of Stross. After all Stross was the focus of my grief; therefore, focusing on him felt emotionally productive.

And so I began to understand the cycle: Tears of pain transformed into righteous anger that was offered to God. Each time the cycle began and ended with a son who deserved a really good mother. Through the process I experienced how suffering produces perseverance, perseverance produces character, character produces hope, and how hope did not disappoint. Stross became my hope compass—my way to rebound from the pain his birth caused.

During the first two days of Stross' life Mark and I waited for his physical recovery if not for his healing. During the waiting, his pain and ours mingled, silently acknowledged and shared through subtle gestures of our daily existence.

•    •    •

# Chapter 7

# Celebration of Motherhood

...

O n the first Wednesday of Stross' life, I was inducted into the sorority of motherhood. There was no official ceremony, and I did not receive a certificate or embossed pin. There was, however, an informal afternoon birthday party for my new son hosted in my hospital room by friends—Rita Pray and Cindy Canoy. They wanted to help me acknowledge a significant change in my life: I was someone's mom.

While Mark and I had spent extended periods of time with family members since Stross' birth, we had not had any lengthy visits from friends. After I had averted an attempt by the nurse supervisor to restrict my visitors to immediate family, she posted a sign on my door. It stated that visitors had to report to the nurses' station before entering. She had also instructed my family that my room door was to remain shut. I asked Mark to take the sign down and then attempted to tell her my door should remain open. I wanted to greet anybody who took the time to come see Mark and me. All visitors were welcomed company.

Her curt response: "You are a recovering surgical patient and a new mother with extenuating circumstances. You need time to be alone and plenty of rest."

Obviously she didn't know me any better than our pediatrician had. I needed to be with people—especially friends who were well versed in Joyisms. Just seeing them and interacting with them would let me know how little I had changed from the woman I was before Stross' birth, and I found that comforting. I may have become a mom, but I was still a very social Joy in need of attention.

Prior to that Wednesday, Mark and I had seized occasions to shower attention on Stross as well.

Since his birth Stross had only been fed intravenous fluids. These fluids had kept him hydrated and his electrolytes in balance. Because the creation of his ostomy was an intestinal surgery, his body needed time to heal before anything of substance passed through his digestive tract. Also Stross' doctors didn't want him using valuable energy learning how to drink—not from a bottle and especially not from the breast.

On Wednesday, May 8, three days after his birth and subsequent surgeries, Stross had his first opportunity to drink milk. While he'd take the easier bottle route, he would drink milk I had created, a personally astonishing feat. Where breast-feeding was concerned, I *was* a changed woman, and I'd come a long way in only a matter of days.

I had begun pumping breast milk the Sunday of Stross' birth. Prior to that, I had not really decided between breast-feeding or bottle-feeding. While breast-feeding was the method of choice among most of the mothers I knew, I had a good reason to depart from the path they'd chosen: I wanted to be a working mom.

All but one of the women I socialized with were mothers who'd had full-time careers before deciding to stay at home. I remained committed to my plan to return to work in eight weeks; therefore, I rationalized, breast-feeding would not be convenient. Plus the idea of a child sucking at my breasts was less than appealing—a view I shared with no one.

Intellectually, I wanted to be a breast-feeding mom. I believed all the messages telling me it was best for my baby. Still I lacked desire. In fact, in the hours after Stross' birth, I'd decided it might be time to formally develop an argument in support of bottle-feeding. Therefore, when nurses on two different shifts asked, "Do you plan to breast-

···

feed or use the bottle?" I offered a vague answer: "Well, Stross can't breast-feed now, and I don't want to put him through any stress."

Because I'd offered no simple breast-or-bottle answer, I received a gentle lecture about the benefits of breast-feeding and an explanation of how a breast pump could be used until Stross and I were able to get together.

Finally one of the veteran nurses simply brought a breast pump into my room and asked everyone to leave except Mark. She knew that amid all the unsettling events that comprised the day of Stross' birth, one basic issue needed to be resolved: How would this baby be fed once he could eat?

She chose a conversational tactic.

"Before he was born, what did you decide about how you wanted to feed your baby?" she asked with one hand on the breast pump. Mark listened attentively. He knew I had not committed to either method.

"I don't really know," I confessed. "I guess I haven't decided."

"How do you feel about breast-feeding?" She didn't wait for an answer. "It really is the best thing you can do for your son right now. I know you may not feel like there is much else you can do."

Her comment nailed it. Breast-feeding scared me; but on the day of my son's birth, not doing the best thing for him scared me more. She did not give me the permission to use formula that I may have looked for. Instead she sat by my bed with a machine that looked like it should be used in a dairy barn and offered me a chance to help my son get better. Basically, she made the decision for me, and I was all right with that. Evidently I needed to get pumping.

"Good, Joy. You are doing a good job," she said. "Just think about your baby, and let the milk come."

Let-down presented no problem. It was as if my breasts were permanently on. Thoughts of Stross were all I had in my head; therefore, once pumping started, milk flowed. Mark looked on in awe and fascination. The nurse made certain he learned how the pumped worked so he could help me the next time.

"Look at this, Joy," said the nurse. "See how it's yellow? It's the colostrum. This is pure gold for a baby—all that good stuff to help fight infections and build immunities. We'll make sure we mark this container well, so it will be the first milk your baby gets."

Her praise softened the awkwardness of a having a stranger handle my breasts. It also eased my uneasiness about breast-feeding. The rhythmic hum of the pump began to sound soothing and reassuring. She had uncovered my primary motivating factors—encouragement and affirmation—then used them to my son's benefit. I may have given birth to a baby with defects, but I could express milk like a professional.

Soon Mark took over the nurse's task of swelling my pride by privately dubbing me "The Pump Queen." While I feigned irritation over my new nickname, both he and I knew I loved it.

By Wednesday I was a veteran. Eight times a day I took my latest installment to the NICU refrigerator, placing it on a shelf next to the other mothers' milk.

Wednesday was my first chance to feed my milk to Stross. When Mark had been down to visit him that morning, Stross' nurse told him we should both plan to come around noon to feed him a bottle. She made a big deal about us coming for Stross' first feeding. About 11:45 a.m. we headed to the NICU nursery, eager to start. Mark carried our camera and the video recorder, so no moment could sneak by us.

The nurse had a tiny bottle warming in a bowl of water.

"He just woke up and is ready," she said. "He should do really well for you. He was eager to eat this morning."

I noticed the milk in the bottle looked whiter than my colostrum, so I asked if she had taken the wrong container out of the freezer.

"No, I fed him the colostrum this morning," she said. "I wanted to make certain he was ready. He did a great job."

After her set up about his first feeding, I was irritated to be playing second string; but those feelings dispersed as she passed Stross to me. She set his bottom onto the pillow propped in my lap and handed me the tiny bottle.

Stross' eyes stared at me, tiny dark eyes. I held his head cradled in my left hand, his feet against my tummy. Gingerly I offered the bottle as Mark recorded his first sucks on video. Stross gulped down the first

100 ml using some pretty hard swallows that made his eyelids squeeze together. Whenever that happened, I'd feel tempted to pull the bottle out, afraid he'd choke. His nurse instructed me to keep it in.

"Let him figure it out," she said. "Eating is a new sensation. He'll catch on."

Burping Stross was complicated since all the leads and IV tubing had to be accounted for whenever he was moved. His entire chest rested against the palm of my left hand; his entire upper back disappeared each time I tapped him with the palm of my right. I burped him high on his back to avoid the column of sutures that lined his spine.

Stross' first bottle was followed by another 100 ml, which he downed as well. After the last burp session, he snuggled in and fell asleep in my arms. I had wanted Mark to have an opportunity to feed him, too, but Stross was clearly worn out.

The prospect of me nursing my son was scarier now. I'd seen how fragile he was and the look of intensity in his eyes as he concentrated on the mechanics of eating, but he had learned quickly.

Stross had definitely locked onto me visually. During his feeding, he had either been deep in thought or extremely observant. A dark side of me wondered if I was romanticizing the blank, empty stare of a mentally retarded child. Until the tests came back, I would continue to wonder.

After the nurse placed Stross back into his isolette, she told Mark and me what a CT-scan of his brain, taken earlier in the day, had indicated. It confirmed that Stross had hydrocephalus—cerebral spinal fluid trapped inside the ventricles of his brain. We weren't totally surprised, since the doctors had warned us of its frequent occurrence in children with spina bifida. Yet the reality that he needed another surgery came as a shock.

Stross needed a shunt placed in his brain to drain the fluid. If he didn't get it, his brain would be crowded by the fluid and become impaired. That's how most spina bifida babies died prior to the 1960s, we were told. Their brains slowly lost function and shut down.

The surgery involved a neurosurgeon inserting a tube through the ventricles of Stross' brain so fluid could be diverted through a valve and down through tubing that ended in his abdomen. The doctor had scheduled surgery for Friday.

Surgery in two days was too much to think about. I focused instead on what had happened. We'd held our son and fed him a bottle of milk.

By the time Rita and Cindy arrived after lunch, I was proudly wearing my motherhood. They'd brought presents for Mark and me as well as for Stross, along with a birthday cake covered in baby decorations and a candle in the shape of a zero.

"We thought we could have a birthday party in honor of Stross," Rita said. "Even if he can't eat it yet, we can."

The party seemed a little silly, but I was glad they did it. Rita had two children, and Cindy had one. This marked the first time I would converse with them about my own child. I was one of them now. No matter what happened—whether my son lived or died—I was a mother. Stross had secured a spot for me in this sisterhood.

Mark had made himself scarce during their visit, choosing to spend male bonding time with Stross. When he returned to my room, he asked Rita and Cindy if they would stay with me while he took the roll of film we shot of Stross eating to the one-hour photo shop. They agreed, and we settled in for a session of girl talk.

We spent time looking at the few Polaroid pictures we had taken and talking about mom stuff. We shared what it felt like to hold your child instead of someone else's baby and discussed the advantages of breast milk. I told them about the past few days and volunteered how well I was doing with my version of pump-to-bottle breast-feeding. When they asked about our parents' reactions, I offered my perspective, as subjective as it was.

As Rita and Cindy listened, I sensed how they hung on every word and noticed their eyes grow moist. Then I began to cry as I spoke. My tears said what my words couldn't: I could never be like them. I never had been—nor would I ever be. I felt more pain than anger and more grief than pain, and I felt as if I'd lost the opportunity to have something they cherished even if I didn't know what it was.

• • •

But the awareness of some unknown loss confused me. I'd not fashioned a traditional concept of motherhood anyway. So what had I really lost?

Maybe, simply, the freedom of unlimited dreams. Or the freedom to dream with the limited parameters of a human mind.

I continued to tell to them about previous days events with fresh tears brimming my eyes. My voice remained measured and controlled, and I felt my thoughts becoming more analytical than my words or moist eyes conveyed. It wasn't just the breast-feeding and career choices that were different for me. My stories about my newborn were different too. Being different was my destiny. I would always be a different kind of mother, and not in a way others found desirable.

I didn't want pity over the injustice of my or my son's differing life circumstances, just genuine empathy. And that's what Rita and Cindy offered: empathy, a gift of friendship. And they also helped me practice a new way of presenting myself to the world. I didn't have to provide right answers or present only the best of what I had to offer. I could simply share what I had—broken parts and all. In fact, sharing the broken parts might even be the best thing to do some times.

I felt myself relaxing into the woman I'd become.

When Rita and Cindy asked about Mark, I took advantage of their interest to ask a favor. Mark had hardly gone anywhere the past few days. He had managed to run home a couple times to shave, shower and change; but I really wanted him to attend the activities at our church that night. I could tell he wanted to go too, but he refused to leave the hospital unless someone stayed with me. Consequently Cindy agreed to come back so Mark could go to church. I was pleasantly surprised he took her up on the offer.

Even though I knew Mark needed to get away, I felt apprehensive about not having him near should something happen with Stross. On a deeper level, I understood he needed his own version of a fatherhood induction, and our friends at church could help that happen.

Mark's time at church gave him a chance to talk with our youth and show everyone he could the pictures of Stross he'd developed earlier in the day. The photos were beautiful, and Mark proudly explained which one we had chosen to send with the birth announcement. He also described how Stross liked his head touched, and reassured all who asked that I was doing well.

While Mark was at church, Cindy picked up where she, Rita and I had left off that afternoon. We chatted a long time about Stross' birth defects. She looked at the book on spina bifida that Stross' nurse had given us the day before and studied the diagrams our doctors had given us. Twice she asked if it bothered me to talk about Stross' health. I assured her I welcomed it, and I did.

The nursery called while Cindy was with me to tell me Stross was awake in case I wanted to spend time with him. I had never made the trip without Mark. To avoid feeling nervous and alone, I sneaked Cindy in with me. She stayed for about two minutes before the nurses figured out she wasn't a relative and asked her to leave. I left soon after, but I had loved showing Stross to her in person. With a big smile, she said all the right things about "how beautiful he is" and "so cute." I asked her if he looked like he had Down syndrome. She thought awhile then concurred with my position: My son looked like Mark.

Mark returned with stories about people passing around Stross' pictures and exclaiming about his beautiful eyes and dark hair. I could tell Mark enjoyed his evening as a father. I had enjoyed my day as a parent too.

●  ●  ●

# Chapter 8

# What Have They Done?

...

By Thursday it was clear that not only had Mark and I found joy in our parenthood status, but our child's grandparents were delighted with their new roles as well. Stross was the sixth grandchild on the Newcoms' side, so Mark's parents were well seasoned. They had both male and female grandchildren. They had grandchildren who lived miles away in Kentucky and one who lived across town. Stross' impending birth had promised no new experiences for them, yet his actual birth brought them anyway. He was their first grandchild born with birth defects.

We had not seen Mark's mom and dad, Carolyn and David, since they had come to be with us the day of Stross' birth. Daily phone calls kept them apprised of Stross' health concerns and our emotional status. They planned a return trip to Des Moines the coming Saturday, two days after my discharge and one day after Stross' shunt surgery. This was in keeping with an informal grandparent agreement: The first days of Stross' life were my parents' time to be with us since their jobs demanded limited use of personal days. Then after they left, Mark's parents would come and leave Carolyn, a stay-at-home mother, to assist us with Stross' homecoming.

This was an experience Caroyln had enjoyed with new grandchildren five times previously. I believed Mark had gotten his nurturing and caretaking skills from her. Now—at least to both sets of grandparents—it appeared we would need Carolyn's extra set of caring hands more than ever.

The parental "exchange of care" was scheduled for the coming weekend. My parents had clearly communicated to me their intent to have at least one of them stay with us until David, a division manager at John Deere's experimental engineering center in Waterloo, brought Carolyn to Des Moines.

But before we could enact any homecoming plans, Stross needed to survive another surgery—neurosurgery. Nourishment from only one day of mother's milk had done wonders for him and his doctors seemed comfortable with plans to proceed. Therefore, he would have the third surgery of his life when only five days old.

Stross had always shown signs of being alert, but having something of substance to eat made him even more so. He liked to eat and when he awoke on Thursday, it seemed like he was looking for a bottle. Mark and I took turns feeding him, carefully avoiding an infringement on each other's time. Even if one of us offered to share the privilege, the other understood the offer was a mere formality.

Mark and I had learned that taking turns allowed both the holder and watcher a maximum experience, since whoever wasn't actually holding Stross would then sit extremely close in order to stroke his hair or slip a finger into his hand and enjoy feeling his grasp.

Sometimes my mother would come to simply see what he looked like when awake. As her first grandchild, Stross enjoyed privileged status even before his birth. His monumental arrival had further sealed his fate.

My father was a more interesting case. Dad had displayed a reserved interest in my pregnancy. When I'd shown him an ultrasound photo taken of Stross at nine weeks gestation, he mumbled about people "getting all excited over a dark shadow on a piece of film." Stross had resembled little more than a tadpole with tiny buds for arms and feet, but to me it was clear evidence that something was alive inside my body.

That had been the whole purpose of the ultrasound in the first

• • •

place. When my doctor had trouble hearing a baby's heartbeat at the beginning of my second pregnancy, I panicked and basically demanded that he prove to me a child was growing inside. He tried to reason with me about waiting until 16 weeks when evidence of birth defects was possible. I'd have nothing of it. Our miscarriage had happened in July and this was only September. I had not intended to become pregnant that early; if I were, I needed proof.

That ultrasound had convinced me that I would really have a baby, but the photos did nothing for my father. He may have faked an inability to read the ultrasound photo to avoid looking like a foolish first-time grandpa. Yet as my due date approached, his interest never increased until it heightened the Sunday Stross was born.

For my Dad, becoming a grandfather appeared as challenging an adventure as sharing my childhood home with all females had been. Raising daughters had certainly been uncharted territory for him, and yet life managed to equip him for a 1970s version of the journey anyway.

Dad, the younger of two sons, was born to parents whose lives had been shaped by Depression-era farming. And while my dad regarded his father with honor and respect, he idolized his older brother, Lee, who introduced him to long horseback rides and games of cowboys and Indians after chores were done. Dad also had regular opportunities to play with his 23 cousins—20 of whom were male.

Lacking sisters or young female relatives as playmates, Dad's primary feminine reference was his mother, a woman capable of intimidating tough hired hands. Relatives who knew Grandma Delma in her prime describe her as forcefully self-confident, abrasively assertive and frustratingly stubborn.

My dad caught glimpses of these traits as a child. When he complained about the way Grandma sewed and mended his clothes, she pointed him to her treadle sewing machine and told him to sew it himself. He did.

So while daughters may have been a novelty for my father, strong women were not. And he approached fathering daughters the same way his mother had approaching mothering sons—by challenging my sister and I to do things for ourselves. I joined him in shoveling snow, mowing the lawn and assisting him in his basement wood shop. While my mother taught me how to cook, my father taught me how to sew, do laundry, fix a flat tire, change the oil in a car and tie a Windsor knot—in case I ever "dated a young man who was unfortunate enough to have never learned how to tie his own tie."

I had discerned my father's hopes and expectations through heart-to-heart conversations held in my room and fatherly lectures offered anytime he saw the need. He wanted me to mature into a strong, independent woman.

Now Dad, too, appeared to be searching for a newly defined role. During adolescent times of crisis he had offered advice and counsel. Stross' birth seemed to leave him without an appropriate anecdote or metaphorical story to offer.

Dad had stayed with Mom through Tuesday of that week—the first three days of Stross' life. He joined her in regular visits to my room and the NICU before leaving in the early morning hours on Wednesday to return to his high school teaching position in social studies. He had left reluctantly, already looking forward to the chance to see Stross again when he would retrieve Mom on Friday. Seeing our son in the flesh—even with tubes and tape—had been much more rewarding than his early ultrasound image.

When Dad left that Wednesday, his 48th birthday, he carried a special set of Polaroid photos that showed off his new grandson. Stross' nurses had made the photos just for him after hearing his dismay about having nothing to show his fellow teachers. Unfortunately they had taken the photos before Stross was removed from the ventilator. I smiled thinking about how he and mom's high school colleagues would react to Dad's apparent pride while being forced to gaze at poor-quality pictures of a tiny baby buried under yards of tape and monitor wires, with a large and awkward tube protruding from his mouth. It was obvious that when Dad looked at the pictures, he only saw the most beautiful baby in the entire world. I hoped his colleagues would see what he did. Dad missed seeing Stross without the ventilator tube by a matter of hours; and while Mom would enjoy holding Stross later that morning, Dad's first chance to hold his grandson was still days away.

Since Sunday, it had become apparent that Stross' birth caused many to redefine their relationship with us. To our parents we'd done more than become parents. We'd achieved a level of maturity they'd never needed. To our friends and coworkers, we became reminders that humans are at the mercy of life's whims.

The vast majority of cards we received were congratulatory, offering prayers for our future while sharing wishes for wisdom and strength. Many were complimentary, stating that Stross was lucky to have us as parents. Some went even further and said that "God knew what he was doing" when he "picked us out" as parents for Stross.

Divine surveillance and providence were predominant themes. Whether written on a card or spoken in person, those who attempted to explain God's methods made me uncomfortable. Many were the same people who, after our miscarriage, had expressed philosophical sympathies stating, "This was God's way of taking care of something that just wasn't right."

Based on that philosophy, I wondered if they believed Stross' life was right and just. Using their theological progression of thought, God had allowed Stross to be born alive; therefore, a life defined by birth defects must be his destiny—an unsettling concept.

I felt like convening a theological discussion on issues like predestination, free will and grace. For me, believing God matched parents to children is the theological equivalent of believing God manipulates every detail of creation, controlling lives like a supernatural puppeteer. With a God like this, if I made mistakes, they were mistakes I had been destined to make, and I am helpless against the course God has charted.

While well intentioned, this theology of predestination felt disconnected from my life experiences then and continues to misconnect today. Broadly employed, this approach means God plans for certain children to be born into families who abuse them. Likewise God must also choose to have some born to parents who would abandon them because of their birth defects. This has never been the God I know. This certainly was not the God who grieved with me over life gone amiss.

No matter the inside sentiment, every card and note we received gave us strength. There were joyously happy baby cards—so many of them, in fact, we did not have enough room to display them—and there were cards and handwritten notes that told us the sender was thinking of us. The thoughts, we believed, were actually prayers on our behalf.

After receiving triplicates and even quadruplets of several cards, I started to think about the difficulty people must have had in selecting a greeting, and I imagined bewildered shopping sessions in the baby section of the local Hallmark store. I also imagined them with worries about the kind of message to write. Some people tackled that task head on. About a dozen greetings came on generic blank cards sent with a personalized message. These senders talked about loving us and not knowing what to say. They also requested that we let them know if we needed "anything at all."

One day a large envelope arrived from Fort Worth filled with notes from friends we'd made during our carefree, newlywed life. Could they even imagine how our lives had changed?

Mark and I most enjoyed children's homemade sentiments made with construction paper flowers and button decorations. We disliked the three sympathy cards sent with messages of condolence. To appreciate these greetings, we considered the senders and accepted the cards for what they were—messages of concern for us.

Each piece of correspondence—even the condolence cards—buoyed our spirits. Each told us our lives mattered; our son's life mattered. The messages, indeed the cards themselves, validated our interconnectedness. People were praying for us, and we truly felt a divine presence as we tackled the challenges of each new day.

We loved our baby, and we loved the fact that our baby meant something to others: close friends, casual friends, immediate family, distant relatives, coworkers, even business associates. They shared words of faith, love for our family, expressions of inexplicable grief and promises of emotional support.

Not only was our faith being worked out, our child had given them a reason to examine their own faith more fully. Who is God? How do we define God's character? Does knowing God ever mean understanding God? Where is God when bad things are happening to good people?

On one of our pastor's trips to visit us in the hospital, he filled us in on the everyday business of church. As youth directors, our main concern centered on the youth and how they had been affected by Stross' birth. A few youth— both boys and girls—had visited us. For some it was their first trip to a hospital. Their relief at seeing us with smiles on our faces was obvious. Fears eased as we shared tears and laughter with them and explained the details of Stross' condition.

We shared with our pastor ways he could describe our feelings to the youth we had not seen personally. We wanted them to know we were not angry with God but felt loved and cared for. We wanted to tell them that life gets messy sometimes and that ours felt a little messy, but we felt strength and peace in the midst of it all.

While my faith asserted that trials can have a higher purpose, I needed evidence of some greater good. I needed to know that the trials we faced were being used to minister to others, so near the end of our conversation I asked our pastor, "What are people saying?"

His response included anecdotal stories of interactions with parishioners, and one story stood out from the rest. An elderly couple in our church, each more than 70 years old, had wondered aloud what Mark and I had done in our lives to deserve this. God must be teaching us a lesson, they'd said, and they were curious to know if our pastor had any idea what our great wrongdoing might have been. In response he used their question as an opportunity to challenge them about the nature of God and how God continued to work in the world. He reassured us of his attempts to help them understand that Stross' birth condition had not been a result of God's intervention because of our life choices.

Still I was incredulous. Even dumbfounded. Did this man and woman worship the same God I did? Did they read scripture from the same Bible but come away with a fully different meaning?

Mark and I were increasingly aware of how rapidly our spirituality was changing.

A card we received from Mark's parents pointed to a scriptural passage that held an entirely new focus in light of our son's birth. His dad, unaware of this elderly couple's reaction, had scrawled a simple message in the card:

> *I've looked at the baby pictures of Mark and Stross. You*
> *all sure look alike. We're claiming John 9:3.*
> *Mom and Dad*

The reference to Stross' family resemblance seemed to be David's way of saying, "Hey, I don't believe all this talk about a chromosome abnormality. Your son looks like you."

The reference to scripture seemed to speak directly to the elderly couple, answering their question. It referred to Jesus' healing of a man born blind. The disciples had asked Jesus, "Rabbi, who sinned, this man or his parents, that he was born blind?" In verse three, Jesus seems to conclude the matter. "Neither this man nor his parents sinned," said Jesus, "but this happened so that the work of God might be displayed in his life."

Mark and I knew his father was more focused on the opportunity for our lives to be used by God than deflecting blame for Stross' defects. But did David believe that God had intentionally given us Stross so our lives could be a divine example for others?

That conversation remained for a later day. It didn't matter now.

For whatever reason, Stross came to us as he did. We loved him and knew our lives could be a blessing to others. We could honor God just by helping Stross become all God intended for him to be. This was the dream our parents had held for us, and it was the dream we now held for our son. It was the primary reason we gave him a unique family name.

I've learned to spell his name voluntarily. I have also learned to point out that Stross is my son's first name. His last name is Newcom. And sometimes even my best proactive measures don't work.

• • •

Scott? Ross? Strauss?

"No. It's Stross. S-T-R-O-S-S. Like Ross with an 'st' in front."

"Stross. I've never heard that before. Did you make it up?"

Or, "Stross, what an interesting name. It must be a family name."

Yes, it is a family name, and while we did not make up the name, someone in Mark's family did—his great grandmother.

Until our son was born, Mark's grandfather Stross Newcom was the only one I'd ever known by that name. The two Strosses would eventually meet in the fall of 1991 and again in the summer of 1992, but first we needed to find a new vocabulary or a new manner of speech suitable for describing what it felt like to be Stross' mom and dad. And our friends helped us with that.

If you ask them today what they remember about their introduction to Stross' life, most recall the details of his birth circumstances in sketchy detail, yet nearly each person can remember what Mark said about how he looked: "He has lots of dark hair, and he's beautiful."

•    •    •

# Chapter 9

# Sister Mary Pull-Me-Down

...

Joyism. A joyism is term I created and only use myself. Having the word helps me during times of personal evaluation, for it's usually a joyism that causes momentary times of agitation in my relationships. However a joyism—I've been told—can also make me endearing. And so it is with the frustratingly paradoxical nature of joyisms: Some of the things I do cause others simultaneous feelings of delight and distress. Like when a person really appreciates what I have to say but they can hardly wait for me to shut up.

That's what it was like with Sister Mary Pull-Me-Down.

Sister Mary Pull-Me-Down, a name jointly bestowed on her by Mark and me, was a product of the same generation as the elderly couple from church who were eager to know what we'd done to bring calamity to our lives. The sister's actual name, printed on a hospital badge, wasn't of interest. To me she was Sister Mary Pull-Me-Down, a woman whose saccharin kindness genuinely emitted from every part of her body.

I found the sister uncomfortably kind, and Mark and I regarded her expressions of sympathy and concern as pity. I did not feel pity for myself, nor did I want to be pitied for anything, especially by her. Her presence magnified my pain and renewed my anger. Somehow, seeing her tempted me to be angry with God—a paradox itself.

The sister, an occasional visitor to my room, peppered her conversations with phrases like "such a shame," "so, so sorry," "hard to understand," "nice," and "must have faith." Her visits with Mark and me came after her visits to Stross in the NICU and, for a reason known only to her, Sister Mary Pull-Me-Down took a personal interest in our son's recovery. Spina bifida babies were rare, and one born to "such a nice young couple"—to use Sister Pull-Me-Down's jargon—warranted uncommon attentiveness. Radiating holiness and compassion, the sister floated into our lives to be of spiritual assistance. I know I should have felt grateful. Instead I prayed my lack of gratitude was hidden from her.

Stross' birth condition had not shocked me. I had no impulse to ask God, "Why me?" Instead my reaction had been, "Why not me?"

I knew no one could plan to live a life free of uncommon grief or extraordinary strife. However, I had liked my odds.

As an adult I'd managed to continue living by principles that had served me well through childhood, adolescence and early adulthood. I lived clean, played fair and picked up messes of my own making. Often I even helped others clean up after themselves. I came from a good family, had married into a good family and had charted a worthy career. I believed that someone who had in mind my higher purpose knew my comings and my goings; I understood I could never flee from that presence. Therefore, what had I to fear?

Nothing, I supposed.

And I didn't feel afraid. Not for my physical self.

And I didn't feel abandoned by God.

So where did my anger come from? What fears had I not identified? What was the source of the pain Sister Mary Pull-Me-Down so easily brought to the surface?

My best guess was this: I was deeply sad that this broken world had managed to touch my son even before his birth. I had done everything possible for him while pregnant, and it hadn't been enough. But I wasn't mad at God—not for what had happened. I was distressed about the world he'd created. That kind of anger felt different to me. I hated brokenness and how it robbed lives of safety,

... —

health and a sense of wellbeing.

The only thing left for me to do, it seemed, was to protect Stross and give him the best life possible. The sister could not know this kind of pain for a child, I thought. Surely she couldn't understand the burning desire I had to protect him. I didn't want her constant reminder that things had gone awry. She personified qualities I had not yet learned to value: mercy, meekness and submission. I didn't believe those qualities could move me forward—whatever forward meant.

I believed that interactions with the sister threatened to undermine my resolve. When she visited, I saw things I didn't want to tackle. The strength I gained physically paled with reminders of what I faced emotionally, and I just didn't have time for that. Not then.

Perhaps this resolve contributed to my speedy recovery. Clinically, it would have been possible for me to go home on Wednesday, one day ahead of schedule. Of course that would have meant leaving Stross alone one day earlier. My doctor really had no intention of sending me home before Thursday, but I enjoyed knowing that my body had rebounded so well. It felt good not to be pregnant anymore. It felt good to start gaining control again.

In truth more credit for my recovery belonged to Stross. To visit him I had to get out of bed and walk. The exercise for my body carried over into healing of my spirit, wholeness—not brokenness—in my life.

Our son truly was the word Mark and I kept calling him: beautiful. He was resilient, strong and determined—a fighter. I beamed with pride over our survivor.

My last day as a patient in the hospital was strange. Thursday morning Mark and I packed my belongings then questioned my discharge nurse about the latest possible time I could leave the room. She informed us that we would be charged for a full day that, according to our insurance plan, ended at midnight.

She then reminded me that I was a recovering cesarean patient and needed my rest. In turn I reminded her that I already was taking it easy since others were primarily caring for my newborn. Besides Stross would be taken to surgery early on Friday, and we wanted to be with him as long as possible. I needed to be there.

We would stay until midnight.

Mom questioned our decision too, since it gave her new reasons to worry. Without Dad, Mom was more unsettled than usual. We strained through guarded conversations about big issues like the assurance of eternal life for a child who had not been baptized (she wanted him baptized that day; we didn't see it as necessary), and little issues like how to get the dozens of flower arrangements and gifts from the hospital to our house (she wanted Mark's help that afternoon; he didn't want to leave).

Not yet skilled at identifying anger as pain, I frequently used Mom as the target for my anger. Had I been proficient at the transformative process, we could have shared our feelings and deepened our relationship. Instead I relied on behavior patterns from my childhood. I knew that she worried about saying the wrong thing and upsetting me, so I relied on her to back down when I became agitated. However, backing down was not part of her nature anymore than it was mine. Plus her coping skills—like mine—had begun to wear down.

Mom spent an extended amount of time next to Stross in the NICU on my day of discharge. Her desire to have private grandma time allowed Mark and me quiet time together.

With the lights out, my hospital room was nearly as dark as night. For the fourth day in a row, rain clouds deadened the early afternoon. Mark and I sat in the darkness talking quietly about a lot of things: our most recent visitors, items we needed to keep until our midnight exodus, Mark's supper plans, and whether or not my sister and her husband would drive Mom home for us. Jill and her husband, Greg, would be arriving just before supper. We wondered how to sneak them into the NICU for a firsthand look at their new nephew.

Mark and I also talked about God and the validation of salvation many associate with the act of baptism. We wondered about parents whose children died minutes after birth, and how they reconciled those beliefs with the realities of the moment. Neither one of us believed that Stross, unbaptized as he was, would be barred from entering heaven should he die in surgery. Yet we were keenly aware that many in our own family did not share our belief.

The foundations of our own baptisms had been laid years earlier by our respective parents, products of their mothers and fathers. Now it was our turn to be the grown-ups. Stross was ours to love, guide and protect. The faith Mark and I shared created the family Stross had been born into, and it filled the home that would shape his spiritual development.

In the comforting warmth of Room 403, we resolved that Stross was more God's child than ours. The task laid before us was the acceptance of a calling. We were Stross' parents. Confident of his future and ours, we believed that no matter the outcome—should he live or die—all would be well. If that weren't true, we asked ourselves, what kind of God—what kind of faith—did we have?

Mark came over to me as I sat in bed and kissed the top of my lowered head. It signaled the tears that began to streak my glasses and dim my vision.

"I love you, Joy." His voice said it would be okay. "You need a nap and so do I. Get some rest."

Mark tucked me in and then snuggled up on the couch. I'm not certain how long we both slept. I awoke when I heard Mom crack the door open and quietly enter. I didn't move but opened my eyes to watch her walk across the room. Her body language told me her time with Stross had been upsetting.

Sitting in a mauve-colored recliner near the window, Mom started to cry quiet tears that demanded an immediate inquiry. I popped up as quickly as my healing abdomen allowed.

"Mom, what's up? What's wrong?"

"I'm sorry. I thought you were asleep." She wiped her face and regrouped.

"Is Stross okay?"

"Yes, he is fine. He's sleeping now."

"Did something go wrong?"

She didn't really want to talk, and her less-than-forthcoming answers courted doubt. Mark was sitting up now too.

"Mom, are you all right?" I finally allowed for the fact that her feelings could be about her.

"It's what the sister said," Mom answered, obviously distressed. Mark and I knew which sister she was talking about, Sister Mary Pull-Me-Down, the nun who had taken so much interest in our family.

"What was it?"

I felt myself growing irritated. I did not want to go through the baptism issue again. Surely the sister had not ventured into that with my mother.

"Oh, she went on about how you were such a nice-looking young couple and that this didn't make any sense that it would happen to you."

"Oh, Mother," I said in a quietly exasperated tone, my way of scolding her for buying into such a butterflies-and-roses approach to life. Yet I was relieved.

"I know, I know," she continued. "It's not just that."

I emotionally braced again.

"She said he was so little and that it was awful to think about him having to go through such a big surgery."

So the sister had dared to think all of our thoughts aloud. Mom's voice trailed off and her next words caught in her throat.

"And...and, did you know they are going to shave off his hair?"

With that final pronouncement, Mom started to cry harder. She didn't worry about being quiet this time.

Her fear had brought anxiety over Stross' hair? Or perhaps his impending hair loss a safe diversion to cry about.

"Oh, Mom," I laughed in relief. We would not have to talk about baptism again. "Of course they will have to shave his head. It's a little hard to operate on a brain without doing that."

In truth I had not thought of it.

"I'm sure they won't shave off all his hair, just the part of his head where the shunt will go," I said, making a mental note to ask the neurosurgeon and even Stross' nurses about this. I didn't want a bald son any more than Mom wanted a bald grandson. We all took pride in his full head of dark brown hair.

···

"Fran, he'll just have his first haircut a little earlier than most kids," said Mark. "Even if they take it all off, it will grow back fast."

"It's just not very fair," said Mom. I was convinced she had cloaked her fears about Stross' surgery and his assurance of salvation with superficial concern over his hair.

None of what had happened in the last few days could be classified as fair. I wasn't even certain what the standards of fairness were anymore. Sister Mary Pull-Me-Down, with her comments about "such a bad thing happening to such a nice, young couple," seemed to struggle with this world's disregard for fairness too.

"Mom, just promise me something," I requested, mocking a subdued sense of seriousness. "Promise me you'll stay away from Sister Mary Pull-Me-Down."

Mom laughed. We all did.

Four years passed before we learned that my mother baptized Stross that afternoon using a bottle of sterile water she'd poured into a basin next to his bed in the NICU. He had looked into her face while she placed water on his head and prayed in the name of the Father, Son and Holy Spirit. Then she sang to him: "Jesus loves me, this I know." I imagined her kissing him and holding him close too.

So my mom had baptized Stross while they were alone. God served as their sanctifier and witness. Any surprise I had was for her confession itself. I understood her regard for baptism. I also knew it was a familiar and personal ritual for her. Stross was actually the second newborn baptized by her hands. One day after my birth, my mother had baptized me, three weeks before my church baptism celebrated in the sanctuary of her home congregation. She had kept my private baptism a secret until Mark and I married 21 years later.

In a world void of true fairness, Stross was blessed to have a grandmother who loved him as deeply as the daughter she bore. Sister Mary Pull-Me-Down would surely be pleased with this.

"How nice," she might even say. "How nice."

●　　●　　●

# Chapter 10

# A Bad Day

• • •

E very nurse on duty Thursday knew our goal was to remain at the hospital with our son for as long as possible. The nurses began to wean Stross from bottle feedings in preparation for his shunt surgery scheduled for early the next day.

Because Stross had lost a small amount of blood during the two surgeries performed the day of his birth and because he'd had little opportunity to take in calories, his weight had dropped from 5 pounds 10 ounces to just over 5 pounds. The neurosurgeon ordered a small amount of blood, a portion of a test tube, to prepare Stross for surgery. Once again one of us needed to sign a form, this time giving them permission to give Stross the blood. We had already signed permission for the surgery itself when the neurosurgeon had come earlier to explain the procedure. He also had made certain we understood that surgery carried its own particular set of risks.

We knew. We even knew the most serious risk was death. We endured his explanation anyway. That was part of our new job as Stross' parents, perhaps even part of the wild ride I'd been promised the day of his birth. The events of this day were beginning to feel like the slow, anticipation-filled climb to the top of a roller coaster. I hoped the trip down would be more thrilling than life threatening.

I swallowed hard as I signed the second permission form,

pushing back thoughts of AIDS.

"Is the blood really necessary?" I asked the nurse who had brought the form. Mark's head turned sharply in our direction. His alert eyes told me he was pleased I'd asked the question.

"The doctor feels Stross will handle the surgery better with the extra blood," she replied. "Everyone loses some blood during the process of surgery, and babies cannot afford to lose much. Because Stross has been recovering, he just has not had enough time to rebuild his blood supply."

It made sense. I would have preferred postponing surgery. In fact no surgery at all sounded good. Unfortunately, I could not ignore his hydrocephalus. The CT-scan had shown a build up of cerebrospinal fluid in his brain. I feared mental retardation, something that— pending the results of his chromosome analysis—might soon be real anyway. Choosing not to act was not an option. The fluid had to get off his brain, and the sooner the better.

Once again we were being asked to make a decision that could greatly impact Stross' life. In spite of reservations I signed my name and behind it, the word "mother."

"Joy, we are in Iowa. We probably have a safer blood supply here than in many other parts of the country," said Mark as he took the clipboard from me and added his signature.

I glanced at the nurse hoping for some indication of agreement. She gave none, but now she knew what I had been thinking.

Mark handed back the consent form. We understood it was our legal agreement to abide by the consequences of the actions we had requested on Stross' behalf. This form, like all the others, bore both our signatures as a symbolic pact.

This decision had been made without a conscious prayer for guidance. If God had spoken to us, it was through jumbled images and emotions pulsing through our separate minds. In the fullness of the moment, we were feeling more than hearing.

Having faith, however, did not prevent negative thoughts: Sister Mary Pull-Me-Down's notice about my baby's shaved head, the effect it had on Mom, the uncertainty of Stross' surgical consent

...

form, the horror that he needed neurosurgery at all, and a growing awareness that Mark and I would soon sleep miles away from Stross. Each one added to a very heavy day. I steeled myself against further irritants by taking a nap. It served two purposes: I could mentally escape, and I could shorten a dreadfully long day. Mark, once again, headed for the NICU to join Mom with Stross.

While I napped Jill and Greg were on their way to the hospital from their home two hours away. Jill and I had chatted by phone a week earlier, but this would be the first time I'd see or speak to her since I'd become a mother; therefore, I had no idea how news of Stross' birth had impacted her or if she harbored concerns related to me.

After watching Mark suffer through his long-distance conversation with Jason the Sunday of Stross' birth, I had been willing but not eager to call my only sibling. As it turned out my parents volunteered for the job and encouraged me to focus on matters at hand. They would keep Jill apprised of our situation, they had assured me; and then subsequently told me of her plans for this Thursday visit.

In fact my parents had self-appointed themselves the task of sharing our news with everyone on my side of the family. But, unbeknownst to me, they had then deferred the responsibility of telling Jill to Grandpa Fred and Grandma Delma. My father's parents decided to drive to Jill's home to deliver our news in person. Only months later would Jill tell me how their body language and the way their words stumbled forth had led her to believe, for at least a few minutes, that I had died.

Jill admitted that it had taken her awhile to rebound from that unnecessary shock.

I sensed that Jill's regard for me, four years her senior, was a complicated mixture of awe and resentment; for throughout childhood and adolescence she evaluated my achievements using terms that indicated this belief: things came too easy for me. Therefore, I was neither perplexed nor hurt by Jill's seemingly tardy arrival. I understood she needed time to reconcile all that had happened to her big sister. However I wasn't having a very good day this particular

Thursday. Stross' impending surgery, my impending discharge and an accumulation of fatigue had me feeling impatiently anxious. In short, I had become short-tempered; I had hoped a nap could rectify my mood.

Unfortunately for Jill, it hadn't.

I had just awakened when she and Greg entered my hospital room. It was near suppertime, and they were clearly awkward and uncomfortable. I wasn't interested in making it any easier for them. In the next moments, I apathetically responded to things that I regarded as inane talk about everyday trivialities.

In fact it was difficult to listen to anything she was saying because my mind was racing with the nightmarish reality of my day. I vaguely heard Jill tell about Greg working a lot of hours and her own hectic job schedule and the fact that she wasn't certain her boss understood what she did. Plus, she added, they had sorted through several mounds of unfolded clothes before dressing for the drive to Des Moines; and because their dishwasher had broken, Jill had washed dishes by hand.

After the last in this string of what I interpreted as benign complaints, Jill blew a puff of air out her mouth as she exhaled and rolled her eyes.

"This has just been a really bad day," she said.

I snapped. I had been waiting for an opportunity to talk about how I felt and seized her innocent two-word invitation.

"Bad day? A bad day?" I taunted. My voice was poisonous.

"I gave birth to a child who is handicapped, and tomorrow he is headed into surgery. Brain surgery. Do you know what I had to do today? I had to sign a form that said—basically—that I wouldn't sue the hospital if he died in surgery. A bad day? Do you want to talk about bad days with me? Why don't you stop being so shallow?"

The room was stone silent. Jill hadn't seen it coming. Neither had I.

"I'm sorry," she said very quietly. The silence continued.

Nothing in our lives had prepared us for the conversation we should have had. When things come too easy for you—real or

...

imagined—conversations about calamity don't wear well. Instead you resort to what you know—talking about your work and daily chores or spitting back an angry response.

But I knew what I had to do next. I was her big sister. So I found her eyes and mustered an apology—rather a huge understatement. But my voice, while softer, still sounded angry.

"I guess I'm not in a very good mood right now."

Unlike Jill, I left my "sorry" unsaid.

Greg, who had basically been silent since his arrival, guided Jill out of the room stating they should probably find Mom to let her know they had arrived.

There were no tears from me, and I wasn't sure how my words had impacted Jill. I noticed that she didn't talk much the rest of the day. Had I been wiser, I'd have recognized my anger as pain—emotions that magnified with the realization I was deeply alone. I wanted to have an older sister, not feel the need to act like one. I wouldn't—couldn't—help my little sister navigate the awkwardness.

Ten minutes later, the entire clan came back. Mark acted as a warm host and informed me of his failed attempt to sneak Jill and Greg in to visit Stross. After a while Mark and Mom headed down to the hospital cafeteria while Jill and Greg kept nervous company with me.

Greg, a paramedic by profession, began asking technical questions about Stross' condition, interested in details of his impending shunt surgery. I answered with a polite dryness. Jill asked if they could help cart our flowers and gifts home, and then offered to bring back a comfortable sweat suit I'd said I wanted. I needed something more appropriate for our late night camp out than the celebratory outfit I'd packed.

As soon as Mark and Mom came back to my room, Jill and Greg headed to our house in West Des Moines. Mom left also. Mark sat with me as I ate dinner alone in my near empty room. We were only hours away from taking a lonely and weary walk to our car.

•   •   •

# Chapter 11

# Breathe, Please

...

Even the mere idea of sleeping in my own bed felt good. Fortunately by midnight I was too tired to fully comprehend how sad it was to have an empty nursery at home. Semiconsciously I understood that the longer Stross stayed in the hospital, the longer Mark and I could hold off the fear of becoming his caregivers. Our son promised to remain a complicated, little mystery man.

Upon entering our home, I noticed the preparations for Stross' arrival that my family had begun. Jill and Greg had tossed the hospital's gift bags into the bottom of the nursery's closet, while Mom had done her part finding homes for stuffed animals and the other baby items we'd received. The balloons, plants and floral arrangements that had decorated Room 403 now reminded us that a family of three belonged here—in this home, on this suburban cul de sac.

One detail had eluded Mark and me as we'd planned for our transfer home: I needed a breast pump of my own. A nurse had helped Mark make the necessary arrangements, and he'd driven to the medical supply store just before it closed to pick up my rental unit, but neither of us had taken the time to learn how it differed from the hospital's industrial-sized version. Comforted by a promise that my pump pieces would fit, we had simply driven home. With engorged breasts telling me it was time to express milk again, I suddenly wished one of us had asked for more specific instructions.

Mark urged me to get ready for bed.

"You get your pajamas on, wash your face and stuff. I'll get your pump hooked up," he volunteered.

The gaskets, a piston unit and tubing made the project seem well suited for a guy who loved mechanical tinkering. Besides if Mark could get the pump put together while I readied for bed, I would feel relief that much sooner. I reached into my travel bag, tossed him two bottles with breast horns attached and headed for the bathroom. It felt fabulous to be taken care of by the one person in the world who came closest to knowing what I felt like that night (engorged breasts notwithstanding).

In the comfort of my own bathroom, I splashed warm water on my face, washing away traces of the day's tears. My recently purchased maternity bra outlined breasts that were much larger than I remembered of my pre-pregnancy body, and a lumpy profile of excess skin hid the figure that matched the smaller-sized chest I'd left behind. I reluctantly lowered my eyes. It was time to examine my incision in detail. A red line crossed my body, evidence that a doctor's scalpel had sliced me open from side to side. This huge cut had enabled the doctor to lift out a living baby, my first child—a son. His cut, now my scar, served as proof my body had borne life.

I knew Mark's eyes wouldn't allow him to see what I did. Incredibly, no matter how large I'd gotten while pregnant, Mark looked at me as if I were the sexiest woman he'd ever seen. In five years of marriage, I'd learned that Mark believed I was drop-dead gorgeous every minute of every day, and his genuine adoration often caused me to believe it too. This night I felt that my body's physical condition allowed no room for Mark's love-inspired delusions.

I looked intently in the mirror searching for additional evidence that I'd changed. The last time I'd taken a physical assessment, my figure and my future had been rounded, promising. That night I saw lumpy contours more suited for a woman whose life would be far from smooth.

• • •

The rhythmic whir of my new breast pump called me back to more immediate concerns. I quickly searched through my toiletries for a toothbrush so I could finish a more familiar part of my nighttime routine.

"Ouch! That hurt."

I jumped at the sound of Mark's loud yelp and hurried to check on him. He sat on my side of the bed, breast pump dutifully working on the nightstand beside him. How he was sitting there made me laugh aloud. Mark was rubbing his chest with both hands, one nipple covered by each palm.

"What happened?" I asked. He moved his hands to show me two circular pressure sores, one around each of his nipples. I reduced my laughter to giggles, holding back loud peals of laughter.

"There wasn't enough suction at first," he said. "So I adjusted it. Then I was worried it seemed too strong. I didn't want you to get hurt."

"Oh, baby, that is so sweet," I managed to get out between giggles.

"I thought it'd be safer to try it myself first," he said sheepishly.

"I'm so glad," I said, stressing my pleasure.

"I couldn't get them off," he said, still rubbing his wounds.

I carefully selected my next words, unsuccessfully suppressing louder giggles. "You know, there is this little trick I could have told you about." I was laughing hard enough to bring tears now.

"Don't laugh," he said and started to smirk himself.

"I know, I'm sorry," I said with better vocal control.

"It's just, when we moms are done pumping, we press on the skin next to the horn to release the pressure."

"Really?" he said.

"Yes, really," I answered.

Sleep came easier than I'd expected that night.

It didn't matter that we had not gone to bed until after midnight. By 7 a.m. Mark and I were headed for the hospital. As a newborn Stross would be first in line for surgery. We needed to spend time with him before he'd be taken into the surgical suite.

There would be no private room to hide in during this surgery. Mark reminded me to pack busy work for the hospital waiting room. I counted on productivity to safeguard me from anxiety, so I grabbed a box of envelopes and my address book. While Stross was in surgery, I would address envelopes for his birth announcement. I had no idea how the actual announcement would take shape, but I knew who should get them and which photos we'd enclose.

Mark and I had selected a gorgeous headshot of Stross taken after we'd fed him for the first time. His eyes were big and dark, his nose and mouth adorably petite. The photo conveyed the beauty we saw. Because Stross slept so much, I taped a duplicate of the photo onto his bed so all could see how incredibly adorable he was when awake. I also wanted to include a nice family shot, so I chose a photo that showed me feeding Stross a bottle while Mark looked on, stroking his head. Mom had taken it for us. In the photo, both Mark and I looked like kids with a new toy. I hoped it would show how deeply we loved him.

Stross was sleeping when we got to the NICU. The nursing staff had just changed shifts, and we learned which nurse was assigned to Stross. We liked her. She had been with him on some of his other big days. Today she would accompany him into surgery as a protective surrogate mother.

"Could they please save his hair for me when they shave it off?" I asked. "You know, it will be his first hair cut."

"Well I guess it will be," she replied. "I'll get an envelope right now. That way I won't forget."

"Yesterday they said they won't shave it all off, right?"

"Right. Just where they need to make the incision for the shunt. Probably this much," she said indicating a swath two inches wide.

It seemed small enough.

"You will be with him the whole time, right?"

"Oh, yes. We don't like to leave our babies alone," she assured me. "Those doctors sometimes like to have the operating room too cool for little ones. Don't worry, though. I'm not shy about speaking up. We

• • •

know our babies better than anyone on the surgical team. Babies need a warm surgical suite, and the doctors can just tough it out."

I liked her attitude—protective, assertive—just what Stross needed. I also liked how freely she shared information, making us feel included in his care.

"Not only will I be with Stross in surgery, I'll be with him when he comes here for recovery," she said. "It's better for our babies to recover here where we can take care of them best."

Stross continued to sleep. I softly stroked his hair, tears welling with each stroke. My eyes grew red, and my breasts tingled. My body was betraying my false sense of resolve. This was my son. I loved him. I did not want him to die. I did not want him to be retarded. I did not want the world to see him as less of a person because he would never walk. Yet if any of those things occurred, I trusted the outcome.

Days earlier I might not have been as bold. Until Stross, faith existed as an untested truth. I had believed in God because I had no reason not to. Now Stross' life testified to life's higher purpose.

Until Stross I'd never relied on a divine partnership 24 hours a day, seven days a week. I thought I had, but after becoming Stross' mom, I understood what faith-filled reliance truly felt like. Stross, from first breath, swept into my life and exposed life's holy pervasiveness. He helped me understand that life—every aspect of it—demanded authenticity.

The formidable circumstances of Stross' birth validated much of what I'd previously taken on faith, and the power of his life directly transmitted this tested faith into the essence of who I'd become. My life was now filled—not just touched by—the undeniable presence of a Creator at work within human lives. I would never discount the dynamic nature of that truth again, especially in the face of Stross' impending surgery and the helplessness it brought. Regardless of the outcome, my more mature faith demanded that I trust whatever came next. I had become stronger because of weakness.

I knew there would be no way to explain it to others without sounding inaccurately mystical. But maybe someday, I thought, I could try.

Except for a trip to express milk, I stood with Mark by our son's bed for nearly an hour as we waited for his call to surgery. When the call finally came, we rode together in the elevator. The nurse pushed Stross in his tall surgical bed with Mark and me tagging alongside. Three others, two women and one man, stepped onto the elevator when it stopped at the floor below. One of the ladies stared at Stross. I didn't like it, and I wasn't really sure why.

"He's such a cutie. So tiny," she said, "Isn't he a cutie?" she asked the other woman with her. The second woman agreed and joined the first one in staring at our son. I knew Mark wouldn't say anything in response—it really wasn't required. I chose not to speak either in case whatever came out started a fresh crop of tears. The nurse also said nothing.

One of the women looked at my hand holding onto the side of his bed. My armband gave away my identity as Stross' mother.

"Is he your baby?" the first lady asked. Had she noticed my red eyes too? Did they make her wonder about his condition?

I had to respond now, so I smiled and nodded yes.

"Well, he's adorable."

"Thanks," I managed to say.

As the doors opened to the first floor, I thought about launching into Stross' impressive five-day history and then thought better of it. She could never fully appreciate how incredible he was anyway, I decided.

The nurse led us into the white curtained cubicles of the pre-surgical waiting area. Finally a handful of people in white garments came to help Stross' nurse escort him into surgery.

I was glad Stross' photo was taped to his bed. None of these people would have an opportunity to see him alert; however, they could see him bright-eyed and adorable if they noticed the photo.

As they began to wheel him away, both Mark and I kissed Stross on his head and told him we loved him, something we'd never thought of doing only days earlier. On Sunday our son was a stranger. Today he factored as more than one-third of our family.

•••

Our pastor gestured us to a doorway then a nurse guided us to the family waiting area. Once inside, six to eight friends welcomed us. Warm hugs and mutual tears provided comfort. We were not alone.

And these people knew how to do waiting rooms. A man handed me that day's copy of the *Des Moines Register*, and a woman asked if Mark or I needed anything to eat or drink. Mark joined her on a trip to the vending machines, and I took a deep breath and settled in with the front section of the paper on my lap. A couple of women started to talk about their children and the latest news from church. So-and-so said to give us their regards, one said, and thus-and-so was also thinking of us. Another wanted us to know church just wasn't the same without us.

Today small talk was a welcome distraction, and our friends did not mistake silent responses as impolite gestures. Understanding their roles, our friends kept Mark and me engaged in a polite level of one-sided conversation, human white noise to distract us from the loud thoughts blaring in our minds. Occasionally I'd try to read the paper, but mostly I just sat and listened, aware of my own tired sounding breaths.

After a while my breathing quieted and I addressed all the envelopes and read the entire day's news. Mom showed up and enjoyed hearing the compliments as Stross' photos were passed among our friends—couch-to-couch, chair-to-chair. Finally one of the nurses who had been providing regular updates on Stross' surgical progress let us know he was done and on his way to the intensive care nursery. Mark and I thanked everyone and gave quick hugs before heading upstairs. We rushed as quickly as we could to Stross with Mom close on our heels.

When we got inside the NICU, Stross' nurse was leaning over his bed checking his monitor leads and recording his vitals. Every once in a while she grabbed his foot and said, "Come on, Stross, breathe."

"What's going on?" I asked. "Is he okay?"

"He did super," she said. "He did so well getting off the ventilator after his first surgery, we didn't want him to get dependent on it this time, so he's off it already."

• • •

"That's good, right?" I asked.

"Oh, yes," she said. "Stross is a good breather. He can do this."

She flicked his foot again, and Stross took a deep breath.

"Sometimes these little guys just get too tired and forget to breathe."

Breathing had never been a problem for Stross. We'd watched preemie after preemie set off apnea alarms as nurses rushed over to fill their lungs with air. Each time I had breathed a prayer of relief that my son was not like those babies. Today I lived their nightmare.

Stross' apnea monitor was sounding an alarm now; and he continued to lay still. I flicked his foot, and the nurse voiced her approval as Stross' chest began to rise up and down. Mark and Mom both took deep breaths as well.

"That's it, Stross. Stop being so lazy now. You can keep breathing," she said.

I could not believe what was happening. This child we'd spent so much effort on, the child I'd carried in my body for 38 weeks, was now so drugged from surgery that he was too tired to breathe. On top of that his nurse insulted him and us by calling him lazy.

My task became clear. I'd protect him from her rude and unwarranted insults. Standing by Stross' bed, I stared at his chest then flicked and jostled him just as the nurse had whenever his chest paused its rhythmic cadence. I couldn't even wait a few seconds to see if he was breathing the normally abnormal pattern of a newborn or to see if he'd catch himself and start breathing on his own. He needed—*I* needed—a regular, steady pattern. I needed the monitor to be quiet.

As I stood there I took further inventory of Stross' body. His face was puffy again, even more than the first time. A large, vertical band of white sterile gauze was taped to his head about one inch behind his right ear. More than a two-inch strip of his hair was missing, but it was hard to imagine the full effect of his near baldness. In addition, the white gauze hid a large patch of the offensive haircut. The envelope with his trimmings lay on a shelf under his bed.

As I kept watch, I peppered the nurse with questions. Besides breathing, what needed to happen before we could officially believe Stross was out of danger? Had he lost blood during surgery? When could he start to drink milk again? How could she tell if he was in pain? What pain medication was he on? Did it seem like his hydrocephalus was extensive?

Still regularly recording Stross' vital signs, she casually mentioned details. The most interesting information came when she described the fluid drained from his brain. "It was clear," she said, "like water."

Even from a layperson's standpoint, clear was obviously better than cloudy. Her lifted eyebrows told me just how important clear was. I thanked God for clear fluid and whatever that meant for my son.

I had grown tired of standing and sat in a nearby rocker, head back and eyes closed. Mark remained by Stross' head, stroking the hair on his forehead. I counted on Mom to keep guard. In less than a minute the alarm sounded again. Mom jiggled Stross and told him to breathe. Seconds later, he stopped again. The nightmare continued.

"Come on, lazy boy," said the nurse. "You've got to remember to breathe."

A lazy boy? This woman needed to know my son was far from lazy. My mind raced in private conversation: Woman (I no longer saw her as a sainted nurse protector of "her babies"), Stross has been through three surgeries in five days. If he's too tired to breathe, just put him back on the ventilator.

"Hey, you, lazy boy," she said tapping his leg. "Get going."

Stross took a deep breath. Mom took a vigilant stance near his feet.

"Why can't he be on the ventilator?" I curtly questioned aloud.

"Oh, we don't want that. That is a huge step backward," said the nurse, "He's doing just fine. Really."

I couldn't talk anymore. I looked to Mom, then to Mark. He seemed worried, but more about me than Stross.

"Joy, you look pale. Why don't you sit down?"

"We need to keep him breathing Mark," I said in a near whisper.

"He'll be fine," said the nurse. "This lazy boy is already doing better."

I desperately wanted to make her stop calling him that.

Ten minutes turned into 20. Stross did seem to be getting better but my fear didn't lessen. My breasts were full now and beginning to leak again.

"I have to go pump," I said and started to cry.

"This has been a big day for you," the nurse said. "You need to get away. Don't worry about Stross. He's doing super."

Mom voiced her agreement and promised to stay right where she was until Stross was breathing consistently again. Mark located the bag with my pump pieces and bottles, then walked me to the door of the nursing mother's room. It was available.

I spent the next 20 minutes expressing milk and crying my eyes out. I prayed in silent moans that words could never have expressed. My 20 minutes, a strange mix of self-pity and maternal compassion, was just enough time for me to empty myself emotionally and physically while Stross mastered the admirable act of breathing.

Stross had passed that day's tests: surviving neurosurgery and resuming the act of breathing on his own. One other test promised to keep us holding our breath the remaining days of his hospital stay. Until the results of his chromosome analysis returned from the Mayo Clinic, we could draw no conclusions about his future.

Physical disabilities aside, it was still possible that a diagnosis of a mental abnormality would derail us. I simply could not comprehend how one blood test might determine whether or not a doctor would offer options for institutionalization. One of my worst-case scenarios had Mark and I never taking Stross home from the hospital, or if we did, it would be only for a few months before he'd die.

To avoid the anxiety of this existence, I attempted to dismiss the evidence they used to warrant the test in the first place. I reasoned that the physical characteristics found on Stross' body were open to interpretation. My thinking went like this: "Stross has a high soft palate and a split uvula, so what? And this business about his eyes being slanty, they only look that way when he sleeps. Mark is supposed to have Native American blood in his gene pool. That should help explain his eyes. And, yes, one ear is a little misshapen, and yeah, I understand this business about one parallel line instead of two across his palms. But Stross' hand is so darn small. I see what you see, but can we really trust that?"

The questions persisted, and my optimistic musings came off as too Pollyanna even in the privacy of my mind. Worst of all I could not interpret what Mark believed true. Did he believe our son was mentally retarded or not? We dared to talk of it only in private snatches of time. Interruptions kept us from fully committing one way or another. Until the results of the blood test, we could only wonder anyway. The thing I knew for certain was that Mark was as scared as I.

•   •   •

# All I Ever Wanted

A s a family of three, our first 10 days can be divided into two nearly equal parts: five days and four nights with all of us in our hospital home, and five days and five nights with Stross in the hospital and Mark and me home only at night.

Every day for five days, we'd drive the 24-minute trek from our house to the hospital so we could share the day with Stross. Car conversation only happened in the first few miles. After our car entered freeway traffic, both Mark and I would fall silent, losing ourselves in private thought.

One compact disk was our CD of choice that week providing background music for each of these hospital trips: Margaret Becker's "*Steps of Faith*." On happy days the sounds filled our car as early morning sun. On sad days the rhythm kept time as wipers pushed raindrops off our windshield. I wondered if God, fate or chance had decided that our sad days would accompany inclement weather.

It felt like God.

In fact it felt as if we were fully connected to a divine presence during those commutes. God was riding with us in our car, talking to us through music and expressing our emotions through weather. God used our travel time to prepare us for each day.

On these early May days, God was far from abstract.

Childhood Sunday school classes had provided me with a masculine image of God; but after Stross' birth, I became equally convicted that God could manifest in fully feminine moments. He was as real as the weather, and she was as comforting as the words and music of Margaret Becker's songs. In our quiet commute, her music—divine music—became a vehicle for our unspoken prayers.

God spoke loudest through the words of a song called *"All I Ever Wanted."* During those first 10 days, it seemed to rotate into play every time we needed the song to express feelings for us.

*From where I lay, I can see the sun*
*rising through the trees.*
*Before I face this morning rush,*
*I get down on my knees.*

Each morning brought a mixture of emotions, familiar ones mixed with unsettling ones. The unsettling ones became familiar. The only prayers Mark and I shared those days were unspoken ones, private thoughts that joined together as we sat—driver and passenger. We were on our knees in spirit.

Our trips to the hospital became familiar too. The parking lot, the lot attendant, the hospital entrance, the bank of elevators that carried us to the fourth floor—each landmark indicated how close we were to our son. Neither Mark nor I took off our armbands that confirmed our identity as Stross' parents. I spent my morning elevator ride looking forward to entering the NICU and casually waving it near anyone who might notice.

Entering the NICU was a ceremonial affair. We each selected a yellow gown to wear over our clothes and assisted each other with tying it. This was followed by a two-minute session of hand washing. We had arrived. We were with Stross again.

Our new son received superior hospital care the entire length of his stay; however, as a new mom, I feared my role suffered whenever I was not physically there to participate in his care or to share in mundane daily decisions. I wanted—I needed—to be in two places at the same time.

Mark had already grappled with these feelings. During my time as a patient, he divided his time between my bedside and Stross'. Now that I was home, I had to face my frustration and sense of inadequacy over divided priorities. When we were all together in the NICU, from early in the day until we tore ourselves away at night, the world made more sense.

*I lift my eyes and I thank you for*
*this life You've granted me.*
*I pray that every day I live,*
*Your heart will be pleased.*

In the first quiet moments of morning, God was there. Mark could hear him, and I could hear her. Together we met each day seeking to remain faithful while caring for a newborn who depended on us. In our hearts, we now understood that the intense, life-changing love we felt for Stross measured only a fraction of the love God felt for us.

We were thankful for Stross' life and eager to take him home and share him with the world. At home, we could be Mom and Dad under circumstances that better matched our emerging sense of reality. We already knew we were different from other parents. Consequently defining our parental role had become a primary focus, an awesome task shaped by what we believed, or thought we believed, about God.

*I pray for hands that hold You,*
*higher than anything else.*
*And a heart that loves You, more than life itself.*

Parenthood had always been part of Mark's and my shared life plan. Had biology or even the miracles of modern science worked against us, we were open to adoption. This type of parenthood—becoming a parent to a child with birth defects—had never been

· · ·

discussed. As real as this truth was, it remained beyond imagination.

> *From where I stand, I can see the dreams*
> *that You have fulfilled.*
> *Such kindness I did not deserve,*
> *but You gave it still.*

Through the lyrics of a song, we repeatedly confronted a truth we could not ignore. Our dreams of parenthood had been resoundingly fulfilled, and our baby was beautiful. He was the baby the nurses lovingly called "Peanut." He was the baby with the eyes that could pierce your heart. He was the baby we had dreamed of, and yet, he wasn't. It was becoming undeniably clear that his life and what we allowed God to do through it would be the best gift we could give to the world. It was a bigger truth, a bigger gift, than we could have imagined.

> *What do I have, that you did not give?*
> *There's nothing that I can see.*
> *So all I have to give to You*
> *is what You've given me.*

While we couldn't always touch Stross, we could spend time just standing by his bed and watching him sleep. We learned to distinguish his restful sleep from his respite sleep, those drug-induced times of unconsciousness that helped his body heal. Even when he made no vocal sounds, we learned to interpret his movements—the twitch of an eye or a jerk of his arm.

A physiological change occurred whenever I looked at Stross. My blood rushed faster, my heart beat in my throat and the edges of my personality softened. When I tried to verbalize how much I loved him, I choked, yet my body spoke of love loud and clear.

Mark spoke through his hands. During the first few days of Stross' life when holding him was impossible, Mark could not keep his hands off him. He would spend hours at a time stroking Stross' hair and rubbing lotion all over his body. When it looked like Stross' tiny diaper was the least bit wet, he'd change it. If his lips were chapped, Mark dabbed on a bit of Vaseline. I knew Mark's loving touch well, and I marveled at this new sensation of seeing Mark and Stross together.

*I pray for hands that hold You,*
*higher than anything else.*
*And a heart that loves You,*
*more than life itself.*

Many things now made sense. Parents would lay down their lives for their child without thinking about it. If it were within the realm of possibilities, parents would change places with a child and live the life laid out for him instead—regardless of surgeries, inconveniences of daily life, medical tests and the uncertainties of science.

Parents would experience prejudices if it meant their child would not. Parents would endure the low expectations, the stereotypes, the unfairness of life. That is what I wanted as a parent—to take on my son's battles. If it were possible, I would do that. I could do that. I really could.

*This is all I ever wanted,*
*this is all I want to be.*
*All I've ever wanted is to love You faithfully.*

When I would lie in my own bed or stand next to Stross', my thoughts came in a jumble. In quiet moments I sorted through them. A certain amount of fatigue worked in my favor. All the high energy I typically relied on faded just enough to better open my channel to God, and the yearnings of my new mother's heart signaled him in spirit at every opportunity. Even though I'd entered motherhood without fully anticipating its impact, I had wanted to be a mom. Now I was one. I was Stross' mom and that was a more important task than I had ever dreamed. Even more than I had ever wanted.

*I know I don't have the power*
*to love You like I should,*
*But every day with every thing I have,*
*I wish I could.*

Already I recognized that being Stross' mom would require diligence. I'd need to press for answers to difficult questions at times when people were uncomfortable. And I'd need wisdom. I would need to think of appropriate questions when it appeared the answers were eluding us. And I'd need patience, for even if I'd done all of the other things well, answers might not come quickly.

"We have to wait and see."

"That's not something we can answer now."

"When Stross is older, we'll have a better picture of what we are dealing with."

I also needed tolerance. Not everyone saw how wonderful Stross was. His defects seemed to disqualify him as the model of a perfect baby—yet he was. While no one spoke of it, I was aware that the paradoxical nature of his existence was lost to many. They did not see Stross as Mark and I saw him: beautiful. He was an incredible fighter with a sensitive soul.

Our little mystery man promised me lessons about how to live in concert with others. But to learn these, I would need the ability to see him for who he was, without limiting him or what he aspired to be. Piecing that concept together made me realize how normal a parent I really was.

What traits were evident when my parents first encountered me? What emotions had I unmasked in them? How often had they not understood my desires or underestimated my abilities? Did they struggle with perceptions of who I was and what they believed my limitations to be? Had they gotten everything they'd wanted in me?

. . .

# Chapter 13

# A Miracle in Hand?

...

S tross and I finally got the opportunity to try nursing on Mother's Day, one full week after his birth. I was nervous and afraid to admit my preference for keeping things the way they were. I had become a master milker, a Pump Queen who appreciated electronic convenience.

Incredibly cooperative and efficient, the breast pump gave me the control I craved. In fact I thought putting my breast milk in a bottle gave Stross and me the best of both worlds. I could stay on my schedule and he on his. Yet the majority of women I'd known advocated breast-feeding, and for them it meant putting a baby to the breast. The act, they claimed, was natural and nurturing.

Since Stross had dealt with enough abnormalities in life already, emerging maternal instincts told me I owed it to him to try breast-feeding the traditional way. So after church that Sunday Mark and I drove through McDonalds, then straight to the hospital. I gobbled down a high calorie meal with extra fluid. But I hoped Stross would be sleeping when we arrived. He was.

Stross' isolette was decorated for Mother's Day with balloons and a message facilitated by the night nurse. His tiny footprints signed my first Mother's Day card, an act that for some mothers, perhaps, might have brought on a bout of tender tears. But I was too anxious for sentimentality. I was about to try nursing—real nursing—and had no indication if I'd be good at it.

Stross' day nurse had learned from his chart that today was the big day. I noticed the brightly curtained accordion wall she'd already pulled near his isolette. Soon it would become Stross' and my hiding place as we attempted the fine art of breast-feeding. Hardly a private place, it was the only place to nurse in the NICU.

I looked around the room at other mothers visiting their children, many who had been NICU residents for several months. In my heart I knew these women envied my ability to hold my child and attempt nursing. Many had given up on the process long ago, overwhelmed by the uncertain lives of their preemies. Others were veteran pumpers with months of experience compared to my measly seven days. They dreamed of the day that was mine—a chance to breast-feed on Mother's Day.

Eager to help me get started, Stross' nurse, a mom of two breast-fed children, volunteered to wake him for me.

"Oh, just let him sleep now," I demurred. "We can do it when he wakes up."

"Okay," she said. "Just let me know when you are ready to pump again, and we will make sure to do it before then."

"That's not for a few hours," I said with a little too much enthusiasm. "But I'll let you know."

Mark's mom and dad arrived in the next half hour, and we chatted about the events of the past week while waiting for Stross to awaken. It wasn't long. Stross somehow sensed the excitement and opened his eyes to check us all out. This would be the first opportunity David and Carolyn had to hold him. That easily took precedence over his first nursing session. The rocking chair was pulled into place while Grandpa and Grandma gowned and washed their hands.

Today, like all the days before, we examined Stross whenever he ventured out of the isolette. He still did not wear clothes, only a doll-sized diaper and a comparatively adult-sized ostomy pouch. All other parts were open to inspection: his nose, his ears, his toes, his arms and chest, his fingers, the palms of his hands—the palms with one line where two should be. I didn't regularly look at his hands. I was more interested in his eyes. Today he seemed more alert—his eyes intent, searching. I wondered what he thought about all the fussing and cooing.

Several photos and yards of videotape later, Stross indicated he was hungry. A tiny thumb found his petite mouth, and he made a small noise—barely audible but enough for the nurse to bring us back to the task at hand. Mark came up with an excuse that gave him and his dad a reason to step out leaving only the nurse, Carolyn, and me beside Stross. Carolyn politely volunteered to make herself scarce as well, but her presence was the least of my worries. Any and all moral support was welcomed.

So there we were, three women and one tiny baby behind a thin, brightly colored curtain wall. I awkwardly sat in the hard rocking chair, my elbows uncomfortably resting on its arms. A pillow in my lap provided a supportive and soft place for Stross, now being gently laid in my arms. He was really hungry now. It was time to set modesty aside, expose a breast and revel in the womanly art of lactation.

The nurse grabbed Stross' head with one hand and pinched his jaws open with the other. She pushed his mouth over my nipple, and he locked on, hard. A few sucks later he pulled off and wildly turned his head side to side, searching for a better source of nourishment. Drops of milk dripped onto his face, and his search grew more frantic. The nurse repositioned him tighter against my chest and pushed him on again. Again he locked on, sucked three or four times and released. He became more frantic now. He smelled the milk and had even tasted it. It just wasn't coming out the way he believed it should. This scenario repeated itself more than a dozen times, and I started to revere Stross more as a force to be reckoned with rather than a child seeking nourishment.

In order to match his formidable energy, I mastered all the methods for holding a baby while nursing and learned strategies that were supposed to help me overcome any difficulty. I alternated breasts in case he preferred the landscape of one more than the other. I tried on nipple shapers and enhancers, even though the nurse and I both doubted that was a problem. Eventually I resorted to placing a bottle nipple over my own. Stross happily sucked the familiar texture and calmed down. Too tired to eat his full meal, he fell asleep and the nurse took him back to his bed with plans to wake him in an hour. Even then, she explained, the stress of nursing may be too tiring for him.

I agreed to her plan to give him the remainder of his allotted milk from a bottle and tried to think of ways to alleviate my own stress. As I tucked myself in and re-buttoned my blouse, I wondered what the point had been. Neither Stross nor I had enjoyed nursing, not in the least.

The nurse offered words of encouragement and reassured me that Stross would catch on. After all, he had only been bottle-fed a few days during his first week of life; and he was a fantastic eater. He knew what to do. He just didn't know how to do it with me. She asked me to try again that evening. I reluctantly promised and took my engorged breasts to the pump room for relief.

I did not look forward to upcoming sessions or any advice I would receive from the seasoned nurse practitioners that were coming later to help. I sensed that nursing, supposedly a normal part of motherhood, would be far from normal for me. In fact I doubted it would happen at all.

Over the next few days, Stross and I attempted to work through the issues each of us had with nursing. A handful of nurses and lactation specialists made attempts to assist us as well. The sessions always ended the same: Stross falling asleep from fatigue, then a breast pump finishing the job he'd begun. Once Stross awoke, his nurse filled his tummy using a bottle—Stross' preferred mode of drinking. He ate extremely well from a bottle. Apparently he didn't like doing things he wasn't good at either.

Nourishment aided Stross' healing, and his health improved quickly—so quickly that his discharge was set for Tuesday, May 14, Mark's 28th birthday. The date seemed too early, only four days after his shunt surgery, and only nine days after the surgeries performed

• • •

on the day of his birth. To prepare for this transition, we spent the rest of Sunday and all of Monday learning Stross' life care skills: how to empty and change his ostomy, how to order from the medical supply company, how to identify signs of a shunt malfunction, how to avoid skin sores on his paralyzed legs, how to bathe him, how to store and thaw breast milk at home and, of course, more lessons on how to nurse babies who were reluctant learners. I didn't believe he was reluctant. I believed he'd made a choice and was sticking to it.

We reread our manual called *"What You Should Know About Your Child With Spina Bifida"* and brochures we'd been given about hydrocephalus. We worked with doctors and nurses to schedule follow-up appointments and observed Stross' first hearing screen. A full eye exam was scheduled for the next week along with his two-week check at the pediatrician's office. There were also upcoming appointments with the pediatric surgeon and the neurosurgeon as well as plans to get Stross started in a physical therapy program through the school system's area education agency, or AEA.

A pediatric cardiologist wanted to see Stross on a follow-up basis since a diagnostic test on his heart showed a ventricular septal defect or VSD. Basically, Stross had a heart murmur, a hole in the wall of his heart. The cardiologist explained that it should close on its own, but the outcome should not be left to chance.

All of Stross' doctors were anxious to know if the chromosome study had come back from Mayo. Depending on the results, there may be a need for more tests. Stross' doctors seemed cautious and pessimistic about the outcome; his nurses seemed optimistic. Mark fluctuated on what he believed day to day. I, on the other hand, became Scarlett O'Hara: I wouldn't think about mental retardation now; after all, tomorrow was another day.

Fiddle-de-dees aside, I did give a damn about the results. In one week I'd risen to the challenge of parenting a son with a physical disability. I wasn't prepared for anything else.

When Tuesday arrived, the day we'd take Stross home, Mark and I dressed up. I selected an outfit even nicer than the one I'd chosen before Stross' birth. Today was more significant than

...

previously imagined. We weren't taking home an ordinary baby. We were taking home a survivor.

Mark and I rode together to the hospital that day—just like the days before it. We spent time talking to Stross before dressing him in a cuddly yellow sleeper and took turns videotaping each other holding him. He watched intently as Mark adjusted the straps of the car seat we'd brought, then we sat together waiting for Stross' discharge papers. We felt like the family of three we'd become.

A nurse we had not met before was on duty. Stross was healthy enough to share this nurse with two other NICU residents. In fact our son was so healthy, his bed was now a standard bed, the kind most newborns enjoy immediately after birth. He looked so different with clothes on and no barriers to keep us from touching him.

We were eager to just take Stross and leave. We were tired of hospitals, tired of doctors and tired of everything different reminding us how far off course our life had ventured. Going home meant getting back on track somehow. Comfortably away from all things different, we could better assess what had happened to us and then decide the best way to move forward—Stross and Mark and me. But first we were being asked to wait.

Mark and I had no idea why we needed to wait. Both the pediatric surgeon and neurosurgeon had come earlier and left notations in Stross' chart. However, according to the nurse, there were more things to be done; and our pediatrician wanted to see us.

A few minutes later the pediatrician came. He looked Stross over, studied the notes on his chart then pulled up a stool and sat down. He repeated the instructions for discharge and asked if we had questions. We had none, other than an obvious one. I'd asked every day if the chromosome study from Mayo had arrived? Today the answer was "yes." Mark and I made an immediate, emotional connection. We didn't look at each other or even touch. We simply breathed—our chests rising and falling in syncopation.

The doctor looked at his clipboard. Finally he lifted his head, glanced in our direction and began to speak, but then hesitated. After a three-second eternity, he spoke.

"It was normal," he said plainly. His expression and tone of voice were difficult to read. Was he pleased about the normal report or perplexed?

"Normal?" I asked. "What does that mean? Stross will have no mental problems?"

"None that are related to a chromosome abnormality," responded the doctor.

"So he is normal mentally," said Mark, attempting to get a "yes" or a "no" by rephrasing the question as a statement.

"You see, what this test does," said the pediatrician, using an explanation for his answer, "is watch how the chromosomes divide as blood is grown in a laboratory. Stross' cells did not show any abnormal divisions."

"That's good," I said tentatively, working hard to press the pediatrician into a more concrete response. "So Stross doesn't have Down's or a trisomy syndrome? Can we believe Stross' biggest genetic problem is that he looks like his dad?"

The pediatrician smiled without responding. Mark chuckled. I still had not heard the conclusive answer I longed for. Physical disabilities aside, I wanted the doctor, any doctor, to say my child was not mentally impaired.

"Can we take him home now?" Mark asked. "There aren't any more tests related to that, right?"

We needed conclusive clarification of his discharge.

"Oh, yes. Of course, you can take him home," said the pediatrician. "Take him home and enjoy your baby."

Maybe the pediatrician was more relaxed than I first thought. Yet something still seemed to be bothering him. Mark and I started to pack the last of Stross' care items into the hospital's complimentary diaper bag. The doctor stayed a while longer, making notes in Stross' chart and reminding us about the upcoming check up. As he started to leave, he offered one last piece of information.

"There is another test that can be done for chromosome abnormalities. It is very similar to this one, but it uses skin cells," he said. "If you'd like, we can schedule a skin graft in order to send those cells for observation. Then we can be even more certain."

The term "more certain" indicated what he'd left unspoken. Either he or another doctor—or all of our doctors—retained doubt. Neither Mark nor I said anything, so he continued.

"Stross had a variety of birth defects that do not seem to be related," he said. "They may not be, or they might be part of an even more rare syndrome that we have not explored. You don't have to let me know today. Just think about it. We can always schedule the test if you want."

We thanked him as he said good-bye and left. I made a mental note to ask each of Stross' doctors about the report so I could assess what each believed it meant. I now had an agenda for the follow-up visits.

Stross' trip to the neurosurgeon would be the most interesting. He had called Stross' facial features "Mongoloid"—a term I thought no one used anymore. I believe his exact words had been, "Well his face is very Mongoloid. Just look at him." Of course, the neurosurgeon had been extremely careful not to rule out an error in his judgment. I looked forward to a conversation about chromosomes with him and mentally filed away my joke about Stross' and Mark's shared genetics for future use.

After our pediatrician left, Mark and I were alone with Stross. It felt different to look at him. The report gave us permission to see only what was in front of us.

"Do you think the report missed something?" I asked Mark. "It seems he thought so."

"I don't know, Joy," Mark said. "Let's just be thankful for what it said. Let's don't borrow trouble."

Mark already sounded like a dad, in fact, a lot like his own dad. I'd started to obsess about something not within my control, one of my mother's traits. Perhaps Stross, like Mark and me, would resemble parts of his father and parts of his mother—nothing more or less.

Thirty more minutes passed before the nurse let us fasten Stross into his infant seat to exit the doors of the NICU. Hospital regulations

• • •

required her to walk us out the front door and push Stross, now fastened into his seat, on an official hospital transport cart. However, until she finished helping another baby, we had to wait.

Stross quietly slept while I held his left hand with my left index finger—tiny fingers wrapped around my large one. He had magnificent hands, short and strong. They looked the same as the day he was born, yet different somehow.

Everything was different today. It was Mark's birthday, and we were taking Stross home for the first time. Best of all, we no longer had to wait for the report from Mayo. It was back, and it brought good news—at least Mark and I thought it did.

No one saw me slip Stross' fingers from around mine to pry open his tiny palm. I needed to examine our little mystery man myself. I needed to stare at that one line in the palm of his hand again. I had not looked since they explained its significance to me the day he was born. I needed to see it again to decide if another test was in order.

I didn't look just once. I looked twice and looked a long time. I looked at both hands. Both palms had two lines across—parallel lines. I opened Stross' left hand again, wider this time, then blinked his tiny palm into focus. There really were two parallel lines. I looked at my own hand. I had two also. I already knew that, but it seemed necessary to check again. After all Stross had only one line there 10 days ago, and now he had two.

I immediately began rationalizing. Perhaps Stross had developed more since birth, and this second line had simply not been mature enough to notice. But that seemed as likely as his fingerprints changing their pattern. So if that wasn't the explanation, perhaps the doctors and nurses who had noted this abnormality were mistaken. That seemed more likely and yet equally improbable.

Stross' palms now had two lines that ran parallel. They only had one line 10 days ago. My mind entertained a startling possibility. Our family had received a miracle. If this were *not* true, we'd endured a gross misjudgment. A misjudgment was easy to believe. A miracle was mind-boggling.

I decided not to show anyone Stross' hands, not even Mark—not now. It might have meant more tests. Mark could see Stross' hands when we got home. And I did need Mark to verify my confusion—my conclusion.

Way too many unsettling things had happened in the past 10 days, events I could never have imagined—events I would never have willingly participated in. I wasn't even certain I wanted a miracle. I just wanted to take my baby home.

•  •  •

# a Career

# Chapter 14

# With Mixed Feelings

...

Y ou would think a miracle—one that you had secretly desired but never overtly asked for, one so enormously life changing that it made the difference between taking your son home to grow up or possibly finding a place for him to live where he could get specialized care—you would think that a miracle of this type, even the possibility of this miracle, would carry significant memories.

It doesn't.

Mark and I recall strikingly similar details—and we share a strikingly similar sense of ambivalence. Mark wasn't sure what to make of Stross' hands either. Still isn't.

It seems disbelief has clouded our memories—not unbelief in miracles, but disbelief in the magnitude of one child's life. And our disbelief tangled with seemingly unbelievable things.

We had a child and had become parents. Unbelievable.

We had a child who had been born with birth defects. Unbelievable.

We saw that child through three surgeries in five days. Unbelievable.

We became adept in medical procedures that were part of his daily care within 10 days. Unbelievable.

We received hundreds of cards and dozens of phone calls from across the country—from distant relatives and from friends we had not spoken with in years. Unbelievable.

Love could be tangible—that we believed.

In fact loving and raising the child who slept in the nursery we'd decorated had become the most rewarding and most challenging part of our lives—a complicated combination that kept us somewhere between moments of heart-breaking anxiety and heart-racing euphoria.

Perhaps Stross had been transformed from a child with both intellectual and physical disabilities into a child with only physical ones. If so we had, indeed, been the privileged recipients of a miracle. As magnificent as that prospect was, we were too tired, too worn down, too shocked to share any form of exuberance with others.

Based on the results of a chromosome study, we could believe—at least for the time being—that our son would not be mentally retarded, only physically disabled. How this situation had come to be, we did not know. Whether the second lines across Stross' palms had gone unnoticed or whether they had arrived divinely late, we could not know. We simply accepted their existence as our reality like we had so many other things during those first two weeks of May.

There was no time to analyze how we were coping. We were simply thankful for all we'd be given—for all we'd survived. At that time surviving *was* coping. But we were still grieving things we couldn't adequately identify—things we'd never had in the first place. And when you don't know what you are missing—like what it feels like to become the parent of a child without physical abnormalities—it's difficult to recognize that you are grieving things you can't explain. In fact it's difficult to recognize grief at all.

Stross was our first baby. We didn't know what it was supposed to feel like to bring your baby home from the hospital. We knew what it felt like to get him home: We were relieved. He was alive. According to the medical tests, he would not die before his first birthday because of any chromosomal abnormalities; and now that the surgeries were over, we could focus on getting to know him.

In a way, bringing Stross home was anticlimactic. The experiences surrounding his birth had been so poignant, so moving, that carrying

· · ·

him into our house and nestling him into his own crib didn't feel as momentous as other things we'd experienced in recent days. And it was a little scary. The first time either of us held Stross, he already had IV lines and monitors attached. I wasn't certain this version of Stross was ready to be tether-free.

Besides we just wanted to hold him. That's what we'd been missing: feeling him snuggle into the crook of our arm, making eye contact while cooing and cuddling and watching him sleep on our chest after a feeding. We were his monitors now.

Mark, who regularly let Stross sleep on his chest, seemed to have always appreciated tactile experiences that evoked the power of human touch. When we were dating I noticed that Mark was usually photographed with his arm slung around a person's shoulders or, particularly in some photos taken with former girlfriends, gleefully holding a hand. According to his siblings he was also the brother with an affinity for pinching, tickling and wrestling.

I was quite different as a child. I used body language to inform family members I did not want to be touched. While my sister readily crawled into my parents' laps to sit and cuddle, I preferred merely sharing the same couch. My mom figured out I'd let her massage my sore feet after a long day of waitressing, but other than that, I was my family's one-second-hug child who then darted out the door. I had learned to appreciate touch as an expression of affection because of Mark; in a matter of days Stross accelerated my lessons ten-fold.

Because we were beginning the fun parts of parenthood, life felt a bit surreal. We were away from all things hospital. And even though Stross was more baby than patient, there were still many things to remain on guard for regarding his health. Therefore the hospital never really seemed far away.

I had always been a person who kept a to-do list, but Stross made me aware of how truly task-oriented I was. I approached one process-driven duty related to his physical needs—caring for his ostomy—with particular care for detail. At the hospital the nurses had changed his ostomy appliance when needed. At home its management was our responsibility.

• • •

The doctor had said Stross' ostomy (colostomy) may become a permanent bowel management solution, but that decision existed years into the future. We understood that meant we should incorporate its care into our lives as if it were permanent already.

Because Stross' fecal matter could be drained from a plastic ostomy pouch at our convenience, his version of a dirty diaper was quite manageable. However, unlike other babies, when Stross smelled of fecal matter, it meant the seal of his ostomy appliance was leaking and needed immediate attention. If we could smell feces we knew stool had found a way under the pouch's seal and onto his skin and clothes. Therefore all other tasks were immediately on hold until he was cleaned and a new pouch system was put in place.

Mark and I had learned that with ostomy care, experience begat skill. And we had learned that skin care was the greatest related skill we'd acquired. We had developed particular techniques for cleaning the skin around the stoma and took great care not to touch or irritate the blood-rich opening, which was actually the end of his large intestine exposed. We preferred to use tissues for large amounts of stool then baby wipes for stool residue. Next we used adhesive remover to rid his skin of residual adhesive paste followed by a warm washcloth rinse. Finally, a medical supply called Skin Prep was wiped on as both a finishing touch and a first step for the new appliance.

While the solution left by the Skin Prep air-dried on Stross' tiny tummy, we would stand right next to him and cut the seal for a new pouch system. The pouch's opening needed to match the circumference of Stross' stoma and fit snuggly without rubbing the stoma's intestinal tissue. Should his body begin to discharge stool before the new appliance was in place, the entire cleaning process had to begin again, and likely with more soiled changing cloths and clothing than before.

Knowing where to stand, where to place the necessary supplies and how quickly you needed to work became keys to success. It was a job you wanted to complete swiftly, but moving too quickly circumvented a successful outcome. A secure seal only happened

· · ·

when a well-cut appliance with just the right amount of stoma adhesive paste was gently pushed onto clean, dry skin. Then the ostomy pouch could be comfortably positioned inside a fresh diaper, and Stross could be dressed in a fresh baby outfit.

With Stross now clean the work area had to be cleaned too. So while he waited in his cradle, soiled tissues and soiled laundry were properly disposed; hands and surfaces were disinfected; and paste, scissors and supplies were returned to their places.

A well-affixed ostomy appliance could last for two, maybe three days. But leaks could develop for seemingly no apparent reason and under the best of circumstances. Stross' creamy, breast-milk stool frequently found ways to break through even the best seals, making it necessary to change his ostomy even several times a day. However, changing it too many times could damage his delicate skin, so Mark and I learned to read the contours of his growing tummy and adapt the process—how we cut and pasted—as we saw need. We never wanted to learn firsthand about skin breakdown.

Even though his ostomy care resembled something more suited to a doctor's procedure room, Stross, and everything that came with him, made our house feel even more like a home. A baby lived in our house now. And Mark and I were the dad and the mom.

Mark had gone back to work the day after Stross came home; and Carolyn had left a few days after that, leaving me as Stross' primary caregiver. It was time for Stross and me to get to know each other as mother and son, and I sensed him pulling me in as a moth to a flame.

In many ways I regarded Stross as a life force that required engaged interaction rather than a gift to enjoy. And he had survived so much—had presented such a powerful life force—that I wasn't sure how to enjoy him. I'd stare at him while he slept, attempting to learn how to read his needs. I wanted to hold him when he was fussy, feed him when he was hungry, change his diapers when his unfeeling bottom was wet and drain his soiled ostomy pouches when they had stool. And I also wanted to guard his soft, seemingly pliable head against injury.

Ever since I'd first learned about the plates of the human skull and how they functioned in babies, I'd been utterly astounded by soft spots. It seemed inadequate that only skin and a few layers of membranes protected the brains of the world's smallest humans. My baby's soft spot was even a bit scarier. His was slightly larger than most, widened by the pressure of hydrocephalus.

Stross' recent surgery had corrected the build-up of fluid, so his soft spot was no longer dangerously taut. Now the plates of his head could fuse normally as he grew because a valve drained the excess cerebrospinal fluid. I couldn't determine which was scarier to think about—his soft spot or his valve.

A bandage on the back of his head covered both an incision and a bump of skin that hid the shunting device inserted days earlier. Evidently manufacturers did not make pediatric-sized valves to treat hydrocephalus since, under the best of circumstances, one valve could operate for life or at least make it into young adulthood. Stross' valve protruded from his head—the size of an extra large grapefruit—making it appear as if we'd tucked a baby carrot under the skin that covered his skull. The tubing that was attached to the valve also bulged under his skin as it ran behind his right ear then down and over his collarbone before obscurely entering his abdomen.

To casual observers the neck tubing merely looked like a pronounced blood vessel that was noticeable only when Stross turned his head to the left, pulling the skin taut. After his hair grew back the valve would be equally obscure, but during Stross' first days home the white bandage marked its location. Because I knew it was there, I regularly noticed it and regularly braced for a major case of the heebie-jeebies.

Compassion for my son kept me from fully freaking out. He'd endured greater things than I in his short life. I admired this child, less than one month old, and was fiercely proud. Stross proved he could do more than survive. He could thrive. He was eating well and tolerating all the ways Mark and I had invented to hold him.

We both liked to tuck him close to our chest, yet facing forward. Sometimes Stross nestled in the crook of Mark's arm or snuggled close to my breasts. No matter the method of cradling, Stross looked out at the world, taking in everything we saw.

At home I took Stross everywhere—positioning him next to me on the sofa while I folded clothes, lying him on a floor blanket while I read the day's mail and situating him in the center of our bed while I expressed milk. He napped at least once a day in a cradle my Grandfather Fred crafted out of walnut, but other naps occurred in my arms because I had a hard time letting him out of my sight. Moms are supposed to be enamored with their newborns, but I felt extraordinarily captivated—and overprotective.

Stross, born with a cherubic face, appeared to have an old soul living inside his miniature body. His dark eyes penetrated deeply, and he appeared to have the wisdom of a sage, making me wonder if he already knew what the future held.

Sometimes Stross and I could spend a portion of our day with Mark. Doctor visits scheduled during Mark's lunch hour kept us together as a family and warded off overwhelming feelings of responsibility when I was alone with Stross. I measured my Stross-time in two- to three-hour portions, small segments used to orient me to motherhood.

My leave was to last eight weeks, and more than one-fourth of it was gone, so I filled each day with Stross duties that comprised a new kind of to-do list. The item at the top: childcare.

I found nothing life-giving about the process of finding childcare. Being able to return to work felt life-giving. And childcare, by anyone's standard, was a prerequisite for that privilege. So I couldn't really explain why I'd tabled such an important task until now. In fact both Mark and I had regularly avoided the topic before Stross was born, choosing instead to focus on home buying responsibilities. Now, finding adequate childcare—a daunting task with near non-existent prospects—loomed as an unwelcome challenge. And I normally thrived on challenges.

My best explanation for why I never considered myself our family's best first choice—either before Stross' birth or after—is this: I didn't want the job. And not because I thought being a caregiver was beneath me. I honestly didn't think I was the best candidate for the job. I did believe I could be a fantastic mother in the off hours: evenings and weekends. But when using other women for comparative analysis, I believed I wasn't very nurturing and didn't have the patience or selflessness necessary to meet the real demands of Stross' most productive times of day.

In fact I recognized an incompatible truth: I needed the stimulation of an office workday in order to be any good during my mommy hours at all.

Ironically, the most thinking I'd done about work and motherhood had occurred a few years earlier in relation to someone else.

While living in Fort Worth, I had served on the board of a professional communicators' organization and had gotten to know an officer named Renae fairly well. She managed part of Burlington Northern Railroad's communications department, and the company I worked for helped produce her company's employee magazine. She was an excellent writer and a meticulous editor. I knew Renae was regarded as somewhat of an annoying perfectionist among our colleagues—and could tell by comments that she'd made that she knew it too—but Renae was also the kind of person most would want using her skills for your benefit.

When Renae became pregnant, I watched her make detailed plans for her maternity leave. She had appointed a coworker to oversee her magazine's production schedule and tapped me to step into her board position while she was away. I received detailed, written instructions during a one-on-one lunch meeting in the last month of her pregnancy and felt honored that she entrusted her responsibilities into my care.

Near the end of our meeting Renae handed me a phone number and said she could be reached at home if necessary. Otherwise, I could plan on her coming back eight weeks after giving birth.

She didn't come back. Instead she resigned her job and came to one more board meeting—along with her newborn daughter— to resign from the board as well. Everyone was clearly in shock. We had heard of her job resignation but had been fairly certain she'd maintain her organizational membership as a way to stay professionally viable. No one begrudged her choice to leave. It just seemed highly out of character.

But I understood. And as the meeting died down, I worked my way over to her, both to admire her daughter and to offer encouragement. Her demeanor indicated how conflicted she felt, and I wanted to recognize her internal turmoil.

"It must have been a tough decision," I said. "I know you loved your job at Burlington Northern. Now that you won't be coming to these meetings, I guess I won't see you much anymore. But I think I understand your decision."

"You do?" She was clearly surprised. My career trailed hers by about four years, and I imagined it was easy for her to doubt my ability to connect to her station in life.

"Sure," I said. "You've always struck me as someone who wants to be the best at whatever you do. It only makes sense you want to be the best mother."

As the words slipped out, I feared they might be misinterpreted: Perfectionistic Renae wants to be Perfectionistic Mom. Fortunately that is not how she received them.

"Thank you, Joy. That's exactly it. I hadn't really thought of it like that," she said.

Her face did show a measure of relief. I had no idea about the individual circumstances that had led to her decision to step away from her career for awhile. I only knew that my words had provided her with context. And she rewarded me with a hug.

I don't know if Renae ever did resume her career. I know that had been her plan—to take time off and then come back someday. But I doubted she'd been able to make it happen. Since that day I'd maintained a heighten awareness to news stories about working women, glass ceilings and difficult re-entries into the work force. Based on what I'd heard, I believed the mommy-track could derail even the most talented Burlington Northern professional.

Now the same decision stared me in the face multiple times a day—dark-eyed and adorable. And like the moth and the flame, I drew close to Stross but feared what might happen if I got too close.

• • •

My identity was at stake. If I stepped away from my career to fully enter his world, would I even exist anymore? Didn't he deserve more than the shell of a mother? Something beyond charred pieces—mere dust in human form? I knew that countless women gave birth and then returned to the workforce without taking years off to raise children. I'd identified with them, and I'd imagined becoming one of them. Why did I have to change just because my son had disabilities?

Soon returning to work became a symbol of my ability to overcome adversity. I didn't want to succumb to any perils that might have befallen Renae. At the core I was still the little third grade girl who—affected by images of Vietnam bloodshed, campus uprisings and women's rights marches—wrote down the words "role model" as my answer for what I wanted to be when I grew up. I wanted to know it was possible to lovingly care for your son, lovingly support your husband and still love who you were as a grown up. I wanted to overcome—and to me, at that time, overcoming meant returning to the place I had been, and then finding my way forward.

I knew that Joy. But I couldn't comprehend the Joy—or even the joy—that I would know in the future.

The few conversations about childcare that Mark and I had before Stross' birth told me my husband understood he'd married a woman who would become a working mother. And he continued to be fully supportive of that type of planning now. We simply needed a qualified caregiver to help us raise Stross. Our family needed a modern Mary Poppins—the West Des Moines version.

Because Mark had already exhausted his leave time, the primary burden of finding childcare fell to me. The pressure of this personal crisis did not invigorate me the same way a professional crisis could. But fortunately everyone around me was understanding, including my boss.

Mark had called both bosses at their respective homes the Sunday of Stross' birth, and he'd done his best to explain the circumstances that altered our plans to return to work. Both bosses thanked Mark for informing them so soon.

Mark and his boss comprised their company's entire video

production department. She had little need to share the news of Stross' birth with others. My boss, however, needed to inform my colleagues about Stross' arrival.

Peter King, the association's executive director, arrived at my bedside at 8 a.m. that Monday, 24 hours after Stross' birth. I can still see Mark, smiling in anticipation of my surprise, as he escorted him through my hospital room's door and to my bedside. Mark, like me, was clearly impressed that Peter had made me the priority of his day.

My boss was congratulatory but spoke few words. His countenance conveyed kindness, empathy and concern. His presence was a link to my life before Stross and a time when my future was what I made it, not what happened to me. A small part of me longed to get out of bed, join him on his commute to the office and tackle the familiar responsibilities of my job instead of my inherent duties as Stross' mom.

I welcomed conversation with Peter. I'd last seen him when we'd left work three days earlier. Standing next to each other as we waited for the elevator that Friday, neither of us could have known that my leave would begin the next business day. We had joked about how I'd be missing "any day now," and in previous conversations, we had discussed how certain aspects of my work would be completed during my leave. Each time I'd assured him that I'd planned well, and that the association's publications and annual convention would remain on schedule. He hadn't seemed concerned, but I'd wanted to reassure him anyway.

With Peter at my bed rail, I picked up where our conversation had left off. Rather than begin a dialogue about my new parental status, I launched into an explanation of the arrangements I'd made to publish the next issue of the magazine and outlined additional information about notes I'd left on my desk for my intern. These were topics I was comfortable discussing. They made for better pleasantries than the medical prognosis of my first child, but we soon talked about that too.

Peter listened politely and waited silently when my voice cracked and my eyes welled with tears. He asked informed questions about

Stross, evidence that he comprehended what Mark and I faced. As he left he assured me that any problem at work could be handled by staff and encouraged me to take as much time as I needed settling into my new life. He said my job would be waiting for me when I was ready to come back and let me know I wasn't to worry about our group's insurance plan or my job security. Peter wanted me to know that he understood Stross was my first priority.

Nearly a year later I'd learn how the rest of Peter's day had gone. As a dad who'd lived through several miscarriages, he wanted the news of our son's birth announced to my co-workers with clarity and respect for our circumstances. If there were questions, he wanted to help answer them; so he had gone from office to office personally announcing Stross' birth. When Peter entered the last office to tell our business manager, a grandmotherly woman near retirement, he began to cry. My boss had openly cried for me.

Later that week Peter wrote a letter to the members of the association's executive board. It announced Stross' birth and explained the situation Mark and I faced as his parents. Peter began by stating that it was "with mixed feelings" that he wrote to report on the birth of my son. He shared that the staff's "excitement and happiness" for us had been "tempered by the fact Stross was born with physical difficulties, the extent of disability which is not yet fully known." He concluded with wishes for them to "join in hoping for the best possible outcome."

Peter's letter illuminated what happens when personal lives impact professional responsibilities. It acknowledged that one Friday I had left work as a young professional who was looking forward to the birth of her child, and by Monday, I had become a working mother facing unimaginable circumstances.

Now I only wanted to forge ahead with life as I had planned it—to return to work and be Stross' mom too. But first I had to find childcare. As understanding as Peter had been, my leave time was running out. I appreciated his words about my job security. Yet I understood that I would not be able to collect pay for work I had not completed or maintain insurance coverage as a benefit of a job I could no longer do.

The bills for both my and Stross' ambulances had arrived the day I'd been released from the hospital—one week before Stross came home. Bills and insurance statements filled our mailbox nearly every day, and I began to worry about expenses that weren't covered. For the first time, I realized why it was important to learn how to read the insurance company's explanation of benefits: Catching mistakes could save us money.

Even though I'd been instructed to not worry about my job, I kept tabs on the intern whose first day of work was my first day of leave. I wanted the magazine to meet its deadlines and plans for the convention to remain on track.

Each day brought me one day closer to returning to work. I simply had to find childcare within my allotted leave time. That's what I'd intended before Stross was born and that's what needed to happen now. If I could make that happen, then maybe Stross wouldn't be such a different child to rear after all. Perhaps our most horrible experiences were over. If I could find the perfect caregiver for our son, he'd be better for it and so would Mark and I.

●   ●   ●

# Chapter 15

# Nightmares

• • •

A few months before Stross was born, I had one of those nightmares to which pregnant woman grow accustomed—the kind where a woman dreams of giving birth to a full grown child or spawning so great a number of children that the delivery is noted in a book of records. Sometimes a hormone-induced nightmare might involve giving birth to a child who has unmentionable abnormalities.

My nightmare found me giving birth to a cyclops baby. I became the mother of an adorable child who had one huge eyeball in the center of his or her forehead. The sex of the child remained hidden from me, but the eyeball could not be missed. In my nightmare I was the only one who noticed the deformity. Even Mark was oblivious. I carried the baby around receiving compliments on him or her, questioning others if they noticed anything different about the child. No one seemed to, yet I couldn't tell if they were lying or not. In my nightmare mistrust and fear bred a fierce protectiveness. I loved my cyclops baby. I could see him or her clearly and was afraid that if others began to notice the huge solitary eye, the child would be labeled an outcast.

Before Stross was born, this dream was a source of uneasy amusement. For all of the strange ways children come into the world, I had never heard of a cyclops child. After Stross was born a few people with whom I'd shared my pre-birth nightmare labeled it a sign that I had intuitively known about Stross' defects. I do believe I knew something was wrong. However, my baby's lack of activity was a more likely reason. If the nightmare had any significance, it was in illuminating how extremely protective and possessive I was.

I can now understand how arrogance fed these qualities—even spiritual arrogance. Since childhood I had believed God intended for me to do great things—that I had been set apart for a purpose greater than I could comprehend. Who I was and what I possessed represented God's best. In its most innocent manifestation this ideology reflected a healthy interpretation of humans as the Creator's best offering to the world.

However, if something is regarded as best, did that mean other things were necessarily less?

Because of Stross I was growing toward a more egalitarian understanding of creation with nothing or no one any better than another. Only the diversity of the universe, I believed, could reflect the fullness of creation; therefore, small and great needed to be regarded as equal parts of the whole.

But I was aware that some were attuned to a graded spiritual order. In their hierarchy some select humans were regarded as God's ideal; some readily received human affirmation because of a perception that they had more to offer. Fiercely protective, I felt a need to guard my disabled son from others' perceptions. As was true for the cyclops baby of my dream, I was concerned that only I could see who he really was: part of the world and all things best—nothing more and certainly nothing less.

Stross had arrived like a loud wake-up call, and in this newness of life, I could see his wholeness and testify to his beauty. I understood my role was to share who he was with the world.

Until the end of May family members came to see Stross in the more natural surroundings of our home. Even friends from college and seminary days came great distances to meet him. While guests in our home, they lived through our new daily routine taking interest in Stross' ostomy care and allowing us to therapeutically relive the drama of his first days.

... ————————————————————————————————

By the Memorial Day weekend, our parental warm-up period had ended. I'd fully abandoned attempts at traditional nursing a week earlier, continuing the unconventional practice of expressing milk.

But even feeding Stross with a bottle had become a problem. He continued to chug his breast milk eagerly; but within minutes his small tummy tightened in pain, and he squirmed in our arms. The miniature features of his face wrinkled in a wince, expressing his discomfort. Stross didn't cry out in pain, but he groaned and contorted, making awkward and jerky movements with his body. Casual observers diagnosed colic. Mark and I studied his body and diagnosed a greater problem.

Stross' stoma had partially retracted inside his body making it hard for his intestines to rid his body of stool. Stross' appetite was healthy, but feeding him meant living through nearly one hour of heartbreaking pain as he wiggled and used abdominal contractions to force excrement out of the now tiny opening to the left of his belly button. There was little we could do but softly empathize, gently rub his tummy and brace for the next feeding.

An appointment with the pediatric surgeon confirmed our diagnosis. With words of compassion, he told Mark and me of the need for another surgery to correct this rare misfortune; and we quickly went from shock into action. If Stross needed surgery, the sooner the better. Our son had become part of us. His life mattered more than it had four weeks earlier. If his life were again in danger, we wanted to get through the ordeal as soon as possible—before we became more deeply entangled.

This was a Wednesday, the day before our fifth anniversary. Personal holiday aside, we pressed to have surgery scheduled for Thursday. The pediatric surgeon explained how at least one day was needed to clean out Stross' intestines in preparation for the colostomy revision, so the next day wouldn't do. In fact all the doctor's surgical days were full for the week. According to his appointment nurse, Stross couldn't be scheduled until early the week after next.

I asked the surgeon how dangerous it would be if Stross refused to eat because it hurt too much. He didn't answer. Mark started to talk now. He shared how horrible it was to feed Stross and to hold him as he writhed in pain. The doctor looked at us, deep in thought.

"Couldn't it be any sooner?" I asked. He paused, sighed and then spoke.

"You are right. That stoma is barely functional. I'll see what I can do." That was the answer we wanted. "Let's try for a week from today. I will see if I can adjust my schedule."

The idea of sending our newborn into surgery again was numbing, but there was no alternative. Stross' body could not correct itself.

Mark, Stross and I waited alone in a small consultation room while the doctor's appointment nurse adjusted the schedule. Within 30 minutes, we learned the surgery was set for Wednesday the fifth of June—the day Stross would turn one month old.

There was a flurry of activity now that surgery was a week away. A nurse came with information about hospital admission procedures and a consent form. Mark and I listened to her read through a list of pre-surgical instructions. We needed to stop by the pediatrician's office for blood work, and Stross had to be weaned from milk and placed on a clear fluid diet again.

Mark and I spent our anniversary together without fanfare. He worked, and I endured a day of uncomfortable feedings. Apple juice seemed to be easier on Stross, so I began alternating a bottle of milk with a bottle of juice. Anything to help the week pass more quickly.

On Friday Mark approached his boss with a request for more vacation days. She reluctantly granted them while making him promise to work additional hours to make up for the lost time.

When Monday arrived, my intern spent most of her day at our house going through the next issue of the association's magazine. Then she held Stross while I sorted my stack of mail. I enjoyed the productivity, even though our time together was strained. I barely knew this 21-year-old, yet I was forced to rely on her during the most trying time of my life. Watching her hold Stross took me back to my own college days, and I wondered when I'd begun to think about having a child. I couldn't remember.

And now I was preparing my one-month-old son for the fourth

...

surgery of his life.

Even though Mark's sister, Iris, had seen Stross on his first day of life, she had not had an opportunity to hold him. She really wanted to see him before surgery, and her best opportunity was the morning before we left for the hospital. Iris spent nearly an hour that Tuesday holding Stross and checking him over. But then it was time to get him to the hospital.

This time Stross was a pediatric patient in the same unit as children and adolescents. He had graduated from the hospital's NICU simply by going home. Walking the hospital's halls this time, Mark and I felt like veterans. It was against hospital policy for both parents to sleep in the room with their child, yet both of us managed to stay with Stross that night and every night after.

Caring for him and assisting the nurses with his pre- and post surgical care eased our feelings of helplessness. It was obvious that we'd attained expert status concerning his ostomy care. Because we were more relaxed than the nurses when changing the appliance or draining stool from the pouch, we took full responsibility for his bowel management.

The surgery on Wednesday went well, and Stross moved from intensive care to a private room the following day. He began eating that evening and was discharged into our care by noon on Friday. This three-day hospital stay was a breeze compared to what we'd experienced a month earlier.

Meanwhile my maternity leave had dwindled to only three weeks, and Mark and I had yet to make a decision about childcare. Many commiserated with our dilemma but no one offered suggestions. We could not imagine finding a day care center that would take Stross. Even if such a place existed, I did not want to deal with the countless germs found in that environment. Exposure to childhood diseases threatened to further complicate our lives.

I looked to Deb Davis for guidance. She and Steve had been in our position before and both of them were employed full-time. Deb recounted the details of their own search and told how Austin was still being cared for in a family day care by the same woman who took him in as a newborn. Deb had high praise for the woman who cared for Austin, sharing with us how she participated in his intermittent catheterization and even assisted with therapeutic exercises. Intermittent catheterization, a urological management procedure, was standard care for children with spina bifida, so Mark and I began to mentally prepare for this even though it was not yet medically necessary.

Deb volunteered to ask if her provider would agree to add Stross to her care should an opening arise. Unfortunately, when asked, the woman said no. She feared caring for two special children would drain her physically. Besides Stross had an ostomy, something beyond exercise and catheterizations to work into a daily routine. She felt she owed it to the other children to avoid taking on a more demanding situation.

We were beginning to learn how unique Stross' needs were. And while Deb continued to be a great source of moral support, her version of motherhood was nearly as far removed from mine as mothers with able-bodied children. As with the other mothers, our family's unique challenges set us apart. Deb and I both had sons with spina bifida, but my son also had an ostomy. Where childcare was concerned, that difference was significant.

Sharing the benefits of the Davis' childcare arrangement had seemed too good to be true anyway, and now we learned it was. However, hope remained. Home care now seemed a viable option. We just needed to find someone like that woman.

It felt as if everyone at church knew of our childcare dilemma. While many had offered to "do anything we can for you," we understood what anything meant. It included running an errand, cooking a meal or even giving us some money for bills. Yet I still hoped for a Mary Poppins-in-Training who would step forward as a caregiver for Stross.

With no such woman presenting herself, Mark and I asked flesh-and-blood women who exhibited similar qualities. We singled out women who had decided to stay at home to raise their own children. We hoped one was looking for extra income and that she would consider our need her opportunity.

That would not be.

One by one, we were turned down. One by one, we were told how honored the woman was by our request, but she simply could not take on the awesome responsibility of caring for Stross. Each said she would love to baby-sit for a few hours from time to time, but full time was out of the question.

I found the explanations excruciating. I did not want to hear about family responsibilities, fears about doing it right or a commitment to give more time to her family. When a woman said, "no," I wanted that to be the end of it; their decisions had been based on their families' needs. Their explanations illuminated my divergent perspective and augmented my pain.

Later at home I'd cry to Mark, attempting to rid myself of feelings like helplessness and frustration. But pain doubled in intensity as he took it in. Mark, if it were possible, felt more helpless. He envied my time with Stross and the luxury of purpose I felt both at work and at home. Instead he spent his days advancing a mission he didn't believe in while tolerating workplace practices that were inconsistent with his values.

Lacking solutions based in reality, I'd fantasize about rectifying our family's desperate situation. I'd vividly scheme of ways to find a new job for Mark, then I'd concoct a way to locate the ideal caregiver for Stross. I still believed the most loving thing I could do was to find someone incredibly nurturing to help raise him. He deserved the best chance of realizing his full potential just as Mark and I did.

My fantasizing took place while Stross and I napped. When he was tired, I'd rock him to sleep after a bottle, then lay him on our bed so I could sleep too. I'd lie facing him so I could study his innocent face, attempting to discern who he was and what his life meant. Eventually I'd close my eyes, either in exhaustion or prayer. My prayers for Stross were the most fervent. I implored God to bless him with health, social acceptance, worldly intelligence and a life partner who'd love him and care for him as long as he lived. The prayers made it easier to sleep.

Most days I'd awake first, but sometimes when I opened my eyes I'd see Stross intently looking at me. My son's fascinated look unnerved me. This tiny sage appeared to know what I felt and wanted to communicate what he knew of life for my benefit, if only he could speak. Perhaps he prayed on my behalf, as I did for him.

The challenge of finding adequate childcare was a greater strain than seeing Stross through surgery. The energy I spent in private despair left me fragile. When family asked about our progress, I offered defensive explanation. Where once I welcomed opportunities to call the office for updates, I now avoided contact out of fear they would ask when I'd be back.

Eventually I negotiated an extended leave by offering a way to fulfill my responsibilities while caring for Stross. Under my proposal, I clocked about 20 hours of work at home each week of July including a few hours worked in my office with Stross. I enjoyed having Stross with me at work. It provided me—truly—with the best of both worlds. Since the surgery for his ostomy revision, he'd exchanged his pacifier for his thumb and exhibited an uncanny ability to soothe himself when bored or tired.

Rather than being an office distraction, Stross seemed welcomed. Co-workers took turns playing with him and were genuinely interested in his development. Hardened lobbyists stopped in my office to talk baby talk or shake a rattle at him. Stross could be easily won over, conveying his appreciation with a smile. Several women in the office were grandmothers who enjoyed holding him in their laps. They took turns nestling him on their shoulders and caressing his back as he fell asleep.

After several weeks I sensed his novelty wearing off. I could tell at least a few of my colleagues wondered if I planned for him to permanently hang out by my desk. Working from home and trips to the office had kept major setbacks at bay regarding the convention and the monthly publications. Yet there were tasks that would soon demand my sole presence.

The annual convention, an event that encompassed one-half of my duties, loomed only two months away. The monthly publication schedule was nothing compared to the annual timetable this event mandated. By September nearly 600 individuals would attend the association's annual meeting. In order to achieve our attendance goals, I would need to manage facility and speaker contracts, organize the workshops, write and publish the marketing materials and plan several special events. Budgets, media coverage, décor arrangements and more would either originate with me or need to pass my review.

And I loved the challenge of making each piece work differently—better—than before. It felt satisfying to hear that things ran a little more efficiently, inspired a little more involvement and were a little more profitable than the previous year. Of course I knew what it felt like to be overwhelmed by details too. But even the logistics of troubleshooting for a major event were nothing compared to the nightmare of finding childcare.

Still Mark and I were committed to the search for we believed childcare was the one puzzle piece that could help all other things fall into place.

At the end of the third week in July, Stross had what Mark and I believed to be a seizure. While Mark was holding Stross on his lap, Stross thrust his arms straight out at his side. His eyes became fixed, his cheeks taut and his whole body rigid. The entire episode lasted what seemed one full minute (perhaps only a few intense seconds) but it was enough for Mark and me to get scared. We had both seen it and both believed it to be more than an exaggerated startle reflex.

I called our pediatrician. He cautioned us to not overreact and then thoroughly questioned us about the episode. He asked us to closely observe Stross during the next hour and call him if we noticed it again. We did, so we called and made plans to meet our pediatrician in the emergency room at the downtown children's hospital. After a complete evaluation, our doctor found nothing too compelling but, based on our descriptions, decided to admit Stross overnight for tests and observation. Fortunately it was the weekend, and Mark did not have to worry about taking a day away from work.

We did not feel at home in this unfamiliar hospital and spent an uncomfortable night taking turns at Stross' bedside in intensive care. Since there was room for only one parent to sleep in the room's recliner, the other took up residence on a sleeping cot in a room down the hall that was shared by half a dozen other parents. Stross only had one seizure in the hospital, and it did not last long enough for a nurse to see it. An EEG showed no irregularities in his brain waves, so we returned home the next day with instructions to keep an eye on him and call if we noticed anything worrisome. We didn't.

Returning to work part-time had helped me regain equilibrium. I felt stronger and took comfort from familiar feelings of productivity. Church activities became an outlet too. Near the end of July Mark and I helped our youth with a penny carnival to promote Vacation Bible School. Sometime that afternoon a mom of one girl told me about a couple in our church who might be willing to become our childcare provider. She knew the couple had adjusted their own work schedules to accommodate care of their five-year-old son. Rumor had it the mom was trying to have another baby, but things weren't going so well. Perhaps taking care of Stross would appeal to them.

I cautiously moved into action hoping that, at last, we'd find what we'd been hoping for. I began with a fact-finding mission then reported my findings to Mark. The woman and man alternated days at home to care for their own kindergartner. She was employed in a grocery deli; he was an MRI technician who worked out of a hospital's mobile unit. The alternating schedule worked well for them, she'd said. If we were open to them both caring for Stross, they were open to discussing it with us. When we learned their house was only a three-minute drive from ours, we started to hope that this lead would not play out as yet another too-good-to-be-true scenario.

I hedged over one detail. As liberal as I believed I was on gender stereotyping, I hesitated to have the man as a caregiver for my son.

"Mark, for some reason I'm not sure how I feel about having them share the job of caring for Stross," I said. " I don't have a problem with the wife, but I'm not sure about her husband. If Stross were older, I think it'd be easier; but he's a baby."

"No, I know what you mean," he said. "I thought about it too."

"Am I more sexist than I thought?' I asked.

"You don't have a problem with me taking care of Stross."

"Of course not, honey. That's entirely different."

···

"But even if I weren't Stross' dad, I'd be able to focus on caring for a baby, right?"

"Yeah," I said quietly.

Mark spoke as our voice of reason. "Let's just check it out and see what we think. Who knows, they might not even want to do it after we talk more."

I called their home and spoke to the wife about arranging a time to meet. As we chatted I could tell that she was open to further discussion, but if we asked them to care for Stross full-time—from 8 a.m. to 5 p.m.—they would turn us down. Their daily lives divided into segments of time, and our best opportunity to use them was to match their segments. Mark and I had more negotiating to do with our employers before we met with the couple.

I casually observed their family during worship the next day— the Sunday our family gathered to celebrate the dedication of Stross' life. The service was an official acknowledgment of Stross and his significance to us and our family of faith. On that day, faith billowed forth in huge clouds. Doctors, nurses, coworkers, countless friends, both sets of parents, my paternal grandparents and each of our siblings and their families testified to the power of an individual life. The beauty of this simple revelation brought tears of joy and gratitude.

I cried. Mark cried. Our family and friends cried, and our pastor's eyes brimmed with tears as he spoke. We had felt guidance in the midst of our living nightmare so maybe we could trust all that awaited us in the future.

•    •    •

# Chapter 16

# Uncomfortable

• • •

At 30 weeks Stross smiled most of the time. He expressed his likes and dislikes well, helping us discern his favorite activities through giggles that came from deep within. I liked to sit him in my lap while I sat cross-legged on the floor and watch his eyes dance across the pages of brightly colored board books. He'd gaze intently at pictures of farm animals while I mooed and clucked us through the pages.

Music shaped much of Mark's time with Stross, and I loved watching Mark sing to him. He'd position him in the crook of his arm, and Stross would tilt his head back to stare at Mark's mouth. If Stross could have spoken, I imagined him saying, "How in the world do you do that, Dad? It's so cool."

Mark found it easy to hold the attention of his captive audience. He'd scat words to make his lips move faster then watch Stross' brow furrow in wonder. Sometimes Mark would unnecessarily fluctuate the dynamics and rhythm of a song to watch Stross' head jerk in startled surprise. The heartwarming grin that followed told us he loved being surprised.

Stross had become his own person—a child who would grow, mature and eventually separate from us in a celebration of independence—at least that is what Mark and I believed parents were supposed to work toward. But we were parents of a different kind of child—one that made thinking about the future more difficult. Playing with him and enjoying who he was came easy, but planning for his future—even a future as close as my return to work—was overwhelming.

After playtime the fact that Stross was an intense 24-hour-per-day-365-days-per-year responsibility hung over us. Simple household chores like grocery shopping, sorting the mail and stocking shelves with his supplies reminded us of our increased financial need which, in turn, reminded us that we had 8 a.m. to 5 p.m. responsibilities that didn't accommodate him. Somehow we needed to responsibly provide for his care while responsibly managing our employment commitments.

Mark had already been pulled back to work by a societal expectation to provide for his family. I was being pulled back by a force that had commingled my love of self with my love for Stross. Somehow my self-identity (career woman) and my genetic identity (Stross' mom) had enmeshed in a way that demanded I provided for both his and my futures by successfully completing the plan Mark and I had intended to complete before his birth: We'd find childcare so I could return to work.

The time I'd already spent back at work had helped me reestablish a sense of equilibrium. Therefore, asserting my need to work came easy. So did more practical reasons for my return: I provided more than 60 percent of our family's income, and my employer provided our medical benefits.

The married couple we'd learned of through church seemed our best (and only) childcare possibility; therefore, Mark and I needed to propose a caregiving arrangement that appealed to them and then hope everything else fell in line.

I called my boss and proposed yet another plan for special work hours. However this one, I assured him, could be thought of as my return-to-work schedule—at least for the time being. As proposed, I would arrive at work by 7 a.m., work through lunch and then complete another two hours at home after picking up Stross around 1:30 p.m. My boss, perhaps also feeling limited by my options, agreed while cautioning me to remember that my proposal was to be regarded as a temporary solution. I assured him Mark and I would continue to look for a full-time care solution that kept me at the office during regular working hours.

Mark, likewise, negotiated with his boss to arrive at work around 9:30 a.m., work through lunch and leave at 5:30 p.m. This allowed him to drop off Stross at 9 a.m., reducing the time our son would be in someone else's care: only four hours each day. We now had an attractive schedule in place for a potential caregiver. After reviewing our family budget, we decided to offer an hourly fee that was slightly greater than minimum wage. It was just beyond what we could comfortably afford, but we didn't feel as if we could afford not to offer an amount that expressed how important we regarded a caregiver's role.

We scheduled a late afternoon visit to the couple's home. With Stross looking his most adorable, Mark and I headed to the meeting feeling cautious and noncommittal, yet hoping to make a positive impression. Certainly they needed to convince us they could provide quality care; however, we had the burden of convincing them Stross' daily care was not an overwhelming proposition.

The meeting went well. Their home was clean and well kept, a typical suburban split-level. Each of them was genuinely interested in Stross' history and spent time playing with him. The wife fed Stross a bottle while talking about how much she had enjoyed spending time with her own son when he was a baby. She also told of their difficulty in conceiving a second child and then showed Mark and me a room she volunteered to transform into a guest nursery.

I joined in these tentative plans saying we would buy a second bouncer seat, a spare bottle steamer and another set of monitors to leave at their home. During our intentionally casual conversation, the wife seemed uncomfortable about her husband caring for an infant. She admitted to his inexperience with their son explaining that, as a very hands-on mother, she had left him without opportunities to change diapers or take part in feedings. Still, she continued, both of them believed this would be an excellent chance for her to nurture a child again and for him to experience that aspect of parenthood.

I appreciated the wife's talkative nature. Her husband, on the other hand, was non-expressive and painfully quiet. While he would answer direct questions, he was mostly silent; often she shared feelings for the both of them. She invited him to respond, but he didn't really have much to say. He did offer that he was willing to give it a try and was pretty sure he'd do fine. I longed for him to speak even more, voluntarily supplying his own endorsement. So did Mark.

It was evident both the husband and wife were pleased about our proposed schedule, because it fit with their care schedule for their 5-year-old son. So we delved into details. For instance, if they agreed to care for Stross, he would need to ride along in their car when they dropped off their son at school around 12:45 p.m. Mark and I were open to such a trip—mere blocks in their car—provided Stross rode in his own car seat. We vowed to leave the seat each day and to teach them how to fasten it into the center position of their back seat.

Before we left Mark and I expressed how we felt about leaving Stross in the care of others. We explained it was a choice we felt compelled to follow and said we viewed Stross' care as a partnership between us and his care providers. As his care providers they would become an extended part of our family. Furthermore, we understood that Stross was still somewhat of a mystery. There were things we did not fully realize, like how to identify a shunt malfunction or to gauge his moods as a way to diagnosis his health. Thinking of the recent seizures, we acknowledged there might even be disabilities and defects we had yet to uncover. Full communication was extremely important to us, and we wanted them to know that we considered no question "dumb." After all, we were still full of questions ourselves. Our work phone numbers could be used at any time, we told them. We believed there was more to learn about Stross, and we welcomed any observations they could provide.

Feeling vulnerable and misunderstood somehow, I launched into a sincere speech about how I knew I could come across as assertive and overprotective. I implored them to understand that Mark and I depended on their open communication, and it seemed my comments were appreciated. We parted with an agreement to

●●●

think things over. I promised I would call soon to share our decision and then call again, if necessary, to learn of their response.

Mark and I were cautiously optimistic. It truly seemed like the perfect situation. This couple's home was only a few blocks away from ours. However, while their family appeared loving and stable at church, the husband's quietness made us uncomfortable, and we still didn't have a sense for his personality. It was difficult to know if he felt as strongly about this prospect as his wife did. Perhaps he did not feel capable of taking care of a baby. Still, he cared for their son, a kind if slightly rambunctious boy.

"Mark, didn't it make you nervous that she did most of the talking?" I asked.

"Yes, but you do most of the talking for us too," he countered.

"But Mark, even you talked 10 times more than he did today," I said.

"We knew he was a quiet guy, maybe even shy, before we got there, and he seemed interested in everything we were saying, even if he didn't ask questions."

Because Mark always attempted to balance negatives with positives, I stuck to my role of primary inquisitor.

"Come on. You don't mean to tell me that you're not the least bit uncomfortable about him, do you?" I needed to press Mark on this.

"Truthfully, I'm a little uncomfortable, but I keep reminding myself that being quiet isn't bad. He may turn out to do a better job than she does."

Mark's point left me without a rebuttal. I understood that my husband had incredible insight on this topic. His caring personality could make others perceive him as a whipped puppy. During public conflict Mark played the role of peacemaker, often placating others at the risk of denying his own interests. At home he'd share his insight with me about how the offender in an argument will probably meet their undoing. But then in subsequent weeks or months, I'd watch a situation play out almost as if Mark had scripted it from the privacy of our living room. Quiet wisdom served Mark well.

In social situations Mark clammed up, causing me to flit about as our family's conversational butterfly. He knew I seized opportunities to turn storytelling into dramatic productions—in truth, another joyism—and he ambiguously loved watching me perform. Sometimes—in the midst of a performance—I'd glance at my husband and then notch up the level of animation in flirtatious interplay. The subtleties of our relationship were lost on others. No one else knew Mark gave me permission to enjoy this role with a simple phrase: "You go ahead and tell it, honey. You'll do it much better."

Based on these interactions, others simply saw me as outgoing, extroverted and domineering. Therefore, by default, Mark was passive, introverted and compliant. Only friends who had lived through our early years as a couple comprehended how equally passionate, driven and self-assured we were.

Realizing how mischaracterized we were made the couple's relationship and their individual personalities less suspect. No other choice had presented itself in the past few weeks, and I had to return to work in a matter of days. Lacking an audible message from God or even a quiet sense of peace, I rested in a rationalized theory that God had led us to this couple by process of elimination.

I had yet to learn that rationality and instinct have little in common, or that rationality—given too much credence—can hinder instinct's ability to protect.

After a very rational conversation, Mark and I decided to officially ask the couple to care for Stross, and they accepted. I spent the next week gathering things to help make our son comfortable in their home. By the last Monday of July, I worked partial days in the office, using that week to train the couple on Stross' ostomy care and feeding preferences. By the second week of August Stross was three months old and Mark's and my new work schedules were functioning as we hoped. Best of all, two other people now knew how to care for Stross.

I was so ready to return to work on a near full-time basis, that I suffered little of the mother guilt many woman report. During the first week I called their home once a day. However, the calls tapered to nothing as the association's annual convention neared. With it less than a month away my workdays flew by, leaving little time to worry about Stross' wellbeing. Admittedly Mark, as drop-off parent, had the harder role, while I had the joyous task of rescuing Stross and whisking him home.

In the evening Mark and I compared notes about how we believed the couple was doing. He shared information about their home's atmosphere at the morning drop off, and I filled him in on what happened during the pick-up time. To aid our communication with the couple, I created a tiny notebook with a daily log that was kept in Stross' diaper bag. Whoever cared for him was to note details of his feedings, ostomy care and playtime. Both Mark and I appreciated the role the notebook played in eliminating the need to ask the same questions daily. The book helped us keep track of how much Stross ate and drank while providing little reminders about possible playtime activities. After all playtime for Stross was therapy. Batting at toys from his infant seat or looking at pictures in books were all ways to engage his mind in learning, a mind we believed had already been changed in inexplicable—perhaps even undetectable— ways by congenital hydrocephalus and a plastic ventricular shunt.

In September an AEA physical therapist began making weekly visits to our home. So did an early childhood instructor. I had initiated the paperwork within weeks of his birth. I believed that utilizing our AEA (like the Davises had) was the best way to ensure Stross did not fall behind his peers any more than necessary.

Both of Stross' caregivers indicated they were open to suggestions about how to help him therapeutically, and it was a relief to know they were helping us. I believed we had found the childcare solution I'd desperately wanted in this couple, so it got easier to spend large portions of my workday thinking only of my profession.

As a result my job was going well in spite of everything. In fact the convention's success—record attendance with enough profit to seed the following year's event—amazed me. I deeply appreciated all the ways coworkers had accommodated my altered work schedule, expressing their support through their willingness to adapt.

During the actual week of the convention, I'd been emotionally supported by Mark's and Stross' presence on-site. When they attended general sessions, I found moments to introduce Stross to city officials from across the state and then, after each evening's festivities, all three of us would retreat to our hotel room to relax as a family.

In keeping with the convention's '50s theme, I'd even secured a "Happy Days" era costume for Stross: jeans, a white onesie and a baby-sized green and gold letter sweater. One day while I was buzzing around with officials duties, Mark dressed Stross in his "baby greaser" costume, then the two of them came to find me at a sock-hop reception held in an antique auto showroom. Stross and I posed for pictures with my custom poodle skirt. I'd made certain it had been sewn with both a mom poodle and a baby one, my public expression of pride.

During my few days off the following week, I cared for Stross myself again and drew comfort in the familiarity of him. I didn't need to mess with the notebook. I knew Stross' every feeding and could practically predict every diaper or ostomy change. According to the notebook's growing stack of notations, Stross' days were orderly and predictable—if we could believe what was recorded, and neither Mark nor I felt we had a reason not to.

The husband and wife did not seem to mind my quest for full disclosure. In fact when I picked up Stross, the answers to my questions were already written down, and he was usually already dressed in his coat and strapped into his car seat. More often than not, particularly on the days he was in the husband's care, Stross—in his car seat—was already waiting for me by the door with his diaper bag packed.

I shared with Mark how thoughtful I believed this gesture to be, and then Mark, with a grave look, provided more data. His additional information made me uncomfortable. According to Mark, he left the diaper bag right inside their front door, at the base of their split-foyer entry—approximately the same place I found it each afternoon. Coupled with the fact Mark didn't fully get into the house each morning, he sported seemingly irrational fears. What if Stross hardly ever got out of that seat? He needed to stretch and exercise his tenuous muscles. Since he had no feeling on the back sides of his legs or his bottom, he needed to be moving as much as possible to avoid pressure sores. Neither one of us could fully believe that Stross sat in his infant seat all day. If so, there would be more substantial evidence. However, the thought allowed us to give weight to other concerns.

As Mark described it, the husband's morning routine was to meet him at the door and take Stross from him still buckled into his infant seat. He also instructed Mark to leave the diaper bag and cooler of milk just inside the door. Mark wanted to believe it was because the husband was being helpful, yet he felt like he was hiding something. Mark wondered if it was because, on most days, the husband wasn't yet dressed for the day. This was very likely the explanation. Still the reason he wasn't dressed by Mark's arrival at 9 a.m. was a mystery. Conversely the wife was more welcoming. On her days to watch Stross, Mark felt better. By 9 a.m. she met Mark at the door and escorted him all the way into the house along with the bottle cooler and diaper bag. She was dressed, wide awake and ready to take Stross into her care.

When autumn turned colder, the wife loaned us a knitted blue coat with a hood for Stross to use. She had found it among her son's baby clothes and took obvious delight in seeing our son wear it. Stross loved the coat too, at least its metal zipper. He'd chuckle each time we zipped the coat closed. If we ran the zipper halfway up and down repetitiously, the sound of the zipper's rhythmic ripping caused him to deepen his chuckle until he laughed uncontrollably. He'd close his eyes and lean his head forward as if to capture the mirth-filled memory for safekeeping. Stross never grew tired of the routine.

The act of sharing the coat and her friendly demeanor encouraged us, but increasingly, more discouraging aspects of the husband's behavior dominated Mark's and my conversations. We rationalized it was possible for the husband to dress for the day while caring for children. We did it every day, so who were we to question the choice he'd made to dress after receiving our son into his care? Was it our right to infringe on his daily routine? Telling him we didn't like it might have caused conflict; so instead of talking to him about our concerns, we made adjustments to our routine.

Since it wasn't possible for Mark to arrive at work any later, he suggested I leave work early a few days to see how the husband's or wife's routine differed if I arrived before anticipated. So I began to come at 1:15 or 1:20 p.m. On the wife's days, nothing appeared too different other than her surprise at my early arrival. On the husband's days, I often greeted him in the driveway as he returned from a late drop off at school. This gave me several opportunities to see how Stross rode in their car.

On my first early arrival I noticed he had Stross' car seat buckled incorrectly. I politely pointed out the error and demonstrated the correct way as I placed Stross into our own back seat. The second time it happened, I found a magazine ad of the car seat being used properly and taped it to the side of the car seat. I then pointed out the illustration to him and politely asked him to use the car's seat belt properly again. No matter what I tried the error remained; and on days the husband cared for Stross, I knew our son rode loosely secured in their back seat.

Mark and I were very pleased with the wife's care skills but remained skeptical of her husband's abilities. We weren't certain if his heart wasn't in it, if he was simply incompetent or if he was dealing with depression or something worse. We wanted to make things better but didn't know how. We vowed to give him the benefit of our doubt and planned to patiently work with him. I also looked for an opportunity to discuss our concerns with the wife. Before I had that chance, something worse happened.

The second Monday in November was a holiday—Veterans' Day. I was running behind and did not arrive to pick up Stross until 1:35 p.m. I went to the door, rang the bell and waited for an answer that did not come. Anxious, I started to walk around the side of their home. Perhaps the husband had taken Stross outside for some fresh air. Nothing. I went back to the door and strained to look in the window. No movement. I looked for a way into the garage to check on the car. It wasn't there. Panic started to set in, and my pulse raced. The husband regularly took their son to school late but never this late. I sat on the steps and prayed for my son's safety as I waited. Soon their car entered the cul de sac and came into their drive. I spotted the car seat, thankful I would soon be holding Stross in my arms.

I was at the car door even before he'd placed the car in park. One look at my baby told me he was not happy. Stross was beyond fussy. His face was pinched, and his body strained in agitated contortions. His expression let me know he felt extremely uncomfortable. When I opened the car door, the sound of his strained whines made my heart beat faster. I unhooked his ill-buckled seat and lifted him out. Nothing had appeared to be pinching him, yet he still did not quiet. I became very conscious of the tone in my voice.

"I was getting pretty worried," I said to the husband.

"Oh. Yes, well, we were just running behind," he said.

"Stross seems upset. Anything happen today I should know about?" I wanted an answer.

"No, nothing out of the ordinary," he responded. "I couldn't get him to drink his second bottle, that's all. Here it is. Once he drinks that, he'll probably feel better."

The husband appeared as if he was feigning a sense of calm, and my concern for Stross made me want to believe nothing grossly wrong had happened.

"Maybe so," I responded, performing mental time calculations. Stross normally drank his second bottle of the day around 11:30 a.m. or noon. It was very late for a second bottle. "What time did you start trying to feed him?"

"Oh, about 11:30. I didn't write it down yet," he said. The bottle felt cool. Either he was not being truthful about the time, or he had placed it back in the refrigerator after Stross had chewed on it hours earlier.

"That's okay. This breast milk is old by now anyway," I reminded. " I'll get him a new one at home."

There was nothing more I wanted to do than get out of there and get home. Things just didn't feel right. I needed to get Stross into familiar surroundings and assess the situation. I needed to call Mark. I buckled Stross securely in our car, gathered his things and took off.

Twice during the short drive home, Stross cried out loud enough to scare me. The first time I tried to reassure him that home wasn't far away, and I'd feed him as soon as we got home. The second time I pulled the car over and got out to examine him. Had I put him in so quickly I'd pinched him? Was he hurt in some way and just couldn't tell me? He refused to be quieted, so I got back in the driver's seat and drove the last few blocks even faster.

Once home, I examined Stross again while a new bottle warmed in the steamer. I couldn't find anything wrong so I simply held him and comforted him hoping my soothing tones would ease what ailed him. I wanted to call Mark right away but wasn't certain what I would tell him.

I offered the bottle to Stross, and he tried to take a few swallows; but stopped after only one-half ounce. If what the husband had written in the notebook was true, Stross had not eaten since 9:30 a.m.; therefore, he had to be hungry. I decided to try again after I opened the front window shades to watch for the physical therapist's car. She was due to arrive at 2 p.m. and apparently was also running behind. I carried Stross to the window to look for her car.

The clattering of the metal blinds rising caused Stross to jump in my arms. Now I was really scared. Intuitively I knew something bad must have happened, or at the least, Stross was sick. An illness might delay his next surgery—a simple circumcision procedure—that we'd scheduled for the third week of November in Iowa City. Feeling helpless, I placed a thermometer under Stross' arm to take his temperature. It was a normal 97 point something.

In search of more facts, I nervously called the husband to ask more questions. I asked the same questions in a new way, and I asked new questions with new intensity. I needed him to start talking. He quietly responded to each of my inquiries, claiming nothing unusual had happened. I suggested that maybe something had scared Stross: a strange show on television or loud music or a neighborhood dog or even one of their son's playmates. No, nothing like that had happened, he said. The only strange thing that had happened that day is that Stross wouldn't eat.

I apologized for bothering him, citing my fear that the next week's surgery would need to be rescheduled if Stross fell ill, and

• • •

then I thanked him for his time. Just then the physical therapist arrived, and Stross again lurched in my arms—this time at the sound of her knock on the front door. I told her of my unsettling concerns, and she tenderly took him and checked him over. She too could not find anything amiss but noticed how upsetting it was for Stross to be manipulated during exercises. Typically he lit up for her and loved being played with and talked to. He was not as responsive today, and she elected to end the session after only 10 minutes.

I finally called Mark. I described our son's behavior, told him he had no fever, then told him the husband's answers to my questions. Mark agreed that something seemed amiss and told me I was right to be worried. He offered to come home, but neither one of us knew exactly what that would accomplish. Instead I reassured him I could tough out the next few hours. Stross seemed ready to take a nap. I would just sit, rock him and hope he acted better after he slept.

Stross fell asleep after about 15 minutes, and I found myself wanting to call the husband one more time. I didn't know what I'd say differently. I just needed to call because I felt there was more to his story. When I did call, I got the same answers—the same unrevealing responses. There was one small difference, however. The wife, home from her job, answered the phone. I seized the opportunity to share my concerns with her before she handed the phone to her husband.

I learned later that after my conversation with him—the third we'd had on this topic—she'd conducted her own inquiry. Subsequently, 20 minutes later, I heard a knock at our front door. When I opened it my heart dropped into my stomach. I saw both of them standing there. Tears brimmed her eyes, and he stared forward focusing just below my eyes.

"There is something we need to tell you," she began. I became numb.

"Stross fell off the changing table today, and he didn't want to tell you. I'm so sorry," she finished, nudging her husband to speak.

"I'm really sorry," he said. "I checked him over, and he seemed fine. I didn't want to worry you."

· · ·

Worry me? Surely he had noticed I had gone way beyond worried without him even saying a word about the fall. He checked him over? There were parts of Stross we couldn't see. I immediately thought of the shunt and wanted to get Stross to the pediatrician and possibly even his neurosurgeon. Stross' small, soft head needed examining. I wanted to kick them out of my house quickly, but they held answers to questions I knew the doctors would ask. They owed me answers now.

About what time did it happen? How did he land? Head first? More importantly, how did he act immediately after the fall? Had he lost consciousness? Had he cried a lot?

The husband wasn't certain about anything. He thought it happened about 12:30 p.m. When he found Stross, Stross was lying on his side.

Still feeling the husband wasn't forthcoming, I pressed more. What did he mean: "when he found him"? Where had *he* been when Stross fell? And which side did he find Stross on? The shunt side? Stross' right? How could the accident have happened at all?

Thoughts filled my head: Our six-month-old son had yet to roll over. Changing his diaper was incredibly easy. Without substantial leg strength, he never kicked or wriggled away. Had he been left totally unattended? Had he been placed near the edge of the changing table? Had something else happened? How could I trust anything he said when he had told me so many lies?

The wife was crying now and responding to some of the questions even though her knowledge was second hand. I continued to direct my questions straight at the husband, asking and re-asking until I was satisfied the responses were as complete as I could expect. The husband offered to pay for any doctor's visits we might need. In the midst of it all, the wife mumbled something about her husband running late when getting their son ready for school. There was also something about the husband checking on their son while he was in the bathtub to hurry him up.

The only scenario that made sense to me was that the husband had left Stross alone on the edge of a dresser—nearly four feet high—while he went into the bathroom to check on their son. I was certain of the height, because the spot used by the husband for diaper changes was already one of my concerns. The wife preferred to change Stross in the crib while the husband used the top of a dresser. They had no true changing table, a fact that had nagged at me.

I felt myself beginning to relive every haunting, uncomfortable, uneasy detail of the past few months. To snap myself back into the moment I quickly said some comments to assuage their guilt, then hurried them away: No, paying for the doctors would not be necessary. Our insurance would cover it. No, we wouldn't be bringing Stross by tomorrow. We would call to let them know of our plans. Yes, we had known things like this could happen. I was personally disappointed the husband had not felt he could tell me about it. From the beginning we had stressed that Stross' health and development were our primary concerns. If the husband had felt overwhelmed by the circumstances, we should have been told.

My six-month-old son had taken a hard enough blow to his body to cause several hours of agonizing and obvious discomfort. How could this man have ever believed that would remain hidden? Was I such an imposing person that he felt he could not have called me at work as soon as it happened or, at the least, confess wrongdoing the first time I asked? During the 12 weeks Stross was in his care, what else had I not been told?

As soon as they left, I called Mark and told him to meet me at the pediatrician's office. We were there by 4 p.m. and then consulted with the neurosurgeon by phone shortly thereafter. Nothing showed up during a physical examination, and the pediatrician reassured us that babies were resilient. The neurosurgeon reiterated the standard signs of a shunt malfunction and scheduled an exam later in the week. At that appointment he found nothing amiss either, and we were not savvy enough advocates to press for a CT-scan or MRI.

Friends filled in as our childcare providers the rest of that week, and Stross' circumcision went almost without incident the following Monday. The procedure—about one hour in length—took place at the university hospital in Iowa City where we had taken Stross for

• • •

their specialized spina bifida clinic. In recovery he got a dose of intravenous antibiotic before we left, then we were given a doctor's prescription for a different antibiotic to be given intramuscularly in the emergency room at our hospital in Des Moines. The arrangement allowed us to leave for home four hours earlier than if we stayed for the second drug.

The only uneasy moment occurred when Stross went limp in my arms 10 minutes after getting the injection in his thigh. Mark and I located the first nurse we could find, and she worked with us to waken him. He had either passed out or had a drug reaction; it was difficult even for her to tell. When he regained consciousness after a few long minutes of poking and prodding, we went into minor shock ourselves. His fall a week earlier multiplied our anxiety. Uncertain times and uncomfortable feelings were, once again, our reality.

Oddly, surgery brought a comforting familiarity. After guiding our son through five operations, Mark and I had become experts on that issue—but not childcare. We had failed miserably at obtaining childcare and were now faced with another search. Even though we had made a gallant effort to make a situation work, we had been betrayed. I struggled with my belief that we had misread an answer to prayer.

Somehow not having a caregiver was not as uncomfortable as it once had been, but mentally preparing for a new search was. We had regained temporary control over who would care for our son: we would or, once again, more trusted volunteers. In a strained meeting with the couple the day after Stross' fall, I paid them for the previous week and told them that Mark and I no longer trusted them. The meeting occurred in our home while Mark was at work, which was to their benefit. Mark silently wore his anger like a mother lion, ready to pounce on those who threatened his young.

The couple had brought with them the baby items we'd taken to their home, so before they left I collected them and tried to return the blue coat with the zipper that made Stross laugh. The wife pleaded with me to let Stross wear it as long as the weather required it. I agreed but soon purchased a winter snowsuit for Stross so I could return the

· · ·

coat and rid our home of any physical links to their family.

The succeeding months found us piecing together childcare by relying on five of the women we'd approached earlier. These friends took one day a week for a few weeks. Then Mark and I spent one week alternating care of Stross ourselves by carting him to work again. While we looked for a more permanent solution, Stross' daily notebook continued to provide continuity and written assurances that helped us glimpse what life was like for him when we weren't there.

Because we did not want to appear to smear the couple in a slanderous way, we avoided speaking of it. But we shared our version of what happened with those who had stepped in to help us with Stross. Our friends, our employers and our relatives knew the magnitude of our troubles.

Our hurt over what happened to Stross ran deep. The married couple hurt deeply too. Their pain kept them from coming to church; our pain drove us to church for solace. Beneath the pain, we'd grown wiser. We'd learned that fear did not justify lack of action and that helplessness could be self-imposed. We'd also learned that we could not spare another's feelings at the risk of our son's health. Life circumstances, it seemed, had placed us at the mercy of something beyond providential directives—if there had been directives. Had we been warned something wasn't right? Had we ignored it? If so, shame on us. Could we have instinctively known our son was in danger? Had we ignored our feelings because they weren't convenient? If so, double shame on us.

We struggled with the reality that Stross had suffered because of us somehow. Our lessons had come at his expense.

Mark and I agreed that, this time, we owed him our best without error. We vowed he would be cared for in the manner he deserved. I still felt Stross deserved someone more nurturing than me—someone more diligent about giving him dedicated attention during the most productive hours of each day. Mark wanted someone like that too.

• • •

# Chapter 17

# Leap of Faith

...

When I turned 18, I stopped by my hometown post office to fill out a card that explained why I was ineligible for the draft. I placed a mark next to this statement: I am female. As I did, I felt guilty. My male classmates had to register for the draft or face a penalty; yet I was excluded simply because I had been born female—and I was grateful. My guilt was real; my gratitude for exclusion was real. Yet as someone who took pride in passionately fighting injustices, the conflict was unsettling. I had never experienced this type of egocentric hypocrisy and didn't like my newfound self-awareness.

In the first weeks of Stross' life, I pondered draft exclusions again. I had given birth to a son—a male more qualified for the draft than me, a female. However, birth defects excluded him from enlistment and possible war. He couldn't enlist in the army even by choice. I embraced that. My child would never leave home—voluntarily or involuntarily—to fight a war.

There were other scary things my child would not—could not—do. He would never lie seriously injured on a football or rugby field facing the possibility of paralysis. His paralysis had arrived at birth, prohibiting him from those sports in the first place. I would hold my partially paralyzed son, thankful for those small consolations in a world often void of consolation. I welcomed those injustices and offered thanks for a child who would never dart into the street or fall off a climbing tower, even if that meant he also would not enjoy the pleasures of running or skipping or riding a traditional bike.

But I had also believed my child could never fall from a changing table, so even the military's draft and rugby became scary again. False security had fostered idealistic—unrealistic—notions. I now wrestled with the reality that our son had been injured in the home of people we'd chosen to care for him. If that could happen, virtually anything could happen.

An ad placed in our neighborhood shopper resulted in two calls. The first call was from a mother of two who—as she said it—"took care of four children in her home" on the west edge of Des Moines. I returned her phone call, distressed by the din in the background and by my inability to determine whether she was caring for four children including her own or four in addition to her own. No matter how I asked the question, I was unable to clarify this fact. She seemed uninterested in learning details of Stross' medical conditions but money interested her. When I tried to explain about Stross' ostomy and how it factored into diaper changes, she offered assurances that it was "probably no big deal." I wanted the next caregiver we chose to think it *was* a big deal but a big deal she could handle. There were distinct differences between this woman's philosophy and mine.

The second inquiry was from a woman who lived five minutes away. Her two children were attending college in another state. While she was a native Iowan, her family had lived in Colorado for many years but had moved to Des Moines 10 months previously. She did not need to get a job but looked forward to having something to do with her day. Our ad had caught her eye. She was warm, friendly and cautious on the phone. We set a time for her to meet us in our home and learn about Stross. If things went well, we would visit her home to see where Stross would spend his days. We had used this same interview procedure with the married couple but hoped for a better outcome this time.

Mark and I liked this woman as soon as we met her. She seemed

···——————

like a young grandmother and was well dressed. She asked a lot of thoughtful questions and was forthcoming with answers about her own children (no grandchildren yet) and home. She seemed lonely and homesick for her friends in Colorado. I hoped this was a sign that she had been providentially led to us so we could fulfill each other's needs: ours for quality childcare and hers for companionship and purpose. The fact that she had a dog was slightly unsettling, but she tentatively offered to keep him in another room until Stross and he became acquainted. As non-dog owners, Mark and I weren't sure how to introduce her dog to our baby, but we trusted her instinct.

We parted with an agreement to think it over a few days and to arrange for a meeting at her home. Mark and I liked the idea that she would care for our son. She had spent her childhood near my homctown, and while she wasn't the Mary Poppins I'd originally hoped for, she did match the more realistic caregiver profile I'd reworked in my head.

When the woman called the next day—earlier than anticipated—she informed us that becoming a caregiver was not a good idea for her right now. I cautiously lobbied for a change in heart. Nothing I said persuaded her to reconsider. She explained that a serious conversation with her husband led her to believe that caring for Stross would not be good for him, her family or their dog. I couldn't change her mind, and I wanted to. For almost a full day I had enjoyed simply the thought of her.

Within days one additional lead came from a friend at church. An acquaintance of hers had recently talked about a surgery her one-year-old granddaughter had needed to reverse a colostomy put in place at birth. When told about Stross, she showed interest in considering our proposition. Our friend arranged a meeting at our home.

A few days later we met this woman, an actual grandma—not just a grandma-type—who knew firsthand how to care for an ostomy. I dismissed the faint smell of cigarettes, assuring myself we could talk her into not smoking around our son. Concessions may be necessary, I thought, if we were to get someone who wouldn't shy away from our son's special needs.

The conversation was natural and comfortable. Mark and I learned her granddaughter had been born with an imperforate anus, the only birth defect on an otherwise able-bodied little girl. Her surgeon but another pediatric surgeon had created her ostomy and then, about the time her granddaughter turned 18 months old, had created an anus that the little girl was now successfully using as she potty trained. The grandma reported it was going well, and we all laughed about how much greater an accomplishment this girl's first "poop in the potty" was than other children's.

It was an encouraging conversation. The family used the same kind of ostomy appliances we did, and the grandma had been one of this child's primary caregivers. She even described how she had cared for her granddaughter's ostomy using nearly the same techniques. We joked how others could never understand how changing a baby's ostomy pouch was easier than cleaning a baby's messy butt. We readily connected on these issues, until she told a story about her granddaughter's ostomy and called the pouches "shit bags." Her comment negated everything else. I no longer liked her, Mark no longer liked her and the fact that she smelled of smoke was no longer tolerable. As soon as she left, Mark and I knew there was no need for a second meeting.

When our leads for home care ran out, we set our sights on a nanny. To adequately explore the nanny option, I spent time researching state and federal employment laws and reading suggestions for screening procedures. Our combined income paled in comparison to lawyers and doctors, the stereotypical families with nannies. Regardless, we fully examined the option.

I sorted through minimum wage requirements, unemployment insurance, liability coverage and suggested policies for vacation days and sick leave. Then I reviewed regulations regarding quality care for children. I found myself wondering: What was the point? No legalities or precautions would protect Stross from an abusive caregiver. We had learned that heeding our basic instincts would surpass even the strictest regulations. Besides my homework proved that a nanny was too costly anyway, even if Mark took on another

• • •

job and I trimmed my work hours just enough so I could care for Stross part-time while maintaining our insurance coverage.

While we worked for a solution, Stross stayed with friends. I toyed with the idea of regularly employing a weekly rotation of friends but knew the likelihood of such an arrangement was slim. These friends had willingly sustained us through a time of need. If one had felt able to offer more, she would have voluntarily made it known.

In the weeks after Stross' accident, Mark and I honed our introspective abilities and new questions arose. Were we capable of trusting someone to care for our son? What were we willing to do for the next five years until he entered all-day kindergarten? Was it unrealistic to believe Stross could enter school then? Would we be able to find an answer during his foundational years that would serve him well throughout his life? The stress of searching for answers nearly immobilized us.

Because the Thanksgiving and Christmas holidays hampered our ability to have friends as substitute childcare providers, members of our family volunteered to take one week each: my father, the teacher; my brother-in-law, the paramedic; and Mark's dad, the engineer. Each man (interestingly no women were available) sacrificed a week's worth of vacation, a gesture not lost on us: We now treasured vacation days and sick leave as gold.

Mark's dad was lined up to help the three workdays before Thanksgiving. After the holiday, Greg and my dad were individually scheduled for one week each. Mark and I knew the remaining weeks before Christmas could be managed by us (taking Stross to work) and friends—but only if our employers and friends could see the end of our neediness in sight. The new year became our new deadline.

We spent the weekend before Mark's dad arrived looking at our household budget again. I pulled out two years' worth of check registers and sorted through the numbers, poring over every detail. We created categories of expenditures that were fixed expenses and identified our discretionary spending. Most important to me was determining how much money we typically wasted each month. Every dollar counted.

Exploring the expense of a nanny, then comparing it to our monthly expenditures had already made that decision obvious: There was absolutely no way we could afford one. So with no appropriate day care center, no one emerging as a home caregiver and no way to afford a nanny, the only option left— it seemed—was for one of us to quit working. Oddly neither of us had spoken that choice aloud in anything but a negative context: "What are we going to do? Neither of us can quit our job." But each one of us had privately played out the scenario in our heads, alternating the roles of caregiver and provider as we attempted to envision that type of future.

A sinking realization began. Our dreams—old and new—didn't really matter right now. Stross' future had overtaken ours. Ensuring his wellbeing would lay the foundation for ours. Someday we might have the luxury to fashion new dreams again, but right now our family had to survive. We needed to start the process by determining the best parental caregiver from a pool of two: Mark or me. The prospect that I would emerge as the most qualified aroused new fears, but I feared continuing our futile search even more.

I found a measure of objectivity among the lines of our monthly budget. I used it to run two sets of figures—one without my income and one without Mark's. The exercise highlighted our wage disparity. I generated more income by several thousands of dollars and provided the link to our medical benefits. Conversely, running the figures with Mark as our caregiver almost worked, and fortunately, he read the data as notice of his emancipation.

Mark's career had been stifled by no opportunity to advance and an undesirable work environment. Leaving meant a chance to explore the free-lance market as a weekend videographer or evening video editor. While our budget still required expenses for two cars (and therefore no savings in gas money or auto expenses), we could save money on his clothing and dry cleaning. As Stross' caregiver, suits would no longer be daily attire. Additional monthly savings could come from no more meals out, no more extras for the house, no more extras for us and no more tithing.

Mark's resignation represented both an unconventional and

uneasy choice. Yet it made more sense than anything else. In fact, if I had created a spreadsheet comparing Mark's and my caregiving qualities, the data would have tipped his way again. I believed Mark was more nurturing, patient, creative, disciplined and calm. From my point of view Mark was our family's all-around, best candidate.

We found it intriguing that the practice of tithing stood between us and our ability to care for our son should Mark resign. Were we being tested to see what we valued most? Were we being asked to choose between our church and our child? After shared contemplations, we decided the situation had less to do with pitting the church against Stross than it did with exploring our definition of spiritual growth. Both of us, having accomplished the discipline of tithing prior to marriage, viewed tithing as integral to our faith. Mark grew up tithing his allowance, and I gave one-tenth of my income during college. Once married, tithing became second nature—almost too easy to count as sacrifice. To survive as a family, perhaps we needed to step out in faith again, surpassing what we'd learned by tithing.

Based on our understanding of sacrificial living, it made sense that our spiritual growth might now involve stepping away from practices that had become gratuitous ritual and toward a life lived in gracious response. Living on one income promised to heighten our appreciation of all we'd been given.

Besides by this time only a caregiver as esteemed as Mother Teresa could have swayed us. Mark loved Stross more than his own life. That quality alone helped him surpass even Mother Teresa. Therefore, Mark had to resign. Stross' life deserved it. Stross' life depended on it. Perhaps providence *had* led us to the perfect caregiver: Mark.

The decision brought some relief. Mark began to smile more, imagining the freedom of spending his days as he pleased. I relaxed, knowing Mark's new role brought me freedom as well. With our greatest worry eliminated, smaller sources of anxiety surfaced, like sharing our unconventional decision with others. Without exception, our friends and coworkers encouraged us. Without exception, our parents questioned us.

I fielded questions from my parents over the phone during their Sunday call—my dad on the phone in their kitchen and my mom on the phone in their bedroom. Could we still keep our house? What about both cars? Was Mark really open to this? What if we asked that one lady, the one with the dog, again? Basically the conversation with them reviewed our own deductive reasoning. My anxious mother asked me to promise to continue looking "just in case." My instructional father quizzed me over our budget as if to check my math.

"It'll be tight, Joy," he said. "You will have to be extremely disciplined."

Tight? I'd thought to myself. He hadn't acknowledged we were actually $200 short each month. Our new budget counted on Mark generating free-lance work or me finding an additional source of income. We foresaw the need for a back-up plan, and the most feasible option included asking Mark's mom and dad to supplement us. Mark balked at the idea but saw it as a potential necessary evil.

First Mark had to tell them he was leaving his job. He crafted a speech that covered all the high points financially and then broadened the appeal. Philosophically he could tell them it meant new ventures for each of us: opportunities for him as his free-lance career took hold; physical advancements for Stross because of Mark's attention to daily therapy; and a time of growth for me as I assumed the role of family breadwinner. Practically, he acknowledged, becoming Mr. Mom required risk—financial risk and a career risk. Mark would break the news to his father the week of Thanksgiving, the week David agreed to watch Stross for us.

David arrived that Sunday night and endured a briefing session from us on how to care for this unique grandchild. I used the little notebook as a guide to explain Stross' schedule, and David offered to fill in the blanks just like the others before him. I explained that it wouldn't be necessary since he could answer any questions we'd have in the evenings. He again offered to record the information; and Mark said we appreciated his willingness, but it really wasn't necessary.

• • •

Later that night and Monday evening as well we talked around the issue of childcare for Stross, filling David in on the disappointing details of our search.

While Mark had decided it was best to inform his father of our decision in person, he had trouble bringing up the topic. His hesitation expressed the difficulty of the task. Finally on Tuesday after supper, while Stross slept in his cradle and we adults sat around the table, Mark walked his father through the emotional conclusion of our quest for childcare. As I listened to Mark explain it, I realized he was making it sound like our decision was an idea we were trying out rather than a done deal. In truth, Mark had not officially resigned. Part of our plans included him working through the end of the year, since we could continue to patchwork childcare through December.

David listened and became very inquisitive, even more so than my family. He asked questions we had already provided answers to such as, "What did your ad say?" and "Can't you get him into a regular day care center?" Then he asked a question that made me wonder if he'd been listening. In fact, he asked the same question a few different ways: Why can't Joy stay at home? What does your budget look like if Mark works and Joy stays at home? How much extra money would you need to have Joy care for Stross?

It wasn't just the money, Mark explained. It was the insurance too plus Mark had skills that would allow him to free-lance easily. Mark, appealing to his father's sense of mission, told how we saw this as an opportunity to spend more time with the youth at church and build our ministry. He could take Stross to church with him during the day and work on some things we'd always wanted done there. We would tithe our time, he told his dad, instead of our money.

Then David, in frustration, became angry. He raised his voice, his face became red and he launched into a speech about how tithing personal time was good, but it just wasn't the same. He strongly cautioned us about how hard it was to start tithing again and that it was even harder to get back into the job market once you left it. David, now sounding more like a corporate manager, told Mark he needed to think of his career—after all, potential employers look at time not accounted for on a resume. With each statement, he became more animated, uncharacteristic for this studied engineer. And yet each time David offered more counterpoints, either Mark or I responded by outlining—again—how we hoped to counteract the negatives.

Eventually our round dining room table became a verbal shooting range. David, seated next to Mark and across from me, aimed his eyes at me and launched a string of accusing questions: What could we expect if we showed no trust in those we asked to care for our son? Didn't we know accidents happen? That's part of a normal kid growing up. Didn't we want to treat Stross just like anybody else? How can we do that by being overprotective?

David had stopped looking back and forth between Mark and me in order to aim the balance of his remarks at me: It was ridiculous that I insisted on people filling out forms about what Stross ate or drank, he said, or how many wet diapers Stross had. If we dropped him off in the morning and picked him up happy and in one piece at the end of the day, what more could we expect? And who did I think I was throwing away extra baby food in the jar? All his kids ate out of baby food jars and Carolyn had saved the extra. If it was in the refrigerator, David said, it was fine. This business about bacteria contamination was nonsense. It wouldn't hurt Stross, he said. How could any doctor believe that kind of bacteria could cause an infection?

I'd become silent, recognizing that my words had dug an even deeper chasm. Mark had fallen silent long before. I, feeling like the lone defender of our actions, longed for Mark to speak, at least in defense of our notebook and food handling. How could Mark's father not know that Mark was more cautious than me? Why wasn't Mark informing him of that fact? Mark was the one who gave speeches about taking no chances on bacteria from a $.33 baby food jar. He was the one who reminded me to feed Stross out of a dish and to only put the jar in the refrigerator if no saliva had been introduced. I was certain David blamed me for the brick wall we'd hit concerning Stross' childcare. I was confident he believed I'd driven his son down a road to professional destruction, and his son—my husband—offered no retort.

I had never seen David like that. I had never even heard him raise his voice. To have it leveled square at me was unnerving. Had it been my own father, I'd have been on my feet yelling in equal volume, if necessary. But it was David, so I had been shocked speechless. I kept looking at Mark—nothing. Then finally David reached the climax of his exhortation. Wildly invigorated, he rose, leaned across the table, and pointed a finger straight at my face. His next statement held the full measure of his unbridled frustration.

"Perhaps you need to understand," he said, "your expectations are too high. You can only expect the kind of child care you can afford."

He was shaking, and I could tell his anger surprised even him. He made a few more statements—thrown out as emotional asides—then ended by admonishing me "to throw out that little book."

David took his coat from our closet and left. We listened as the sound of his car faded, then Mark found his voice—finally.

"I'm sorry," he said, quietly. "Dad was wrong."

"You're darn right," I said, on the verge of exploding myself. "Can you believe he said that about his grandson? Our expectations are too high when it's Stross' life we are talking about? How can he say that?"

I was on my feet now yelling things at my husband that I had wanted to yell at my father-in-law. In the midst of my venting, I marched upstairs to see if we'd awakened Stross, then marched back to confront Mark with the injustice his father's wrath had wrought. I started to get extremely riled up and planned to launch into an explosive, targeted tirade of my own, but one look at my shell-shocked husband told me it wasn't worth the effort. The person I wanted to verbally rip into had just left.

Instead my angry pain found release as a wall of tears.

"I'm so sorry, Joy."

Mark took me by the hand and pulled me onto his lap. The gesture, like his words, felt too little, too late. My body became rigid.

"I should have said something, anything," Mark said.

"Yes, you should have." I wanted to stand and begin yelling

hurtful things about his father. Instead I sat stiffly and continued to cry. Mark needed to see how badly I hurt.

"I just couldn't believe what I was seeing. I have never seen my dad like that. Not even when he was angry at Mom or us kids," Mark said.

I had to challenge this. "Never? I find that hard to believe."

"Never, Joy. I guess I froze. I wish I'd have defended you. I'm so sorry. It's not right that I didn't defend you. I'm sorry...I..."

Mark was quiet; I filled the silent spaces.

"Well, I'm so glad I have the distinct honor of being the only one who can make your Dad that angry. Do you think I'll earn a prize from the family at Thanksgiving?"

Mark laughed uncomfortably but still didn't speak. David's absence allowed us to regroup. When Stross started to coo in his cradle, both Mark and I began to focus on household tasks and our evening activities, taking more time than usual to bathe Stross and tuck him in. We did not know when David would return.

Mark was finally ready to talk, so we spent the majority of an hour trying to see life from David's perspective. He had just learned that his oldest son, the first child to complete college, would no longer be employed. This son would become a house-dad, an occupation far removed from David's corporate world. As a working father who often worked overtime, David had missed a great deal of the everyday stuff that comprised his children's lives. The choice Mark was making had not been David's, nor would he ever possibly make such a choice if given the opportunity. As such, he could easily believe I had bullied Mark into this decision to further my career.

Part of Mark's pain came from realizing his father didn't really know who he was. His dad didn't know he'd accepted the role of Stross' caregiver freely. Mark wanted to be Stross' primary nurturer. He looked forward to it; he just needed to convince his father of this truth.

David also held no frame of reference for our everyday fears. We dreaded a possible shunt malfunction that could come from injury or illness. If Mark and I could avoid getting symptoms misrepresented by a bacterial bug, we'd gladly throw out extra baby food. Besides diarrhea caused by an intestinal infection made for messy ostomy changes. We'd also defend our little book. With a different care provider every day of the week, it had been the only way to maintain confidence in how we provided for Stross.

After an intense reexamination of the most important decision of our lives, Mark and I were exhausted. The privacy of our bedroom is what we needed.

Before we readied for bed, David returned. He quietly apologized for his behavior and asked for my forgiveness in a conciliatory tone. I gave it. He assured both Mark and me of Carolyn's and his support and requested that we keep the lines of communication open. Then he gave me a hug, and he gave Mark a hug. As we headed toward our respective bedrooms, he told us again he was sorry and that he loved us. No one wanted to talk anymore. Instead we silently acknowledged topics for conversation in years to come.

●　　●　　●

# Chapter 18

# Hello, Mr. Mom

• • •

The beginning of Mark's Mr. Mom days brought back memories of our newlywed days in Fort Worth. While Mark took courses toward his master's degree in communications and religious education, I spent eight-hour workdays nurturing a professional career. Because Mark could only work a certain number of hours at his student job each week, he'd spend his extra hours in our apartment studying or cleaning. Mark enjoyed cleaning, not the everyday stuff of dusting and vacuuming, but the deep-down stuff like scouring decades of grime off paneled walls or meticulously cleaning the tiny panels of our indoor shutters.

At the end of his day Mark would pick me up in the El Camino and attentively listen to the misadventures of my job in Color Tile's public relations and advertising department. No matter the topic, Mark listened intently. I reciprocated by listening to his theological insights from a recent reading or lecture and stories about the guys he'd eaten lunch with. Sharing each other's day this way introduced us to a new type of emotional intimacy. By the time we arrived back at the apartment, the conversation may have just begun or have transformed into what we'd cook for supper. We'd continue to talk as we prepared our meal, sharing details of our day.

Once in a while I messed up this intimate time by not noticing things Mark had done around the apartment. However, I was at a disadvantage. Because I don't regularly notice dirty windows, I don't notice when the dirt's no longer there.

One day after opening our apartment door, Mark stepped back and motioned me in with a sweep of his hand. I smiled at his playfulness, walked to the kitchen counter and dropped my yellow, insulated lunch box.

"Well," Mark said. "Do you notice?"

"Oh…" I said, in an immediately heightened state of awareness. "Notice what?" I quickly scanned the tiny room.

"I can't believe you can't tell. It makes such a huge difference!"

I made a slow, visual sweep including the floor and ceiling.

"You vacuumed," I said. "It looks great. Thanks."

I smiled, hoping I'd found what he wanted me to find.

"Yeah, I vacuumed, but that's not it. You really can't tell?" Mark asked with a mixture of disappointment and disgust.

"Um, I'm not sure," I said, making another visual sweep. I started to walk around a little, too, wishing he'd offer clues about whether I was hot or cold.

"You…dusted?" I questioned.

"Oh, don't even try, Joy," he said. "I can't believe you can't tell. It's the windows. I washed the windows inside and out. They were filthy. It is so much brighter in here. I even chiseled away the paint that made them stick shut. We can open them now."

Mark equated not noticing clean windows as great a sin as forgetting his birthday or not acknowledging a haircut. Not noticing how he'd improved our standard of living had been a personal affront.

"I'm so sorry, Mark."

"That's okay," he returned, but I knew it wasn't.

After that I learned to be preemptive during our ride home by asking Mark what he'd done that day. Sometimes he'd tell me; other times he challenged me to notice for myself. The ritual made me more observant and much better at guessing.

Once at the apartment, we cooked our evening meal together. He took charge of things like chili and fried chicken, and I took over on

• • • ——

baked dishes and vegetables. During our early years of marriage, I learned that Crisco cooking oil, Blue Bonnet margarine and Morton's salt were Mark's three favorite cooking staples. Before moving back to Iowa, I had conducted fairly successful culinary negotiations about the privilege of adding my own margarine or salt to my portions yet had failed to convince him to cut back on his own.

Now five years into our marriage and only two years since our Texas sojourn, Mark was Mr. Mom. Our home—our kitchen—was again his domain. Mark's days consisted of feeding and changing Stross, paying our bills, helping out at church, taking Stross through his physical therapy routine, vacuuming, dusting and doing our laundry. Mark also planned our meals, shopped and did the majority of the cooking. Cooking offered him a break in routine that had nothing to do with caring for a baby. Supper was his time of respite because once I got home, Stross was mine.

Adjusting to Mark as Mr. Mom meant leaving work early enough to be home by supper. If I found myself running behind schedule, I called. If I forgot to call, I spent my commute thinking of ways to compliment my husband and let him know how much I loved him—another preemptive strike.

It took nearly three months to transition into our new lifestyle. Mark had quit his job just before Christmas, his two-week notice directly coinciding with the holidays. It had not been the best time to give notice to a retail employer, even for a corporate videographer, plus the motivation behind Mark's decision escaped his boss. When he gave notice, she warned of the professional and financial setbacks Mark would suffer by removing himself from the job market. He politely pointed out that her estimate of gross revenue lacked perspective without the benefit of also projecting a decade of expenditures that now included long-term medical expenses. He also assured her his skills would sharpen, not stagnate, by taking on free-lance jobs and that, above all, Stross' and my well being came first. Because we needed him at home, that's where he'd be.

During Mark's last two weeks with the company, he brought Stross to work with him. Stross played with toys in his infant seat or slept on a blanket while Mark finished editing the next month's training video and completed paper work. Mark, practically flaunting his new life, enjoyed having Stross with him as a reminder of what he gained by quitting—an opportunity to improve life for his son. Seeing the two of them together made sense of Mark's career shift for those who cared to see it.

By the second week of January 1992, Mark stopped going to the office. When he woke up in the morning, he was already at work with his boss waiting for him in the next room. I tried to do as many Stross-things as I could every morning but found anxiety kept me distracted. Though I was not in danger of losing my job, performing poorly enough to lose it seemed possible now, even if an extremely remote possibility. We needed my job. It was our family's only substantial source of income.

Mark enjoyed the freedom of his first week at home. He organized the house and took Stross on trips to the ice cream shop at the mall and to Menards, a large warehouse hardware store, to buy supplies for a building project at church. A handful of doctors' appointments dictated a portion of their days but the balance was Mark's to fill with fun endeavors like planning for youth events or simply playing with Stross and his toys.

Now 9-months-old, Stross adored slapstick humor. Bopping a sponge ball against your head and adding Batman-like sound effects could keep him belly laughing indefinitely. Stross never quit laughing before an entertainer quit entertaining. In fact Stross, a baby-sized proponent of laughter, created ways to make himself laugh. Mark and I marveled at how our son never tired of laughing at the way a rattle sounded when he banged it on the floor or how hilarious he thought it was to call a red ball an "ah-pul" (apple) and then pretend to bite it.

We counted on Stross to make us laugh several times a day, and Mark enjoyed spending part of his days inventing new ways to elicit giggles and laughter. After I arrived home, the pair included me in their mirth making by performing new tricks for my benefit. Stross was hitting so many developmental milestones on target that it was

• • •

easy to forget what he physically lacked.

Mark's second week of life as Mr. Mom had a decidedly different tone. On Monday I joined him and Stross for a scheduled trip to Iowa City for our second visit to the spina bifida clinic. We had appreciated our first visit to the clinic three months earlier . It seemed possible to forecast Stross' future by observing the other children in the waiting room.

Babies in strollers wore eyeglasses over their crossed-eyes and young adults in wheelchairs independently rolled down the hall. Other children—toddler age—sat in large strollers wearing leg braces while still others, many school-aged, wore leg braces and ambled along with crutches. Observing these children—how they played and talked with their parents—introduced us to life with a disabled child.

We trusted the things these doctors and nurses told us. Stross was only the most recent in a long line of children they had seen. The physical challenges caused by his spina bifida—leg paralysis, muscle weakness and hydrocephalus—were nothing new to them; therefore, we accepted his prognosis as statistically and clinically sound. According to their testing, Stross' defect occurred somewhere in the lumbar region, possibly the L3 vertebrae. This meant he would have some control over a portion of his leg muscles and could be fitted with leg braces someday. Based on their experiences, they believed Stross could learn to walk using leg braces and a walker.

They also tested Stross' sensation levels by poking the sharp end of a broken tongue depressor into various places on his feet, legs, and buttocks. The doctor observed Stross' reaction and wrote down a sensory level of L4, one level lower than his motor level. This meant Stross could feel more sensations than we had previously believed. Using an anatomical diagram, the doctor shaded the portions of Stross' lower extremities and buttocks that were without pain sensation. He cautioned us to protect these parts especially from severe hot or cold (including sunburns and frostbite), bug stings, slivers, clothing irritation and anything else that may hurt him without his knowledge. He also admonished us to warn anyone who took care of Stross for us to do the same.

Every clinic visit included consultations with a nutritionist, urologist, orthopedic specialist, physical therapist, a pediatrician who specialized in children with myelodysplasia disorders and a social worker. Typically children with spina bifida visit the clinic every six months for a routine follow up of their health. Additional visits are scheduled if there is a need for more specific medical follow up.

On this trip we returned to the orthopedics department to report on a bracing device prescribed for us to place Stross in at bedtime. The brace, called a Rochester HKAFO, was shaped like an "A." When Mark and I first saw it, we both thought the technology for its manufacture originated in some medieval torture chamber. When strapped into the brace, Stross' legs were held out from his body in what appeared to be a 60-degree angle and a large Velcro® strap across his chest kept the upper part of his body against a back plate covered in fuzzy fake fur. Even his feet were fastened into place with the aid of tiny, Velcro®-bottomed, open-toed, white leather shoes.

The thought of strapping our child into this bedtime contraption horrified us. The brace effectively immobilized Stross' lower body and trunk, making it impossible to roll over or stretch his legs. The device forced Stross to sleep on his back all night, his legs secured at obtuse angles. Deciding when to place him in the brace each night was difficult.

We understood the importance of the brace. Children with spina bifida are more prone to hip dislocations and a type of growth imbalance that causes scoliosis. Our orthopedic specialist believed that using this brace during Stross' first year, typically the year of most rapid growth, would reduce the likelihood of these complications.

The first night we had the brace, we tried to put Stross in it while he was awake to continue our practice of letting him fall asleep naturally. He looked up at us through the dark of his room and held out his little arms as if to say, "Okay, that was fun. Now get me out of here so I can sleep." When we tried to leave the room, he started to loudly protest—not a cry, just grunting sounds to let us know he wasn't happy with this new game. By then I'd started to cry, so it was up to Mark to go into Stross' bedroom and rectify the situation. Mark's solution: Take Stross out of the brace. We would hold him and rock him to sleep and then decide what to do next.

As the Mommy, I had the pleasure of rocking Stross to sleep while Mark, the Daddy, watched from a nearby couch. The cute, white, open-toed shoes added nearly two pounds to Stross' lower body. Because even a wrinkle in his sock could cause Stross a foot sore, we had carefully cut out the toes of his socks so we could keep track of his tiny digits. His feet looked normal, but the way they hung—heavy and limp—felt abnormal. Still Stross soon fell asleep, oblivious to his footwear.

Mark and I waited several more minutes before deciding what to do next. Recognizing our attempt to delay the inevitable, I carried Stross up to his crib and gently laid him down. While I cradled the upper half of Stross' body, Mark helped position his legs and then secured his feet, legs and chest with the brace's straps. When I backed away, Stross started to open his eyes so Mark bent over him, whispered quietly in his ear and stroked his hair.

In less than a minute Stross nestled into sleep. As we drew the blanket to cover him, Stross placed his chubby hands behind his head with his elbows pointing to the sides of his crib. He cocked his chin into the air. He looked comfortable. The blanket hid the things that made us uncomfortable—things Stross seemed oblivious to. Mark placed his arm around me, and we stood watch for five, maybe 10 minutes. I rested my head against Mark's chest and let his shirt absorb my tears. My hair caught his tears.

Our son still looked angelic when he slept.

After we'd laid Stross to sleep this way for three months, it was time to return to Iowa City so his doctor could verify that our diligence was helping. We needed to be on the road by 7 a.m. to arrive on time. I had already informed my boss that I would use one of my remaining sick days for the trip. Waking that morning at 6 a.m., I knew I really was sick. I felt nauseous and warm. A thermometer confirmed a fever. A trip to the bathroom to empty the

· · ·

contents of my stomach confirmed a virus.

"Joy, you can't go. Maybe we can reschedule. What do you think?" Mark asked.

He already knew what I thought. He didn't need to ask. We would keep this appointment no matter what. In fact we had been looking forward to this visit, not because of the brace check but because we'd also see the pediatric specialist for a regular check up. He would measure the circumference of Stross' head during his exam, and we really wanted to know how that measurement would compare to the previous one. Stross' head had appeared oversized in our Christmas photos, causing Mark and me to speculate about his growth—particularly the growth of his head. We had wondered whether it was normal or not. We'd been cautioned to watch for abnormal head growth as a sign of a shunt malfunction. We just didn't know if we were looking for a big change in size or an extremely big change. The exchanges went like this:

"Does his head look big to you, Mark?"

"Yeah, sort of. But not extremely big."

"But do you think it's too big?"

"I don't know Joy. What do you think?"

"I don't know."

"Well, he is growing. He's gained a pound to two hasn't he? Makes sense his head will get bigger, too. Let's not panic."

Panic was something I was good at.

"Okay. You're right," I'd conclude. Even after I'd agreed with him, Mark still looked worried.

Sometimes we switched roles and Mark would begin the big-head conversation with me offering the reassurances. But then something happened that had stopped these conversations altogether. During our youth snow sculpting contest two days before this Iowa City trip, one of our male youth commented on Stross' head. After that neither one of us could reassure the other. We both kept hearing that 14-year-old boy say, "Man, look at his head. It's HUGE." The comment had been delivered with honest tact as only a teenager could.

We had to make the 120-mile trek to Iowa City. We needed those

• • •

doctors—not some kid—to tell us if Stross' head was abnormally big or not. And we both needed to be at the appointment, even if that meant Mark had to become my caregiver as well.

Upon arrival Mark filled out the necessary paperwork, pausing occasionally to ask me the date of Stross' surgeries, his own Social Security number or medicines to which Stross was allergic. When our assigned case manager learned I was sick, she asked if we would prefer to reschedule. Mark answered.

"No. We just drove two hours from Des Moines because we have some questions."

So she took us into a side room, then asked: "Do you feel well enough to answer questions, Joy? If so, I can stay with you while Mark takes Stross to get weighed and measured."

I assured her I could talk as long as I could stay lying down, so Mark and Stross headed off for our moment of truth. Meanwhile I filled her in on what had happened with our family during the previous months. Even she was surprised at how much had changed, primarily our income and the fact Mark had become our Mr. Mom. The remainder of her questions focused on how Mark enjoyed this new life and how I was coping. I reminded her—and myself—he'd only had one full week in his new role.

It wasn't long before Mark, looking concerned, came to take me to see the doctor. The doctor looked concerned too.

"His head measured 44.9 cm today," he said. "It was 40.0 cm in October."

I needed no translation. Stross' head had grown nearly 5 cm in three months.

"So what does that mean?" I asked the question anyway.

"His fontanel is open, and it's very tense and full," he continued. "Last time you were here, his spot had nearly closed. I believe it has enlarged to accommodate a build up of fluid in his brain."

"So the shunt isn't working," Mark said, confirming my fear more directly than the doctor. "Shouldn't he be vomiting and stuff?"

Projectile vomiting and listlessness were the warning signs we remembered most from the hydrocephalus brochures we'd received when Stross was born. Stross had not shown any of those. He had taken longer naps lately and been quieter, but it was still possible to pull a belly laugh out of him by adding sound effects when zipping his coat. Once Stross started laughing, as he had that morning, he ran on his own giggle-steam for minutes.

"He should be vomiting from the cranial pressure, but he is probably fortunate his soft spot is relieving that pressure," said the doctor. "The shunt doesn't seem to be doing its job, but we need a CT-scan to know for sure. We can get you into radiology as an emergency case here, but your neurosurgeon is in Des Moines, isn't that right?"

Mark and I nodded.

"How quickly can you get back to Des Moines?"

Things were accelerating faster than we could think.

"As fast as we need to," came Mark's response. I laid down on the exam table and focused on taking slow, deep breaths. The doctor made no move to leave. I sensed he was waiting for us to grasp what we had just been told.

"Does this mean surgery?" I asked. "Is there any other way to fix a shunt?"

He paused, looked down and then found my eyes.

"Yes, it means surgery. I'm sorry."

He waited for us to speak again. We didn't. Mark looked at Stross sitting in his lap and gave him a sad smile. He kept Stross busy playing with his toy.

"I'll go call your neurosurgeon," the doctor said, and then left us in a place we'd been nearly nine months before.

"How are you doing, Joy?" I wasn't sure if Mark was asking me about the flu or the news I'd just heard.

"I could be better." My answer sort of choked out.

"You gonna make it?" This was a bona fide Mark question. I'd heard him ask it other times when I'd felt sick or stressed. I wondered if he understood that simply asking this question begged the response: Do I have another choice?

I chose to smile and say, "Yes."

· · ·

I spent the next 40 minutes answering other questions about Stross' general health and willing my body's recovery. At some point another nurse entered the room to say our neurosurgeon had ordered a CT-scan that afternoon. We were to arrive as soon as possible and report to the outpatient procedures desk. So after 90 minutes in Iowa City, we were headed back to Des Moines.

As we drove I thought Stross looked as if he was staring. If so, his shunt problem was worse than we'd thought.

"Mark, do you think he's staring or looking?" Stross didn't change his expression, and Mark didn't answer.

"Stross? What do you see, Baby?" No response. "Stross?"

Stross turned his head to look at me and offered a tired smile. The third time I began this routine, Stross ended it by closing his eyes and starting a nap. I reached over the seat to wiggle his leg.

"Joy, leave him alone. He's had a long day."

But really our day had just begun. We arrived in Des Moines in record time and drove directly to the hospital. Soon Mark was telling the woman in admitting that our doctor had scheduled an emergency CT-scan for our son. He offered our name, Stross' name, the doctor's name and the name of the doctor in Iowa City. But the woman couldn't match anything to the information in her computer. Mark's body language conveyed nervous impatience. The woman, now flustered, started to question Mark. She asked questions for which he had just provided the answers.

"I just told you," Mark said, and then gave her the names again. Finally she located Stross' name but nothing about a CT-scan.

"Shouldn't he look sicker if his shunt isn't working? Shouldn't he be throwing up?"

Her transformation into a neurological consultant was not appreciated, and Mark let her know it.

"Do you want his head to explode or something?" he barked. "Just get him in—for the CT-scan. His doctor ordered it. That's why we're here."

Mark spoke in concise and demanding sentences. His tone made her speechless. Stross, still sitting on the counter and leaning against Mark's chest, looked with interest at the people around him. I pulled myself off the chairs and slouched to Mark's side. It was my turn to step into a role Mark usually played.

I began by quietly outlining the events of our day; and while I talked, Mark calmed, she regrouped and the woman sitting next to her called our neurosurgeon. By the time I finished the second woman had printed out orders for the CT-scan, and the first woman apologized for the confusion before giving us directions to radiology. Mark, far from appeased, told her we already knew where to go and that we had just needed her permission to go there. Finally, papers in hand, we were on our way.

During the CT, the radiologist had told Mark that our doctor would call us the next day. Our doctor, in fact, called us only two hours after the scans were made. He asked about Stross' behavior and if we'd noticed any of the signs for shunt malfunction. We told him the same things we'd reported in Iowa City. Stross seemed to be himself, just quieter and more tired. The neurosurgeon seemed surprised and skeptical. He asked to see us the next morning, a Tuesday.

We arrived in his office at 11 a.m. He confirmed the need for surgery but wanted to schedule it so the pediatric surgeon could assist with the placement of the shunt tubing in Stross' abdomen—the same arrangement used for Stross' first shunt surgery. Even though Stross had had no abdominal problems since his ostomy revision, the neurosurgeon wanted to be cautious and invite the other surgeon to assist. We agreed.

The neurosurgeon explained that he was willing to cancel other surgeries to open a slot that coincided with the pediatric surgeon's schedule. Unfortunately it wasn't that easy. His scheduling nurse informed him that the two doctors' operating days did not coincide. Therefore the pediatric surgeon's scheduling nurse offered Saturday as a possibility if the neurosurgeon was willing to come in on Saturday. He was. The neurosurgeon delivered the news to us in person. I received it in the spirit offered: Two doctors would operate on a Saturday to help my son. Still the five-day wait seemed an eternity.

"Five days?" I asked the neurosurgeon. "Can't it be any sooner?

• • •

Isn't sooner better for Stross?"

He glared at me and then spoke in very measured sentences.

"Yes, sooner is better. But what would you like me to do? I said I'd clear any spot in my schedule, and I tried to do that. The other doctor just isn't available. Would you like a different neurosurgeon? Maybe his schedule will work better," he asked.

The doctor was clearly impatient and irritated. I had not anticipated a confrontation with my son's doctor. Mark looked at me with wide eyes of caution. He knew my response needed to be as measured as the doctor's.

"No," I said softly, then paused. "We want you to operate. We trust you. I just hoped it could be sooner."

The doctor softened too.

"If you can call and get something else worked out, fine. I told you I'd open my schedule."

We took the admission sheet for the Saturday surgery and left the office. Mark and Stross went back home, and I went to my office. I spent the remainder of the day clearing my schedule and trying to speak to the pediatric surgeon.

His scheduling nurse recognized my name and could tell by the tone of my voice that I was upset. I wanted to talk to the doctor myself. When he called 30 minutes later, I thanked him and then tearfully unloaded all that we'd experienced in the last two days. I apologetically begged for a way to schedule surgery sooner, relaying the conversation I'd had with our neurosurgeon and his offer to open his schedule. When the doctor got a chance to speak, he offered swift reassurance.

"Joy, I'm so sorry. I did not understand how serious the situation was. Do not worry. I will open a time on Thursday."

He then promised he'd see me sometime Thursday, but the nurse would tell me when.

In about 10 minutes the nurse called back to report the shunt revision had been scheduled for Thursday at 3 p.m. We were to check in at 1 p.m., and Stross was to visit his pediatrician's office for a pre-surgical exam on Wednesday.

After I hung up, I quickly called the pediatrician's office and then called Mark with the news. The following 10 minutes I spent head down, sobbing into my desk calendar. Gratitude and grief mixed equally. I'd nearly moved heaven and earth for my son. I had altered the lives of two surgeons and families of unknown patients who were now displaced from the surgical calendar.

Evidently I could change many important things—all but the one thing I wanted to change most.

And so Mark's second week as Mr. Mom ended with his son in the hospital again. This time for another surgery—his sixth. Mark spent three full days at the hospital, sleeping by Stross' bed as he recovered from his shunt revision. Mark took care of Stross' feedings, diaper changes and ostomy care. I also slept at the hospital but managed to put in a few hours at work the next day and even Saturday. Stross was discharged into our care on Sunday.

By Monday, Mark's third as Mr. Mom, Stross developed a raging case of diarrhea. At our surgical follow-up that day the neurosurgeon expressed his pleasure at how well Stross' scalp incision was healing. The diarrhea did not concern him since it was not a sign of shunt malfunction. He reasoned that Stross must have caught my flu virus—a logical prognosis, but I'd had no diarrhea and Stross was not vomiting.

By Tuesday he was vomiting—projectile vomiting. Mark called me at work to inform me that as soon as Stross drank an ounce of breast milk, he threw it back up. Mark wanted to know what I thought he should do. Stross' diarrhea looked flaky and yellow now, he said, and it was emptying from the ostomy pouch as more liquid in consistency than solid. I reminded Mark of the BRAT diet (bananas, rice, applesauce, and toast) and spent my lunch hour making a round of doctor's calls.

The neurosurgeon was still not concerned, but our pediatrician said to bring Stross in. So I called Mark to inform him of the 2:45 p.m. appointment, and Mark gave me a full report of the visit at supper.

The pediatrician had encouraged Mark to eliminate solid foods from Stross' diet and to alternate between feedings of Pedialyte and breast milk. If Stross refused the Pedialyte, Mark could mix it with breast milk. He cautioned that Stross needed hydration, especially since he was recovering from surgery. Therefore Mark appointed himself to a 24-hour care schedule. Every two hours—through Tuesday night, Wednesday, Wednesday night, Thursday—Mark fed Stross. He slept while holding Stross in our family room recliner and took over the room's adjacent guest bath.

The cold, bleak days of January conspired with the illness that invaded our home. Both coldness and disease impaired our ability to function. Mark kept a fire burning in the fireplace night and day to ward against physical and emotional numbness. Stross' health threatened to paralyze us again; and Mark, as the parent closest to our emotional ground zero, grew fatigued. When I volunteered to spell him, he deferred. I had just been sick, he told me, and I needed to stay healthy to work. Caring for Stross was his job. He'd survive by sleeping when Stross did.

By Thursday I worried about them both, so I called periodically from work for updates: Stross' diapers were damp, but he still had liquid diarrhea. Mark said he had a hard time keeping Stross' ostomy appliance on since stool easily seeped in around the stoma and under the seal. Stross still had playful times, he said, and he would still laugh; but our son appeared even more tired than before his shunt surgery.

When I got home that Thursday, I saw my husband dressed in a dampened sweat suit with dark circles under his eyes. His puffy cheeks sported three-days' growth of beard. My son's eyes, peering up from his head as it nestled against Mark's shoulder, were sunken and his cheeks pronounced. Stross looked like the child of a Holocaust victim.

The first words out of my mouth resembled an order: "Mark, we've got to take Stross to the hospital."

"Really?" he asked, unbelieving. Mark could not see the baby I saw.

"Honey, he doesn't look good."

Mark sensed my worry but couldn't fully connect.

"I sort of thought he was getting better," he said, sounding exhausted. "He didn't throw up as much today."

My husband's sensibilities drained with each tired word of rebuttal. I hoped to gently overcome his insufficiencies.

"Mark, something's not right. Let's go, honey, please."

I couldn't wait for Mark to relent, so I took Stross out of Mark's arms and laid him on our bed. Stross felt empty in my arms. I feared that part of him had slipped away.

Stross watched quietly while I packed his diaper bag and expressed milk. I thought about packing a change of clothes and the breast pump but resisted the urge, believing it catered to a panicked overreaction. Within 45 minutes we arrived in the emergency room at the children's hospital. Stross' weight was 14.5 pounds. He had weighed 19 pounds prior to his surgery the week before.

The staff called our pediatrician who met us there and told us Stross would be admitted for dehydration. A culture of his stool would tell us what kind of virus he had. The best thing we could do was get an IV started and give his body the fluids it needed.

After he left Mark and I talked about which one of us would call our parents and the church and who would go home to bring back clothes and the breast pump. While we waited, Mark emptied Stross' ostomy pouch two more times. The first time he poured its contents into a specimen cup that we gave to the nurse. Finally, with nothing left to talk about, we waited.

Stross sat at the end of Mark's knee and batted at a toy of colored wooden beads threaded through colored, twisted wire. One of his hand movements caused the beads to topple all the way to the bottom, clinking as they went. He started to laugh, just a little at first, then harder. It sounded like one of Stross' characteristic belly laughs, the infectious ones that make you laugh no matter how bad you feel, but it echoed as he continued. Both Mark and I laughed, feeling permission to relinquish our sober feelings; but I soon stopped. The echo of Stross' mirth haunted me. I wanted his sick laughter to stop.

The first nurse who came to start Stross' IV couldn't find a good vein. With Mark and me holding Stross down, she tried two times in one of his hands anyway, hoping to hit something that looked like it might be there. Both times Stross cried screams that came from a hollow place deep inside him. Finally she left and returned with another nurse who looked over Stross' body. That nurse decided she wouldn't try but recommended calling for a neonatal intensive care nurse, someone who excelled at starting IVs on preemies with paper-thin skin. However, she cautioned, sometimes these nurses resorted to attempts on the scalp and that might mean shaving Stross' hair. She shared the information to prepare us, just in case. I wondered if she'd noticed the patch of hair Stross had lost from the previous week's surgery.

When the neonatal nurse came, she looked over Stross' feet and vetoed the possibility of starting one there—poor circulation. She surveyed other options and made a failed attempt in the hand that had not yet been stuck—then she looked at his scalp. Stross' veins were not as close to the surface as preemies, so she feared failing an attempt there. Because I'd watched her face when Stross wailed during a previous failure, I also suspected lack of courage. My job of holding Stross while he wailed inhuman sounds of protest was hard enough. I couldn't imagine how she felt.

Our admitting nurse enlisted the head of the ER department next. This doctor, commanding and bold, made four attempts—three in the emergency room and one in the pediatric unit's treatment room. Mark and I continued to hold Stross as still as possible. I had his head, Mark had his legs and two nurses were on hand to steady the hand or arm that contained the targeted vein. Even though Stross looked emaciated and tired, he managed a vigorous rally against every needle stick. My son was still a fighter. After each attempt, the doctor stepped back, the nurses released their hold and Stross became quiet. He'd shut his eyes and lie limp on the table, exhausted. Between each of the doctor's attempts, Stross entered a deep, scary sleep.

Finally the ER doctor announced that if he couldn't get a needle placed, he'd have to start a mainline IV through Stross' chest. I asked him what that involved—but after hearing his first sentences, I shook my head and waved him off. The little I'd heard sounded awful. Mark faced the wall near one corner of the room in an emotional retreat. No one could see his face.

The doctor left the room saying he'd be back in a few minutes for one final attempt. He wanted to give Stross time to rest. I plopped down on a foot stool that was about 12 inches off the ground and looked up at the nurse who stood next to my son. I'd seen tears in her eyes during the last attempt, but the evidence was gone.

"What happens if he can't start one?" I asked. The nurses looked at each other and didn't say anything.

"Is there even another place on Stross' body to try?"

More silence and then, "Oh, yes, there's another location," one of them said. "He's the best doctor we have for IVs. Sometimes he gets them started when no one else can."

If that had been true, I'd wondered, why had he been unsuccessful so far? In a few minutes the doctor returned with an alternative.

"Hey, what's that kid's name? The one on Life Flight? His name is some sort of initials. J.I., J.R.? You know the one I'm talking about?" he asked the nurses.

"You mean, A.J.?"

"Yeah. Is that it? Call him. He's good. I'll try one more time, but let's call him just in case."

The doctor did make another attempt. Stross awoke to wail in protest, then fell asleep when it failed. Emotionally drained, we resumed our positions—Mark against the wall, me on the stool, the nurses by the exam table—as the doctor went looking for A.J.

When the door opened, we stood at attention. The doctor escorted A.J. into the room. Calling him a kid had not been an understatement. He looked like a teenager wearing his father's Life Flight jumpsuit.

"I left you a spot," the doctor told A.J. "Don't blow it."

I couldn't believe what I heard. The kid had to have felt enough pressure with two panic-faced parents staring at him, and the doctor had dared to up the ante. A.J. studied Stross' arm. The doctor *had*

• • •

left him a good place—a vein inside the crux of Stross' right arm, one of the veins phlebotomists typically use to draw blood.

Everyone but A.J. held his or her breath as he opened the needle package and approached the area of skin prepared for him. As the nurses took their positions at Stross' arm, and Mark and I took our positions at Stross' head and legs, Stross sensed something big was about to happen and opened his eyes. When A.J. pricked through Stross' skin with the needle, Stross let out a long cry, then fell silent as a small amount of blood indicated the needle had hit its target. The nurses helped A.J. tape the needle securely in place and attach the IV tubing with its life-restoring fluid. The doctor slapped A.J. on the back. A.J. beamed.

"Good job," the doctor told him. "I knew you guys thrived under pressure."

Mark thanked A.J. I thanked A.J. Mark leaned over Stross to kiss and stroke his hair. I cried. The nurses—each with tears in her eyes—adjusted the intravenous fluid and set the pump's monitor. Glucose began to flow into Stross' body. We all felt a little more life coursing through our veins.

• • •

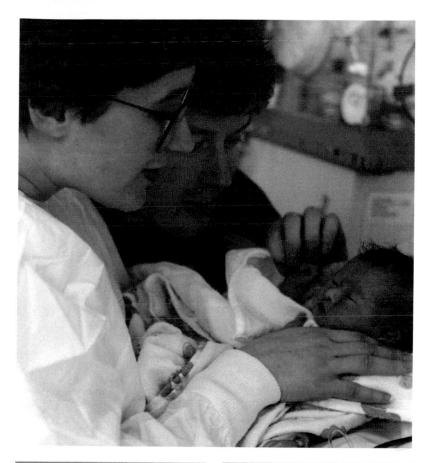

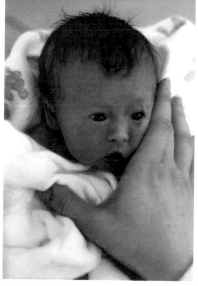

*From top, left to right:* Mark and Joy, shown feeding Stross (3 days) for the first time, found him captivating. ❯ This photo of Stross (3 days) helped introduce him to family and friends in his earliest days. ❰ Mark's ability to connect with Stross (4 weeks) was evident from birth.

*From top, left to right:* Stross (14 months) looked forward to helping Mommy get ready for work every day. ❦ Stross (10 months) learned to army crawl then quickly developed the muscles for crawling on all fours. ❧ Stross, shown on his second birthday, has always enjoyed playing dress up. ❦ Mark made therapy fun for Stross (18 months), shown here using a parapodium to practice standing.

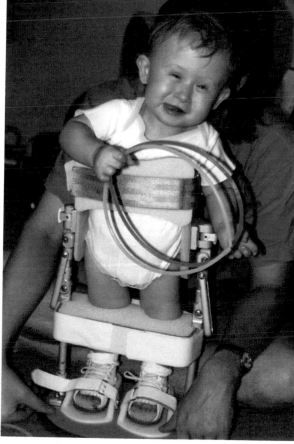

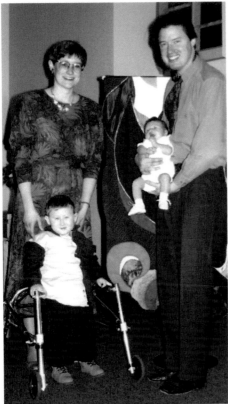

*From top, left to right:* Stross (4 years) welcomed his little brother, Skye, by joyfully introducing him to life. ❧ Our family celebrated Skye's baptism (October 1995) while publicly acknowledging Stross' baptism—conducted in the hospital by Joy's mother in 1991. ❧ Stross (3 years) began regularly using his walker around Christmastime—his second December in Forest City.

# Chapter 19

# Crying

· · ·

As fluid poured into Stross' body, his arms began to fill out, his cheeks began to look the right amount of puffy and his eyes began to emerge from dark sockets. Late on Saturday we learned the cause of the severe symptoms that had brought us to the hospital three days earlier: rotavirus—a nasty illness caused by an opportunistic germ. The virus had eaten the good bacteria in Stross' digestive system, making it difficult for his body to fight back.

Our pediatrician explained how rotavirus could be tracked geographically as it spread throughout the United States each year. Children in the Des Moines area had been getting sick from rotavirus for several weeks. He also explained how contagious and destructive the virus could be to infants. This virus, far different from the one that caused my stomach flu, didn't disappear in a mere 24 hours. It inhabited Stross' body for as long as it could, depleting him of valuable fluids.

Because Stross had spent all his waking hours with either Mark or me since late December, I was at a loss as to how he could have contracted the virus. Our pediatrician said the hearty germ could live on hard surfaces for days making contact possible by touching something as seemingly benign as a shopping cart. This scenario seemed highly unlikely to me. I believed a more probable hypothesis: One of the nurses at the hospital where Stross had his shunt surgery had contaminated him after visiting the room of a sick child. Even if true, what would that matter? Nothing but fluids, rest and time could hasten his recovery.

While Stross regained his strength, my parents came to spend a day in Des Moines. They offered to stay with him in the hospital so Mark and I could feel free to leave. So we sat in a movie for about two hours and ate in a restaurant for an hour. Knowing we could stay away longer did not matter. We needed to get back to Stross. It didn't feel right having fun without him.

The rest of that weekend we sat in Stross' hospital room with my parents who talked to us and entertained Stross between his naps. Mark read some trade magazines about computers and video production while I used the extra patient bed in Stross' room as a cutting board for a church sewing project. Our individual efforts were wonderful diversions, for this hospital stay bored us. All it required of us was to be quiet as Stross slept, watch him plump up from IV fluids and feed him as his appetite allowed. Periodically we checked his ostomy bag for signs of solid stool.

Coming back from this bug was no small task for Stross. His body had just started bouncing back from surgery when his immune system began combating rotavirus. By Sunday—three days after he'd first arrived—Stross kept down small portions of applesauce and small bottles of breast milk. By breakfast on Monday, he kept down his normal meal of a banana half and some cereal. When we took Stross home Monday afternoon, Mark and I held our emotions in high alert, uncertain whether the new week would bring yet another adventure.

Nothing significant did happen—not really. At least nothing we hadn't experienced before.

A few weeks after Stross' hospitalization, our pediatrician delivered news of a second chromosomal study. Stross' pediatric surgeon had taken a skin biopsy and sent it to the Mayo Clinic on one of the days Stross was in the hospital rehydrating. This test had come back normal too. Therefore we could continue to believe Stross' only limitations would be physical ones.

And so we fell into a normal routine, at least a routine we thought of as normal. Each morning Stross woke up first, talking to himself and gurgling happy sounds into the baby monitor. He woke us about 10 or 15 minutes before the alarm every day. Mark would get Stross from his crib, then change his diaper and empty his ostomy pouch while I sat in our bed expressing milk. Then I'd crawl back in bed for snuggletime. Games of Peek-a-boo, Where's Stross' Toe? and Thumpkin served as the official start to my day. When Stross started to make hungry sounds, Mark took him to the kitchen to warm a bottle while I showered and dressed. By the time I was ready to brush my teeth and put on make up, Stross was fed and dressed. Mark then passed Stross to me while he took his turn in the shower.

Stross loved to sit on the counter and hand me things out of my make-up bag. Some of our 10-month-old's first words included the names of facial products. He soon learned the difference between a tube of mascara and a tube of eyeliner. If I reached to grab something out of my bag instead of asking for his assistance, he'd let me know I'd crossed a line. Stross also let me know he wanted to assist with the application of my blush by reaching up to run the compact's small brush across my cheek.

Because he took such joy in helping, I devised a way he could assist me with teeth brushing also. I'd hand Stross the toothbrush, and he'd try to hold it steady while I squeezed toothpaste onto the bristles. His eyes danced as they focused on the blue gel. My "all done" indicated it was nearly time for him to hand me the toothbrush. As I screwed the cap back on the tube of toothpaste, Stross always echoed, "ah duhn."

When we finished in the bathroom, I'd carry Stross in to sit on our bed. He'd babble excitedly, anticipating what came next—an opportunity to rifle through my jewelry box and help me select earrings and a necklace. Best of all, Stross got to wear bright, yellow, clip-on earrings and a gold chain of leaves on his head. The choker-sized chain capped his head, resting across the center of his brow.

The adornment made him look like a tiny, baby Caesar. The clip earrings became his toy: I'd put them on my ears; Stross would pull them off and then insist I put them back on again. I happily obliged.

This newfound daily peace made it difficult to interpret what happened to me on one of the last weekdays of February, the day I couldn't finish getting ready. On this day I followed our family's morning routine until it was time to dress. I only got as far as donning my undergarments—then I could do no more. I sat on the edge of our bed and stared into my closet. I stood up, then sat down again. The next time I stood I managed to take a few steps toward the closet before sitting back down. I wanted to cry, but I didn't know why.

Whatever was happening to me, I knew I didn't want to be alone. On my next attempt at standing, I walked onto the landing at the top of our stairs. I looked over the top of the split-foyer, half-wall into our kitchen where Mark held Stross. The two were patiently waiting for a bottle. I wanted to call out Mark's name but feared that speaking would cause me to cry. Mark glanced up and saw me. A flash of concern crossed his face. I still couldn't speak, but my lip began to quiver and tears started streaming down my face.

"Joy? What's wrong?" Mark's voice was quiet, strained.

I moved my head from side to side and lifted a shaking hand to push back the bangs of my hair. The tears came faster, and I heard a whine push through quivering lips.

"I don't know."

I heard my voice, but it didn't sound like me. I tried again. "I don't know."

"Are you sick?" Mark asked, ascending the stairs. I didn't respond right away. Stross, still sitting on Mark's hip, looked back and forth between Mark and me. This was new.

"Are you sick?" he asked again.

"No, I don't think so," I said.

"Why are you crying?"

"I don't know." I didn't know, but the act of crying felt strangely good.

"Is there something wrong?" Mark asked, desperately trying to

· · ·

find the cause of my crying.

"I don't know, Mark. I don't know."

My voice sounded tired, desperate. Mark guided me back into our bedroom where all three of us sat on the bed. Stross looked around and started to coo a word that sounded like "pretty," our cue that it was time to pick out jewelry.

"No, buddy, no pretty yet," I told him. I smiled to let him know his Mommy was still in my body somewhere.

"Do you plan to go to work?" Mark asked.

"I guess so," I said. "I don't think I'm sick." With that a new wave of tears began. "I just...can't...stop crying."

"Do you want me to call someone?" Mark asked.

I shook my head "no" and then asked, "Who would I call?"

"Your mom, maybe?"

"No, not my mom."

"Maybe a friend? Rita or Michele or Charlene?"

I shook my head "no." Mark sat quietly while I cried.

Stross looked at Mark and asked, "Ba-ba?" He wanted his breakfast.

"Just let me sit here a while, Mark. Maybe I just need to cry. I can't cry forever. I'll try to get ready some more."

Mark took Stross back to the kitchen to retrieve the bottle and mix a bowl of cereal. He placed Stross in his high chair.

I continued to sit on our bed and regained some control. Tired, I willed myself to rise, then walked back to the bathroom. I shut the door, turned on the water faucet, and started to cry again. My crying accelerated into sobs, full-bodied sounds that reverberated in my chest. I stayed in there as long as I could, then decided to reemerge—I didn't want Mark to be scared.

My time in the bathroom had been productive. I'd decided I could not go to work, at least not before noon. While I had no idea why I was crying, I determined the tears would not go away quickly.

"Mark," I again called down from the top of the stairs. "I'm not going to go to work. Can you call them?"

"Are you sure?" he asked.

"I guess so. I don't have any more sick days. But I guess I am sick. I mean, I think I must be. I don't know. I just can't stop crying." I not only heard the confusion of my statement, I felt it.

"I don't think you *should* go to work, Joy," said Mark. "I'll call." He left Stross playing with dry cereal and walked up the stairs again. He gave me a long, tight hug.

"You're scaring me," he said. "We need you. Do whatever you need to do. Are you sure you don't want me to call your mom? Maybe it will help you to talk to her."

I could not understand Mark's insistence that I call my mother.

"Mark, are you worried I'm having a nervous breakdown?" My tone was indignant, even accusatory. He didn't answer, so I tearfully pushed the issue. "Do you?"

"Joy, I don't know. I don't think so. Maybe your mom could help you figure it out."

"Don't call anybody, Mark. I don't want to talk to anyone right now. Just let me lie down. I'm going to put on some sweats and lie down," I pleaded.

I was still crying, but it came in quiet streams now.

Mark looked scared. I learned later how scared he was— scared enough to call my parents behind my back. While I was upstairs changing, Mark called my office to report my absence and then immediately phoned my parents to fill them in on what had transpired that morning. My dad, responding to Mark's concerns and my apparent need, stepped into a role he'd played countless times during my adolescence. As Mark spoke Dad transformed into my personal counselor, giving Mark reassuring feedback.

Mark listened then suggested Dad call me later just to talk and be supportive. My dad told him a call would give him a good excuse to let me know how much he loved me and that he was proud of me. Dad promised Mark he'd call from his office before his first-period class. The call came 30 minutes later while I lay on the sofa in our family room under an afghan knitted by my Grandma Delma. After Mark answered the phone, he handed me the receiver. I didn't want to take it. My involuntary weeping had not yet subsided, and I still

● ● ●

found it difficult to talk. Mark forced the phone into my hand.

"It's your dad. He loves you," Mark said.

I spent the next few minutes listening to my dad talk and making feeble attempts at verbal responses. While I listened, I looked at the fire Mark had built for me in our fireplace and watched the flames dance through liquid pools that welled up, spilled out, then welled up again. I imagined the flames as waves of gratitude for my father; my husband; the health of my son; a job I enjoyed; and a home where I felt safe, warm and cared for.

I couldn't remember what my dad had said after I hung up, but I did remember how it felt to talk to him. It felt just like the times he had come into my bedroom when I was in elementary school to tuck me in at night and the times he had sat on my bed consoling me after a fight with a junior high friend or after a dating relationship ended. I'd grown so much since Stross' birth, but not so much that a call from my dad couldn't take away some of the hurt.

I let myself cry all day and tried not to worry about Mark worrying about me. I knew I'd be able to go to work the next day even if things remained unsettled, and I also knew that I'd be okay—eventually.

● ● ●

# Chapter 20

# Everyday Stuff

...

I f I'd experienced a nervous breakdown, I'd also made a remarkable recovery. My crying fits disappeared by the next day except for occasional bouts of tears that would usually come during my commute. On weekends Mark would fall witness to these bits of release when I'd start to cry during our drive to the mall or Target. For some reason I felt comfortable crying in the car, especially on the freeway. The familiar route could take me to work or to one of the downtown hospitals. My two second homes comfortably existed merely exits apart.

While I didn't know what brought on the tears or why I cried so freely, I looked forward to how I felt once the tears dried. The more moisture I lost, the less stress I felt. I could never have produced enough tears to eliminate all the stress, but I was able to reduce it to manageable portions. The songs off our Margaret Becker CD once again became a tool for therapy.

I scheduled a visit to my gynecologist in case my emotional state had organic origins. A blood test indicated my hormones were within pre-pregnancy levels (just within) and my pituitary gland seemed to be doing its job. The doctor asked questions designed to assess my mental state. We both concluded that I was not clinically depressed. The feelings I'd experienced had been a genuine reaction to the very real demands of my life. He offered to refer me to a counselor, but I didn't think it was necessary. I had my car rides, Margaret Becker's CD, an attentive husband who cared for me, a happy son and a job I enjoyed.

Mark worried that my new role as breadwinner weighed heavily on me. A few friends speculated that as well. I knew the truth. I loved being at work. There were no demands there that I deemed unconquerable. My job was to manage things. I managed multiple things simultaneously, and I managed them well. I had a budget—someone else's money to spend—and colleagues who enjoyed their jobs also. I felt happy there.

I loved conferences and business lunches. I loved doing business over a meal so much that I started to schedule meetings over brunch. I'd head out of our building and down the lamp-lined sidewalks of Des Moines' historic Court Avenue District. The hustle and bustle of the city's skywalk system—a corporate fantasyland of connected businesses—were only one block and one elevator ride away.

On workdays, my office became my respite. It was peaceful and busy—an intoxicating paradox. To review magazine copy or brochure layouts, I'd sit at a drafting table placed by a window so I could look out at the Des Moines River as it flowed under the Court Avenue Bridge. Occasionally I'd pretend to work on copy or layouts just so I had a reason to sit in my office and watch the moving water.

Mark and Stross were a constant presence at work. Photos of them lined my window seat and filled the corner of my desk. At least twice a day, I intentionally looked at an 8 x10" photo of Mark whispering in Stross' ear when he was 4-weeks-old.

Looking at the photo became the start of my 20-minute breaks for nursing. I'd look at the two of them, wonder how they were spending their day, and then grab my portable pump unit for some mommy time, a daily ritual that linked me to my son and my husband.

Mark and I talked on the phone at least twice a day—once after I'd pumped in the morning and once after I'd completed the task in the afternoon. If Mark and Stross' day included a doctor visit or a therapy session, I'd time my call so I could hear an immediate report. About once a week the two of them came downtown so we could lunch together. In the spring and summer we'd choose a meal from one of the dozen food vendors in a nearby plaza, then sit on a terrace near the plaza's fountain. Stross loved the moving water and laughed whenever Mark or I reached down to splash water at his face or legs.

When a downtown visit wasn't the high point of their day, Mark arranged for something else to be a high point: a visit to McDonalds for a taste of "frenfriez," a trip to church so Stross could greet office staff and visitors while Mark prepared youth mailings or a wagon ride around the neighborhood that included a stop for swinging in the park. However, our local Menards reigned as Stross' favorite destination. Mark made regular trips to Menards for a construction project at church. We'd incorporated youth musicals into our ministerial programming, and Mark decided the church needed a portable set and lighting kit. Soon he was making daily trips for supplies.

Mark noticed that the store's bright lighting display with its moving ceiling fans and reflective mirrors was Stross' favorite department. They'd walk the aisles, and Stross' face would become more animated as he spotted colorful streamers dancing in artificial wind. Even if Mark did not need anything from that section of the store, he'd carry Stross through the aisles to watch him cock his head back and laugh as the breeze from dozens of fans hit his face. His sounds of glee—ranging from squeals to peals of laughter— grew louder with each visit.

Before long Stross began snapping his head in the direction of the lighting display as soon as Mark passed through the store's entry. Stross' best view of the display came, not just inside the doors, but just after Mark passed through the security turnstiles. Anticipating the sight, Stross strained in Mark's arms to get closer—his body language expressing his sense that the lights and fans could not be seen soon enough. Therefore, no matter what Mark had to buy at Menards, his first stop had to be in electrical lighting.

It wasn't long before Stross' squeals and giggles began in exuberant anticipation at Menards' door. His eyes squinted under the strain of an ear-to-ear smile, and his body grew tense with excitement. Since his feet had limited movement, Stross' arms took on extra duties. In excitement mode, this meant Stross' arms—bent slightly at the elbow—flailed up and down, wildly expressing his joy. He punctuated his rapture through the independent movement of each tiny, extended finger. At peak emotion, Stross looked like a large hummingbird struggling to stay near the sweetest nectar ever tasted.

"Ummmmmm, uhh, ummmmmm," Stross intoned in various high pitches. "Ummm, uhhmm, uhhmmmmm."

He struggled to get some of his new words out, words adequate to describe the splendor he saw.

"Oooo, ummm, priddy," he'd say using the same word reserved for my sparkled earrings or necklaces. "Ooo, ummmmmm, ooo."

The thrill nearly caused him to burst. It was large enough to draw the attention of shoppers four or five aisles away. Men and women found reasons to drive their carts into the lighting section and then stand at a polite distance, smiling at our effervescent son as he bounced up and down in Mark's arms. Stross' communion with this world of light was intoxicating.

Soon store employees joined in Stross' visits. When I tagged along once I heard one employee say to another, "Here comes the Ceiling Fan Baby." Then they set aside what they were doing to nonchalantly follow us as we carried Stross to the lights.

As his first birthday approached, I entertained ideas for an elaborate celebration. First birthdays were supposed to be big. Because Stross had survived an amazing year, he deserved not just a big celebration, I thought, but an enormous one. To make certain I conceptualized the perfect event, I planned for his birthday as I did the association's convention. I began by identifying audiences and some objectives—not a typical mom approach to birthday planning.

I easily identified our family's primary objective: to acknowledge all that had happened in the past year and to offer thanks for having survived it. Clearly we had not survived on our efforts alone. The quality of Stross' life—perhaps even his life itself—had been made possible through the work of skillful doctors and caring medical personnel. We had to thank them.

We had to thank our entire congregation as well. Individual members had joined to collectively sustain us through every obstacle that had come our way. With each hospitalization only one phone call set in motion a chain reaction that instantly buoyed our spirits. We'd receive personal visits, phone messages and notes of encouragement. In addition snacks would show up at the hospital, and meals would arrive at our home for weeks after the immediate crisis ended. Sometimes a check or a stack of food coupons appeared in our mail, making that month a little easier than the last. Most of all the knowledge that others were praying for us brought a sense of comfort. Our strength and courage rose on the power of their prayers.

Stross' birthday also gave us a chance to thank our immediate families as well. Each set of parents planned to come to Des Moines on separate weekends, one before and one after his birthday. Mark and I knew private celebrations with them in our home—cake and all—would suffice. They simply needed time alone with their grandchild to discover how he'd grown and appreciate who he'd become.

We needed time alone with Stross too. His birthday fell on a Tuesday, and I planned to take the day off to commemorate it with Mark and Stross. In one year of life, he'd survived six surgeries, two additional hospitalizations, and a fall from a changing table that had redirected the course of his parents' lives. In addition, he'd begun a program of weekly physical therapy and educational sessions and had made countless trips to half a dozen doctors for follow-up appointments including visits for regular stuff like ear infections and well-baby exams.

Because Stross had lived a lifetime in one year, his birthday celebration could not be contained to one day; so I decided we'd begin the Sunday before—52 weeks since Stross breathed life for the first time. At the end of worship that Sunday, Mark and I thanked the entire congregation for all they'd done. Both of us spoke only briefly. I began and then Mark picked up when my voice trailed off. We attempted to express our deep gratitude and then treated the whole crowd to juice and cupcakes in Stross' honor.

On Stross' actual birthday we went to breakfast at the Iowa Machine Shed, a restaurant that had become an important Saturday morning ritual regardless of the strain on our budget. From the time Stross was 8-weeks-old we'd eaten breakfast there each Saturday, sitting in the same booth with the same waitress serving us. We'd feast on our favorite breakfast comfort foods—Mark's pecan pancakes and my ham and cheese egg scramble—while Stross either slept or cooed at us from his infant seat.

The staff here, particularly our waitress, Stefanie, had watched Stross grow also. Each week he'd brought new skills to show off. Now at one year of age Stross sat in a high chair feeding himself bits of eggs, pancakes and country potatoes. He'd stop occasionally to put on his toy sunglasses and utter, "Cuhl, doood" (a trick taught to him by some of our youth) or to drop a brightly colored toy off the tray of his chair then peer down at it—laughing. "G'in, g'in," he'd call to us or Stefanie, asking us to retrieve the toy so he could throw it then laugh hysterically again. His birthday warranted an extra trip to the Iowa Machine Shed that week—a Tuesday trip to celebrate.

After breakfast we made a round of visits to Stross' doctors in their offices—first the pediatric surgeon, then the neurosurgeon, then our pediatrician. At each stop we shared words of gratitude and then gave the doctor a ceramic photo mug that held a birthday cupcake. Each one seemed genuinely touched.

Finally we took Stross to the neonatal intensive care unit to visit his nurses. Two of our favorite nurses were on duty that day, and each took time to talk with us, hold Stross and thank us for coming. I knew we'd only be able to extend our personal thanks to one shift of nurses, so I'd written a thank you birthday card and included a photo of Stross for their unit's bulletin board. I'd looked at the photos on that board many times during the first nine days of Stross' life. The success stories that smiled back from photos and personal notes offered comfort. Now our story had become part of the unit's legacy.

With our round of thank you visits completed, Mark and I took Stross to play by a set of fountains in a West Des Moines office complex. He giggled at the dancing water for several minutes before we headed

••• ————————————————————————————————

to McDonalds so he could enjoy his other favorite restaurant.

Stross' first birthday was a sunny day, a perfect day for driving with our windows down and breathing in aromatic wafts from apple blossoms and springtime flower beds. As Mark drove I occasionally looked back at Stross now peacefully napping. Every so often a breeze from our open windows lifted his hair off his forehead, and he'd move slightly. He looked even more beautiful than the day he was born.

Stross awoke rested and ready for more adventure, so Mark pointed our car in the direction of Menards. We wanted to take him to the best place we could think of for our private birthday celebration, a place that, to him, was as much a wonder as he was to us. We spent the best part of an hour blissfully walking the aisles of the elcctrical lighting section and basking in the glow of our son's life.

•  •  •

# Chapter 21

# Suffocating Guilt

...————————————————————————————————

The word "survival" sums up our family's first year of life with Stross. He'd survived surgeries and life-threatening illness. Mark had survived a career change that would make many men depressed and angry, and I'd survived watching Stross and Mark conquer those things. However I did not know how closely my survival was linked to theirs.

By the summer of 1992 I was ready for life to move on, whatever that meant. Often during Stross' second year of life, I felt suffocated; but I'd adopted a coping mechanism that kept me from feeling hopelessly stifled. An evening spent with high school photos, college keepsakes and albums from our early marriage always cured what ailed me. During these times I'd travel to a previous era of life in an attempt to recapture the euphoria of untested hope. These binges of nostalgia were an unconscious attempt to drink in my youthful, more naive state of being.

Without fully understanding my compulsion to revisit those times, I managed to transform any guilt related to these nostalgic longings into benign regret. Regret over what, I wasn't sure.

Like a character from Thornton Wilder's "Our Town," I identified with a regret-filled Emily who asks the narrator: "Do any human beings ever realize life as they live it—every, every minute?"

His response: "No...the poets and saints, maybe they do some."

Perhaps I had not realized my own life back when it was carefree and pregnant with possibilities. Or maybe I had...at least some. I was certain Stross' birth had not left me void of hope, nor had his life left me without promise for the future. I still felt like the same girl who spent afternoons in my family's backyard singing Broadway show tunes at full voice or reading a biography about someone—Malcolm X, Marie Antionette, Judy Garland, Grace Kelly, Maya Angelou—who had left an imprint on the world stage. I could remember what it felt like to move through my family home, my neighborhood, my school and my hometown wondering how I, too, would imprint the world. I was still wondering.

While coming of age in the '70s and early '80s, I imagined myself as a television producer (ala Mary Tyler Moore), a television reporter (ala Barbara Walters or Jane Pauley), a politician (ala Geraldine Ferraro), and an actress in regional and national theater companies (ala SuEllen Estey from my hometown). I was impassioned in the midst of musical and dramatic endeavors and was happiest considering creative livelihoods. However, I lacked the type of reckless confidence necessary for unconventional career choices. My confidence was more studied, more measured. So even though I loved the romance of a career that could connect me to others via a stage or television camera, I lacked the daring resolve necessary to bring those dreams to life.

Consequently I drifted to more traditional career paths that presented emerging opportunities for women. Like most young feminists, I believed that I, too, could advance women's causes in a manner that would make Justice Sandra Day O'Connor proud. My new ideal was something that could link a love of stories and storytelling with a desire to shed light on injustices. Believing I could do that in a behind-the-scenes broadcast career, I decided to pursue a degree in journalism and discovered that I could, in fact, tell a story. Unfortunately the college I chose didn't have as strong a broadcast program as it did print journalism.

My career pilot then became a beloved adviser who encouraged my writing. He encouraged me through several campus editorial positions before I gravitated to the field of public relations. I had not known anyone who claimed to have such a career and wasn't even certain of its practical applications. Still, it seemed like a fit—my way to employ communication skills while advancing causes in which I believed. In addition, I could become someone who—like so many who had gone before me—enjoyed the best of both worlds professionally and personally. At least that is what I'd been led to believe as a daughter of the '70s. I could "bring home the bacon, fry it up in a pan," and never let my husband forget he was a man. It's what I'd strived for then, and it's what I continued to hope for in spite of new life circumstances.

Unbelievably, none of my life planning exercises had included concrete thoughts of motherhood. I had not imagined myself as a mother, yet I believed that I'd eventually be one—a working one. My mother had worked as a substitute teacher when I was in elementary school, then began working full time when I entered junior high. I was convinced that she would have worked full time from the beginning had someone informed her generational peers that women could indeed have it all.

Now I was a mother. A working mother with a stay-at-home husband. And my husband was fully supportive of what I wanted to do with my life. I just wasn't certain what that was anymore. Revisiting former times seemed my best opportunity to get back on track; therefore, I enjoyed my periodic mental escapes without regard to their meaning. All I knew was that I breathed easier when reliving what had come before, and I could better remember what it meant to feel safe, innocent and full of potential.

I didn't feel my life was in danger, but I couldn't escape the reality that tenuous days stretched before me.

As a young girl, sometimes an adult would tell my parents that I seemed wise beyond me years. Now—in limited ways—I actually was. Life had granted me a degree in hard-won wisdom—a brand of wisdom honed by hardship. It lay on my heart like a stack of overpriced textbooks, tempting me to memorize each edition from cover to cover until I became an unquestioned authority.

But my wisdom had come through life experience; it would

forever be how I learned best. Stross had given me a way of looking at life that uncovered hidden ways of knowing. I could now see when people expressed a sense of indifference to things that mattered. I could also recognize injustices born of apathy and inequities propagated—unknowingly—by misguided intentions. I could see when people didn't get it, and I had a deepening appreciation for what "it" actually was. I just didn't know what to do about it; therefore, the mastery of "it" remained annoyingly elusive.

I continued to maintain faith that God held my future, but I liked to remind the Creator of plans set in place previous to Stross' arrival. What I wanted out of life seemed to dominate jumbled conversations with the One who created me.

I felt restless professionally and anxious about my personal life. I worried about Mark feeling fulfilled in his role as Stross' primary caregiver, and I worried about losing my desire to better myself as a person. I worried about the act of worrying and how it could hurt me physically.

Professionally, I'd taken my career about as far as I could at the association. I reported directly to the executive director and had no desire to become an executive director myself. Therefore, advancing professionally either meant a lateral move to a larger not-for-profit organization or to a company with a defined corporate ladder, but now the idea of leaving my job scared me. I needed the emotional support of my colleagues and the mental assurance of medical coverage for Stross. In addition to the benefits, I needed the fulfillment I got from meeting the basic responsibilities of my job. Therefore, the association appeared to be my indefinite professional home.

Thinking dominated many of my days, and I contemplated who I was as much as who I was becoming. Because I'd not contemplated the realities of motherhood before becoming a mother, I'd never personalized the concept either. Now I was inventing a whole new version vastly different from the playhouse variety I'd practiced as a babysitting teen. And while many of my childhood friends had speculated about their progeny's appearance, I'd avoided forming images of children or conjecturing personality traits. Amazingly

• • •

Stross had filled the void spaces within minutes of his birth. I could see the fullness of him and was able to instantaneously define what it meant to be his mother—specifically his. The only detail lacking: whether being his mother involved working fulltime.

Mark suffered his own identity crisis. As Stross' primary caregiver, he borrowed from the best parts of motherhood to form his brand of fatherhood. When we attended a social outing just for grown ups, Mark and I began the evening by wandering off to the areas spontaneously divided for men (in a den or around a barbecue grill) or for women (in the kitchen or circled in lawn chairs). By night's end, one of us crossed the gender barrier to join the other's conversation as a way to bridge our lives with our peers. Soon conversations mixed topics like office politics, hunting or fishing with anecdotal stories of children or the latest round of conflicts caused by someone's mother-in-law.

On many occasions, we lacked the desire to share with our matched gender group at all. When I offered stories about my child, it felt like my contributions were too different to be valid. Mark grew tired of using old office stories (and he didn't hunt or fish) for his contributions. As Mr. Mom, he lacked new office stories, plus he worried that tales about his current work might generate awkward pauses from men unable to cobble an adequate response. The fear of being vulnerable kept Mark from attempting to share those kinds of stories with other men at all.

Our awkward moments at private parties mirrored awkward moments in public. As Stross grew, these moments magnified. During the first months of Stross' life, I suspected that taking him out in public would grow increasingly difficult. I just didn't know how. There were little clues from time to time. For instance, Stross attracted attention with his smile. He smiled at everything and everyone. He especially enjoyed conversing with employees at cash registers.

Both Mark and I recognized that Stross liked to be freed from a shopping cart's child seat as soon as possible so he could sit propped against us as we paid. He watched the entire transaction while smiling at the cashier as if he or she were a long-lost friend. If the checkout line had a counter or even a small table for writing,

• • •

either Mark or I sat him on it so he could lean back against our body while our left arm served as his safety belt. Stross' sock-covered feet—never moving—either dangled over the edge or stuck straight forward from his hips in the direction of the cashier. Cashiers took this as an invitation to play with his feet.

"Are you ticklish?" they'd ask. Stross' smiling expression never changed, and Mark and I learned to ignore their attempts and keep writing our check. Some cashiers were persistent.

"Well, look at you. You just aren't ticklish, are you? I bet I can get you to laugh," they'd say as they wiggled their fingers against the soles of his feet. Stross kept the same smile but looked with more fascination at the person talking to him.

"What if I get your toes? Oops! Got your toes."

A funny word like "oops" could get Stross to chuckle sometimes, but no amount of tickling would ever get him to giggle with laughter. He could not feel his feet. Never could; never would.

Once or twice when confronted with the question, "He just isn't very ticklish, is he?" Mark and I tried to stop a cashier's tickle game by informing them that Stross couldn't feel his feet.

"Oh, really?" was the usual reply. "Why not?"

"He was born with spina bifida and is partially paralyzed."

The typical response?

"Oh." Then silence. "I'm so sorry. I didn't know."

"That's okay," we'd say sounding intentionally cheerful. "That's just why he won't laugh for you."

"That's such a shame. Well, he sure is a cutie. How unfortunate."

Instantly the game of Tickle turned into a game we recognized as Pity. The encounter typically ended with us finishing the transaction in awkward silence, gathering our purchases and heading for the car—one of us carrying Stross with his limp feet dangling and the other carrying our bags hanging limply to one side.

Until I'd spent days, then weeks, then months staring at Stross' unmoving toes, I'd never noticed how much other babies' toes wiggled. I marveled at how other babies could make each individual digit stretch or arch in concert with its neighbor toes even as they slept. Stross' lack of toe movement spawned a keen appreciation of that miraculous ability. To this day, staring at a sleeping baby's naked foot elicits a melancholy joy. I long for others to experience the thrill of intentional purpose that a tiny toe—one intricately formed without error—can express. This is when I take my turn in pitying others: Moms and dads whose children have the ability to move their toes are unable to appreciate the gift they've been given. I, a mom whose child can't wiggle his toes, can.

The more Stross grew, the more his physical inadequacies stood out.

"Boy, he looks like a mischievous one. I bet you have to chase him all over your house," I'd hear from a stranger making small talk in a checkout line.

"Yes," I'd say, having learned it was easiest to pass on opportunities to educate strangers. I'd been a similar stranger myself once.

Before Stross gave me an appreciation for infants' individual body parts, I'd encountered a baby whose face still lingers in my memory, a baby who confronted my courage at a time when I only wanted to focus on designing the best nursery any mom had ever seen.

One Saturday when I was about five months pregnant, Mark and I spent nearly one hour in the local fabric store. As parents-to-be, we'd adopted a very hands-on approach. No decision was small and no detail was overlooked. The nursery was our first parent project, and together we fashioned a beautiful room decorated in a farm theme. It was a tribute of sorts to our parents' agricultural heritages.

On this Saturday I searched for more adornments for our nursery and found an adorable pattern for a play structure shaped like a barn. For the barn roof, Mark found some wonderful fabric with black-outlined, cartoon cows all over. It had an occasional red, blue, yellow or green cow that accented the primary colors found everywhere else in the nursery.

Mark's mom had already crafted a bumper pad and ruffle for our crib that used similar fabric plus, as a surprise, she'd tied our look together with a quilt whose squares were of red barns and tractors in John Deere green. Carolyn had also used the fabric's cartoon cows to accent the quilt's barns. This day I returned to the fabric store to buy enough material to make matching curtains and floor pillows.

As I stood in the checkout line, it was impossible to ignore the woman's child in front of me. He quietly waited in his infant seat while his mom casually talked with her shopping companion. I guessed him to be maybe four or five months old, it was simply too hard to tell because of his grossly misshapen head—huge and bumpy. In fact, he had what appeared to be a cleft down the center of his skull. He resembled a child that might be born to the Klingon character of Whorf from "Star Trek: The Next Generation."

I desperately wanted to know the name of his condition. Instead of asking, I intentionally smiled at her baby and made sure I talked to him as I would to any other baby. As I talked, I scrutinized his strange features. He looked like an elephant baby. I had seen a movie about an elephant man in junior high and wondered if he was one of those. An internal debate played out on whether or not I should engage the mom in conversation. I didn't want to embarrass her but surely she knew that when she went out in public people were curious about her son. More than one year after that Saturday afternoon, I had no doubt this mother was aware of others' stares. While her body language never indicated such then, I now believed she had elected to ignore my inquisitive and overtly friendly behavior.

At the time I had wanted to have a long conversation with her about so many things: her pregnancy, diagnostic tests she may have had, her reaction to her son's birth, any indications she'd had that something had gone incredibly wrong inside her body. As I waited in line behind her and her son, I wondered if the material she was purchasing was for his nursery or special clothes to fit over his extra large head.

My unasked questions remained unasked. Had I said them aloud, it would have been out of callous curiosity. Yet if I'd had an opportunity to stand in line behind that woman months later, an infant who had formed abnormally would be riding in my cart also. Any questions I'd have asked then would have originated from my identification with her as a mother. She would not have ignored me even though, compared to her, my type of motherhood was easy for public consumption. I had the benefit of a slow, public warm up. My son's deformities could stay relatively hidden until his inabilities to move the same as other children became noticeable. Her baby had been a spectacle from the moment of his birth. Also her baby didn't have my son's personality.

Stross eagerly embraced the world, at least everything except small animals. During stroller or wagon rides, Stross became agitated if we passed a bird standing on a lawn or if he saw a squirrel run across the sidewalk or up a nearby tree. Several times he'd become so upset during one of our leisurely neighborhood strolls that Mark or I had to take him—crying—out of the stroller to carry him all the way home.

Stross also seemed apprehensive of other small creatures, particularly human ones. He had a ready smile for any adult or child who chatted with him or played games, but he stiffened at rigid attention if we carried him into close proximity of another baby or toddler. This made his time in the church nursery particularly difficult.

The nursery was never one of Stross' favorite places. He preferred attending worship with us and going to our adult Sunday school class. He also went with us when we taught the junior and senior high youth. Tagging along worked out okay when he was still small enough to sit in his infant seat or when his naps coincided with the worship hour. But as babies at our church grew, they were supposed to spend time in the nursery while Mom and Dad learned about God with other grownups.

Mark and I wanted our family to behave within normal social boundaries as much as possible. There was no medical reason Stross couldn't be in our church nursery, so we took him there as often as he tolerated it. The easiest days for Stross (from our perspective) were when Mark or I was scheduled as one of the parent workers. When I was one of the workers, it might have been good for Stross; but it was hard on me. During my hour or two on duty, I would be reminded of how difficult it was to pay all babies equal attention and how our son—with paralyzed legs and an ostomy appliance hiding under his onesie—could scare and even intimidate volunteer workers.

I first suspected this on days when we'd been brave enough to pass Stross through the nursery window just like other parents. After handing him off (with his diaper bag), both Mark and I would assure the worker that one of us would be back in 30 minutes to check his ostomy since his diaper change was different. Then we'd watch the worker place him on the floor to play. Once Stross got settled with toys placed all around him, we'd wave bye-bye and head for the door. Later one of us would return to sneak a peak at our pride and joy through the nursery's little square window "just to check."

We repeated this ritual every time we left Stross in the nursery. Both Mark and I were overprotective and especially curious about what we'd see through the window. Nine times out of 10, I'd see Stross still lying on his tummy, apparently content to watch the world go by. Occasionally I'd see him grab toys within his arm's reach, then mouth them or study their shape and color. If the toys happened to roll out of reach, he simply looked around the room at the other children playing.

I was often tempted to rush through the door and bring the toys back to him, but I comforted myself by believing these were early life lessons for our son. If a toy fell out of reach, Stross would have to figure out what to do on his own in spite of his physical inability to crawl toward it. Even if he couldn't crawl, he had to try. It was good for him developmentally.

Observing Stross in the nursery was good for my own development as well. I obtained the ability to provide self-comfort even when I felt like irrationally yelling at the parent volunteers—my angst about unconventional motherhood spilling over as misplaced anger.

"Hey, you, you nursery ladies. Look at Stross. He needs a toy to play with. Hey, lady. He can't crawl. Notice him, please. Get him a toy."

The longer I'd stand at the secret window watching Stross exist toy-less, the greater my desire to yell.

"Oh, sure. The crying kid is getting tons of attention. So is the curly-haired, smiley girl. Woman! See that baby on the floor? He won't cry for attention. I know him. He saves crying for surgeries. He has had six of them. How many have you had? Get - him - a - toy."

• • •

Sometimes I'd stand at the window for 10 or 15 minutes hoping Mark was not worried about my absence. I'd stand watching my son and feeling comforted by a release of anger that came through loud admonishments spoken only in my head.

"Listen, ladies. You call yourself nursery workers? Stop talking to each other and talk to my baby. He's the one giving you no problems on the floor. You know, just because he is content to lie there without a toy all day doesn't mean that it is good for him. Pick - him - UP. Please play with my son. Give him mental stimulation. He has a lot of work to do. You can help us. He loves books and music. Read to him. Sing to him. He will smile real big at you. I promise."

Sometimes standing there was pure torture but turning away from the window didn't lessen the pain. I desperately needed someone—another mom—to fawn over my son in an irrational way. Many women held him, cared for him and talked to him as they would any other baby; but I wanted someone to champion my child as incredible—a child she was privileged to know.

When I was one of the nursery workers on duty, things were different. I'd begin by choosing the most exciting and colorful toys for Stross to play with. Occasionally I'd turn my focus to some other children, but Stross was my ever-present concern. If I played ball with a child, I'd teach him or her how to roll the ball to Stross. After a few passes, the child would lose interest and cross the room in search of more exciting games. Part of me wanted to play more intentionally with the other children, but usually it was clear that whoever I was paired to work with assumed I was Stross' primary caregiver when I was in the nursery. Should I leave him to play with other children, I was not confident my counterpart would help Stross if the need arose while I was busy with another child.

Once when I allowed my attention to stray from Stross, a chubby kid stepped on the back of his legs and stood there. Stross made no sound.

"Stross, did that hurt?" I'd asked loud enough for the other nursery worker to hear. She sat three feet away, oblivious to what happened.

I knew kids stepped on or even hit other kids all the time, but this kid—my kid—was different. He couldn't feel when it happened. I wondered how many times something like this had happened without Mark or me knowing it. I mentally bristled at the thought of all the pinpricks, wood slivers, bee stings, and hot dishes that might unknowingly injure him in the future. Didn't this other woman know how special my child was?

By the end of Stross' time in the nursery—whether I was there or not—every toy placed near him managed to walk off, taken by another infant at play. Even toys Stross held in his hands might be carried away, grabbed from his grip by an early walker who had yet to develop a conscience. That was the hardest act of all to observe. It was not fair that some kid months younger than Stross could cheat him out of a toy simply because Stross couldn't defend it.

I wanted Stross to chase after those kids—to get upset at them.

I wanted to cry but I had grown tired of crying.

One morning when I worked in the nursery, church seemed to drag on. I had not wanted to be there, having spent my morning choking on a ball of emotions. All the things I wanted to say aloud to someone were stuck fast. I wasn't even able to yell them clearly in my head. It felt difficult to breathe.

I couldn't talk during our short car ride home either. Mark filled the silence by singing to a song on the radio. I pretended something out my car window was incredibly interesting. I did not want Mark to notice I was on the verge of tears. Safely inside the confines of our home, I dropped into the nearest chair—our blue recliner—and waited for Mark to free Stross from his car seat. I hoped Mark would take him immediately upstairs and into his room to play. I needed more time to collect myself.

Mark had other plans. Stross suddenly appeared on my lap right where Mark placed him, feet toward my tummy, his face lighted by a huge smile and bright eyes that looked for my approval. I couldn't look at him at all.

"Hey, Sweetie," I managed to say as I turned his body away from mine. While Mark returned to the garage for the diaper bags and Bibles, I repositioned Stross' bottom in my lap, and a relaxed

• • •

Stross leaned back against my chest, his head nestled between my breasts. My tears started. I was glad Stross couldn't see my face. I couldn't bear to have him see evidence of my guilt and self-pity. I didn't want Mark to see it either.

A soft ka-boom let me know the garage door had closed. After carrying our last load into the house, Mark walked behind my chair. I held my breath, waiting to see what he would do next. He came around to the side of the recliner and knelt at my side.

He knew. How had he known?

My tears came harder and in sobs now. Tears fell on Stross' hair.

"Joy, you have a beautiful little boy," Mark said. "He's just on his own time schedule."

Somehow Mark had known exactly what I was thinking. Somehow he had spoken the very words I needed to hear. Instantly I could take a deep breath again. The guilt I'd been carrying for the majority of a year lifted.

My guilt had never been about any role I may have had in causing Stross' birth condition. I knew I'd had the healthiest pregnancy possible. The origins of my guilt came from a deeper source, my self-pity. I felt sorry for myself. My baby had birth defects, and life wasn't what it was supposed to have been. Week after week, the church nursery magnified that reality.

The previous year we had been a family surviving against incredible odds. The novelty of us had worn off, and this year we were just the Newcoms, the family whose son was different than other babies. I loved Stross. I did not want a different son. I just wanted the son I had to behave differently. I wanted him to be different in a good way. I wanted him to be more normal. If he were, then I could be too.

Instead my son lived life on his own time schedule, a different time schedule than anyone else's. Because he did, I did too. Somehow Mark's words gave me permission to let go of the feelings that had torn me up inside and accept the reality of my life. I had always loved my son. Now I could see that his kind of different was okay—that I was okay—just as things were. The realization freed me from guilt.

•••

I had been guilty of so much: of denying the beauty of what I'd been given, of fighting against the way life was by believing I was fighting for it and of wanting more miracles than the one who sat on my lap. When Mark knelt beside the recliner and listened to me cry, I realized I had been guilty of denying God. Depriving myself of that relationship had caused me to suffocate emotionally. I'd allowed myself to drag down in the mire of daily therapy exercises, messy ostomy changes, difficult doctor appointments and uncomfortable public conversations. I'd forgotten how to celebrate life's simple moments.

The very next day, Monday, I came home from work and was met in our living room, as usual, by a smiling Stross in the arms of his adoring daddy. I looked forward to this welcoming committee every day.

"We have something to show you, Mommy," said Mark.

"Oh? Okay, what is it?" I asked, enjoying the aroma of our supper cooking on the stove.

"Well, Stross has something he wants to show you."

"Stross does?" I asked, realizing the surprise had nothing to do with food.

"You do, don't you buddy?" said Mark, confirming it with Stross. "Let us get ready first."

Mark got down on the floor and placed Stross on his tummy. He laid him in a prone position, his arms out in front with his feet sticking straight out behind him. Stross cocked his head in anticipation. Next Mark backed up about three feet from Stross' face and held out a ballpoint pen.

Very deliberately Stross pulled in his chin to tuck his little round head. He reached out an adorably chubby forearm, pressed it into the carpet, and then pulled himself toward Mark. It was the first pull of an army crawl and with it, he moved forward. Stross was moving. He made awkward, little movements—fractions of inches really—but he was moving forward. He was crawling.

As I watched my son move with intense and intentional motions across our floor, I acknowledged a presence I'd first sensed the day of Stross' birth; and it spoke to me through the actions of my son.

"See what I can accomplish?" it said. "Keep your eyes right here, Joy. Keep your eyes right here. I'm not finished with you either. Your son can help you understand what it means."

Then Stross smiled at me, proudly lifting the pen in his hand as an offering.

•   •   •

# Chapter 22

# New Mental Images

•••————————————————————————————

My ability to recognize how Stross impacted me grew steadily that summer. Now the time I spent observing him in the church nursery helped me realize that the world hadn't changed as much as I had. I no longer saw the volunteers as antagonists but as fellow sojourners in life. We each had things to learn.

From the moment he first breathed life, Stross helped me better realize that to live was to learn. The moment I'd closed myself to life's lessons was the moment I'd stopped living. I just didn't know when or how it had happened. I'd been so focused on survival that I hadn't recognized how internalization of self-righteous anger had shut off my ability to dream new dreams. Deep cleansing breaths of permission renewed my spirit. I was free to focus on me again—free to relax and accept, to discard old ways of thinking in order to risk adopting new ways of relating to the world.

It began with self-realization. I despised self-pity as much as I despised others pitying me.

Like my favorite arcade game, I'd attempted to whack down pity whenever it reared its ugly head. But it had become an incredibly exhausting game. I now understood I needed to regard my self-pity as a channel of rising but navigable water. Whenever I

• • •

felt pity pushing in, I simply had to keep moving in the direction of the current until I found a channel that promised easier travel and forward progress.

I felt as if I'd begun a new journey. Simply stated: I had learned to go with the flow.

This didn't mean everything became easier overnight for I had also discovered that personal resurrection came through deliberate intentionality. Therefore, to aid my self-enlightenment I had to avoid simply going through the motions of daily responsibilities. Monotony, callousness, inattention, guilt and anger—any emotion tied to a negative existence could court pity and cheapened the richness of life. What's more, I learned the value of my life was based on my treatment of others—imperfect children worthy of respect and celebration.

Because of this heightened awareness, I began to appreciate what I could learn from others. I also learned to appreciate time to relax and have fun. That summer my parents offered to help us go on a seven-day vacation. They suggested the five of us ride in one car so they could pay for the gas, and we could share driving duties. If Mark and I were willing to sleep in the same room with them, they'd also cover the cost of lodging each night. My dad pointed out that—with them on the trip—Mark and I were free to go out in the evenings while they cared for Stross.

Mark and I had not traveled anywhere for that length of time since our honeymoon. Our biggest vacation had been a five-day trip to Knoxville for a reunion of Mark's World's Fair musical performance team, but since returning to Iowa, even our weekend excursions had waned. Now the demands of our life made any type of getaway a volatile topic.

My parents' offer of a nearly all-expenses-paid vacation was too good to pass up, so I asked for a week off near the end of June. My dad and Mark agreed on an itinerary that took us to Kentucky to introduce Stross to Mark's extended family and then to Texas to visit friends. On the way home we planned a stop in Wichita to visit more family.

Mark and I thought of this vacation as Stross' Victory Tour, a chance for us to introduce our son to friends and family and a chance for them to marvel at how amazing he was. The trip accomplished that purpose while restoring our sense of healthy adventure. Taking Stross to see people who had only heard about him helped erase any images they had of a deformed, sickly child who'd needed multiple surgeries.

I'd learned the importance of redrawing people's mental images of Stross the first day I returned to work. Someone in the office had tacked up Stross' birth announcement and photo in a prominent location. I'd been told that during my maternity leave, visitors who asked about me were updated on Stross and then taken to the workroom to see his picture. My coworkers shared some of those reactions with me after I returned. Evidently hearing about Stross brought grave expressions and clumsy questions. Showing those same individuals photos of Stross enticed smiles and surprised compliments such as, "Why, he's adorable. You'd never know anything is wrong," or "What a pretty baby. He looks like his dad."

For meetings out of the office, I learned to carry a photo of Stross in my purse. If the topic of children came up, and if the fact that my child had birth defects made it into conversation, I pulled out the photo to show a colleague who had yet to hear about Stross or to meet him in person. Expressions transformed from furrowed brows of concern to grins of relief.

I enjoyed my job more each week. Before vacation I'd spent one week at a video production house overseeing the taping of a training video that would debut at the annual convention. I also joined with our legislative director and technical services director to create printed training material to accompany the video as well as materials for our lobbyists to use with state legislators. These were new experiences and new challenges—my professional frontier.

The association itself also headed for new territory with plans to make its home on the top floor of a building located in the center of downtown. I worried about losing the sedative effect of my river view. However my new view—14 stories higher—was of downtown Des Moines' south end and the same section of river I'd come to know intimately. The height, however, caused a dramatic shift in perspective. While I was too far away to see the movement of the water, I could trace a portion of the river's course as it headed for its eventual meeting with the Mississippi River. So I did look at the same river that flowed by my old office window but saw new things.

The association's new offices would not be finished until the beginning of October, one week after the convention. When Peter made the announcement, he also informed the staff that he would not experience those significant events. He had taken a job in Colorado and would soon move. It was difficult to see him go. His support during trying circumstances had been part of my healing.

I now worried that a new boss, one who had not shared the most significant part of my life's history, would find me a professional nuisance. During the first year of Stross' life, I had been out of the office nearly four months' worth of working days. An extended maternity leave, Stross' hospitalizations and the roller coaster adventure of our child care search had kept me juggling office hours well into the night many weeks and even some weekends. When I was in the office, I arrived on time, did not miss meetings and fulfilled my social role in daily office banter. As for the duties required of my job, no one else at the association could perform them.

At 27 years of age, I had overcome incredible personal adversity to accomplish goals. The magazine had won awards from a state organization for communication professionals, and the annual convention had netted more than $20,000 over the previous year and exceeded its attendance goals. The video, "Nightmare on Main Street," earned national recognition from the American Society of Association Executives. I could still take care of business. I simply needed the freedom to take care of my family in the process. And I hoped a new boss would see things the way I did.

Mark's boss had changed as well—he'd grown from an infant to a child the age of a toddler. Because Stross' physical limitations prohibited him from toddling, Mark made accommodations by transporting him to fascinating locations multiple times each day. Once in a location Mark made certain that Stross—either sitting in his infant seat or on the floor—was surrounded by visually

• • •

stimulating sights. If a room or workspace were too bland, Mark chatted or sang to Stross while he worked.

Now that Stross could army crawl, Mark had to baby-proof places previously out of range. Crawling brought Stross more independence, and his learning curve was swift. Captured by the excitement of this new activity, his crawling improved daily. We soon noticed that growth in his coordination accompanied intellectual growth as well. Communication was easier, and Stross' functional vocabulary enabled him to share his delightful sense of humor with us.

On an overnight trip to my sister's, Jill arranged for our family to sleep on a mattress on her living room floor. Stross spent the entire night between Mark and me. The next morning Jill woke us for breakfast and, while Mark showered, she sat next to me on the mattress talking and watching Stross crawl in and out of the sheets.

On one of his undercover expeditions, Stross crawled too far and plunked, head first, into the floor. His knees and feet remained propped in the air, resting on the mattress edge. His hands and arms stuck where they had landed, wedged between his chest and the side of the mattress. All we could see of Stross' head was a mop of fine, blonde-brown hair on the back of his skull. His forehead appeared embedded in the floor. Jill quickly reached for Stross, and I put out my hand to wave her off, shaking my head "no." I wanted to see what he would do next. If he'd not hit hard enough to hurt his head, I wanted to know if he could get himself out of the predicament he'd created.

I waited, listening for a shocked, delayed start to tears. Nothing. Seconds more passed and still nothing. Jill and I looked at each other. I quickly looked back at Stross and began to reach for his body. Perhaps he had knocked himself unconscious.

Just before I lurched forward, Stross made a sound.

"Ohhh, maaan!" his soft, nasal voice intoned. He sounded like a shrunken teenager embarrassed by an uncool mishap.

Jill and I burst out laughing as I picked up Stross and turned him around to face us. He beamed. He'd gone farther than his current abilities could take him, but he'd made us laugh in the process.

Stross sounded like a teenager because he learned to talk from teenagers. He learned the phrase "Oh, man" from some youth at church. Mark and Stross were regulars there each day, and the agenda invigorated Mark. Plus he was proud that we'd set a new standard for what a traditional family could be. Not one of our youth came from a family where a dad stayed home while the mom went to work. Mark and I became more than a fascination. We were a study in role reversals. Mark even spiced up the lesson by growing his hair long. In fact, a ponytail was his daily hairstyle now, and he shelved his suits and ties in exchange for jeans and tie-dyed or screen-printed t-shirts. His new look complemented his free-spirited way of life. Mark's days were full and productive.

For physical exercise, Mark joined our church's men's slo-pitch softball team. We had played on a coed team in Texas, and Mark wanted the same kind of reckless fun for us again. (We share a fond memory of me throwing him out of a game for yelling at an umpire the year I was a coach.) But I was a mom now, and I didn't see my body as athletic anymore. I didn't think like an athlete anymore either. I was certain that—if I played again—I'd only spend my time on a ball diamond scanning the bleachers to watch Stross and the person taking care of him. Softball became Mark's time for fun. He needed it, and a mishap during one game reminded me just how much I needed him.

About one year before Stross' birth, Mark began experiencing strange episodes of fatigue and light-headedness about three or four times a month. Nausea and hand tremors signaled the start of these bouts. Soon after, color would drain from his face and he'd perspire. The occurrences became so frequent that Mark agreed to see a doctor. A review of his dietary habits and family history of diabetes made the doctor believe that Mark was a candidate for hypoglycemia or low blood sugar. He built a strong case and encouraged us to try diet modifications before subjecting Mark to any tests.

For nearly two years Mark, a fan of Coca Cola and a confirmed chocoholic, eliminated all sources of refined sugar from his diet. When he'd start to feel bad, Mark would either eat an apple or graham cracker or drink one of the bottles of 100 percent apple juice we always had on hand. Mark would then lie down and within

• • •

30 minutes to an hour start to regain strength. Since the treatment had appeared to work, we'd trusted the diagnosis. Apples and apple juice had helped Mark maintain his strength through his first year as a dad. Now well into his second year of fatherhood, Mark experienced signs that something more serious was going on.

During the second game of a springtime doubleheader, Mark, in centerfield, noticed his hands trembling. He started sweating profusely and came to me between innings to ask for juice or a cracker. He'd already used what I'd packed in the diaper bag during the first game. Another player's wife volunteered some breath mints that Mark took, and then he began to climb back down. I grabbed his arm.

"What's going on? How do you feel?" I asked.

"I'm okay," he said, "really," and then he leaned up to kiss me as a sign of assurance.

Mark's time to bat came in the bottom of the inning with the bases loaded. After two called balls and two swinging strikes, Mark connected with the ball and hit it long into deep right field. He easily ran to second, and then began to stumble between second and third base. The opposing team had difficulty hitting their cutoff, so our team's coach motioned Mark home. He crossed the plate just before his legs gave out.

Half the bench cleared, not only because Mark had cleared the bases but because he clearly had a physical problem. The first two guys helped him to his feet. Mark legs bent at the knees, and his upper torso bounced above them like rubber. He laughed through tears, finding it hard to catch his breath. Stross had been sitting in my lap, and when I saw Mark go down, I'd grabbed the diaper bag and was already standing behind our team's dugout.

The guys who held Mark by the arms took him over to the grass behind the dugout where he laid down next to our diaper bag. I crouched in a semi-sitting position beside him with Stross propped on my knees. Mark couldn't talk. When he tried, he laughed. Laughing made him cry, not because anything was funny but because his body was temporarily out-of-control.

"What's going on, baby?" I asked him. The sound of my voice

told him I was scared. Mark's eyes were closed and his right hand was holding his ball cap at the crown of his head. His left had rested on his chest which was rising and lowering in jerky, deep breaths. Mark could only shake his head from side to side and moan.

"You are scaring me, Mark," I said. Mark moved his chin up and down. I knew he was scared too.

"Let me know when you think you can walk to the car," I said. Mark's chin moved up and down again. He covered his face with his cap now, and I heard him crying softly. We sat there for five or 10 minutes. The guys from our church team glanced over occasionally to see what we were doing. I'd smile and wave back. After Mark sat up, our pastor walked over to see if I needed help getting Mark home.

"No, we'll be okay," I said. Mark found his voice too.

"Yeah, I think I'm ready to go," he offered.

"You headed home for some apple juice?" our pastor asked.

"At least that," I joked. The two of us helped Mark to his feet, then he leaned on my left side while I carried Stross and the diaper bag on my right.

Mark sat quietly on the ride home, and Stross fell asleep in his car seat. I talked periodically to fill the silent spaces.

"Now I know how you felt when I had our miscarriage," I told him. After I'd started to bleed at church, I'd gone home to check in with my doctor and wait for Mark. The doctor told me to come in if my bleeding got heavier or if I did not feel well. The next morning Mark had entered our bathroom to find me passed out on the floor. He carried me to our bed where I regained consciousness as he slapped my face and repeated desperate sentences: "Wake up, Joy. Don't do this to me. Where's the doctor's phone number? You have to wake up." Mark had thought I was dying.

I hoped Mark wasn't dying on me now. I needed him more than ever. I could not imagine being Stross' mom without him. The man sitting in the passenger seat of our car with his eyes closed looked weak and fragile. I didn't like it. For weeks after that ballgame, I wanted to yell at Mark the way he had yelled at me the day of our miscarriage. "Snap out of this," I wanted to tell him. "Don't do this to me. Don't do this to us."

Whatever was happening to Mark left him helpless, and whatever was happening to him accelerated. He began to have episodes several times a week. They started with a mild headache, nausea and a shaky feeling—sometimes with obvious hand tremors. Once he began to feel bad, Mark would—as usual—eat apples or drink apple juice and wait to feel better.

I blamed Mark for making himself feel bad, certain he had cheated on his restricted diet. I knew how hard it was for Mark to give up regular Coca Cola and sweets, especially donuts. I also knew Mark might believe himself invincible and think one donut couldn't drop him.

As the episodes worsened, Mark came to expect bouts of diarrhea and vomiting as his headache diminished. The sensations made him so uncomfortable, he'd strip off his clothes and lie in his underwear on our bathroom's cold vinyl flooring. He did not want me near him during an episode. The external stimuli of a spoken word brought agony. I tried to comply but fear kept me close. I believed there was something I could do to help him—some clue I could uncover that would aid in his diagnosis.

Once I convinced Mark to take his temperature while the symptoms were at their peak. His temperature was 102 degrees. Hours later the symptoms disappeared, leaving Mark weak and tired. His temperature returned to a normal 98.6. I thought this information could be helpful in the hands of a new doctor, so we shared Mark's mysterious medical history with a different physician. Because Mark had so many intestinal symptoms, this doctor suggested we keep a food log to see if certain foods or ingredients triggered the episodes. The food log only made Mark's condition more confusing. He could go for days without any symptoms and then have a string of episodes, days in a row. Once a type of food became suspicious, he took it out of his already limited diet. Soon simply seeing a billboard or storefront for certain restaurants made him ill.

Mark often woke up feeling nauseous. If he felt ill when I left for work, I'd call him several times during the day to see how he was. When there was no answer, I'd regard it as a good sign believing Mark and Stross had left the house and were spending the day running errands or going on an adventure. At supper I'd drill Mark with a series of questions about how he'd spent his day, what he'd eaten and how he'd felt.

One day Mark confessed that he had not answered the phone because he was lying on the floor of the bathroom.

"You cannot do that. What about Stross?" I spoke in a forceful stage whisper. I wanted to yell at him, but he seemed fragile.

"He was asleep, Joy," Mark said. "I knew it would pass."

"This time, Mark. But what about next time?" Panic took over, and I loudly slung horrific hypothetical situations at him. "What if you passed out? What if Stross is crying and needs you and you can't help him? What if something serious happens, Mark?"

Something serious was happening. Life was messing with our family. We needed help. At a minimum, we needed witnesses.

Mark agreed to call me at work if he ever felt that incapacitated again while caring for Stross. If he called, I would come home. If he called when I was out of the office, Mark agreed to call our pastor or Charlene Horak to come sit in our house until he felt better.

Charlene's family had just joined our church and her two children were in our youth group. She was one of our most supportive and kind parents. Best of all, she delighted in following Stross' developmental achievements and had become our most willing ad-hoc baby-sitter. Charlene's husband was a bank president, and she spent her days assisting with various volunteer boards and charities.

Everything Charlene did or said illuminated a heart filled with mercy and compassion. She regularly spent time in Des Moines' inner city handing out food or assisting with a special activity. A manicurist designed her fingernails once a week and her black, sculpted hair was always in place. Yet Charlene had readily absorbed the lessons we'd given her about emptying the stool from Stross' ostomy and willingly took on this sometimes-messy task.

It felt good to pick up Stross after he'd been in Charlene's care. His ostomy bag was always flat against his body, a sign that she'd not avoided the task of releasing trapped flatulence, and he always smelled of her perfume—Estee Lauder's Private Collection—a sign that he'd been held and snuggled while we'd been away. The way she talked to Mark and me and the questions she asked us were clear indications that Charlene loved our son, and she loved our family.

Going to work got easier again. Knowing that our pastor and Charlene served as my back up comforted me. For nine hours, five days a week, I could work guilt-free. Stross was in good hands, even if Mark fell ill.

I needed to be at work. That's what I kept telling myself and reminding Mark. We needed the money, and I needed to spend my days there. Mark's condition had made home life unpredictable, and the time we spent together was draining. Because Stross' medical emergencies had dramatically reduced, my attention shifted to Mark and his medical needs. I worried about what Mark ate and how often he went to the bathroom and why. My husband had become as much a liability as he was an asset.

Stross wasn't our family's medical project now: Mark was.

I returned to coping tactics that proved useful the previous year. In survival mode I focused on what Mark needed, then worked to accomplish it. I did not consider Mark's feelings about his health or wonder if he worried about what was happening to his body. I simply wanted him to regain his status among our small band of survivors. I wanted him to make himself better. Fear kept me from asking him if he believed something more sinister caused his body to lose control. I only talked to him about how his days went—his good days and his bad days. I wanted him to understand how his health affected our lives.

In the midst of Mark's health problems, we got a phone call from my cousin Monte, an assignment editor for an NBC-affiliate in Waterloo. He knew that Wartburg College, Monte's and my alma mater, needed someone to teach a broadcast class; and he had thought of Mark.

Mark was flattered. He asked Monte to give him one day to talk things over with me. If I was open to Mark making the two and one-half hour drive to Waverly, Mark was open to teaching the college's class each Monday and Thursday night. Mark knew I'd have a soft spot for Wartburg, but he also knew I'd be nervous about him spending that much time on the road. His enthusiasm was palpable, so I endorsed the plan to submit his name. If the college elected to call him, Mark promised we'd talk again.

They did call, and the proposal wasn't for just one course. They needed someone to teach television production during the fall semester and corporate video during the winter semester. Mark's expertise matched the content for both courses. With excitement building, Mark prepared for our next conversation by pulling out a map and identifying the best roads for the trip. He determined that it was possible for him to teach the 6 p.m. class if he left by 3 p.m. each day. The class dismissed at 8 p.m., which would get him home well before midnight. All he needed was someone to watch Stross until I came home from work.

By the time Mark presented his case, nearly all the details had been thought out. He would ask Charlene's eighth-grade daughter, Jenn, to baby-sit after school on Mondays and Thursdays; and he would drive our '78 El Camino, leaving me the Honda Accord we'd purchased new prior to Stross' birth. Not only that, he estimated his pay would cover our baby-sitting and car expenses with a little left over.

Mark was excited and confident, and he looked strong. Because he wanted to make this happen, I wanted it to happen for him. I reluctantly agreed to all the necessary life-style adjustments provided Jenn agreed to baby-sit and Mark agreed to drive the Accord. I did not want him navigating Iowa's winter highways in a 14-year-old pick-up that wasn't weighted in the back; he didn't want me driving the El Camino either.

The next day Mark and Stross toured the lot of a West Des Moines Honda dealer and looked into purchasing a mobile phone. He learned that Jenn could babysit after school if Mark dropped Stross off at the Horak's home on his way out of town. When a $1,000 gift arrived from his parents, Mark convinced me to use it for the down payment on a new Civic. Nothing stood in Mark's way now. Not even me, so he agreed to take the adjunct position and looked forward to the fall.

During the summer Mark's health rebounded. Capitalizing on his feel-good days, he took on freelance video projects that allowed him to work as a professional again. Sometimes Mark operated camera for the in-house production staff of a major insurance company; other times he served as a grip on location for Iowa's public television station. He even rented editing time from a small production company to edit a commercial for a local furniture store.

Mark made certain his freelance jobs started after I got home from work or near the end of my working day so I could justify leaving early. Once or twice Charlene, Jenn or another friend from church served as our day care provider so Mark could take a freelance job during the day and —as a bonus—add to our family's bottom line. This small amount of additional income empowered Mark. Stross' life guaranteed we would pay the full amount of our medical deductible and out-of-pocket expenses every year. Plus, gas and hotel expenses for clinic visits in Iowa City also stretched our already tight budget. Even extra doctor appointments around Des Moines noticeably increased our monthly expenses. Mark took pride in his newfound abilities to offset these costs. He talked about expanding his freelance opportunities, but my caution dampened his enthusiasm.

Mark still had episodes of fatigue and crampy nausea, and he still needed to watch what he ate and when. Freelance jobs typically occurred during off hours and often demanded that crew members work long hours without food. Mark promised he'd keep an apple or bottle of juice with him at all times and that he would only agree to take a job if he could find someone we trusted to care for Stross.

By the end of August, Mark's health seemed manageable. He still had bouts of nausea and diarrhea, but they were back to once or twice a week. We celebrated my 28th birthday over Labor Day weekend, then initiated a new weekly routine that accommodated the evolving interests of our unconventional family patriarch.

Mr. Mom was moonlighting. By night Mr. Mom was a professor.

•   •   •

# Chapter 23

# Drives and Determinations

...

B y the fall Stross' favorite days of the week were Mondays and Thursdays. So were Mark's. Stross looked forward to riding in the back seat of Charlene's Cadillac to pick up Jenn from school; Mark looked forward to driving his new, red Honda Civic to teach at Wartburg College.

Soon after purchasing the car, Mark found a stereo on the discount shelf of an electronics warehouse and spent one Saturday installing it. With its stereo cranked to full volume, the car literally rocked. CD versions of albums featuring Mark's favorite '70s and '80s bands kept him awake on his late night treks across the Iowa countryside. Vanity plates that read "4RE 1AB" let patrol cars know that Mark's heavy foot came from his boyhood fondness for fast cars—namely Ferraris. Three times during those eight months, Mark and his Ferrari Wannabe were pulled over by highway patrol. Two times they got a speeding ticket.

At least twice each semester, Stross and I joined Mark on one of his Wartburg trips and sat in on his class. The familiar buildings and comforting sights renewed memories of a time when I was certain my life exemplified promise. They were flesh and blood trips down memory lane, enhanced versions of my nostalgia therapy. Mark's illness had caused me to revisit this coping technique, and I found these trips therapeutic.

At Wartburg I'd found my wings, and after graduation, I'd married Mark and flown far from home. The flight had instilled courage, making me believe there was absolutely nothing I couldn't do...then. But things were different now. I'd experienced the dangers of flying; I now knew fear.

I'd sit awake, anxiously wondering if my husband wasn't answering our mobile phone because he was out of range or because he'd had a car accident.

I'd grow faint every time my son vomited, thinking he may need another surgery for the shunt in his brain.

I'd worry that coworkers would not cooperate with plans, resulting in the need for relentless follow-up.

I'd feel personally affronted if two or three junior high girls had a hard time getting quiet for a Bible study or if a high school boy didn't join a circle within five seconds of me calling his name.

My shoulders and neck ached with tension whenever I sorted the monthly bills, choosing which ones to pay in full and which ones to set aside for the next round.

I lived each day in fear of Mark's illness and the ruin it threatened to bring.

After all, my body had failed to protect my son from unknown external factors. As a result he'd been cheated out of biological wholeness—a phenomenon billions took for granted. An unknown factor had robbed him of abilities he'd never fully know. An unknown factor was also haunting my husband. He'd done so well the first years of our marriage, but now I couldn't count on him making it to bedtime without collapsing from an illness of unknown etiology.

Maybe I was next. Maybe my short-lived resurrection had been nothing more than respite before a mighty downfall. Maybe an unidentified factor was waiting to rob me of my future.

Frozen by fear, I couldn't find a way forward. Instead I lived vicariously through the lives of others. The Horaks and the Griswells, another family from church, became my ties to a life that might have been—if only.

Before Stross, Mark and I spent time together riding in the El Camino (our only vehicle at the time) looking for the most expensive homes in West Des Moines. The homes on Green Gables Drive looked as majestic as the street's name. Green Gables, a long sweeping cul de sac, was the address for houses that towered as regally as the stately oaks that lined the street. Our two favorite homes were a tall, white one with regal pillars and a brown-red brick one with a pool in the backyard—nearly mansions by Iowa standards.

By contrast, our first Des Moines' home was a one-bedroom apartment in a no-frills complex on the south side, four blocks from the scene of a shooting our second month there. The apartment complex itself was in a relatively safe area, but the neighborhoods and business district that lay between our apartment and downtown were questionable. We dreamed of an address in West Des Moines and the lifestyle and status we assumed came with it.

My job at the association, our reason to return to Iowa, headed us in the right direction. I'd held my first paycheck a long time to make certain they had not paid me too much. I had never made that much money before; neither had Mark. On my second payday, we'd jumped in the El Camino and driven through West Des Moines neighborhoods. We'd started in a low-income neighborhood and moved to the upscale modular housing of more developed sections. Finally we'd driven past the mansion-like homes of Green Gables. Taking the El Camino onto this cul de sac had felt daring because we'd feared our old truck would draw attention to our gawking.

Mark and I used these expeditions to dream and romanticize about life's what-ifs.

I'd say things like: "Can you imagine cleaning that house?" and Mark would say: "Joy, if we could afford that house, we'd have someone to clean it for us."

Then I'd say: "I suppose they don't mow their own lawns either." And Mark would say: "If you could live there, would you?"

To make us feel better, I'd pontificate about wealth and its responsibilities. I'd say things like: "Well, if you had enough money for things like that, shouldn't you choose to do your own caretaking

• • •

so that you can give more money away to charity?"

Then Mark would respond: "Joy, if they did that, they'd have no time to work at the jobs that made it possible for them to buy the house in the first place. Besides it is possible for wealthy people to tithe and still have enough money left over for housekeepers and grounds keepers."

That remark staggered me, since a tithe large enough for that kind of lifestyle could fulfill the entire annual budget of a small congregation.

On each drive one of us would muse about the kind of wealthy people we'd be. We'd question whether money would change our priorities or affect our spirituality. We'd wonder about it, then assure ourselves wealth was a risk worth taking.

We weren't inclined to contemplate the spirituality of poverty.

Only five months passed before we had an occasion to enter a house on Green Gables. Our most faithful and dedicated volunteer mom—Michele Griswell, a fellow Sunday School teacher—offered to host a pool party for our youth, so we took her up on her offer. After the youth had met at church, we and the other volunteer drivers headed for her home. She suggested Mark and I follow her so we wouldn't become lost. As she drove, Mark and I began to recognize landmarks. We had driven by them on previous expeditions. When she turned onto Green Gables Drive, Mark and I smiled. Michele lived at 725 Green Gables Drive, the brown-red brick house. We would get to see how she lived.

Michele was the consummate hostess. She directed kids to the bathrooms for changing and invited them to snack in her kitchen or around the pool. At the end of the event, Mark and I joined the Griswell family for a relaxing chat by the pool. She and her husband, Barry, the CEO of an insurance company, were genuinely caring people. We'd felt that before coming to their home, but now it was obvious. For five months we'd had no idea how affluent they were; and now that we'd learned the truth, we discovered they weren't the arrogant, selfish, materialistic snobs that we'd imagined as residents on Green Gables Drive. These people were our friends.

• • •

That afternoon Michele asked us to add a prayer to those Mark and I said during our personal prayer times. She told us she'd met a woman who had quickly become her best friend. The woman's family lived down the street and was considering joining our church. Michele thought her children would enjoy our youth group too. She was essentially telling us that we might also get to meet the family in the tall, white house with the pillars.

I'm not sure I would have believed it that day if someone had told me how supportive this as-yet-unknown family would be to us in the coming years. On that day it was enough to learn that wealthy people thought about life and selected churches the same way we did. However—only one year later—it was Michele's best friend, Charlene Horak, that I counted on to come to Stross' rescue if Mark had a day where he couldn't leave the bathroom. And it was Charlene's daughter, Jenn, I counted on to care for Stross on Mondays and Thursdays when Mark headed to Wartburg.

Jenn was incredibly responsible and mature for her age. This 13-year-old showered our son with unconditional love and undivided portions of attention. She read to Stross, helped him play with his toys, fed him snacks, held him while he drank his bottle, sang to him and rocked him to sleep.

Actually to rock Stross was to sing him to sleep. The acts were inseparable. During the first two years of his life, the strains of a lullaby he helped invent were our best sleep offense:

*Oh, Daddy-O.*
*I love him so.*
*He's my Daddy, Daddy-O.*

The older Stross got the more creative our collaborative song writing became:

*Oh, Daddy-O.*
*Call him on the telephone.*
*He's my Daddy, Daddy-O.*

• • •

Some nights, the variations and rhyme combinations were endless. Even Jenn learned how to spin the tune to its most effective conclusion—Stross asleep in her arms.

Well before his first birthday, Stross showed signs of musicality. He hummed, bobbed his head to hymns or songs on the radio and swelled his body in animated movement when we held him to dance or moved his hands and feet in rhythm.

Not long before Stross' second birthday, our children's choir at church performed celebration songs with a spring theme on the Sundays prior to Easter. Music had always been something Mark and I regarded as a hope-filled endeavor for Stross. We saw it as a great equalizer—an activity where his physical abilities wouldn't set him unduly apart. However during this particular service, the words to one of these hope-filled selections introduced me to a new kind of anguish.

About two dozen human cherubs sang their hearts out about how special it was that God had formed their bodies so perfectly. The verses outlined God's creative handiwork, especially the creation of little children. Then the children sang through an entire list of things that testified to their special place in God's kingdom.

The chorus' lyrics haunted me. After each verse, the children sang about how wonderful it was that God had made them to walk and jump and run, things my God-created son might never do. The children's choir director had even choreographed the song. As a result these miniature adults sweetly pantomimed each action verb, assaulting my feelings with musical motion.

I'd only known music as something healing, but on this day it brought pain.

Fighting an urge to leap from the pew, I chose instead to think of ways I could change the world. My thinking was philosophical and grandiose. I was determined my son would never be offended by insensitive lyrics that circumvented awareness of the beauty that existed in all of God's creation. I vowed to find songs about the awe-inspiring movements performed by the world's physically disabled and mentally retarded citizens. But the longer I sat there, the deeper

• • •

I felt despair. No one wrote songs like like.

I had learned to set my jaw in order to hold back tears. Clenching my teeth in response to building rage helped me fight feelings of inadequacy. The world was not right, and I could not fix it—certainly not by myself. I hoped someone could help me fix it in the future. This injustice had to be corrected by the time Stross was old enough for the cherub choir. I might never be wealthy, but my child could live a rich life despite experiences that excluded him.

I stayed lost in my thoughts the rest of the worship service, bracing for future days. I saw myself as the mother of an older Stross trying to verbalize why a song like the "walk, jump, run" could be insensitive. Then there was me in conversation with the choir director discussing riser placement, because watching the children on the risers had made me aware of how inaccessible choir performances were for a child who used braces or a wheelchair. So I envisioned how to tackle the issue. I'd request that the choir director use vertical placement of children by grades instead of automatically placing the older children in the back.

My last futuristic scenario was the most outlandish, for in it I saw myself rewriting the lyrics to children's songs and directing all the choirs Stross would ever be in. I could do that—if I had to. It's how I'd change the world: all by myself.

I was too grieved to recognize how isolated I'd become again, and I lacked a safe place to share the things that caused me stress. Mark was my only refuge, and I worried that my anguish would intensify his already poor health. I looked for an opportunity to express my feelings to him anyway.

Unwilling to release pain in return for simple joy, I sacrificed a chance for renewed spiritual enlightenment. I still believed I could sidestep pity. And I believed I could change the world without changing myself first. God and I had made a small degree of progress in two years, but I still clung to the illusion that I could control life.

I conceded my humanity in small moments that chipped away at my obstinance. For instance, the personal and financial demands of Stross' life made it fairly certain that our family would never live like the Horaks or Griswells. I had dreamed of that lifestyle once but not anymore. Those aspirations vanished the night Mark and I drove home from the hospital, planning ways to care for our son.

That night we'd agreed that no matter what—a potential move to a smaller home or trading our car for a big, old van or working at the same job for decades to maintain insurance coverage—we could never divorce each other because of hardship. We had vowed to such during our wedding ceremony; but when faced with the reality of sickness not health and poorer not richer, Mark and I were compelled to privately renew those vows. During that nighttime drive in May 1991—one year after buying our first car and three months after buyind our first home—on that night people became more important than possessions. The realization came instantaneously, and I vowed to never look back. Practical insight said that prosperity would be an internal reward. But it was time for practical insight to give way to more profound enlightenment and learning.

It was time to reconcile seemingly contradictory truths: I had a child with disabilities; I had a bright future.

To start this reconciliation I would need to articulate the things I believed I had lost: the freedom to move my family in response to a career move; the freedom to buy a home without regard to steps or entrances; the freedom to buy a fashionable car without regard for its capacity to carry a wheelchair; the freedom to travel without worrying about accessible bathrooms, airplanes, hotel rooms and tourist attractions; the freedom to plan for future children without worrying how their older sibling had altered their lives before birth; and the freedom to save for a retirement that would reward Mark and me for all the ways we'd denied ourselves decades before.

Would my life and Mark's forever be lived in a state of constant denial? Would we ever learn to refashion new dreams without revisiting the past with regret?

My response to the choir had renewed an internal desire to better the world, linking me to the heady days of college and newlywed life. I remembered my younger self as brimming with ideals yet lacking in purposeful direction. The cherub choir's song promised to solve that. It gave me causes to champion; I could take on injustice as I found it. Stross could set my course, and I could take it from there. I'd tackle the cherub choir and work my way up as he grew. The inequities were sure to go beyond church walls. I foresaw conflicts over Stross' right to be included in a regular education classroom and battles connected with infringements of the newly passed Americans With Disabilities Act. It was possible my life's higher purpose existed in my ability to pave pathways for my son.

I believed I could excel as a catalyst for change, yet I remained uncomfortable at the thought I'd need to change as well. However Stross had instigated personal transformation before. Because of him, I was more open to new ways of experiencing grace. He had pulled my life into focus, expanding my concept of creation while enlarging my sense of the Creator.

Still I lacked lessons beyond this fundamental knowledge. Pity, pain and anger continued to be my greatest obstacles. I needed more tutorials about identifying grief and more lessons about submission. Most of all I needed continued instruction in how to relinquish control. My life's purpose could not be discerned on the whim of emotion. Instead I was beginning to suspect that personal revelation would come in small moments of everyday life. And through sweet, involuntary instances of pure, unadulterated joy.

•   •   •

# Chapter 24

# Dreaming

...

M ark's academic year progressed into the spring semester, and he courted ideas of continuing his professor role for another year. I was pleased about the sense of purpose that teaching had given him, but I was concerned that the time and energy it demanded worked against our family somehow. Mark was becoming weaker while Stross was growing stronger. My developing maternal instincts now included a desire to protect both my husband and my son.

I had determined that my obsession over Stross' physical limitations originated with my fierce protectiveness. I wasn't obsessed about what he couldn't do. I obsessed that others would unduly lower their expectations of him or have none at all. Of course, the difficulty lay in helping others fashion realistic expectations about his abilities—ones based on our understanding of what doctors believed was possible and what we believed. (And, of course, I believed I could shape others' beliefs.) I wanted others to see what Stross *could* do rather than focus on what he *could not*. So did Mark.

Neither of us had unrealistic notions that Stross would be lifted out of his crib, propped on his feet and coaxed to start walking one day—but it was tempting. We were able to track Austin's physical improvements nearly every Sunday. As more-than-interested bystanders, we'd seen—through Austin—that large gains against incredible odds were possible.

Early on I'd get a phone call from Austin's mom, Deb, about every few weeks. Our conversations focused on what we shared in common: sons born with spina bifida. Within a few months we began to only converse at church. Mostly we compared notes about our separate trips to the spina bifida clinic in Iowa City during snatches of conversation in the church's hallways. For instance Deb shared her excitement when Austin was chosen to participate in an experimental clinical trial. The trial tested a new kind of leg brace, one crafted with a special cable system that assisted its users with balance and reciprocal gait training.

Even though I knew every child born with spina bifida was totally different, I hoped the proximity of Austin's lumbar-region defect was similar enough to Stross' to indicate we'd also have a child skilled at walking with crutches someday. I was incredulous and even more hopeful when Austin showed up one Sunday using no crutches at all. With the aid of the cable braces, his new gait allowed him to lop his balance from side to side in an awkward, yet independent, motion. He looked great.

"Deb, when did this happen?" I asked, my mouth unable to close. She'd beamed with pride, clearly enjoying the sight of her son as he amazed all who were assembled in the church foyer.

"Just this week," she said. Her soft voice lilted.

"But how?" I hoped I didn't sound like I had shortchanged her son's abilities.

"Well," she spoke in quiet tones that I always found comforting, "we were at the mall, and our friend John teased Austin a little about not needing his crutches, and then he dared him to try walking without them. So Austin just put them down, and he did it. He's not used them ever since."

"Deb," I paused, uncertain of what to say next. "That's so wonderful. I'm so happy for you."

Her face continued to beam as she watched Austin disappear

down the hallway to his Sunday school classroom.

I wanted to be her—so badly. And I wanted Stross to be five years old like Austin was. And I wanted him to walk down the hallway to his classroom like Austin had done.

Stross made his own gains, but nothing to show off in public. Shortly after his first birthday he no longer needed his sleeping brace and was fitted for a standing brace called a parapodium. (Austin had never needed one.) The orthopedic specialist (same as Austin's) told us the parapodium would help develop Stross' leg strength and his concept of standing.

Because Mark had to facilitate a church youth event, Charlene drove Stross and me to Iowa City for a fitting of the custom brace. Charlene proved to be an easy person to spend time with in a waiting room or small exam room. When Stross napped, we quietly conversed. She drank coffee from a travel mug, and I leafed through magazines.

The entire fitting process took nearly three hours, and Stross slept through most of the middle part. He had fallen asleep with his head on my shoulder, and I'd laid him on the exam table to free myself of his limp body weight. Periodically a grandfatherly like gentleman came to measure Stross, who was still sleeping, and align metal pieces against the linear contours of his body. The metal sections grew each time this man entered the room. When the piece was nearly assembled, he announced it was time to measure Stross in a standing position.

I placed Stross' socked feet in his tiny plastic AFOs (a plastic molded brace called an ankle-foot-orthotic) then slipped his artificially stiff foot into small tennis shoes. The act awakened him, and he quickly revived.

"Hey, Baby. Did you have a good nap?" I asked.

The orthotist stood near the exam table while I picked up Stross and placed him in a sitting position. Stross smiled his characteristic ear-to-ear smile, making it look like he was experiencing the afterglow of the goofiest dream imaginable.

"Are you ready to stand up, Kiddo?"

Standing without a parent's support is a huge developmental

milestone for children—the moment a baby learns he is his own person, an independent soul. Stross had never experienced that sensation before because most of his leg muscles did not work. Therefore, Mark or I or someone else had served as Stross' transportation since his birth. Crawling had afforded him a portion of self-sufficiency, but standing with no human assistance would give him a full measure of independence. No words could explain to my 14-month-old son how technology made it possible for him to stand. I hardly understood myself.

"It's time to see if this thing works, Big Guy," said the orthotist. I liked how he acted grandfatherly and professional at the same time.

"Oh, Joy. Your baby is going to stand up today," said Charlene, now smiling with anticipation. Her sentimental comment penetrated the softest part of my resolve. I appeared to barely acknowledge her remark while assisting the orthotist. He placed Stross' body inside the parapodium and checked for proper alignment. My understated reaction warded off tears. I did not want to cry today.

The orthotist demonstrated how to bend the brace while aligning Stross' body. I helped him place Stross into the brace's center and position his feet onto a pre-formed platform where they were secured with a Velcro® strap. Then the orthotist showed me how to lay Stross' back against a padded bar and fasten a wide, seat-belt strap called a thoracic pad against his chest. The man cautioned me about proper leg placement stating that if I recklessly performed the next step (turning the brace's side hinges to a vertical position) I could snap Stross' leg bones when I snapped the hinges in place. He assured me he'd coach me through the act several times so I'd be able to confidently teach Mark.

With the last of his directions completed, the orthotist slowly raised a compliant Stross, who now looked patiently amused, to a standing position. We three adults waited for his reaction. Instinct told me to stay near Stross, but intuition told me to back away. As I moved closer to Charlene, a look of wonder crossed Stross' face. He'd never seen me at that distance or height, and he'd never felt straps supporting his body, only human arms.

• • •

I smiled, and my plan to avoid crying dissipated. I tried to smile really big to let Stross know everything was fine knowing he held no reference for tears of joy.

"Hey, Stross," I warbled. "What do you think? You're up."

The word "up"—as it does for most babies—served as Stross' signal for us to lift him, except when Stross used it, the word did not mean he was tired of walking. He just wanted us to hold him. Now I wanted Stross to know that "up" had new meaning.

"Oh, Joy," said Charlene, handing me a tissue while wiping her own eyes. "He looks so good. You look good, Stross. Do you like it? What do you think?"

Both Charlene and I asked questions Stross could not answer. He shifted his glance between us looking for a visual cue as to what he should think. Were we sad? Happy? Stross couldn't tell.

Stross froze his smile in place and cocked his head. He started to reach for me and felt the tension of his body against the brace as he stretched. The sensation caused him to pull back, but he soon reversed course and attempted to lurch forward again. His smile vanished, so I drew close, taking his hand.

"Stross. You are up. You're up, Stross," I said, attempting to let him know "up" was good. "Good job."

"We need a picture for Daddy," said Charlene, who then snapped a photo. I looked at my upright son again—at the joy-causing image that would be captured on film.

Mark and I photographed all Stross' milestones—good and bad. Hospital shots dominated his photographic records. These pictures would record a happy medical excursion—an "up" time—to our body of work. The photo would give Mark joy too, but not like seeing his son standing with his own eyes. I looked forward to sharing the experience with Mark and feeling the elation together. Because I'd seen our son standing, I believed he would walk one day too. We could share that dream.

I'd begun to learn that dreams rode on whispers of joy. Months earlier on an afternoon in late winter, Stross rested on my lap while I watched a professional figure skating competition. Since childhood, figure skating had fascinated me. Packaged with beauty, grace, athleticism, romance, music, fame and fortune, the sport captured everything I aspired for as a child. It's why I'd spent several winters on ice pretending to be Peggy Fleming, then a couple as Dorothy Hamill—with hair to match.

Each winter I'd spend entire outdoor recesses practicing my famous move, the angel glide—at least that's what I called it. Real skaters called its authentic version a camel.

I was really good at angel gliding, and after several tutorials from two helpful sixth grade boys, I even learned to skate backwards. As a fifth grader I knew I was behind on my journey for Olympic gold, but it seemed possible at times. Because it wasn't an impossible dream, those afternoons on the ice rink were positively glorious.

I'd long abandoned my Olympic dreams by the time I had Stross. Now he enjoyed watching figure skating too. He'd visually lock onto Nancy Kerrigan and follow her path across our television.

"Ooo lights," he'd say, honoring her with his universal phrase for all beautiful things.

"Yes, pretty," I'd say.

Once, as I watched him enjoy all the beautiful aspects of my childhood fantasy, I felt myself begin to dream on his behalf—but then I stopped. My son, I realized, would never know what it felt like to glide across ice like an angel. And for one moment, that was the only thing I wanted for him in the entire world. To experience the freedom, just once, of gliding across the ice on one leg and believing an Olympic medal could be his someday if he just wanted it bad enough.

The pain of this realization almost caused me to stop a prayer before I could pray it. After all, I had no right to tell God or my son what was possible. Only my son could choose his dreams; only I could censor my own. Stross probably would not court dreams as Olympian as I had. But faith, even a small measure, allowed me to reshape my dream for him. If faith as small as a mustard seed moved mountains, my minuscule portion of faith might help my son walk someday, and even—should he desire it—slide across the ice in his

• • •

own version of an angel glide. If his version could bring him joy, that joy could breathe life into a dream.

I was learning that motherhood meant giving your child opportunities to experience joy and to dream. Not dreams born of my joy, but his own. And then, it seemed, a mother needed to safeguard her child's dreams until he no longer needed them. I had only wanted to be an Olympian for a very short time—three or four glorious winters. Having that brief dream had been sufficient. It had carried me to new joys and new dreams. Stross would need the privilege of his own joy-filled experiences that would grow into his unique dreams. Therefore, I needed to be both a joy enabler and a dream protector. If I could accomplish that, I surmised, then my own feelings of joy would multiply a hundred fold.

However my simplistic dream formula left out two important things: hard work and faith. I'd never become an Olympian because I'd never really tried. I'd never worked for the goal—just dreamed of it—and probably because I lacked faith in my ice-skating abilities. Perhaps, I hypothesized, once a dream is born, it requires equal portions of work and faith to keep it alive. And perhaps we'd need each other's help.

I was beginning to recognize how my capacity to dream had waned while Mark's had helped Stross accomplish the hard work of learning to crawl. I felt spiritually quiet but not empty. Mark appeared more alive spiritually, but I couldn't determine if it was real or an illusion—or even if it mattered. Certainly the joy of spending time with Stross made the difference. Still a baby, he couldn't articulate an outlook on life, but he certainly lived one. He awoke each morning joy-filled, eager to live each day's experiences. For him every moment presented an opportunity for a dream to be born.

Joy-filled moments weren't coming as easily to me. I now feared my ability to squelch all the wonderful things that could happen, and I hoped the promise of brighter days would be enough. Mark had given me a gift of joy the day he showed me Stross could crawl. I hoped I could rely on Mark to get us through Stross' walking project, also, unless his life was becoming as oppressive as my own.

• • •

The Wartburg teaching job made for some long days and nights. For eight months Mark traveled to Wartburg twice a week, struggling through periodic days of bad health. He now had to prepare lectures and lab exercises, write and grade tests and be available for students who needed one-on-one assistance. Meanwhile his most important student now needed standing lessons that, if successful, could lead to walking lessons.

So Mark, in addition to cleaning, cooking, and caretaking duties, made time to take Stross in and out of his parapodium every day—well, almost every day. Working with Stross in the complex contraption was time consuming. Therapy sessions could devour half hours and hours at a time. The therapy involved tipping Stross from side to side to imitate a reciprocal gait then encouraging him to mimic the action. As Stross began to tolerate the device longer, Mark increased his time in it to encourage his sense of independence. I served as a cheerleader for the pair on weekends.

"Rock, rock," we'd say, using a term for movement he understood. "Rock, rock."

Stross soon mastered his therapy goal to rock from side to side. The motion resembled walking movements, and Stross thought it was a blast. Especially after the doctor prescribed the addition of a swivel base. The swivel base, engineered to propel the parapodium forward, allowed Stross to move forward. Now the parapodium took him places. When Stross was fully braced, Mark or I couldn't be far away. Stross could rock the parapodium hard enough to tip over, falling like a tree. That's when we started making him wear a helmet.

For motivation we allowed him to play with objects that other parents childproofed against. Ball point pens and sharp, shiny things like paper clips or eating utensils had enticed Stross to crawl. When he was in the parapodium, we pointed him to greater dangers like introducing him to kitchen drawers with shiny, thrilling enclosures; the knobs of our oven; the refrigerator door handle; some strategically placed refrigerator magnets and our stereo's control panel and turntable.

The oven knobs and turntable were our most successful

motivators. Stross could stand for many minutes turning our electric burners on, then off, then on, then on higher, then off, then on again, then on more, on still more, then off. After a full minute or so, we'd back him away and let him "rock, rock" his way toward it again. Stross couldn't reach the heating elements, so the danger factor was low; and our oven appeared no worse for the wear.

The stereo was another matter. Stross moved its levers and knobs in every direction. Nothing remained preset during his parapodium-era. Within weeks, he disabled our stereo cassette deck by holding a small plastic man hostage inside. After torturing the man with the cassette deck's broken door, Stross gave him a ride on the turntable. Many Hot Wheels also took a spin, courtesy of Stross.

Each adult-oriented appliance helped Stross master rocking. His new interest in movement motivated him to refine his crawling as well. Under Mark's supervision Stross learned to crawl while propped on his hands and knees. This refined method prepared him to conquer the seven steps to each of our home's split-levels. Learning to ascend stairs was easier than descending, but after a few soft tumbles, Stross understood why "feet first, feet first" became our mantra for descent.

Stross became a busy child. He'd hustle into action as fast as his hands and knees could carry him. In fact, Stross crawled so efficiently that if his pants had a loose waistband, he'd crawl out of them. If pants slowed his travel in any way, he'd turn onto his left hip and pull them off with his right hand. Having been freed of the inconvenience, Stross would crawl on. By the summer of 1993 it appeared as if we had Stross' medical needs and developmental goals under control; however, Mark's medical needs remained a mystery.

I could tell Mark thoroughly enjoyed teaching, and the students clearly enjoyed him. Even those who grumbled about Mark's tough testing standards respected him for his obvious knowledge, enthusiasm and dedication.

Mark's health only kept him from teaching once, the day students were scheduled to come to Des Moines and tour corporate in-house production departments and video production facilities. Mark had

· · ·

scheduled the day as a field trip, but I ended up using a sick day to escort the students. I called Mark periodically to check on him and Stross. He reported feeling better by day's end, so after the last stop on the tour, I invited the students to our home for pizza.

When the semester ended in May, Mark turned 30 years old, a melancholy milestone. Since the beginning of April, an increasing amount of episodes had left him weak and scared. The bouts provoked a sense of vulnerability. Mark believed age 30 should not feel like it did, and I, nearly 29, agreed.

I'd experienced my own periods of questionable health that winter and spring. My symptoms manifested as irregularities in my monthly cycle. However, not trusting the OB-GYN who had delivered Stross, I chose to return to one I'd used prior to marriage. That meant driving more than 200 miles on several occasions for blood tests, biopsies, X-rays and even laparoscopic surgery. Finally I was given a diagnosis: stress. I hated the diagnosis, because, as I saw it, eliminating stress wasn't an option. The concept of managing stress eluded me.

Mark began a new round of doctor visits too, hoping for a diagnosis we could live with. Mark's newest physician speculated that the fuzzy, tunnel vision Mark experienced could indicate a brain tumor or that his muscle weakness could mean the start of MS—multiple sclerosis. We needed a CT-scan to help us confirm or eliminate those possibilities. So I took a morning off work to escort Mark to the hospital.

While he was in radiology—sedated to ease his claustrophobia— I sat in the waiting room playing with Stross and talking to Joel Dale, our church's education director. He'd come to offer moral support and to keep me company. The nurse who escorted Mark back told us he'd be out in about 30 to 40 minutes.

After one hour I got nervous, and because I was nervous Joel was too. Just before my nerves peaked, Mark—the wobbly six foot and two-inch frame of him—entered the waiting room leaning on the arm of the five-foot tall, nurse who'd first taken him back. The nurse struggled to negotiate Mark's awkward body through the maze of waiting room chairs. He smiled like a Cheshire cat.

"Mark, how are you? Are you okay?" I asked.

He sheepishly looked at the floor, still grinning, and deliberately nodded his head up and down in slow, large motions. My anti-alcohol husband, the same man who'd refused to take cocktail orders, appeared falling down drunk, and he was a funny drunk.

"We gave him a little something to relax," said the nurse. "He should be back to normal in an hour or so."

"Two little somethings," Mark corrected her. "The first one didn't work."

"Well, it looks like the second one did," I said. "When will you know what they found out?"

"I don't know," Mark slowly nodded his head. He seemed calmly perplexed. "I think they'll call me tomorrow."

Anxiety-relieved Mark couldn't have cared less.

The next day we learned the results of his scan were normal, but the doctor wanted Mark to come back. He had another idea. This time Mark would take a five-hour glucose tolerance test to learn—for certain—about his blood sugar levels. Mark could endure this test with the need for a driver, but he needed someone to care for Stross. Feeling like he'd bothered Charlene too much, Mark found another friend to watch Stross, then reported to the hospital at 6:30 a.m.

Not having consumed refined sugar in more than two years, he found the glucose drink more thrilling than revolting. In fact, his body loved the contents of the beverage too and processed it fine. Still, after Mark was four hours into the test, the hospital called me at work. They did not believe Mark could drive himself home when the test was finished.

When I located him, Mark was lying on an exam table with perspiration on his brow. His hands and arms were shaking so badly, that the nurse had a hard time entering a vein to draw blood according to the test's schedule. Mark was pleased I'd come. He looked scared.

"Is he having a diabetic reaction?" I asked the nurse.

"No," she assured me. "For some reason, he isn't tolerating this test as expected."

"What does his reaction mean?"

"I'll have the doctor come talk to you. He's looking at the readings now."

When the doctor came, he explained that Mark's blood levels were normal, and he wasn't sure why he'd had this reaction. According to the test, Mark was neither diabetic nor hypoglycemic.

With the test completed I gathered Mark's things and helped him from the exam table. He leaned on me all the way out of the hospital and through the parking lot to the car I'd driven. Mark's tremors were intense.

"I hate this feeling. I hate it," he said, starting to cry. Mark cried more frequently now but always in correlation to an episode. The episodes regularly disrupted our lives; I hated what this mystery illness had done to my husband. I had married a sensitive man, not a weak one. Unfortunately Mark felt like he had little strength left. Life had gotten so complicated, so quickly.

As I drove Mark reclined the front seat and shut his eyes. I decided I could not go back to work, and I could not let him drive. I waited for his tears to subside.

"Hey," I told him. "That doctor said you can eat anything you want. You have to be hungry."

No answer.

"What would you like to eat?" I asked.

Mark opened his eyes and rolled his head toward me. His eyes conveyed fatigue.

"I don't know. I'm hungry, but I'm afraid to eat," he said.

"What about something safe? A burger and fries?"

"Yeah, I guess so."

After purchasing lunch in a drive-through, I drove to the empty parking lot of a vacant office building, and he ate while I talked about my morning. Neither Mark nor I were ready to give up on a diagnosis. Mark's restlessness since turning 30 could ease, it seemed, if we devised a new plan—a new dream—for our future. Mark needed to do something in addition to caring for Stross, something he could do at home to bring in additional income. Mark proposed a loan to purchase video editing equipment—a huge financial risk made even riskier if his health didn't improve.

We discussed those plans even more on a business trip to Chicago that I took as president of Iowa's chapter of professional business communicators. Mark and Stross went with me to this international conference along with my parents who again served as traveling companions and baby-sitters.

Driving north on I-35, Mark and I became so engrossed in discussion that we missed the exit we usually took for the route to my parents' home. Instead we exited onto Highway 18 at Mason City and decided to turn our mistake into a sight-seeing adventure. We followed signs to Meredith Willson's boyhood home and drove past buildings designed by Frank Lloyd Wright. These drive-by side trips helped us feel like we were already on vacation, and we wondered aloud why we had never ventured into this part of the state before. To us the area seemed like a great place to visit and—from appearances—a great place to live.

We eventually arrived in West Union, and my parents drove the rest of the way to Chicago. Our early June excursion to the Windy City provided a well-timed respite from Mark's doctor visits and inconclusive tests. I hoped the trip would bring us moments just to enjoy simple pleasures. Mom and Dad took Mark and Stross on sightseeing ventures while I attended workshops. Our last day in Chicago, my parents took us to the Museum of Science and Industry.

Mark had felt ill all week, and at the museum, he became shaky. I'd fed Stross his lunch from an assortment of baby food jars, but we'd postponed lunch for the adults. At some point Mark wandered off and did not answer when I called for him. My father and I began a brief search, and Dad found Mark about two minutes before I did. He admitted to walking away and getting lost. The incident took me to the brink of hopelessness, as keeping track of my husband became one more thing to add to my to-do list.

On our drive home Mark and I attempted to complete the conversation begun days earlier, only now I felt dark uncertainty. I listened to Mark describe plans that included work related to his professional skills; however, I also heard him acknowledge that family planning was a factor. Neither of us wanted Stross to be an only child, and because he was already 2 years old, it seemed appropriate to plan for our second child. I politely questioned whether Mark was healthy enough to care for two children, and he responded positively. Mark was certain that, with him as our caregiver, this was the best time to expand our family.

Mark spoke of work and family equally, and I did my best to listen to what he was really saying. What I heard was that I might need to prepare—emotionally and professionally—to be pregnant again. Mark was willing to sacrifice his career a bit longer for the sake of building a family; but he had a professional clock, and it was ticking. The sooner we had Baby #2, the sooner he'd get off the career sidelines. Wishing for him the best of both worlds, I resurrected the idea he'd posed earlier: investing in a home editing system. It could serve as Mark's link to a professional life. He could develop freelance clients while working from home—an arrangement I'd always found appealing whenever I'd heard colleagues describe it. Maybe Mark could work part-time and care for two children if everything he needed was in our home. Maybe.

Coming home felt different that Sunday: We'd made some important decisions. We'd made some tenuous decisions. We were making decisions knowing our future was more uncertain than it had ever been. But we were dreaming again—just a little. As we entered our cul de sac, Mark and I vowed to set our plans in motion despite potential obstacles. We needed to feel like we were moving forward.

After unloading our car, I sorted the mail, and Mark wrote down the messages from our answering machine. There were a few from church members and two from a man named Dr. Oscar Lenning. He identified himself as the academic dean for Waldorf College and the father of Chris Lenning, one of Mark's students at Wartburg. He said there was a position open at the college for an assistant professor of communications, and his son had insisted Mark was well suited for the job. Dr. Lenning's second message sounded more urgent than the first. He really wanted Mark to interview for the position as soon

• • •

as possible. The college was in Forest City, 35 miles northwest of Mason City.

Mark, grinning, listened without saying anything, then played the messages again.

"What do you think?" I asked. "Did this Chris tell you his dad was the academic dean of a college?"

"Yes," said Mark. "We talked about a lot of stuff. I'm just flattered he told his dad I'd be good for the job."

"But do you think it's a job you want to take?"

"How can I know, Joy? Wartburg hasn't offered anything for the fall. So maybe."

"But do you even want to go for the interview?" I asked, feeling more and more that the plans we'd made had temporarily gone on hold.

"Sure, I think it'd be a great experience. A real kick," he said. "Don't you think it'd be fun to check it out? I don't really think anything will come of it, so what's the risk?"

Mark was right. Other candidates with more teaching experience had an advantage, making the risk of a potential relocation small. At a minimum it assured Mark of a fun day out of the house.

I listened to Mark return the dean's call. The dean wanted me to come as well. I raised my eyebrows at Mark and got my daily planner. The dean would have to wait until Thursday after Stross' doctor appointments and my meetings with the Lt. Governor. Plus Mark had more medical appointments.

Mark's doctor was nearly out of potential diagnoses and tests to confirm them. The last effort found him headed back to the hospital the day before his interview in Forest City for an MRI (magnetic resonance imaging) and EEG (electroencephalogram). They attempted to trigger an episode while recording his brain activity. As a result Mark was subjected to an hour's worth of strobe lights and strange lighting patterns. Unfortunately it only caused irritation. Left with no other avenues to pursue, Mark's doctor referred him to an internal medicine specialist, but the earliest appointment was three months away.

Shortly after lunch Mark called me at work to report the inconclusive results of his tests; still lacking a diagnosis, I panicked. Life had accelerated, and it felt like we were running out of time.

The next day we were to head back up I-35 so Mark could interview for a position as a professor. We needed answers about his condition—if there *were* answers—sooner than three months. Not knowing where to turn I placed a desperate call to Stross' pediatric surgeon. His kindness had soothed my fears many times before, and I respected his medical insight. Perhaps he could help me know what to do about Mark. When I heard the doctor's voice through my receiver, I dissolved.

The doctor immediately inquired about Stross. I assured him nothing was wrong with Stross, then explained the problem was with Mark. I outlined our recent experiences, describing how difficult it was to work while worrying about Mark's ability to care for Stross. He asked if our family had opportunities for fun, and I stopped crying long enough to tell him about our week in Chicago. Then I shared how returning to work had renewed my anxiety since Mark was alone with Stross again. The doctor empathized and apologized for being unaware of our troubles.

"We have to find out what is wrong soon," I blurted through restrained tears. "We just have to."

Mark was looking forward to the Waldorf interview, and I understood that participating in the process indicated a willingness to consider an offer. The remote possibility that Mark's interview could result in an offer troubled me. I could not tell the doctor about the trip.

"Let me do some calling for you. Is that alright?" he asked.

"Oh, I don't want to put you out," I weakly offered. "This isn't your problem. I just need to know how to get our appointment moved up."

I started a barrage of questions, but Stross' surgeon simplified the process.

"No, Joy," he said. "Let me do some calling. I'll get back to you. Your family needs this cleared up as soon as possible."

...

I started to cry out of gratitude. This man understood my desperation. He wanted to help. He'd volunteered to help. He'd helped Stross before; he could help Mark now.

"Are you at work?" he asked. I could barely talk.

"Yes."

"Give me that phone number. I'll call you back before the end of the day. I may not be able to reach the doctor I'm thinking of yet," he explained, "but I promise I'll call to let you know what has been done."

"Thank you, thank you so much," I said. "I'm so sorry."

"Don't be sorry," he said. "We'll get this taken care of. We'll get it figured out."

• • •

*Part Three*

a Mom

# Chapter 25

# Sacrifice

• • •

W hen I arrived home that evening, Mark was sitting on our living room floor with an Iowa map. He had located Forest City and timed our upcoming journey. The folder of information the dean had mailed was out also. I could tell Mark had fully read every brochure, form and photocopied sheet. He had even stuck several yellow Post-it Notes® in the college's catalog.

After greetings and a kiss from Mark, I lifted Stross off the carpeted floor for a welcome-home hug, then set him down again amid an assortment of randomly scattered toys. I kicked off my heels, hiked up my dress and then joined my boys on the floor. I had a confession to make.

"After you called me about your doctor's appointment, I called Stross' surgeon," I told Mark.

"You did? Why?" Mark was clearly surprised.

"I wanted to see if he could get you to a specialist sooner."

"Joy, you bugged him with our problems?" Mark sounded irritated by my bold act.

"He didn't mind, Mark. Really. He was very kind, and just before I left for home, he called to tell me he'd spoken to a doctor of internal medicine. You have an appointment for July 12th."

Mark offered reluctant thanks. He strongly disliked relying on anyone for help, and now he'd experienced double jeopardy: I (his helpmate) had turned to someone outside the family (Stross' doctor) for help.

"I know it's still a few weeks away, but early July is a whole bunch sooner than this fall," I stated, building a stronger case for having butted in. Mark clearly felt I'd crossed a line. Fortunately he was too exhausted by his ill health and too anxious about the Waldorf interview to rant about my infringement. Instead he changed the subject to the next day's activities. As Mark reported on a conversation he'd had with the dean, I began to realize that the college considered him a serious candidate for the position. Mark sensed my unease.

"Relax, Joy," he said. "We are just going there for an interview and to see what this is all about. Even if they offer me the position—which I doubt—we can still turn it down. Nothing is going to happen overnight."

Caution lights blinked wildly in my head. I had been uncomfortable asking my new boss for a day off so soon after returning from Chicago. Asking wasn't even a correct description of what I'd done. So that I could join Mark, I'd simply informed my new boss that I would use Thursday for my floating holiday. He had looked at me, raised his eyebrows and thanked me for letting him know. I mumbled something about Mark needing my help and assured him I'd be in the following day.

During our two-hour drive to Forest City, I helped prepare Mark for his day. While he drove I reviewed the day's schedule with him and read aloud the names of the people listed as members of the search committee. Mark then asked me to read each person's professional description from the college's catalog. Next he requested that I pose questions of him to help him mentally prepare his answers. Clearly he didn't consider this excursion purely for fun anymore. If Mark were interviewing for a job, he wanted to be the best candidate.

The closer we got to Forest City, the more nervous Mark became.

"Mark, what if you start to get shaky during the interview?"

... 

I asked, hoping that even my question about his tremors wouldn't trigger an episode.

"I've thought about that," he said. "I brought some apple juice, and I'll just try to take it easy. If all else fails, I'll hide my hands."

We both were silent for about 30 seconds, lost in our own thoughts.

"Can you imagine?" he continued, then changed his voice to sound like someone else. "'The guy with a ponytail has shaky hands. He must be on drugs.'"

We both laughed.

Our speed slowed significantly. We were now on a two-lane highway that seemed to have an inordinate number of motor homes traveling on it—particularly Winnebagos. When Mark pulled out in an attempt to pass an extremely large one, he quickly pulled back. Evidently we were part of a caravan of Winnebagos headed for Forest City, home of Winnebago Industries.

When we finally met up with Dr. Lenning, he apologized for not having forewarned us of the local travel conditions. It was rally time, Winnebago's annual meeting of owners. As we followed behind his car to a restaurant—the site of our first appointment—we passed a campground where thousands of Winnebagos in all shapes and sizes were parked side-by-side. The rally grounds were easily a city within a city. The contrast was striking. Mark and I had traveled to a small town of 4,600, but it was home to a Fortune 500 company that doubled the town's population once a year with people from across the nation, even from around the world. Forest City, it seemed, was a small town with big things happening in it.

At the restaurant Mark and I met both Dr. Lenning and his wife, Renie. I immediately appreciated her candor and sense of self, primarily because the characteristics struck familiar chords with me. Our sense of fashion differed dramatically, however. I had chosen a business casual outfit. Renie was dressed in a boldly printed, caftan-like blouse with matching slacks. The outfit's earth tones were accented by oversized, exotic wooden jewelry that hung around her neck and from her ears. Throughout the lunch Renie laughed naturally and easily, sharing humorous asides to her husband's remarks.

After lunch Stross and I were left in Renie's company while Mark accompanied the dean to the Waldorf campus. She had me follow her to the Waldorf president's home, a mansion even by West Des Moines' standards. The house was so distinct, it had its own name. Oak Knoll. Once inside Renie explained that the three-level home—built in the shape of a "W"—had been donated to the college by a member of the family who founded Winnebago. Waldorf President William Hamm (Bill, as Renie called him) lived in Oak Knoll. Because he was a bachelor he only lived in one wing of the home and allowed the college to use two floors of guest rooms for complimentary housing. Should we take a position at Waldorf, she explained, our family could stay at Oak Knoll while looking for a house. We'd also be free to enjoy the home's pool.

Should *we* take a position? Her use of a plural pronoun intrigued me.

About that time Renie answered Oak Knoll's doorbell and greeted a woman who entered the house carrying a clipboard. Someone at the college had arranged for me to spend nearly two hours with a local realtor, so I could view various homes from a range of selling prices. I was startled and visibly balked. Renie noticed.

"Oh, don't worry," she told me. "We do this often. There is no harm in looking. Besides if things go well today, you'll be that much farther ahead should you end up moving to Forest City."

If things go well? Move to Forest City? What I had done by joining Mark on this trip?

After I moved Stross' car seat to the realtor's car, Renie shared plans for me to meet her back at Oak Knoll. First, Stross and I viewed three homes during a one-hour tour. The realtor offered to show me more, but I declined. I had no idea what Mark's salary might be as a college professor at a small Lutheran college, and I had no idea what I could earn in Forest City (provided we could find adequate child care for Stross).

I politely took the realtor's card, thanked her for returning me to Oak Knoll and promised to call if we needed her. Stross and I spent

...

the next hour playing together in front of a large, stone fireplace and making small talk with the woman who cleaned Oak Knoll for the college. I learned her name was Shirley and that she was curious about who I was and why I was there. Because she was eager to ask questions, I assumed she would also be eager to answer them. She was. So while she dusted and mopped the floor of the nearby kitchen, I posed a series of questions about Waldorf, Winnebago and life in Forest City.

Question: How many elementary schools? Answer: Two—one public and one private, a small Christian one.

Question: How many grocery stores? Answer: Two—but most people used the one on the highway. Of course, there were good reasons to use the other store as well.

Question: Was there a hospital in town? Answer: Not anymore. It closed the year before and the building was now a clinic. In her opinion, the town's two doctors were really good; and she had heard a third one—a woman—would be moving to town soon.

Question: Where did people go for emergencies? Answer: To the hospital in Mason City about 35 miles away. Forest City had a good ambulance service.

I tucked away her medically related answers, aware I could use them as ammunition for shooting down the prospect of a move.

My questions then shifted focus. I sought information about: the president (what he was like to work for and how it worked to have him living in a place that other people used for public gatherings), her estimation of how many people worked at Winnebago (nearly as many as the population of Forest City, but not everyone in Forest City worked there, of course—hundreds of people drove in from smaller towns every day), names of other large businesses (3M had a distribution plant and there were three banks), the churches in town (one really large Lutheran church, a large Baptist church and several smaller ones of other denominations), and what people did on weekends for entertainment (a lot of people went to Mason City or Clear Lake for shopping, dining out or movies; however, Forest City had a bowling alley and a family movie theatre with an

•••

admission price of $2 for adults and only charged $.50 for a bag of popcorn, plus, a state park was only two miles away).

About halfway through our conversation, she left her cleaning duties to sit near me while we talked. Then she began to ask me questions. Where did we come from? Did I work outside the home? What was my job? What job was Mark interviewing for? Where had he taught before? How old was Stross? What was spina bifida and how did it affect him?

She apologized for asking personal questions about my son's medical condition, and I assured her the topic was comfortable for me. Talking about Stross introduced the topic of children, and she shared stories of her grandchildren. By the time Renie returned, Shirley and I were well acquainted. Talking to her made me feel like I was back in my hometown talking to my girlfriend's grandmother. Only this time, I was a grown up and the town I was talking about could become my child's hometown.

Renie then invited us on a guided tour of Forest City. Stross napped while she drove down the main street and stopped to pick up that week's edition of the local weekly newspaper. Then she drove past the college and promised a walking tour of the campus before driving by schools, churches, the clinic, the library, the municipal swimming pool, Winnebago Industries and a center for individuals with developmental disabilities. As she drove, she pointed out homes of Waldorf professors, the town's two doctors, the mayor and other local community leaders. She also drove us past her home and the homes of several friends.

At the end of the tour Renie asked if Stross and I would enjoy an ice cream cone. When I responded positively she pulled into the drive-through of a fast food restaurant, ordered three vanilla cones and then wrote a check for an amount less than $2. The woman at the window didn't balk or ask for identification. Instead Renie and the worker exchanged pleasantries, and then she introduced her to Stross, now awake, and me.

During the encounter I experienced my own awakening. If Mark were to become a full-fledged college professor, I would be a professor's wife. I quizzed Renie about the careers of Waldorf spouses to see if my romanticized version of that role came anywhere close to Forest City's reality.

Most spouses, she answered, were women although the college held a goal of recruiting more women professors. Most of the women spouses, she reported, worked for the college in administrative positions. Renie taught at the elementary school, and so did the wife of another professor in the communications department, the man who would be Mark's colleague if Mark took the position. She informed me that many people at Waldorf could help me find a professional position in town. In fact, if I was interested, her husband and the college president could begin making inquiries. They would be more than happy to help, she said. Especially if it made the difference in our decision to come here. Being part of Waldorf, she shared, felt like being part of a family.

I was overwhelmed.

The transition from "if Mark were offered the position" to "if Mark took the position" made me wonder if she had already learned the outcome of his interview. My very detailed tour started to feel like an orientation. I couldn't wait to see Mark again so we could compare notes. I wanted to know if he felt—as I did—that a strong magnetic power was turning the invisible hand of our family's compass. Only days earlier I had begun to mentally prepare for having a second child and securing funds for editing equipment. Now that kind of planning felt misdirected—even frivolous.

At 5:30 p.m. I was to meet Mark at Oak Knoll where we'd get into our car and head back to West Des Moines. I could barely wait to talk to him alone. But when 5:30 p.m. came, Dr. Lenning brought Mark to Oak Knoll and asked if we could join him, Renie and President Hamm for dinner at a restaurant in Clear Lake. The president wanted to meet our entire family and treat us to dinner.

"Of course," the dean said to me, "Mark told me you have to work tomorrow and might not want to get back too late."

His comment indicated Mark had already provided me an out. Without the benefit of a private audience with each other, Mark and I

• • •

conferred using wide eyes and lifted brows. I could tell Mark wanted to go to dinner and that he wanted me to verbally give permission.

"Sure," I said, feeling my pulse quicken. "That would certainly be a treat for us. I hope what I'm wearing will be okay."

Assurances were made, and Mark placed Stross' car seat back into our car. While we drove to Clear Lake, Mark told me about the people he'd met, his interview with the full committee, his tour of the facilities and his separate one-on-one sessions with Dr. Lenning and President Hamm, both alumnae of my alma mater. Mark, who'd drunk his apple juice after meeting the president, described the encounter as a theological litmus test that he believed he'd passed.

During the interview President Hamm, a bear of a man with a graying beard and a paunch belly, had grilled Mark about his knowledge of Lutheranism, particularly what Mark had learned at a Southern Baptist seminary about Martin Luther. He had also lectured on the importance of maintaining the mission of the college. The more animated the president got, Mark said, the harder he'd puffed on his pipe, blowing long wafts of smoke into the air between declarations. Mark wanted to offer equally passionate responses but never fully had an opportunity. It had been the president's time to be presidential.

The pipe smoke, combined with unused adrenaline, had caused Mark to get shaky; but he was certain the president had not noticed. As they shook hands at the end of the meeting, Mark said President Hamm had joked that having a professor on campus with a ponytail may help the college fulfill some sort of diversity requirement. He'd even made reference to Mark's earring—something Mark did not have.

Having been forewarned of President Hamm's forceful personality, I sharpened my focus and prepared for my own time of testing. I took my behavioral cues from Renie, who continued to be frank, so I was forthright and assertive too. I'd decided I should be no different in front of Waldorf's president or academic dean than I would be with my own boss. I had nothing to lose here. I was fairly certain I'd obtained Renie's approval—and Shirley's. If the president or dean didn't like me, fine.

Dinner conversation began with stories of our alma mater

and lingered there for the majority of the meal. While we alums reminisced, Mark fed Stross his dinner and excused himself once to change Stross' diaper. Renie bantered with Bill at every opportunity, coaxing me into the role as well.

When the president turned the conversation to my career, listening with interest to my aspirations, I knew I had fared well. Soon he was suggesting jobs I could apply for if we moved to Forest City, apologizing for the lack of ones that matched my ambitions. This man, who had initially sounded gruff and opinionated, now sounded surprisingly softhearted and genuinely concerned for my wellbeing.

After dinner Mark and I thanked them for the day and expressed our need to return home. As we drove south I stared out the window at one of Iowa's incredibly beautiful sunsets. It skimmed the tops of row after row of corn stalks, filling the sky with a scheme of brilliant colors—pink, purple, orange and violet—their powdery brightness too intense for visual absorption.

Mark shared more about his day including what he'd seen and what he'd heard about Waldorf's plans to transition from a two-year college into a baccalaureate institution. The communications department was to be one of the first to offer courses toward a bachelor's degree, and the college needed faculty willing to design a four-year academic program and expand the department's facilities. Mark said that when they mentioned building a radio station and a computer lab, he had suggested adding a television studio as well.

As Mark drove he started a new story about every mile. I listened, keeping my eyes fixed on the fading colors of the horizon. The diminishing luster matched my feelings. Mark sounded happy—happier than he'd been in a while but just how long, I wasn't certain. I couldn't avoid feeling that Mark's future happiness depended on my willingness to fade into the background, sacrificing my career choices for his. Nearly two years earlier he had professionally sacrificed himself for Stross—for me. Now life presented me with a chance to reciprocate. The realization mingled my joy for him with sorrow for myself. Soon I felt the arrival of tears, bringing release and relief of unknown origin. Stross, fastened next to me in the center of the back seat, was too tired to notice Mommy crying, but Mark looked in the rearview mirror and saw me brush tears off my cheeks.

"Joy, what's wrong?" he asked, talking to my mirror image as he drove. He waited patiently for me to form words adequate enough to describe what I felt.

"I'm...," I started, hesitating to share my actual thoughts. "I'm . . . going to miss my parking card."

My comment sounded as bizarre as Mark's reference to baseball had been the day Stross was born. Our family potentially faced a time of unprecedented personal and professional upheaval, but the only words I could summon offered a tribute to my parking card. Until then I'd not acknowledged its status as my personal symbol of success.

"We don't even know they will offer me the position," Mark said. "And even if they do, we can say 'no.'"

"No, Mark," I quickly countered. "They will offer you the job, and you need to say 'yes.'"

"Joy..." Mark's voice lingered, letting me know he really didn't know what to say next. I spoke again instead.

"You belong there, Mark. I can feel it. That job is your seminary, teaching and professional experience all rolled into one. If they offer you that, it's too good to pass up."

I'd finally found the ability to express feelings connected to my husband. Mark used silence to absorb what I'd said and to discern what it revealed, if anything, about me. His next words brought even more clarity.

"I can pass up this job if moving means you won't be happy," he said. "It wouldn't be worth it."

The magnitude of the moment sank in. In the ensuing silence, I thought about things that would be uncomfortable to share with Mark aloud, particularly my awareness of our symbiotic strengths and compatible sins.

From our early days as waiters, I'd recognized how my elevated sense of self fed off Mark's need to deny himself. Mark served others to find fulfillment; I sought ways to achieve. Since my approach felt decidedly less honorable than his, I'd craved not only

Mark's companionship but also his mentorship. Mark's approach to life inspired me, and I hoped it could, in some way, hone my egocentric edges. Still, when I needed something—no matter how trivial—I knew I could find success through Mark. Size didn't matter—substantial or trivial. He'd go out of his way to drive me home in a blizzard as easily as he'd insist I take the last chocolate donut. He was simply wired as a giver from birth.

I, however, arrived preprogrammed to take. This relational imbalance wasn't always unhealthy. In fact, most of the time, it worked beautifully. After all, givers need grateful receivers; however, it took years of married life for us to fully understand the fine nuances of negotiating a relationship that was more 65-35 than 50-50. Eventually I learned how to take my turn on the 35 percent side. But I never liked my turn to last very long, and the burden of understanding my capacity to abuse Mark's willing resignation weighed heavy.

While still newlyweds I'd recognized that Mark had become savvy to my ability to request a rescue without actually asking, and I recognized that he thrived on opportunities to rescue me. In that sense I'd been blessed with the knight in shining armor some women fantasize about—a man who had vowed to make my happiness his business. By the time Waldorf College came calling, Mark had spent more than seven years making certain I'd never had an occasion to be unhappy. Even after Stross' birth, whenever circumstances had threatened to undo me, he had stepped in as an emotional buffer. I hadn't recognized how his pattern of sacrifice had limited my emotional growth. If I could count on Mark catching me, how would I know who I was capable of becoming after a fall—after the pieces of my life were assembled in a new way?

Mark had fallen, I believed, without full provision of the rescue he'd afforded me. He might not have acknowledged the impact of the fall, but his body couldn't hide it. He'd fallen hard. And who had he become as a result? I don't think either of us could know. He needed time to reassemble, maybe even reconnect to what he believed was his calling.

"Buttons and busses," he had told me after proposing, "God has given me a gift for buttons and busses. They are parts of an audio board, and I love working with them." That had been Mark's awkward explanation of why he wanted to get a master's degree in communications from a seminary. Now a church college that wanted to build a radio station—and maybe even a television studio—might offer him a job as a professor. How could I ask him to sacrifice that opportunity should it come?

In his most grandiose act of selflessness, Mark had become the answer to all our family's problems. Becoming Stross' caregiver had fixed nearly everything. He was exactly the kind of father Stross needed and the supportive spouse my career required. Had Mark not given of himself in this way, he would not have been happy. Yet our happiness had cost something he couldn't articulate, and this position—encompassing all he'd studied and prepared for—called to him like a beacon.

On some primal level I understood that Mark could never move forward until he knew I'd be happy. Even then growth would only come by discovering the joy that had given birth to his dreams—not Stross' and my dreams—but his. It would bring him new lessons about sacrifice—about what it takes to bring dreams to life.

I also understood what I needed to do in order to move forward. It was my turn to give—my turn to sacrifice for Mark's happiness while safeguarding our son's wellbeing.

I found a way to say what Mark needed to hear.

"I'll be happy," I retorted, then choked on my next comment, "but I'll miss my office too."

Not as comfortable in the selfless role, I threw a pity party in the back seat, openly grieving a life I felt ill prepared to leave.

"It's on the top floor of a Des Moines office building. A lot of people would be envious of my view, you know."

Talking about frivolities came easier than voicing my thoughts aloud. I pouted now, effectively squelching Mark's freedom to be excited. I pouted and complained…and Mark let me.

"They certainly don't have a view like that in Forest City,"

• • •

he commiserated. "You've had a very impressive career, Joy, and you're not even 30. I'm proud of you."

In the back seat of our car, I faced a stark truth: I had changed very little from the woman Mark married. I'd grown into my role as Stross' mom, but I'd managed to do it on my terms with Mark making it possible to live the kind of life we both longed for. He had facilitated my freedom.

I loved this man more than my life.

"Mark...it's my turn to stay at home and take care of Stross," I said. "I can do that. I'll even enjoy that. Stross needs more 'Mommy time' while he's little."

Saying the words aloud brought me closer to believing them.

"Are you sure? You love working," Mark said. "You'd be happy staying home?"

He lilted the statement as a question allowing me to hear his apprehension.

"I can freelance now." I summoned arrogance in an attempt to feign confidence. "I can write while Stross plays or naps."

Mark nodded to show he'd heard. He wanted to believe me.

"I can even keep my appointment to the Lt. Governor's committee." Now I sounded belligerent. I practically dared Mark to tell me I didn't have what it took to become a working, stay-at-home mom.

We began outlining plans for our future–again. Life had shifted a full 180 degrees in a matter of four days. I looked at Stross' face. His eyelids covered his eyes, and his lips formed a pout that lifted his chin in the air. The back of his head rested comfortably against the side of his car seat. Stross' cherubic face still emitted a godly essence. I sensed a holy presence as we drove and discussed but was unwilling to fully give myself to the moment.

"We have to be smart about this." Tears now gone, my combative tone revealed how threatened I felt. I needed a rescue but understood how unfair it would be for Mark to catch me this time.

The hum of the tires churned my thoughts. I returned to familiar survival tactics and built an effective emotional barrier with quiet but forceful commands.

"You have to earn enough money so I can stay home with Stross, and we have to make certain he will be fully included in the college's group insurance plan."

"Of course," said Mark, fending off a verbal challenge to his ability to provide. "But, Joy, I still think you are getting ahead of yourself. They haven't offered me the position."

I started to cry again, unable to remain distant.

"They will, Mark," I said, choking on the weight of my emotions. "Don't you see? They liked you. Couldn't you tell? They'll offer it, Mark. They will."

My outburst exhausted me; so Mark gallantly filled our awkward silence with a one-sided conversation. When he tired of speaking, he too fell silent.

We entered the West Des Moines city limits in darkness. Within minutes we were parked in the garage of our suburban home. I lifted our sleeping son out of his car seat and carried him into a house that felt much different that it had that morning.

• • •

# Chapter 26

# In Transition

· · ·

The exact moment my life shifted focus is not clear, but if I had to choose, I'd choose the moment I began to grieve my parking card.

As soon as Mark accepted the position at Waldorf, our family began planning our move to Forest City. It was late June and Mark needed to be on campus by mid-August. We had seven weeks to sell our house, buy a new one, sell the Civic, say meaningful good-byes to friends and doctors (who had become as close as family) and identify Mark's mysterious ailment.

I had an additional goal: to resign my position at the association without relinquishing control over the annual convention. Those responsibilities would not be completed until the end of September. Therefore, I needed to devise a plan that kept me in Des Moines even after my home and husband existed in Forest City. In addition, the plan needed to address one specific complication: by mid-August I would be Stross' primary caregiver.

I'd rationalized the need for a custom transition plan as the only way to honorably finish what I'd started. In truth, I couldn't walk away from the chance to add one last accomplishment—another successful convention—to my career vitaé. The convention was my buffer—a way to ease into a new life as I pulled away from the old one.

My letter of resignation, written on June 28, listed a "becomes effective" date of October 1. Fortunately my boss didn't balk at the timing. Instead we discussed ways to avoid having my three-month notice turn into a lame-duck period, and he'd invited me to work with him on restructuring my position for a successor. Most importantly he'd agreed to my request for Stross to come to work with me from mid-August to the end of September with the understanding I would not allow him to distract me or other employees.

"Not a problem," I'd assured him, praying Stross would take long naps and maintain an amiable office disposition. "It's a deal."

I'd regularly demonstrated how little a distraction Stross could be—at least to me. In fact, the day of my resignation, I'd spent the morning with Mark at the hospital while our son had tubes surgically placed in his ears. After Stross proved he'd successfully tolerated the anesthesia, I had signed his discharge papers then headed for the office while Mark took him home. After six major surgeries, tubes in our 2-year-old's ears felt as insignificant as a pebble on a road.

That evening we broke the news of our new life to our families via a series of lengthy long distance phone calls. Everyone sounded delighted for Mark, and Mark sounded full of energy again with a new rhythm and cadence to his speech. The phone transmission only amplified his enthusiasm. Our parents' enthusiasm was qualified, however. They had concerns—concerns that echoed our own: Could we afford this? How would it affect Stross' medical care? Did the college have a good insurance plan? Would we be able to keep some of his doctors or at least find comparable new ones?

Of course there were a handful of specific concerns related to me: What will Joy do? Will she be happy taking care of Stross? Are you sure she won't get bored? That's a pretty small town. What will she do to keep busy?

Who I'd become since Stross' birth didn't always resemble my parents' memories of the young woman they'd dropped off at college. Because I'd married five days after my college graduation, I'd always felt that, in their minds, I remained 21 years old. And based on comments I'd heard them share with their friends and colleagues, I also believed they continued to see me as an idealistic, high-achieving, assertive, driven, young woman who gave them reasons to be proud.

Every time I'd made a career move my parents managed to find a reason to visit me in my office within the first few months—even the jobs I had in Texas. They had taken advantage of their teaching breaks to spend time with us, and part of their visit would include taking me to lunch on days I worked.

I noticed they always wanted to pick me up rather than meet in a restaurant, and I could tell they appreciated meeting my coworkers, seeing my office and being introduced to whomever was my direct supervisor. I believed it helped provide them with context for my work-related stories, but I also believed the experiences were some sort of payoff for their parental investment.

"So you are putting your degree to good use," Dad would state.

"I'd like to think so," I'd return.

My parents had made it known I would need to earn my way through college—working or taking out loans for expenses not covered by scholarships. Therefore I interpreted his comment as a reminder that I should acknowledge the payoff for what I—what we—had accomplished.

I believe my position at the association—working on behalf of Iowa's cities and city officials—had given them the most pride, especially for my government teacher father. Mom and Dad had even managed to bring my father's parents to visit me at work in Des Moines shortly after Mark had begun his Mr. Mom role. I retain a clear memory of my dad standing next to his dad as they looked out my wall of windows in search of I-Cubs stadium.

"Now *what* do you do again?" Grandma Delma had asked. My dad provided the response and then asked a question of his own.

"How much do you make now anyway?"

I paused, not certain how I felt about responding, but then offered a round number for his review.

My parents exchanged glances, while Grandma Delma said, "Oh my!"

306 · Involuntary Joy

"Isn't that something, Fran?" Dad said. "She's on a much different scale than a teacher."

Now my parents were having to deal with the fact that I was leaving my job so my husband could teach. I sensed they had begun to grieve my career shift as well.

After Stross' birth my parents had few occasions to observe me as a mother firsthand—only during times of family crisis or celebration. Not necessarily regular work days for a mother. They may have suspected that marriage and motherhood had taught me how to be less self-centered, but because I'd maintained a never-let-them-see-me-hurting attitude, glimpses of how I'd transformed—while real—were rare. The events that shaped my new identity were not public ones. My maternal achievements had come in intense, everyday moments: kneeling by my son's crib, choosing the questions I'd ask a doctor who was about to enter an exam room, contemplating a stranger's stare or lying awake in my bed wondering how to support Mark as Stross' caregiver.

I learned a lot about myself during those private moments, and I was beginning to understand how they defined the person I'd become more than my professional achievements. They'd changed me in ways my parents—and Mark's parents—seemed unaware of and explained why I freely chose to leave a career that had—until recently—shaped my identity: My husband and my son needed me. I was setting aside my interests for my family's well being, and it had been my choice.

I believed I was capable of such a sacrifice and saddened that others doubted. Because I'd maintained a career focus, my evolution had not been complete enough to be seen by those who'd loved me first. In my early 20s, the process of pulling away from my parents to create an independent identity had been a natural, increasingly sentimental celebration. Then shortly after Stross' arrival I'd recognized the process again, however now it was painful. I'd clung to my professional life after Stross, because I needed its comfort and familiarity. It is who I was. The move to Forest City gave me a chance to pull away and embrace a new identity—one that better resembled the woman I'd become.

Our three transitional months flew by. We'd placed our house on the market within days of accepting the Waldorf offer, and it sold the first day it was listed. Days later Des Moines' great flood of '93 closed off the downtown area, making it impossible for me to go to work. The association, like hundreds of other downtown businesses and organizations, had been forced to close its doors until the floodwaters receded and the city's drinking water was restored.

The unfortunate disaster was well timed for our family for several reasons. First, it allowed me to accompany Mark to his Monday appointment with the internal medicine specialist. After her exam she offered a diagnosis of intestinal migraines. Having read the results of Mark's recent tests and recognizing they ruled out other organic causes, she said her best guess was that Mark had migraines that occurred in his intestines rather than his head. Furthermore, because he'd been so intent on identifying triggers, he may have inadvertently created some triggers that explained why he had physical reactions to lighting conditions and places in which he'd had episodes before.

Her diagnosis, as plausible as it sounded, still seemed like a long shot. We had never heard of intestinal migraines before, and it seemed more like a diagnosis by elimination rather than identification. Still she had been the first of Mark's doctors to pose a full explanation for his combined symptoms, and she had offered a pharmaceutical solution that promised results. We'd told her that, if at all possible, Mark needed to be cured by the time he'd start teaching in the fall. She cautioned that it might take longer than that, but we'd at least know if the treatment was working by then. With that, she handed Mark three prescriptions, and we left hoping we'd found an answer.

My unplanned week off, courtesy of the flood, also became our opportunity to sell Mark's car and shop for a house in Forest City. The fourth buyer to respond to our Civic ad met our asking price. With that transaction complete, we headed north to meet with a realtor and choose a house that would become our next home. We narrowed our hunt to neighborhoods within walking distance of the college. Even though we still owned two vehicles—the Accord and our trusty El Camino—our entire family only fit in the Accord; therefore, our home needed to accommodate a one-car lifestyle.

By Friday we were ready to make an offer on a three-bedroom home two blocks off campus. Built in 1910, it lacked the space and amenities of our suburban dwelling, but its tree-lined street and friendly adjoining backyards made up for the lack of a garbage disposal, dishwasher and fireplace. The home was two stories with a full basement that posed a range of accessibility problems for Stross. But Stross, a 2-year-old crawler, could navigate stairs like an agile toddler. From what we'd seen, there were no accessible homes on the market in Forest City; therefore, we'd have to ramp the entrance to any home we purchased. It might as well be a house in a desirable location.

Mark spent the next weeks packing boxes and sorting our meager material possessions. Books and baby toys comprised the majority of our wealth. Our furniture consisted of a sofa, a bookshelf and a desk left over from seminary days; a bedroom set we'd purchased when I was pregnant; a dining room set Mark's parents had purchased for us after Stross' birth; a set of hand-me-down couches; and Stross' crib and changing table. We owned barely enough to fill one small moving van and the El Camino. But with the process of packing underway, it was time to schedule one last round of doctors appointments for Stross and plan incredible events for our youth to cap off our last summer with them.

By mid-August our heads and our hearts were in Forest City. Mark, who'd been faithfully taking his prescribed medications, had not had an intestinal episode since filling his prescriptions. Our new life showed promise, and the hope it offered gave Mark and me the energy we needed to fulfill our joint and separate obligations.

The last week of August marked our time of greatest transition. That Wednesday we loaded the last box into the moving van and signed over possession of our 10-year-old suburban home to its new owner. Then we drove to Mark's parents' house in Waterloo and spent the night there before completing our trip to Forest City.

Members of the college's staff and faculty helped us unload that Thursday so that Mark could attend his faculty orientation "with one less worry." Plus, they'd informed us, there was a service of consecration to begin the school year that evening, and they "sure hoped" we could come.

While Mark was at the college the next day, I moved from room to room unpacking as much as I could. I only stopped long enough to care for Stross or create a new area for him to play. Empty boxes made great play places, and he'd laugh each time he'd throw toys inside only to crawl in after them. Stross' happy banter buoyed my mood.

Mark and I spent the weekend turning the house into our new home. By Monday nearly all the boxes had been crushed, and Stross and I headed back to West Des Moines to stay with a friend of my parents. Mark began his week by writing syllabi and preparing the media learning labs. We'd never been separated for more than one night during our entire marriage. Now we would spend four weeks apart with Stross and me commuting to Forest City on weekends.

Sobbing, I hugged—more like clung to—Mark. I had never felt so torn. All of a sudden, helping the association have one more successful convention didn't matter. I wanted to be with Mark, reminding him to take his medication and taking our son on the two-block stroller ride to visit Daddy in his office.

So much had changed so quickly. I needed time to myself in Des Moines, and Mark needed time alone in Forest City. We each were designing lives far different from anything we'd imagined. So I drove my child back to downtown Des Moines, pulled into the private parking ramp that I was so proud of, parked our car and packed Stross' stroller with his diaper bag and my briefcase. For four weeks each workday started the same—I'd load the stroller with everything I needed to be both a good mother and a good professional. The load it carried was so heavy that, if Stross wasn't sitting in the seat as counterbalance, the stroller tipped over. In effect, I needed Stross to keep everything balanced.

On Fridays, I'd race back to Forest City, leaving behind any thoughts of the upcoming convention or stories I needed to write for the magazine. But each Monday, when it was time to return to Des Moines, I'd feel my blood course a little faster than it had during my weekend in Forest City. I felt more alive, more invigorated the closer I got to the capitol city, and I wondered if I'd ever match that feeling while living in my new hometown.

Back in my office my two worlds conveniently converged. Stross, born with an accommodating personality, quieted for naps as scheduled, waited to eat until I could feed him between appointments and happily played with toys or drew on paper while seated next to me in meetings. Twice he joined me for meetings at the state capitol with the Lt. Governor, an advocate for women's rights and a mom of three herself. During the second meeting she treated us to lunch in the capitol cafeteria where she and Stross selected the same entrée—a hot dog with chips.

Then during the association's convention (Stross' and my third week as a team), we buzzed through Des Moines' skywalk system checking and rechecking arrangements. Stross—never more than an arm's length away—grabbed his naps on the fly, snoozing in his stroller. Meanwhile I confirmed event plans, checked banquet orders, welcomed speakers and carried out numerous other responsibilities. During Stross' awake times I'd alternate between propping him on my hip while using his stroller as a cart for my planning notebook or pushing him around (one-handed) while communicating with my walkie-talkie. At the end of these incredibly long days, we'd retire to our complimentary suite in the Marriott where I'd treat him to a feast of room-service fare, and we'd take turns talking to Daddy on the phone.

As the convention came to a close, I completed my emotional transition. I couldn't wait for the next week to come and go. All I had left to do was verify final budget figures, write thank you notes and leave instructions about the publications for my successor. I had become more of a mom than anything else. But I knew part of me would always search for ways to communicate and plan. I'd realized those skills couldn't be quieted by a move to a new life, and in my heart I knew they might work to my benefit in our new home.

On my last day at the association, Mark and Stross showed up as surprise guests at my going away party. When the party was over, I cried, emptied my desk of personal items that I placed in a box with some files, and then left amid promises to stay in touch.

Mark volunteered to have Stross ride with him on our trip back to Forest City, but I needed him with me. I needed him close enough to touch when I followed Mark home. Stross was a tangible reminder of the choice I'd made and the life I'd been given.

•　　•　　•

# Chapter 27

# Playing by the Rules

• • •

D uring our month in Des Moines Stross and I had hit our collective stride. My days and his had merged to a point where I could set my work schedule around his eating and diapering. His play times had become my break times, and his nap times had become my opportunities to work feverishly. Caring for Stross while working full-time had honed my multi-tasking ability. After my days had become fully my own, I didn't want to lose any of life's intoxicating intensity. Therefore I'd established some hard and fast rules known to no one but myself.

Had I written these unspoken rules as a list, I would have begun with:

> *Rule #1: Dress for the day as if dressing*
> *for casual Friday.*

I abhorred the stereotype of a frazzled mother hurrying her charges out for the day without attending to her own appearance. And because I didn't want to be anyone's nomination for a mommy makeover, I'd spent time shopping in Des Moines' skywalk mall, purchasing a casual wardrobe to replace the blazers, skirt sets and shirtdresses I'd worn to work.

While none of my casual outfits had needed accessorizing, I kept my daily ritual of selecting jewelry with Stross each morning. No matter what I wore, we managed to find a pair of clip earrings to match. I'd always worn clip earrings to work, and I saw no reason to stop wearing them now that my work happened at home. They were my link to something I couldn't put into words. All I knew is that when I looked in the mirror, I still looked like a woman who had it together. Plus as long as Stross and I kept our morning routine—he helping me with make up, then playing with my jewelry on the bed while I dressed—my day didn't feel different until 9 a.m.

By 9 a.m. I was obviously someone who no longer had a morning commute and had little need for a Daytimer®. So I devised this plan:

*Rule #2: Make a daily list of tasks to accomplish—*
*both household and professional.*

The household chores I listed mentally; the professional tasks I wrote on lined paper I kept in my leather binder. While Stross napped I planned to keep my career alive by working from home and accomplishing this:

*Rule #3 - Maintain contact with colleagues*
*and business associates.*

I was still heavily involved with the Lt. Governor's Committee on Diversity. In fact, I'd accepted an appointment as chair of the committee's first statewide conference which would be held the following October—a little more than one year from our move. Because I no longer planned a convention for the association, I'd jumped at the chance to launch another statewide event. The committee hoped the conference would bring together teams of community leaders from cities of all sizes. After a series of learning events, the teams would have an opportunity to create an action plan to solve a local problem that stemmed from a misunderstanding or mismanagement of their community's diverse citizenry.

Because the conference targeted city officials, I'd convinced my former employer to pay for my expenses as their representative on the committee. I'd originally joined as their representative and, after I resigned, the Lt. Governor had asked me to continue on the committee even though I no longer had a title behind my name. She wanted my "talent, not the title," she'd said. Rather than having the association place another person to the committee, I'd convinced my former boss that I could continue representing their interests.

The arrangement made it possible for me to afford Rule #3. Had the association not agreed to pay for my expenses, I would not have been able to afford my volunteer appointment (with its long distance phone calls and monthly trips to Des Moines) on our family's now-lowered income. Once again, the association had provided a lifeline during trying times.

My next rule recognized that I was now primarily responsible for aiding Stross' development. And while he was my number one priority, I needed the first three rules to get myself ready for this:

*Rule #4 - Engage Stross in several learning activities every day.*

I relied on a bevy of skilled educators to assist with the task. Even before our move I'd made contact with our new area education agency in a most unlikely way. One of Forest City's council members had attended the association's convention along with the city clerk. I'd learned they were there after presenting them with the top prize for a skywalk golf tournament. We'd joked about having rigged the competition, then I'd introduced them to Stross.

The city clerk said his wife was an elementary teacher; therefore, I wasn't surprised when he boasted of the city's fine school system. The council member, however, caught me by surprise. After learning about Stross' disability, he said that his wife would probably be our son's early childhood educator since she was employed by the agency as a special education consultant. He gave me her number and encouraged me to call. I did—the very next day—and she guided me through the process of having Stross' records transferred. Then she arranged for our family's first "staffing" to occur soon after Stross and I had completed our family's move north.

We'd first learned about these specialized meetings when Stross had one at four months of age. At such a meeting all the specialists deemed necessary to assure Stross' educational success gather to meet him (as well as Mark and me) and decide which tests, if any, are necessary to help them determine his areas of need. Then this information is used to decide which personnel should be assigned the job of helping us outline his educational goals. Finally we write goals then decide how many hours per week each specialist should spend helping Stross achieve them.

Our new school system, like our former one, decided Stross needed to meet with a physical therapist one hour per week, an occupational therapist one hour per week and an early childhood special education specialist (or teacher) one hour per week. Because Stross was not yet in preschool, he would not have the council member's wife. (But it was only a matter of time. The city clerk's wife eventually became his teacher as well—in third grade.)

That fall I realized our son had grown and matured more than I'd recognized. Now that I spent the majority of each day with him, the changes became obvious. While I'd been working, he'd been turning into a little boy who had favorite TV characters (Barney and Grover) and favorite books (Dr. Seuss' *Hand, Hand, Fingers, Thumb*) and favorite toys (anything he could pretend was a guitar). He loved imaginary play, especially scenarios full of sound effects, and he could play as easily by himself as with others. I'd known all those things. I'd simply neglected to see those were activities of interest to a little boy, not a baby. Consequently I was spending my days with a little boy who, I hoped, wouldn't make it hard to accomplish this:

*Rule #5 - Start being productive by 9 a.m.*

At 9 a.m. each day Stross and I either welcomed one of the education specialists into our home or headed to the clinic for an hour of therapy. Mark and I wanted Stross to have as much help as possible. So in addition to the hours of PT and OT provided by the education agency, we'd scheduled two hours of PT at the clinic each week. The agency's physical therapist came to our home on Mondays, we went to the clinic for PT on Tuesdays and the agency education specialist came on Wednesdays while the agency occupational therapist came on Thursdays. On Fridays we'd head to the clinic for PT again.

To a person, each professional made therapy fun for Stross. Whether he practiced balancing while reaching for blown bubbles or drew pictures of shapes while singing songs, each man or woman learned to tune into Stross' sense of fun and use it to their advantage. It was clear that I could choose my level of involvement in their activities, and most of the time I joined in. Occasionally I needed to coax Stross into cooperating. He had my tendency to avoid activities that were difficult. By teaming up, the specialists and I were always able to get Stross to an established goal—eventually.

All the agency specialists were women, and I enjoyed interacting with them. They were genuinely interested in our history as a family and were invested in our future. Each woman became a ready audience for our war stories and an eager cheering section for Stross' daily victories. The more familiar each became in our home, the more comfortable I was spending time at my computer or answering my work phone while they worked.

We were always in the same room—Stross, the specialists and me—but as the conference drew near, I started sitting out the imaginary games of hibernation played under our dining room table or games of "Under, Over, Behind, Beside" played with a box and even the games where Stross fitted colored pegs into a foam board according to a pattern. As he practiced bending over to pick up toy dishes off the floor without falling over, I *took* phone calls and *made* phone calls.

When these women overheard me making arrangements for Maya Angelou to come as a keynote speaker or chatting with the Lt. Governor's assistant, I secretly swelled with pride. They got to see I was more than just a mom—that I had an identity beyond motherhood. I'm fairly certain none of the women realized how much I used those moments as an emotional crutch. They became my therapists too as they attentively listened to details of my work while keeping Stross engaged in an activity—their work.

Stross, oblivious to my constant foraging for attention, somehow made my life easier and harder all at the same time. If it weren't for him, I'm fairly certain I'd have continued working full time and enjoyed the rewards of a successful career; however, I'd have missed the satisfying challenges of his life. Still, Stross' accommodating personality made it possible for me to miss out even when, technically, we were together.

After morning "school" or therapies, Stross and I would play, then eat lunch. Next he'd oblige me by taking at least a one-hour nap. While he slept I tackled some of the chores on my list. Then once he awoke we either left the house to run errands or to attend meetings. The rest of the day I'd spend working from home while Stross played. I knew that if I could start Stross building with Legos® or playing tea party with his toy dishes, I could sneak away from the game to work nearly without interruption.

While he happily carried on our game, I'd write at my computer or return calls. Periodically I'd look over to smile at him (thinking how great it was that I could work while I took care of my child) or interject myself into his imagination as some fictional character. He'd delight in the attention from Mommy, and if I became a playmate too engaging to ignore, he'd carry over a book for me to read or crawl over to sit on my lap as I typed. That's when I'd oblige him, and that's when my dual life felt deceptive. Stross' actions— very innocently—pointed out how impossible it was to work two jobs at the same time and perform both equally well.

"Are you my mom right now?" he'd seem to ask without saying a word. "Or do I have to wait until you have time for me?"

Even while reading a book aloud to him, I'd be able to plan my next phone call in my head or outline a section of copy. However some days his persistence would fully win me over, making copy deadlines or returning calls before 5 p.m. irrelevant. Stross' response to my attention—and my desire to respond in kind—superceded anything on my lists. Of all my rules, I think this was the most difficult:

*Rule #6 - Keep mommy guilt in perspective.*

Stross had introduced me to an intense version of mommy guilt. In Des Moines Mark had made it possible to work without guilt. While in Mark's care, Stross had not been forced to compete for my attention against a computer and a phone. I hoped that, on some level, Stross understood Mommy was playing too. It was a grown-up game called "Try to Accomplish Stuff Amid Distractions." I just didn't want him to feel like a distraction.

Many times I found myself fighting to place Stross ahead of work. There was always a crushing sense that if I failed, I'd be the reason he didn't succeed in school or the reason his body didn't work to its greatest potential. But no matter how much I worried about becoming my son's downfall, I couldn't set my interests aside. I couldn't devote even the amount of time to therapy and playing school that I'd imagined Deb Davis had done for Austin.

During the next months I fought to work free of mommy guilt. I secured facilities for the diversity conference and negotiated exhibit booth rentals. I also made periodic phone calls for the communicators' organization and agreed to help a local group with community development efforts. At Mark's urging I also took on freelance jobs for Waldorf to write promotional materials and assist the college with the announcement of its baccalaureate degrees.

This latter assignment was of great importance to Mark. Because his department was one of the first to be restructured, he'd felt pressure to design a competitive curriculum. Now he wanted me creating the marketing materials to support his efforts. I'd also signed on to teach a public relations class. In essence, taking care of Stross soon became what I did when I wasn't taking care of my own interests.

But I don't think I could have managed another way. I'd tied my interests to observing one last rule that echoed one of the vows I'd spoken to Mark when we married:

*Rule #7 - Help Mark become all he intended to be.*

Mark, as he had in Des Moines, made it possible for me to pursue my interests. He didn't teach a class during the hour I taught mine, so he watched Stross. Often I'd have a hard time finding them after class was over. Sometimes they'd head across the street for a snack or over to the campus bookstore to check out the displays. Most times I'd find them in one of the media labs. Typically Stross would be laughing at the antics of one or more students while Mark adjusted the controls to a television camera or loaded software on a computer. Wherever Stross went at the college, he drew a crowd. Wherever we were, you could find Stross.

Spending time at the college was therapeutic, in a way. It was a professional environment where I could feel like a professional again—even with a child nearly three years old alongside. Plus having me there reassured Mark that I was happy and gave him permission to continue forging his new life. He was busily researching and buying equipment for the college's radio station and multimedia lab and revamping the way television was taught.

Having Stross on campus also helped Mark. Our most recent role reversal had been harder on me, but it wasn't easy for him. He missed Stross. Stross had become Daddy's boy, and Stross, in many ways, continued to look to Mark for nurturing. Their bond was evident.

When we all attended the same meeting (Stross arriving with me as the hired consultant and Mark coming as faculty), Mark would insist that Stross sit next to him. He and Stross would share quiet inside jokes and doodle on the same piece of paper. It was amazing what the seating arrangement did for me mentally. All of a sudden, I became a professional again: leading discussions, challenging those in authority when I felt it necessary and posing solutions to potential problems—all without worrying about my child.

Mark accused me of practically ignoring Stross during meetings as my way of ensuring he didn't undermine my credibility, and he claimed it was unnecessary. According to Mark colleagues were capable of seeing each other as complete human beings regardless of gender roles. But I wasn't sure I agreed. I knew I couldn't perform well in a meeting when I was distracted by my mommy responsibilities. I preferred laying down my mommy mantle and becoming fully who I used to be for portions of hours at a time. And during our first year in Forest City my tactic worked.

Stross was thriving. I was thriving, and Mark (who'd taken himself off his medication cold turkey after realizing he hadn't had a migraine episode since accepting his new job) was thriving. I'd credited my secret rules for much of our family's good fortune.

As long as they worked I wasn't about to change.

•   •   •

# Chapter 28

# Learning to Abide

• • •

J ust as I'd learned to merge Stross' and my daily schedules, our family had learned to merge Stross' medical check ups with Waldorf College's academic calendar. I would schedule our biannual trips to the University of Iowa's spina bifida clinic in Iowa City during the summer or over a midterm break. Likewise I'd plan visits to his Des Moines doctors over breaks for holidays or spring term. When that wasn't possible, I'd ask for late afternoon appointments so we could start our travel as soon as Mark finished with his classes.

Except for the medical tests, Stross looked forward to these trips. They made up for the fun travel times he'd lost since our move. I'd noticed his symptoms of car withdrawal because I'd experienced them myself. We simply didn't ride in a car for extended periods of time anymore. Most things in Forest City were within two miles. For instance I would make a list of errands to run—pharmacy, post office, groceries—believing Stross and I would be gone for more than an hour. When I'd pull into our drive after only 30 minutes, I'd feel restless—as if there were more to do. I knew Stross felt restless also because he'd refuse to leave the car.

"No, Mommy, no," he'd say as I'd attempt to unbuckle his seat. "Go more."

"But I'm all done, Sweetie."

"No all-done. Go!" he'd retort. Then usually, especially during the first few weeks, I'd relent and settle back into the driver's seat to spend another 10 to 15 minutes driving him around Forest City.

For a while Stross also preferred our car to riding in his wagon. Since the college was only a few blocks away, I'd thought its location provided great opportunities for leisurely strolls.

"No, Mommy. No wagon—car," he'd lobby. But I was hard to persuade. It didn't make sense to park the car close enough to be seen from our front porch. But for Stross the ride itself was a destination. He valued the journey.

I'd started to appreciate journeys too. Our trips for medical appointments gave Mark and me time to reconnect. We'd talk about recent news stories, stuff happening at Waldorf, updates on extended family and Stross. No matter the topic, I'd goad Mark to share his opinions or thoughts, then journalistically grill him about how he'd arrived at them. Mark persevered as my conversation outlet.

The conversations weren't complete, I believed, until I'd had a chance to launch into spiritual musings or observations about life— particularly if I could relate them to a question of God's providence. I liked to believe I could—retrospectively—see evidence of God's foresight and preparation in circumstances we'd encountered. Not that God had brought them into being but that God had attempted to forecast things to come. Therefore, if that indeed had happened and continued to happen, I also believed that somehow—if I could learn to sufficiently fine-tune or enhance my spirituality, I'd be able to identify God's presence in nearly every moment. The day of Stross' birth had felt like such a day, and I wanted that clarity of vision as my constant life force.

Invariably Mark's seminary experiences would surface, and he'd temper my thinking with cautions about predestination (not something I believed I'd referenced). Then he'd respond to my continued ponderings by listening, baiting me with challenging statements and saying things like: "Joy, I don't think God will tell us exactly what to do or how to do it. I think we can only be assured that He'll be with

···

us no matter the choice we make or what happens to us."

Then I'd say something like: "Well I know that, but I think we can know more than we do if we just pay attention."

Then he'd smile and say: "Just be careful."

The following miles would be driven in silence with Stross asleep, Mark lost in his thoughts and me gazing out the window while engaged in a private conversation with God.

My fascination with God's providence heightened that year after a series of innocent conversations converged. Since moving I'd learned that the man who'd owned Carver's Restaurant and had hired Mark and me as singing waiters had once lived in Forest City. He, Larry Kussatz, had been the high school music teacher. During his tenure he'd had a student teacher named Sandy Fredrickson who had filled his position upon his departure. A few years later she married a man—David Damm—who would eventually become chair of the Waldorf College communications department. He'd help make the decision to hire Mark.

This moment of realization had come when I was unpacking our collection of sheet music. I'd already placed a whole stack of song books on the shelf when I came across a folder filled with music Mark and I had sung at Carver's. Inside I'd also placed some random pieces of music I'd gotten in high school. When I touched one titled "Moving On," I saw something that made my body tingle. Even though I'd seen that piece of music several times over the past decade, I had never noticed that it was stamped: Property of Forest City High School.

Before Mark's interview I'd never been to Forest City or even heard of the town. Still I'd been carrying around a piece of music from its high school for more than 12 years. This song, which spoke of moving and making changes in life, had a connection to the town that preceded mine. I decided to share this oddity with Sandy, wondering if she'd recognize the music. She, now the school district's elementary music teacher, couldn't remember it but asked where I had gotten it.

"I got it from my high school," I'd told her. "The words meant a lot to my music teacher, and when he moved I took a copy so I'd have something to remember him by."

I mentioned that they had attended the same college at about the same time adding, "You may have known him—Aaron Swestka?"

She gave me a look of surprise.

"Really? He was the substitute teacher they hired when I was on maternity leave."

So my high school music teacher had lived in Forest City at some point in his life too. I felt like I'd been used to close a circle—or complete a mission. I wondered if life had assigned me the task of returning music to the place it had been before I'd graduated from high school, gone to college, met Mark, married, lived in three different cities, had a child and then moved to its city of origin.

I saw three ways to interpret my relationship to the music's journey: I could believe all interactions had been pure coincidence; I could believe the music proved I was destined to live in Forest City, and that—unbeknownst to me—this leg of my life's journey had actually started years before; or I could believe that God knew of the music's travels (and its interconnections with people I knew) and then used these things to assure me of His divine presence in my life.

I settled on the last one. I needed to know God was paying attention.

We'd had a great first year in Forest City. Mark was healthy, Stross was happy and I was...well, I was pleased I'd not fallen apart. While I'd left behind a job I loved, my life had not changed as much as I'd feared.

In many ways Mark and I were back to where we'd started the day he'd returned Dr. Lenning's call. We were once again contemplating a second child, and one of us (now me) was exploring additional ways to earn money while staying at home to care for Stross. Having a second child had become a lesser priority in the past year, but it seemed time to revive the topic despite our apprehension. The proposition of creating life scared us for two reasons: We believed the odds were against us for a healthy birth even though common sense told us otherwise, and we were worried about the upheaval a second child might bring into our more settled life.

My desire for more knowledge about our odds increased. We'd gone through genetic counseling after Stross' birth only to learn there was no known genetic link to incidents of spina bifida. A doctor had shared statistics about the frequency of birth defects in general and said that 2.5 percent of all pregnancies end with less than desired results. Since we had been part of that population once, he'd told us, we now doubled our risk with a subsequent pregnancy. He'd also pointed out that double was "only five percent," but I had a hard time getting past the term "double the risk."

After Stross' birth I'd done my own investigation about what researchers believed caused spina bifida, one of several types of neural tube defects. The most commonly tested theory linked it to inadequate levels of folic acid in a mother's system. That factor didn't seem to apply in my case since I'd continued taking prenatal vitamins after our miscarriage. Plus I liked to eat broccoli, and I drank orange juice every day. Both were cited as excellent sources of folic acid.

Other studies were based on a prevailing theory that spina bifida was caused by some factor in the environment (as yet unknown) working against an unknown genetic factor in a parent—most likely the mother. There also were claims of links to people with Scottish heritage or fathers who worked in coalmines or parents who worked with chemicals in printing companies—nothing of significance to us. There seemed to be a cluster of spina bifida babies born in Brownsville, Texas, in the '80s, but many believed that had more to do with a large population of low-income mothers.

The most intriguing study claimed researchers were able to cause spina bifida in brown mice (an animal whose gestation process closely resembles a human) by raising a pregnant mother's body temperature the equivalent of more than 100 degrees in humans. This theory intrigued me because after Stross' birth I was able to think of three specific dates when I'd felt abnormally hot. I had not been ill and had not had a fever, but I'd tried to enjoy summer activities during one of the hottest Augusts on record. It had been my attempt to get past our July miscarriage.

At a backyard barbecue I'd been so hot I'd held my wrists in an ice cooler for soft drinks. Another time I'd kept buying cans of pop from a machine to hold against my wrists and other pulse points while playing miniature golf with our youth. And finally I'd purchased several sno-cones while visiting a zoo—not to eat them but to drizzle the ice down my shirt. Each time I'd say to Mark: "If I could only peel off my skin, I'd feel cool." And, "Why can't I get cool? I never felt this hot during summers in Texas."

Of course I had no idea that—according to my Daytimer®— I'd conceived only days before the first incident. My doctor had advised Mark and me to allow my body to have three menstrual cycles before attempting to become pregnant again, and so, that's what we were doing—I thought. When my period was late after only one cycle, I believed that the stress of preparing for the convention had been the reason, for on the convention's first day, I was five days late. Yet it had not been stress. It had been Stross.

For Baby No. 2's pregnancy, I asserted, we needed to schedule conception.

When Mark and I first discussed having another child, I'd been adamant about not conceiving during summer months. Plus several of Stross' doctors had strongly suggested taking folic acid tablets. I was to take them for three to four months in advance of conceiving. According to the doctors, as a member of the high risk category for spina bifida, I'd need to take a daily dose of 4 mg—four times the recommended dose of 1 mg for normal expectant mothers and 10 times the recommended dose of .4 mg for the rest of the population. After conception I was to continue taking the folic acid at least through the first trimester. I had a hard time believing the prescribed dose wouldn't be toxic itself, but I didn't want to ignore research.

Mark and I agreed to trust our instincts about the timing of a second child and decided to use late summer and early fall as preparation months: I'd prepare physically and both of us would prepare mentally. It was hard to tell if he felt as apprehensive as I did. A few of his comments led me to believe that he was experiencing some of the same feelings but not with the same intensity.

"I'm ready if you are," he'd said.

"Well, aren't you a little scared?" I'd ask.

"Not really. Not about the baby so much, but about us and how it will affect Stross."

We both believed that Stross would benefit more by being an older brother than an only child. In many ways we thought we owed him a sibling—that we'd deprive him if he didn't have one. We also believed the demands of Stross' life would not hinder us from giving a second child all the attention he or she required.

"How do you feel about it?" he'd ask. "You're the one who will have more to do."

Mark knew firsthand the demands of being our family's designated caregiver. He also knew I'd bear the emotional and physical brunt of pregnancy itself.

"If you are up for the challenge, I'll take it on with you," he'd told me one day. "I'd always thought we'd have more than one child, and if we're going to do it, now is the time."

Timing did seem in our favor. I was just shy of 30 years; therefore my biological clock was still wound. Plus, Stross had gone one year without medical upheaval, and Mark had enjoyed a busy but invigorating first year. Taking on new challenges had renewed him. Mark and I had even collaborated on two projects—both promotional videos for the college—for the first time in our professional lives. I'd written the scripts (something I'd never attempted before), and Mark had shot and edited the footage. My other work for the college was scheduled to end just as the final flurry of arrangements for the Lt. Governor's diversity conference began. Once that conference ended, there would be no other obligations to distract me from thinking baby. Therefore, I could take vitamins through the fall, hope to enjoy a successful conference in October, and Mark and I could hope to conceive about Thanksgiving, provided things went as planned.

We decided to ask about the folic acid prescription at Stross' August appointment in Iowa City, thinking that would be our big news at his checkup. However when the report of Stross' urine sample came back, the urologist's recommendation surpassed our news. Stross' urine had an unusually high level of bacteria. The indication of infection, supported by our report of increased incidents of diaper rash, meant it was time to begin our three year old on a program of intermittent catherization. Because we'd avoided the need for this standard procedure for three years, we'd believed medical odds had fallen in our favor for once.

No, the doctor explained. Stross' bacteria levels were too high. He had an infection that had gone undetected because of his lack of sensation. It was time for us to protect Stross' kidneys from infection by helping him totally empty his bladder five to six times each day. We'd be taught to empty it, the doctor said, by inserting a catheter through his penis every four hours.

"Of course," he said, "you will need to teach Stross to do this when he gets older so he can be more independent, and then you won't have to do it anymore."

No, we wouldn't, I thought. But our son will. Stross had just been given a life sentence for intermittent catherization. In an instant our lives had changed forever—yet again. According to the doctor, we'd start our lessons immediately, using supplies they'd ordered for us. A nurse was already in the room ready to teach us how to perform the procedure. I felt like I was being asked to politely follow a bailiff to a cell where I'd spend the rest of my life. There was no time for questions or second guessing. There was no time for tears. It was already 4 p.m.—almost the end of a full day of appointments. The nurse explained that after we observed her performing the procedure on Stross, she would watch each of us do it to be certain we used proper technique, and then we'd be free to go.

"However," she said to introduce an afterthought, "I may run out of time to watch you both, so why don't you pick who I'll observe, and then that person can teach the other."

I looked at Mark, and then, before giving him a chance to speak, I quickly volunteered. I knew I'd have questions, and I knew it would be easier for me to ask them of medical professionals than of Mark who had already begun to sweat profusely. Stross was Daddy's boy—Mark's "Little Man." Mark would need as much time as possible to convince himself that what we were being asked to do was truly in Stross' best interests.

My primary concern about the catherization procedure was that Stross understood we were still his loving Mommy and Daddy even though we were doing something that nurses usually did. Stross had come to associate lab coats and vinyl gloves with pain. As soon as he spotted someone who looked like they might be coming to draw blood, he'd start to grab for either Mark or me and rhythmically call out in an anguished tone, "No, no, no, no, no, no." I needed to know that Stross understood we were not going to hurt him.

"Do we have to wear gloves?" I asked.

"No. That's not necessary. We wear them for our own protection, but this is a clean cath—not a sterile cath—so as long as you wash your hands thoroughly, you don't need gloves," the nurse said.

She had aligned the supplies we would need on a tray next to the exam table where Stross sat immediately to Mark's right. She talked us through what each item was and how it was used. Stross looked intently each time she'd lift something for our inspection. He didn't appear worried, probably because soon after we'd learned of our collective fate, Mark had placed his right arm around Stross and had not let go. When her introductory lecture finished, Mark looked down at the top of Stross' light-brown head and whispered an audible, "I'm so sorry, Buddy."

Stross looked up at him, questioning, and I snapped my head in Mark's direction with enough forceful movement to divert Stross' attention from Mark. Stross looked at me; Mark looked at me too. I gave Mark my version of a stern teacher-stare as if to ask, "What do you think you're doing? Stop!"

The nurse asked if I was ready and invited me to lay Stross down and remove his diaper. She then reminded me to wash my hands thoroughly again before starting. I felt like keeping my hands under the warm water forever. However Stross absolutely hated lying down on a medical exam table, and he had begun to realize this wasn't an ordinary diaper change. So I tried to wash thoroughly but quickly.

Mark offered toys, but Stross wasn't at all interested. So Mark began to coo to Stross, making comments about where we would eat and what we would do when we left. His attempts to distract worked to some degree, but Mark's tone sounded sad. Because Stross' instincts were sharp, he scanned the room to see what I was doing, then looked for Mark's eyes. Stross stopped trying to wrench his hands free only after I dried my hands and came back. I stood in position to the right of Stross' body—his head to my left—then I started to make my own distractive comments that sounded intentionally upbeat.

"I'm back, Kiddo. Hey, we're gonna learn something new today. Mommy is going to listen to the directions. If I do something wrong, you let me know, okay?" I wondered if Stross recognized I always asked him questions when I was nervous. "It's not supposed to hurt, but you let me know if it does, okay? Do you want to help?"

Stross *loved* to help. Even the nurse seemed to notice he had brightened at my invitation, and so she handed him something he could hand me—the urine cup. Mark's banter with Stross grew more intentional, and after I began the first step, I spoke only to ask clarifying questions such as: "Is this right?" or "This way?" or "Like this?" Each time the nurse offered encouragement.

Even filling a small syringe with lubricating jelly didn't cause great anxiety. The hard part mentally was inserting the lubricating jelly into his penis then inserting the catheter. Stross was growing restless, and even though the nurse assured me that Stross had reduced sensation and couldn't feel the catheter, I had a hard time believing it. I could not stop myself from imaging how it felt. She encouraged me to push the catheter in farther than I felt comfortable. Mark evidently was empathizing too, for he had visibly winched and blown air out of his mouth like a pregnant woman in labor. As the catheter started to disappear into our son's body, Mark—with his hands still holding Stross' hands—laid his head down on his forearms just off to the side of Stross' left leg. Then Mark began to nervously tap his foot and shake his leg, as if that could discard his feelings.

"Ugh, I can't stand it," he said, his head still face down against Stross' leg.

"Maaarrk… " I drew out his name in a forceful but quiet tone. Seconds later the nurse lifted her hand to indicate I should stop. She believed the catheter had passed through the entire urethra and into the bladder.

"There. That's enough," she said. "We should see some return soon. Why don't you sit up, Stross? That will help."

Mark simultaneously lifted his head and released his grip on Stross' arms. The nurse helped Stross into position, and then Stross—without prompting—set the cup between his thighs and smiled at me, pleased that he'd been such a good helper.

"Hey, thanks, Stross. That's right," I said. The nurse added her encouragement. Stross beamed.

"All done?" Stross asked.

"Almost," the nurse said, smiling back at him.

That's when I began to wipe tears from the inside corners of my eyes. My son had offered me a gift. My son was a gift. He had helped me do something I'd never imagined. I'd worried my new role would destroy his ability to trust me. Yet he—through the simple gesture of handing me a cup—let me know we continued to travel as trusted companions.

"You're amazing, Kiddo," I told him.

"Darn right," Mark said with more force than necessary.

The nurse walked me through the final steps, then asked us if we had any questions.

"You're gonna be fine," she said to Mark. "Joy can walk you through it whenever you're ready, and if you have any questions or run into any problems, just call."

"Oh, he's gonna do the next one," I announced to both the nurse and Mark.

"Yes, Joy. I hear you. I already planned to," said Mark.

"Well...I...well, we're gonna take turns, don't you think?"

"Joy, I'll do them all if I need to once you teach me."

"Oh, no. Turns are okay," I said. "They're only fair."

I started to hear what I sounded like. I was treating my son like a project or a task in contrast to Mark's benevolence.

"Joy, let's just get going."

The agony of Mark's first time was four hours away, just prior

• • •

to Stross' bedtime. Instead of driving to Forest City, we cut our trip in half by stopping at Mark's parents for the night. That gave us the luxury of performing our first unsupervised cath—Mark's very first—in a clean bathroom and not some public rest room between Iowa City and our home.

During dinner at Mark's parents, we shared the news of our day. Both Mark and I picked at our food and spoke in tired tones that told how defeated we felt. Our late meal was cut short by the clock because at 8 p.m. we needed to take Stross upstairs for his catherization and then put him to bed.

I concentrated on fulfilling my responsibility of teaching him what the nurse had taught me. Mark was clearly more nervous than I had been.

"I'll do this, Joy," he asserted. "Just don't mess with me."

Since we didn't have a medical exam table, we laid down a bath towel, positioned ourselves cross-legged by Stross then turned the floor of their guest bathroom into our work area. I simultaneously distracted Stross while guiding Mark through his preparation steps. Stross was tired and seemed a little bored with all the attention we'd been giving his diaper changes. His only curiosity appeared to be Daddy's strange behavior.

Mark was breathing heavily and talking to himself. Large patches of sweat were now visible under each arm of Mark's dark shirt. He barely noticed that Stross was helping him as much as he'd helped me. For the next 10 minutes we collaborated, supporting Mark through each step. When Mark finished, he gently slid out the catheter then flopped backward onto the bathroom floor with his eyes shut and his hands flailed straight out above his head.

"Oh, God. It's over," he said. "I'm done. Thank you, God. Thank you."

Mark's behavior startled me, and I worried that it would scare Stross. Stross still needed a new diaper, so I turned him to face me, smiled at him, then finished as if everything was normal. I carried him into our bedroom and laid him on the bed before returning to Mark.

"Honey, are you okay?"

"Just leave me alone a little bit. I made it," he said.

"Well, don't get too excited," I cautioned Mark. "You're up again in a matter of hours."

I regretted the words as soon as they spilled out of my mouth. Retraction was impossible. Mark opened his eyes and gave me the full benefit of his irritation.

"You know, Joy," he shot at me. "You could have gone without saying that. I know this isn't really over. I know it's a lifetime thing. Can't you just give me this moment now?"

"I'm sorry, Honey. It's just that Stross doesn't seem to mind as much as we do, so maybe we need to take our cue from him."

If Mark's weakness was excessive empathy, mine was minimalist sympathy—and not knowing when to keep my mouth shut.

"Joy. Just be quiet," Mark implored. "This is not an easy thing— especially something for a guy to do to another guy. Stross is just too little to know yet. We guys are just not used to putting things in our bodies like women are."

I burst into laughter despite possible repercussions.

"Well, laugh if you want," he told me (and I did want). "That's how I feel."

We both went to bed soon after—me with a stay of eight hours before the next cath procedure (at bedtime, the time interval doubled) and Mark with a full 12. Our verbal warfare indicated how trapped we felt. We couldn't be as free with our family's daily schedule anymore. Our days were now divided into four-hour segments. Any plans we made for travel or work or fun had to take Stross' cath schedule into account. And because baby-sitters didn't know how to do the catherization, we couldn't leave Stross with anyone for more than four hours at a time.

As we adjusted to this restriction, Mark and I kept our shared schedule for several months with us shifting times so he could take his turns before and after work. After a full month we did feel comfortable performing Stross' caths—nearly as comfortable as we did changing his ostomy. But two more surprises soon added even more stress to my baby preparation months.

•••

Just before Labor Day we took Stross to Des Moines for two appointments: an ophthalmology exam in the morning and his annual neurosurgical checkup in the afternoon. At the eye exam the doctor confirmed something I'd suspected since Stross' birth: Stross' eyes were crossed. I'd been asking each of his physicians about the possibility since his birth, but each had cautioned me "to not be hypersensitive to things being wrong." Being right was small consolation now.

Because the bridge of his nose was tiny, Stross' eyes appeared close-set. Therefore his strabismus had been difficult to detect. This physician was a trained pediatric ophthalmologist with instruments that could determine the truth. Even she admitted to being surprised at the degree of misalignment. If we wanted to give Stross a chance to use his eyes together, or in stereo, we needed to schedule surgery to have them straightened. We were probably too late already, she said, but statistics showed that children had a better chance of correction and achieving the ability for depth perception if surgery were performed before age five. Plus, she reminded us, it was a cosmetic issue; and kids could be cruel. Other children might tease a child because his eyes looked different.

Our child, we knew, was already different enough. We decided we needed to schedule the eighth surgery of Stross' life for October.

After that appointment we headed to the familiar office of Stross' neurosurgeon. Everything was routine—the questioning, the measuring, the examination of his spinal closure site. Nothing happened to further aggravate us until the doctor—offhandedly— asked what we'd been told about the notation in Stross' chart about possible microcephalous. Mark looked at me. Before I answered I ran a terminology check in my head: if hydrocephalus meant "water on the brain," microcephalous had to mean "small head." No one had told us anything of the kind. We knew he was small overall but nothing disproportionate.

"Why do you ask?" I questioned.

"Oh, no reason," he said. "It's just noted here, and I wondered what you'd been told."

"Well, does he have microcephalous?" I asked.

"His head is rather small," he said. "But usually there is a big

···

difference between body size and head size with microcephalous. We'll have to wait and see how he grows. As long as he grows proportionately, he'll be fine."

Mark and I couldn't get Stross out of there fast enough. We just wanted to take him home, far away from doctors who might tell us more things we might need to do with him or to him. Inside our car Mark, sitting in the driver's seat, started to laugh in a release of emotion. Then he started to laugh a strange, weird laugh that caused me to laugh nervously too. Stross began to laugh at both of us. I hoped he believed we were laughing about some big hilarious joke. Everything did seem preposterous. Stross was our adorable little boy—not some physical anomaly.

Mark spoke through uncomfortable giggles.

"This morning we had to watch a video with kids in it who couldn't catch a ball because they were so cross-eyed they'd let it hit their faces," he said, bubbling with odd laughter. "Now this afternoon some doctor tells us our son might grow up to be a cartoon creature with a big body but a pea-sized head."

"Ahhgghh. What's next?" Mark asked, then stopped laughing. We all stopped.

All of a sudden Mark exhaled a huge gasp of air that sounded like he'd emptied his chest completely. He then threw his head back and yelled to God through the ceiling of our car.

"I'm tired of the surprises," he shouted. "Can't you just give it all to me at once?"

Our ride home was quiet. We both needed time to think and absorb all that had happened to us that day and every day since our visit to Iowa City only weeks earlier. Less than one hour into our drive, a colorful bumper sticker on a car in front of us caught my attention. It read: "Expect a miracle." Somehow I knew it was a message for us, and I hoped it was our indication that—despite accumulating distractions—we should forge ahead with Baby No. 2.

It seemed that—on this day—the truth of our helplessness became undeniable. But what were we helpless about? And did helplessness advance hopelessness? It seemed it could if we weren't careful.

Fortunately things—somehow—were still right in our world. Perhaps three years of parenthood had honed our ability to adapt. For that great credit was due Stross, our educational collaborator. He personified the power of helpless submission. Like a reed in the wind, he swayed with life's rhythm. And like a violin bow, he helped tight strings sing. Both Mark and I were better because of him. We could move and even sing in spite of ourselves. Stross had shown us how to navigate recklessly shifting streams and how to find currents that could move you forward while enjoying the ride itself.

"No all-done. Go, Mommy!"

Stross knew that just driving around to take in new surroundings didn't mean you weren't going anywhere. It was an important part of gathering information for the next trip. We couldn't let ourselves tire of the surprises.

Every person, every day awakens to face truths uncovered in previously unknown moments. We were no different. Each day had brought us lessons whose meanings could only be known in the fullness of time. Therefore helplessness was an unwillingness to move forward, and hopelessness was merely its consequence.

We could rid ourselves of hopelessness forever, it seemed, if we could learn how to welcome every moment as we had welcomed Stross from birth.

A few Sundays later I heard a solution that came as a promise of restoration. As I sat in a pew between Mark and Stross, I experienced the magnitude of God's presence filling me from the inside and overtaking my feelings of futility. It happened as I joined with the congregation to sing, but then stopped just to listen. They were singing a simple benediction. I'd heard it only a few times before, but I'd never heard it as I did that day. As the lyrics spilled forth, all I could do was quietly weep and feel my body fill with an indescribable blessing.

The lyrics spoke of God's ability to touch humans through love—a feeling I'd experienced when alone and in the midst of others. And the words invited God's spirit to fill my life with joy—a feeling I'd known countless times as well. Hearing the lyrics—in that moment, that day and in that way—reminded me that I could trust God. And in doing so

I would find "peace and sweet release." God seemed to be pointing me in the direction of hope once again. God seemed to be calling: "Let me fill you from the inside so your life can overflow in powerful witness to what I have done, what I am doing and what I promise to do."

All I had to do was rest in the knowledge of that power-filled love—and abide.

With each lyric I grew with understanding that—just as the song said—I could walk by faith in what God had already done. I could not deny the experiences I'd lived through, nor could I deny that I'd felt God's spirit as a permeating presence. Therefore I had to accept the truth that God would permeate any life-altering experiences I'd encounter no matter what. I thought I'd known that. I'd even said it aloud to others. But as I filled with his gentle spirit that day, a sense of peace overcame the doubt I'd denied.

I didn't like admitting it, but I had doubted that I could bear a healthy child; and I had felt more prepared for something to go wrong with a subsequent pregnancy than for things to go right. Of two pregnancies, only one had resulted in the birth of a child; and he'd been born with congenital defects. Subsequently I'd lost confidence in my childbearing abilities.

So many fears and doubts had accumulated that they had become my expectations. I had convinced myself that lowered expectations better aligned me with God's providence—my lot in life.

Now a sense of peace replaced the doubt. I had to accept it as part of my journey as I moved from helplessness toward hope. Who, given our circumstances, wouldn't have doubts? Why did I feel it was necessary to prove anything? I knew I could be a good mother to another child born with special needs or even to one born without them. Did I really believe I could determine the health of the child I would bear? I could only accept my doubts and acknowledge them as milestones. They didn't have to keep me from the joy our second child would bring—birth defects or not.

Besides being the mother of a child with disabilities did not have to be the only way I'd experience motherhood. In fact I needed to prepare for the possibility that it wouldn't. So as the music played

I allowed myself to feel what it was like to abound with hope. I accepted the child we'd yet to conceive. I also accepted the song's invitation to simply rest and abide.

As the congregation sang through the lyrics a second time, I relaxed and cried. The tears rid me of my helplessness, making room for abundant hope. I now knew that I would find—that I had found—peace through believing. I would be touched by love in all circumstances. And so I gave myself permission to relinquish control. I'd succumbed to hope and in the process found joy.

•  •  •

# Chapter 29

# Getting Real

• • •

Life got easier that fall. Stross' eye surgery in October was the first big surgery he'd had since our move to Forest City. As we prepared for the overnight trip to Des Moines, new friends and colleagues shared cards and comments of support. Unlike our private transition into daily catherizations, we felt publicly reinforced for the hassles of this medical hindrance. And while the surgery did not result in Stross getting stereo vision, it did straighten his eyes.

Stross' surgery also affirmed the existence of a new base of support. Dozens of phone calls to friends in Des Moines and continued correspondence had assured us that our old base of support still existed, but we'd had no crisis since our move to verify the new one. Now we knew we had made friends, and the friends we'd made cared for us and our son. That knowledge made it fun to think about how our next child would be welcomed. So I began to tell everyone I thought would care: The Newcoms are planning to have a baby. I felt it only fair to warn others that my mind was preoccupied with pregnancy. I also felt it necessary—when the time was right—to tell Lt. Governor Corning. While I hadn't made a firm decision about staying involved with the diversity committee's work, I knew I could not be involved to the same degree.

A few weeks after the conference ended, I made one of my

• • •

solo trips to Des Moines for a committee meeting. Afterward the Lt. Governor invited me into her office. She wanted to give me a thank you gift and talk about my plans. I'd already told her the association had indicated they were no longer willing to finance my involvement. In effect my former boss was tired of financing the committee's conference planner. Without financial support, I'd had to bear the cost of participating myself; and the Lt. Governor understood the burden that placed on our family. In her office that November she conveyed how pleased she was with my work and the conference's success. To ensure that it would continue as an annual event, she wanted me to think about a proposal.

"Joy, I'd really like you to be able to stay on to help," she said. "The conference looks like it will be a continued success, and I believe we have shown that we can obtain enough donor support to keep it affordable for community leaders and yet hire an event planner."

I agreed with her assessment then braced for what I felt coming.

"Joy," she continued, "I'd like you to consider taking the position as our conference planner. In many ways you created this conference and understand it better than anyone. You would be our first choice, and I think we'd be able to offer you a substantial fee."

She then told me the approximate fee and explained the additional work that would be expected. She also shared her plan to foster growth by forging relationships with other organizations.

"That probably means more time in Des Moines," she said, "but you've already shown how a lot of the planning can be done long distance. Take time to think about it, then let me know."

The fee alone could have made the decision easy. I was basically being asked to do the same work—with only a few additional duties and a little more travel—but get paid for the work. The amount was far more than my other freelance jobs combined. However, even as I sat in her stately office, I knew I had to tell her no. I'd nearly completed three months of folic acid, and within the month Mark and I planned to begin trying to conceive another child. I wanted time to baby myself, giving my body every opportunity to bear a healthy child. So that's what I told the Lt. Governor. I shared our

• • •

family planning efforts and, sensing her personal interest in my wellbeing, described my mental state and how having a second baby had surpassed my desires to do anything else.

"Joy, I certainly understand where you are coming from and wish you all the best," she said. "I want you to know I have admired the way you have combined being Stross' mother with all the other things you do. I know it can't be easy."

Her flattery caught me off-guard. I searched for an appropriate response, then settled on mumbling, "Thanks." Uncomfortable with her unexpected affirmation, I launched into an awkward litany about Mark's support and "not really a choice" and "so fortunate for how things have worked out." It was the kind of response that can make the flatterer sorry they offered a compliment in the first place. When I paused for what appeared the end of my speech, she took on a more reflective tone to ask, "Do you mind if I ask you a very personal question?"

"No, I don't mind," I said eagerly.

"If you would have known that Stross had birth defects before he was born, do you think you would have considered having an abortion?"

The question wasn't new to me but quite bold for someone in her position. Close friends and college students had basically asked Mark and me the same question during discussions about abortion and the right-to-life movement. Because her political opinions made headlines, I began my answer slowly.

"Honestly…I'd have to say I don't know," I told her. "I'd like to think that I knew what I would have done, and I'd like to think that I would not have aborted a child I knew had defects."

She nodded, listening carefully.

"But in the past few years, I've learned that no one can know for certain how they would react in any given situation. You can't know until something happens to you. You can speculate based on who you are now, but you can never go back fully remembering who you were then."

She nodded either as a sign of agreement or as indication that she was listening. It felt like I should continue, so I did.

I told her how I was a very different person today than I was before Stross was born. And how, back then, I had chosen not to have a simple blood test that would have let us know about Stross' spina bifida. I wanted her to know that I now believed that had not been wise—that I now encouraged anyone to take advantage of as much prenatal testing as possible. Those who choose to be parents, I told her, need to understand their roles begin before birth. Had we known, I added, I'd like to think we'd have used the information to plan for Stross' birth accordingly—to schedule his surgeries and choose his doctors instead of leaving it to fate.

"Truthfully," I said, "I think I chose not to take the blood test because I didn't want to know the bad information it might have told me. At the time I said I didn't need it because it wouldn't change anything, but I think I didn't want it because I didn't want to face the possibility that I might not react the way I believed I would. Does that make sense?"

"Sure, it does, and it's very honest of you."

"I don't know how not to be honest about that," I continued. "When I hear strong pro-life advocates now, I find myself wanting to know if they've ever been in a situation where they felt helpless about a child they carried inside their body. And I also have a hard time hearing men talk about it. I know how intense the emotions are when it comes to having a baby or even thinking about having a baby. It's something I couldn't even explain to Mark."

"And you are on the brink of feeling all of that again," she said. "I agree with you, Joy, that too many people don't empathize enough with the woman's point-of-view. It is such a huge decision for a woman to have a child these days."

There was a slight silence, but I didn't want our conversation to end. I wanted this woman I respected—this politician—to know exactly how I felt.

"I know without a doubt what I would—what we would do this time. If we find out our next child has birth defects, there is no way we'd have an abortion."

"Why's that?" she asked. "Because you've seen what a blessing Stross is?"

"In part. He's certainly a blessing, and I'm confident I'm a better person today because of him," I said. "But if I had an abortion because I carried a child that was 'less than perfect,' what would that say to Stross? That's something Mark and I don't want him to consider."

"What do you mean?" she asked.

"If we aborted that child," I said, "what would keep Stross from thinking, 'Well if my mom and dad had known about me, they'd have decided not to have me either'? "

She nodded in understanding so I continued, daring to touch on more political aspects of the topic. She made the conversation easy by sharing as much as I did. We acknowledged that the abortion issue was one of the most difficult topics on which to take a position—political or otherwise—and shared convictions about it as a woman's issue. We also both acknowledged that the topic may never be legislated in a way that would not result in polarization.

I respected her ability to ask a hard question and to discuss a difficult topic in a manner that evoked true dialogue. I was also grateful that her question had challenged me to explain feelings that had crystallized into beliefs. I'd not articulated before how my experiences had made so many issues more real. While driving home I thought about how much Stross' life had reshaped my views on a variety of political issues: insurance reform, access to health care, government waiver programs, rights for the disabled and now abortion.

I believed Stross' birth, as incredibly powerful as it was, had not wreaked total havoc in my life because of my faith. But faith wasn't something I could give to someone else. I could share it, but not give it. And faith didn't seem to be one-size-fits-all. If I needed to insist that others believed as I believed and did as I did, wouldn't my faith lack integrity? Wouldn't I be insisting that they trust in me—in my faith—rather than entrust their lives to God?

My tested faith now allowed me to trust in others' abilities to follow their own spiritual guiding as surely as my faith had guided me. I could only share my story as I had shared it with the

Lt. Governor—not just during one conversation in her office, but during all the conversations and experiences we'd shared. Spiritual messages were God's to deliver in God's time and God's way.

If my life or my words were to be the catalyst for someone else's divine message, they would know; and I might not know it at all. In fact the message might be clearer without me in its way.

I was learning how spiritual messages and their methods of arrival could vary greatly. I'd gotten them while scared, angry, frustrated, joyous, quiet and concerned as well as in the midst of countless other emotions brought on by both mundane and life-changing situations.

And between messages I was learning to abide.

It seemed to me that if I ever felt the need to declare: "God told me to tell you…" I'd also need to ask myself who in the world I believed I was. God?

That day I became aware that—since Stross' birth—something significant had started without me noticing. I'd begun to understand that the greatest risk to my faith lay in not trusting God to be God.

•  •  •

# Chapter 30

# Walking Lessons

...

Now that another academic year was well underway, Mark kept busy with classes and implementing plans for a multimedia lab and a radio station. He had gotten permission to proceed after the college received a substantial donation from John K. Hanson, the founder of Winnebago Industries. Suddenly Mark was researching and ordering more audio equipment than he knew what to do with. But for him that seemed to make the challenge more dynamic. He had the privilege of learning and then teaching others. The buttons and busses of an audio board became his personal playground—the gift of a dream.

Mark walked to and from campus daily, moving in a way that reflected how he felt: invigorated and vitally alive. Stross and I ventured to campus regularly too. Constant companions, we used these stroller or wagon rides as times to talk about anything I could think of that might help expand his vocabulary. Most of the time I kept a running commentary about my observations of the neighborhood.

With my duties on the Lt. Governor's committee over, I shifted my energies to Stross, the public relation class I taught and reading material about pregnancy. I always made sure I had something to read—textbook, magazine, pregnancy manual—whenever I thought I might be left waiting. I strongly disliked waiting. But that's what I'd been doing several times a week in the waiting room of Stross' physical therapy clinic. After the move we'd wasted no time in identifying a local physical therapist (in addition to the AEA's physical therapist) who was willing to work with a pediatric client with special needs. We had not wanted to lose any ground he had—*we* had—gained. If his muscles were capable, we wanted to help Stross learn to walk.

Stross' earliest PT sessions had been painful—not so much physically for him, but mentally for me. Week after week I invented new ways to bribe him—at two and one-half years—to at least stand near his walker with our hands supporting him. Eventually we offered bribes that coaxed him into actually standing inside the walker and touching its cold frame.

Moving the walker forward was never a natural inclination for Stross—not in those first sessions—not when he preferred cruising around our home on all fours. His engaging personality and small stature made it easy to push the limits of socially acceptable crawling. And walking wasn't a need for Stross either. Mark and I transported him through the grocery store, shopping malls, in and out of restaurants and anywhere else we went. Wherever our schedule took us, Stross was carried along.

Therapy sessions became a battleground of wills. We wanted Stross to understand why it was important for him to learn to use a walker. He wanted us to know he wasn't interested—not in the least. Sometimes a stick of gum served as incentive for difficult PT days. If Stross walked the clinic hallway with his walker, he understood that afterward he could chew gum—and have the thrill of unwrapping it. On special occasions, when he worked past the time it was comfortable, I found myself offering even greater rewards: a quarter to ride the toy carousel at a local department store; an ice cream cone at Hardees; or a family dinner of pizza.

Stross soon learned that leaning against the inside of the walker gave him a momentary rest period, and he tried to use these rests to shorten his PT session. To manage this inventive avoidance behavior, the therapist suggested using a more unstable forward-facing version of his walker. He explained that this would, in effect, knock Stross off balance and force him to focus. So during the next several sessions, Stross held onto a miniature version of something typically seen in a nursing home. It was cute in the way miniature things can be cute. I only wished it, and all the other devices he needed, were not requirements for his freedom of mobility.

While Stross didn't like the uneasiness of the unruly walker, it did bring his attention back to matters at hand: learning to balance and willing his body into proper position. The expressions of disbelief he sent my way seemed to inquire, "How can you let him (the therapist) make me use this thing? I'm not comfortable, Mom. Fix it."

"Sorry, Kiddo," I'd telepath back. "This is good for you."

In the beginning Stross resisted using any walker for nearly one year. Then December came, and a lot of things changed. First Mark and I agreed to meet with Georgia Langerud, the director of Happy Time Preschool, to talk about Stross attending her 3-year-old sessions on Tuesdays and Thursdays. Yvonne Nutting, the childhood special education teacher we'd been assigned by the AEA, had been an advocate for our desire to fully include Stross in a regular classroom. Von, as she encouraged us to call her, had allowed us to decide when it would be appropriate to introduce him to a classroom setting. Only months earlier, I'd actually told her—very plainly—that I wasn't ready. She had been extremely supportive, understanding and empathetic. But in December she'd learned of an opening at Happy Time and thought it'd be a great opportunity for us to start "just exploring the possibilities."

"Okay," I'd told her, "but I don't think we're ready."

"I know," said Von, "and that's what you can decide. We don't even have to have the meeting. I just thought it'd be a great chance for you to meet the teachers and visit the school."

So we went to the after-school meeting. To Mark's and my surprise Stross soaked up the school environment like a dry sponge. We'd brought his walker and had encouraged him to use it, but there was too much to see. Stross didn't want the work of using the walker to take away from the fun of playing with toys. To him the walker took too much time. So instead he crawled over to look at the hamster in his cage, the fish in their tank, the dress-up clothes in their storage box, the pretend food in the toy kitchen, the books on the shelves and the chalk in the chalkboard tray. Once at a destination, he'd pull himself to a standing position to grab something of interest, then drop to the floor to examine it.

Somehow the bright colors and shapes of the Happy Time classroom helped us see our son in a new way. He was practically a preschooler. In fact we couldn't explain why we'd thought he couldn't be a preschooler already. He appeared interested in all the things preschoolers did. When he chose to speak, he sounded like a preschooler. Sitting at the tiny table, I feared that maybe I was holding him back.

"Hey, buddy," Mark called. "You need to learn to use your walker so you can come play here with the other boys and girls."

Stross looked at Mark and smiled with his chin poised defiantly.

"That's right," I agreed. "You start working on that and you can come to school here."

Stross said nothing. He liked playing school at home, but we had no indication of how he'd received our challenge. As the meeting ended I told the director, who was also the lead teacher, that we'd think about taking the opening but most likely we'd call her back to say, no. She told us to "take a week or so," but that she'd need to offer the opening to another child if we didn't plan to use it.

That Sunday we traveled to my parents' home and took Stross into church using his walker. To our surprise he finally treated it like the mode of transportation it was intended to be. Once we set him on course, he headed straight down the center aisle following my parents to a pew near the front.

"I didn't know Stross could use his walker so well," Mom whispered to me as we sat down.

"I didn't either," I confessed.

Back in Forest City I told Mark that I believed Stross was trying to tell us he was ready for preschool. He listened to my theory and encouraged me to call Happy Time and let the director know we'd take the opening. I called Von first and ran the idea by her. She was surprised. At the informational meeting I'd sounded like a mom who was reluctant to let her child grow up too quickly. During this call I sounded like a woman ready to kick her offspring out the door.

"What's different now?" she asked.

"Stross. He started using his walker, and I think being with other kids his age will make him want to use it more," I said. "I think he's letting us know it's time."

"Alright," said Von. "Do you want to call the school or should I?"

"I can."

"Are you planning to start during the first week of January?"

"I guess so."

"I want you to know," said Von, "I'll miss him a lot."

Miss him? She couldn't really mean that because Stross would be going to school, she would no longer come to our home? But she did. Von explained that it was time for Stross to meet Deb Price, the wife of the council member I'd met in Des Moines. Like Von, Deb would check on Stross, but she would be doing it at the preschool. In essence, Stross and I were losing Von and gaining Deb.

"Well, maybe we should wait until fall," I said. "I guess there's no reason for us to be in a hurry."

"No, Joy," said Von. "You're the mom and you know best. If you believe Stross is ready, he probably is."

I knew I didn't want to hold Stross back. If he began school now, he could begin making friends. Mark and I knew Stross would need friends as he grew. Plus by starting preschool now we'd have the rest of the 3-year-old year and all of the 4-year-old year to determine if he was ready for kindergarten. Mark and I understood that kindergarten readiness was the greater issue. The crew of educators and therapists who'd been coming to our home for years had all shared that goal with us. Sending Stross to preschool too early was less a danger than sending him to kindergarten too early.

"I guess I'm just a little nervous," I said. "Can we plan to have you help him get used to it? I mean, this will be the first time he spends time away from Mark or me. Can you go with him for the first month?"

• • •

The class only met two days a week. I thought eight days seemed a reasonable time period for his transition.

"Well…," said Von, hesitantly. "I think it won't take as long as you think. I'm sure he'll feel comfortable there within a few days. Plus he'll have Deb visiting, and both preschool teachers will help him adjust."

"I know. It's just—you know him best," I said. I found it hard to begin sharing my son with so many others.

Von heard my need for empathy. "I promise I won't leave him before he's ready. But I think your instincts are right, Joy. I think he's ready too."

Mark and I prepared for the holidays knowing we'd have a preschooler in our home after the New Year. A few days before Christmas I began to suspect 1995 would be a memorable year for another reason. My period was late—only by three days, but like the only other two times I'd been late, my body felt slightly bloated. I was wiser this time. I told Mark we needed to take a longer route to my parents' home for our family celebration. The route included a stop at my preferred gynecologist.

After an exam confirmed a slightly enlarged uterus, the doctor ordered a blood test to confirm I was pregnant and promised the results would be ready later that day. We finished our trip to my parents' home but arrived too late to call the doctor's office. Very early the next day I called his number and heard the nurse's declaration: "Merry Christmas. It's positive."

I was quiet.

"At least I think that means a Merry Christmas for you."

"Yes, it does," I assured her. "Thank you."

I was extremely calm—too matter-of-fact about what I'd heard. I relayed the information to Mark, then together we told my mom— who cried and then went to tell my dad.

Mark seemed much more elated than I did. I was scared. I was pregnant again, and I wasn't sure how I felt about it. Presents and dinners and travel plans provided plenty of distractions. I cried later in the day, but I wasn't sure why.

Stross maintained his motivation for walking through the holidays. After we returned to Forest City, we sought out places for him to practice. The long hallways of the college were excellent practice grounds. Drinking fountains, elevator buttons, sunny windows and offices with candy dishes pulled steps out of him we didn't know he had. Soon he was known by name to nearly every student on campus.

"Hey, Stross. Give me 'five,' Buddy."

"Wow. Look at you go, Stross!"

"You are really moving that thing, Big Guy."

"Hey, Stross. Come here. Come look at this."

These big "friends" were sufficient motivation to get our 3-year-old moving. Soon speed seemed to be his goal, and he kicked out with a military march that left us looking for a way to protect his spine from the backlash of his stride. Moving at top speed, Stross could bang the back of his walker against his backbone with such force it'd leave a bright red mark. We protected him from his unruly technique by placing a bicycle pad over the walker's back bar.

Once preschool started I found myself wanting to protect him from other things as well—namely the unknown challenges of being the most obviously different kid in the classroom. In addition to helping Stross feel welcomed, Mrs. Langerud went out of her way to help me feel at ease. Each day she told me how Stross' day had gone and took time to write a note that I could place in a scrapbook she knew I'd created for him. The first day's note read:

> *Joy and Mark:*
>
> *Stross ate most of his treats—seemed to like the M&M's® in the cookie!*
>
> *He sat through 'Show & Tell' real well. With only one child left to go he said to Von 'Let's go!'*
>
> *We sang 'My Thumbs are Starting to Wiggle' and 'If You're Happy and You Know It.' We can give you copies of our songs if you desire, so you can sing/play along with Stross.*

• • •

*He also sat quietly during story time and seemed to enjoy it. We're off to a good start.*

I treasured her note. It allowed me to see what my child had done when I had not been with him—and all the things sounded so normal. It was easier to believe my son could go to school and be just like the other kids.

Her next note confessed that:

*Stross cried a little when Mom left—maybe one minute! He then played with the Legos® and didn't mention it again.*

This note also mentioned that Von had left him one-half hour earlier than the previous time. I knew that meant she was weaning him from her emotional support. I knew I was being weaned as well. By the fifth class time, Stross was on his own. That day's note read:

*Stross had a wonderful day! He had a job today and smiled all the while he held the American flag for the pledge.*

*When he had 'Show & Tell,' he was very verbal—as he pulled out the baby Jesus from his bag, I asked, 'Who is that?' and he turned and looked at me with a look sort of like, 'What do you mean, Lady?' Then he said, 'Here's Mary, and Joseph is down here somewhere.'*

*He is very observant and doesn't miss a thing!*

*Also, on his paper today, he started a whole table making dots on their papers (loud!). He said he wanted to make stars, and everyone followed his lead!*

It was clear Stross had made a successful transition. He was a preschooler now, and I was the mom of a preschooler with a baby on the way. During one of my conversations with Mrs. Langerud—Georgia—I told her our family's news. She seemed genuinely excited for us. She was also excited about something else. During one of her conversations with the agency teacher, she'd learned we shared a common friend: Lt. Governor Joy Corning. They had been classmates in college and still got together from time to time for the kind of reunions close friends plan to feel young. The bond linked us on yet another level, and I found comfort in our growing familiarity.

We chatted more and more frequently during the drop-off and pickup times. She'd ask me how to interpret certain behaviors that were typical for Stross, and I'd ask her to describe how Stross reacted with the other children and how the other children regarded his walker. Georgia assured me that they treated him "just like any other child." When I worried that other children wouldn't choose him as a partner for games, she assured me the teachers helped with pairing and therefore, Stross was never left out.

The relationship I established with Georgia formed my expectations for the type of two-way communication I'd seek from Stross' future teachers. During preschool I learned teachers would have a perspective that seemed similar to mine but was very different. Stross—I learned—could fool an adult into believing he understood more than he did. I allowed the illusion for as long as possible. I needed to believe he was keeping pace with his peers, so I concurred with his teachers whenever possible and gave him the benefit of my doubt.

For now his education seemed to be doing what we'd hoped—helping him learn how to socialize with his peers and then learn as much as he could from them. It was evident that starting preschool had increased his motivation to walk. As he improved Mark and I gave him more of the independence afforded a typical preschooler.

Because his mornings were filled with preschool or physical therapy, I used afternoons for excursions to the college so Stross could walk its hallways. He still wasn't adept at maneuvering for turns, so sometimes I'd venture ahead so he could feel what it was like to walk and problem-solve himself.

One day I turned the corner and disappeared into Mark's office leaving Stross to follow at his own pace. When he didn't come, I retraced my steps and found him facing the wall with his walker wheels flush to the floorboards. He was staring straight ahead. Thinking he had strayed from course, I rushed to his aid and turned him square to the hallway.

"Come on, Stross. Let's go to Daddy's office."

Again I left him and waited around the corner. One full minute passed without hearing the familiar click of his back wheel locks. So I again retraced my steps and again found him facing the wall.

"Stross. What are you doing?"

Silence, so I repeated, "Stross. What are you doing?"

"Nothing."

I assumed—like I'd assumed the other times—that he'd ventured off course and had lacked the motivation to alter his alignment. As a result he'd ended up a full 90 degrees off, so I again set him back on course. This time he rounded the corner and into Mark's office—home base.

Our next several outings were marked with this same strange behavior. So I began to leave him facing the wall for longer and longer periods of time before coming to his rescue. One day I hid just past the corner to watch this phenomenon happen first hand. I had no idea I would see him deliberately steer off center to face the wall.

How weird, I thought—but then thought again. Stross had few opportunities to stare at a wall up close and personal. I had to admit that walls did have some incredibly unique qualities—color, texture, warmth—an awesome presence. Most importantly Stross' deliberate action let him know what it felt like to arrive at a place he had intentionally chosen to go.

I emerged from my hiding place, preparing to turn him like I'd done so many times before. But first I called to him.

"Do you like the wall?" He looked at me, startled, then lifted his chin ever so slightly and turned his eyes into tiny slits set above a coy smile. His expression acknowledged that I'd discovered his secret.

"You goof ball," I said.

Stross laughed.

"Now how are you going to get turned around?"

I'd never observed Stross move in reverse, but he didn't hesitate, and what I saw him do reminded me of watching Austin in my hospital room on the day I'd given birth. Stross lifted his walker, pulled it back, set it in place and hopped back into position. Two hops back, a 90-degree turn to the left and there he was—back on the straight and narrow. And neither Mark nor I nor his therapist had ever taught him how to do it. He just did it.

Pride—that's what I had for my amazing child—a deep sense of pride. I had given birth to him, but he had surpassed anything I'd imagined a child of mine to be. Stross was cunning and clever and tenacious—a little daredevil in size 6 shoes. I began to wonder what our next child would have in common with Stross, the big brother, and how they'd be different.

My first trimester flew by. I'd gone back to the gynecologist during my pregnancy's sixth week for an intrauterine ultrasound that had allowed Mark and me have a first look at our next child— a bundle of cells attached by a yolk sac. In the following weeks I'd located an OB/GYN in nearby Mason City. She started me on schedule of prenatal exams that included diagnostic tests for high-risk pregnancies. This time I had the AFP blood test, and it returned normal. Then at 16 weeks I had a Level II ultrasound. Everything appeared normal to the doctor of radiology who informed us our child was a boy. As best as he could determine, he'd said, we would have another son.

"What is your track record?" I asked after his prediction.

"I don't call it if I'm not nearly 99 percent," he said. "Of course there is that remaining one percent. Were you hoping for a girl?"

"No. Boy, girl, either is fine," I said, with Mark concurring. "We are just hoping for healthy."

"I know you are."

Not only had this doctor read my medical history, he'd met Stross, the product of my last pregnancy. Stross and Mark had accompanied me to all my appointments including the ultrasound. Stross had watched the screen and met his baby brother the same way we had. The doctor understood what we feared.

••

"Your first son is beautiful, and so is the one you are carrying. And from what I can see, this child," he said pointing to the screen, "will give you nothing extra to worry about."

I wanted to believe what he was saying. Boy, healthy, all of it.

"So what would you name a boy?" he continued. "Stross is a beautiful name. Do you have another boy name picked out yet?"

"Not yet," Mark said.

"I guess we need to focus on boys' names especially," I said.

"You can always use my name," the doctor teased. "It's a wonderful name. Do you know what it is?"

I vaguely remembered seeing his name on the sheet I'd handed to the hospital's receptionist. Now I couldn't see his name badge.

"I don't remember," I confessed.

"It's Emmanuel," he said, "and do you know what that means?"

"God with us," I answered.

"You're right. Very good. You see, it is a beautiful name. You should think about it."

"We will," I promised. "It describes how I feel."

He smiled.

"It is a very good name," he said again, then stood to leave. "You know. I want to do something special for you. There is a type of hydrocephalus that can occur in the latter stages of pregnancy. I don't think your baby will have it. Do you hear me? I truly don't think that he has it. But with your history, I can justify another ultrasound in about 10 weeks to check. Would you like to look at your beautiful baby one more time?"

We did. Mark and I jumped at the chance to peek at our second child again. By then—during my 26th week—the pregnancy would be more than halfway and our child's features more pronounced. So Dr. Emmanuel ordered an additional ultrasound for us and sent us on our way. We felt hopeful and assured. Now that we knew how different this child would be, we could begin preparation for his birth in earnest.

Now I was excited.

Our planning included older-brother training for Stross. As my belly expanded Mark and I searched for ways to impress upon Stross

the important responsibilities of a firstborn. We knew there was a lot
he could teach a baby brother, and Stross was good at helping us craft
the list. He'd turned 4 years old midway through the pregnancy, and
in his young mind he saw himself giving his baby brother lessons in
eating, crawling, joke telling and taking a nap. Stross also vowed to
teach him how to play baseball, how to sing, how to share, and: "I
can teach him how to walk," Stross announced.

Stross had barely learned to walk himself. He'd finally mastered
the walker and recently, his therapist had introduced him to the idea
of forearm—or Loftstrand—crutches. Stross' assertion that he could
teach walking indicated that Mark's and my desire to foster his self-
esteem had worked. But his words stung because their innocence
was poignant. It's not that I had never pondered how we'd deal
with the differences in our children's physical abilities. It's that
hearing Stross plainly state his optimistic self-image increased the
significance of our function as his parents.

To Stross walking lessons meant this: Look straight ahead.
Square your shoulders. Breathe a breath of confidence. Put one foot
in front of the other. And if you fall down, get right back up and start
all over again. Maybe that was the best walking lesson our next son
would receive from his older brother. And if that child was lucky,
Stross would teach him all the other stuff—like how you muster
the incentive to go down the hall one more time when your mind is
tired and your arms and shoulders are aching. Or how even on the
most ordinary of days you joyfully—always joyfully—rise to the
challenge of willing your feet, ankles and legs to take you places
they cannot feel they have been.

Countless afternoons I'd watch Stross stand proud and tall. Coyly
he'd learned not only to master the art of walking but also to capture
the hearts of those he swept into his wake. Essentially Stross' therapy
sessions prepared us for the pain and promise of all his next steps.

The PT agenda now required him to learn how to stand with
forearm crutches, then eventually maneuver—unaided— anywhere
his legs would take him. But Stross had to agree to put on the
crutches first, and Stross hated his crutches. He thought they were

• • •

fine to use as an air guitar or a saxophone or a trombone. In fact the first sessions with crutches involved Stross sitting on the floor and refusing to touch them unless it was for an impromptu air concert. The antics would divert my attention and that of the therapist—but only temporarily. Neither the therapist nor I wanted to waste time or insurance money on games. There was a more refined manner of walking to accomplish.

Sure, Stross was independent in his reverse walker, but we adults wanted more. We wanted him to become more agile, to be able to climb stairs (if possible), and even to look less handicapped. Those were our goals. Those were *our* goals. Stross, now at the ripe age of 4, simply wanted to play games and then go home. But as we'd done countless times before, we'd end up coaxing him onto his feet somehow, then propping him with his crutches.

Those were tough sessions. On the worst afternoons tears brimmed his eyes, and his mouth formed a taut, tiny, quivering pucker. My heart hung heavier and heavier each time he leaned back onto the physical therapist's legs for support. The crutches would fall to the floor; we would all become silent and wait to see who would speak first. Would it be a protest from Stross or a word of encouragement from me or Don Barnes, the physical therapist? Most times, no one said anything. The momentary respites would end quickly with Stross being pushed back into position, handed his crutches and admonished by Don or me to keep moving. Soon Stross was made to pick up his own crutches whenever he dropped them. Often that act alone would result in a stand off eating up several five-minute segments of his one-hour session.

I could sometimes escape by watching Stross from a distance. Emotional detachment allowed me the luxury of an out-of-body experience that brought an unnatural peace. Because the peace came from a momentary avoidance of life, I only escaped for mere seconds. Too soon my mother-guilt would interrupt this strange existence, and I would crash back into myself. My eyes welled with tears to match those rising behind my son's.

"Come on, Stross. Get busy. Let's say the alphabet," I'd coax, and with each step I'd dutifully recite my A-B-Cs. His eyes often locked on mine as if to plead, "Please quit. You are doing this for you more than me. I just want to go home."

So I would quit talking for a few minutes, but I wouldn't take him home—not until the hour was over and we'd worn out "The Alphabet Song," "Row, Row, Row Your Boat," and several other ditties that helped ease his anguished minutes.

To an outsider Stross' internal struggle might have gone unnoticed. He masked his frustrations well. And there were many days only I, his mother, could connect with his fragile bravery.

I wanted to yell at Don.

"Can't you see he's had enough? Just leave him alone. You've pushed too far today. I'm taking him home."

But without fail, every time we'd journey to that emotional horizon, Stross would take a deep breath, look me square in the eye and walk. Finally two consecutive, independent steps turned into three, then four, then more. After months of these twice-weekly rituals, he was walking the hallways of the clinic with Don at his side.

Soon these days disappeared totally, and he was using his crutches with ease, at least during therapy. Out among inhabitants of the able-bodied world, it was another story. It would be years before Stross would use his crutches independently. There would be more lessons about walking and moving forward than any of us could have known.

•   •   •

# Chapter 31

# Just as He Was

$\cdots$

Stross' preferred mobility aid was his walker, not his crutches. And while Don Barnes had taught Stross how to use his walker in the hallways of the clinic, it was Mark's and my job to help him learn to negotiate through places such as church, stores, parks and our house.

Church was one of the more interesting challenges. We usually sat near the front of the sanctuary. We could enter through a doorway in front, so distance was not prohibitive. Sitting just a few yards from the pastor, Stross drank in most aspects of the worship experience, especially the musicians who performed at the 11 a.m. service. He was fascinated by the instruments—a keyboard, drums, a trumpet, a flute, a bass and guitars—lots of guitars.

"Just like Elvis," Stross proclaimed week after week. I had no idea how or why, but Stross had been an Elvis fan since before age 2 and these "Elvis guitars" kept his attention rapt. Therefore sitting through worship was the easy part, but arriving and leaving the sanctuary presented us with a variety of situations that required creative problem solving.

Because Stross was small, we could lift and sidestep him past many barriers. As newcomers to accessibility issues, we were more concerned about Stross' walker getting in the way of other

• • •

worshippers than our son's ability to move unencumbered. In fact it was far easier for one of us to carry the walker and the other to carry pint-sized Stross than to facilitate his independent movement.

Communion was often part of worship, and our first communion post-walker found Mark and me contemplating logistics such as strategic pew seating and the etiquette of the center aisle. Even as a baby Stross had enjoyed joining us at the communion rail. Too young to partake of the wine and bread, his early communion experiences involved having the pastor "talk to me," as he called the blessing individually given to each child. With the aid of his walker, Stross could now take his place at the rail on his own. The way I saw it, we just needed to get him into position and headed down the aisle. I welcomed this moment with pride and recognized its symbolism— the first time Stross would come to Christ's table unaided.

When the pastor finished the communion invitation, ushers came forward to invite each pew of worshippers into the center aisle. Because of our third row location on the aisle, taking our place with Stross' walker would be easy, I'd thought, and I was willing to figure out the details—like how to move against the crowd to return to our pew—as we went.

While I was content to let the experience unfold, Mark elected to proactively attack it. He picked up Stross and mouthed a message to me: "Grab the walker." Before I could protest, the two of them were in the aisle, but headed to the back of the sanctuary, past the growing line. I awkwardly followed in their wake towing the walker to the side of my pregnant belly.

"What are you doing?" I asked once safely in the foyer and out of anyone's earshot.

"We needed to get out of the way," Mark replied. I knew he'd been uncomfortable about our decision to park Stross' walker partially inside our pew because it partially jutted out into the center aisle. However, its wide wheelbase made this half-in/half-out position our best option.

"People can walk around the walker, Mark," I said.

"But we can help them not have to," he responded.

• • •

"Why? Stross has a right to have his walker there. What do Scott and Dave do with their wheelchairs?" I retorted. Scott and Dave were adult wheelchair users in our church who had conquered this particular circumstance years before.

"They sit farther back, Joy. We are way up front." The tone of Mark's voice let me know he was irritated and thought my approach too self-serving.

"So don't you think it's a little weird that we are going to sneak up from behind?" I shot back at him. I was irritated now. Stross, still nestled in Mark's arms, kept his attention on the action up front even though his parents had begun arguing in the church's foyer.

"We'll just wait until the ushers get back here and then join the people from the back rows," said Mark.

"Fine," I snapped, starting to recognize our locale as an unfortunate place for a marital disagreement. "At least put Stross down."

I set the walker on the floor with more authority than necessary, then Mark looked me in the eye for two beats before launching into a tactical explanation.

"I thought we would leave the walker here, and I'd carry Stross as usual," he said.

"Oh, great!" I shouted in a whisper. "So we're supposed to come all the way back here after communion and simply wait for the service to end? Our diaper bag and my purse are up there, Mark. And Stross' church toys are scattered all over."

"There is only one hymn and a benediction left after communion, Joy. It'll be fine."

I couldn't—wouldn't—offer a retort. Instead I leveled an ultimatum.

"Well, we can come back here," I stated, "but Stross is walking up to communion. So put him down."

I would not compromise on this. I needed to have him walk the aisle. I'd worked too long for this day. Mark stared at me in silence, his jaw tight. Stross, having heard his name, was tuned into our conversation now, and I wasn't finished yet. I was not beyond playing games.

"He wants to do it. Don't you, Stross? Do you want to use your walker and go up to communion with us?" Stross' eyes lit, and he gave me an eager "yes." I knew Mark would not fight this.

Mark gave me a disgusted look and placed Stross in his walker. Nearly 10 silent minutes passed as the ushers worked their ways to the back of the church. I spent most of the time on my knees by Stross offering him eager words of instruction.

"Remember to watch where you are going. We will start and stop a lot. Just stay by me and Daddy, okay?"

Stross was giddy with anticipation.

"I'll help you kneel between me and Daddy when we get up to the pastor," I told him. I was excited too. Stross would have plenty of time to practice his new skill.

The ushers had now arrived at the back of our church's long sanctuary. It was time for us to join the line. As I stepped forward, Stross gleefully kicked out behind me but in front of Mark, who now wore a look of frustrated resignation. Thankfully for Mark and me, the reflective tones of the communion hymns smoothed our egos and guided our thoughts back into the moment. Forgiveness certainly was in order, so I looked back to offer Mark a weak smile. Our eyes met in apologetic acceptance, and I thanked God for Mark's tolerance.

Slowly we moved forward with Stross' walker wheels clicking off each step. I used every pause to glance down at my little miracle. I was so full of pride that I could not help but to smile at Mark's and my walking wonder. The smile on Stross' face ran ear to ear. He loved being part of something that felt important, and he wore his new feelings of independence like a fine tuxedo. Shoulders back, chin held high, Stross marched forward as if he were born for this day. The tempo of the music changed with the beginning strains of a new hymn: "Just as I am, without one plea, but that thy blood was shed for me."

The hymn's lyrics, always poignant, seemed to bring even more clarity this Sunday: God—through Christ—offers a profound invitation. We can come as we are, and that included my son who had come forward to commune just as he was. More than that, the invitation included me—a grown, far from perfect 30-year-old who

• • •

was easily irritated. I was a bundle of contradictions. In all, a very "human" human in need of forgiveness for the way I was.

My son was far more pure than me with so much of his life stretching before him. Looking down at Stross' still smiling face, I blinked away tears and thanked God for this graciously expansive invitation. Time stood still as I took in the moment.

That's when I noticed a face just over Stross' shoulder. A face of a man, perhaps mid-60s, with tears streaming down his cheeks. They were quiet tears, and somehow they were connected to my son. I took a visual snapshot of the man before facing forward again. What I had seen told me they were not tears of pity—God had broken into this man's existence just as he had mine. The music, the act of communion, the joy on Stross's face, even the spirited pace of his gait, painted a picture of God's grace bigger than images or words ever could. I knew the man had experienced a "God moment" through Stross. I had too.

That day was the first time I recognized God's ability to speak to others through Stross simply by him being...well...Stross. I had known God could communicate with me through Stross' life. I'd just been egotistical enough to think God would reserve that mode of communication especially for me. The man's tears as he watched Stross walk let me know my son had helped God somehow simply by being who he was at that moment, in that time, in that place. What's more, I understood Stross would be part of many more God moments in years to come. Those times would have nothing to do with me. God, it seemed, would use Stross just as he was.

Wrapped in my own life, I'd become oblivious to the role I too could play as a walking, breathing example of God's grace. My task, it seemed, was to facilitate as I was led—perhaps by me being nothing more or nothing less than who I was. How beautiful. How simple. Yet intuitively I understood how great a challenge it would be. I needed to stay out of God's way.

•   •   •

*Chapter 32*

# Pushing Through

• • •

So much of the first months of my pregnancy had been spent knowing I was pregnant but not fully comprehending its reality. For two months I walked around reminding myself that I was tired because I was pregnant—not because I carted Stross and his walker from place to place and wrestled him in or out of his leg braces several times a day.

It's not that I didn't think about being pregnant. On the contrary, I thought about it constantly. However I didn't know what to think about being pregnant. I didn't want to compare the feelings and experiences of this pregnancy with my previous ones, because similarities could be simultaneously comforting or worrisome—so could the differences. Therefore trying not to think about what I was thinking about became the challenge. It helped that our pregnancy had become public knowledge long before I started to show. Everyone—it seemed—was rooting for us, and many reported thinking good thoughts on our behalf.

As my pregnancy progressed, Stross added to my fatigue. Even after the normal energy drop of a pregnancy's first trimester ended, lifting and positioning Stross around my bulging belly became—increasingly—a logistical nightmare. Mark attempted to do most of the hauling and stroller jockeying, but he was only available over his lunch hour or at the end of his class schedule. So in addition to laundry and general household chores, I'd spend my days packing our son and his gear from appointment to appointment.

The experience made me an expert of sorts on the issue of accessibility. Not only could I readily identify barriers for people with walkers or wheelchairs or a stroller, but because of my heavier, fluid-filled body I could identify with people who struggled with obesity, arthritis or other disabling medical conditions.

That's why halfway through my pregnancy I agreed to oversee a three-year fundraising campaign for accessibility improvements to our 50-year-old church building—a majestic limestone structure that filled one-half of a city block. I wanted our church to become accessible because Stross needed it to be.

Before renovations not one entrance at our church provided access at ground level. In fact all doors but the sanctuary's main double doors entered onto a split-level landing that connected to eight ascending and eight descending steps. The main sanctuary entrance was another matter entirely. It was set above a series of wide limestone steps—nine total—that opened onto an interior landing that served as an architectural preface for yet another set of five ascending steps that ultimately led to the foyer. Basically anyone entering our church from the front had to climb 14 steps before entering the sanctuary proper.

One day during my sixth month of pregnancy, I was to meet Mark in our church sanctuary for a music rehearsal with other musicians. Knowing Stross and his walker would be accompanying me—and realizing that I'd have to lift him and his walker up any stairs we'd encounter—I'd decided to take advantage of his parking tag and park in a disabled parking spot. Our church had only three spots at the time—all located by a side door close to the sanctuary. Unfortunately after parking and unloading, I discovered that door was locked. So rather than put Stross and his walker back into the car, I decided to coax him to walk to the next closest entrance—the imposing front entrance.

I carefully navigated the steps carrying Stross on one side and

. . .

his walker on the other while clutching a small bag of toys. At the top I set him down and tried the doors only to find them locked also. I pounded as hard as I could, hoping someone inside would hear us and come to the rescue. I could faintly hear music, but no one could—even faintly—hear me.

Not wanting to retrace our steps, I carried Stross and his walker down the stone steps and set him in place at the bottom. I hoped to coax him into walking alongside me to yet another side door that led to the church's office. It was still some distance away, and our most direct path was across grass—a surface not well suited for his walker's wheels. Stross tried taking a few difficult steps, then announced, "It won't work."

"Yes, it works, but it's very hard," I said. By this time I was physically tired and becoming angry.

"Where's Daddy?" Stross asked. Stross knew Daddy always helped during times like these.

"We'll see Daddy soon," I told him. "Remember? I told you he's going to the same meeting we are." I used the word "meeting" with Stross often. Meetings were any gathering that required Stross to be quiet while Mommy and Daddy's attention were on other matters. The rehearsal would be such a meeting, but first we had to get there. We were now as far from our car as we were from the exterior door that led to the church's office. While I contemplated our next move, I talked aloud to assure Stross I was working on a solution.

"Well, why do you suppose our church locks the doors by its disabled parking spots—especially on a day when it knows people will be meeting in the sanctuary?" It sounded like I was asking Stross, but I knew he had no understanding of the injustice we'd uncovered.

"Why don't people think of that?" I asked again.

In his distinctive, chirping voice Stross said, "I don't know," then shook his head side to side.

"I don't know either," I told him, "but we should tell somebody that's not very nice, shouldn't we?"

Stross just looked at me wondering what I would do next. I wanted him to know he'd been wronged—to prepare him for a day when he'd approach a building alone, find he had no access and then have to solve his dilemma with no one to assist.

"Well, Kiddo, will you walk for Mommy back that way again, please?"

"No, I don't want to," he said.

"I know you don't want to, but will you? Mommy really needs you to," I told him. His unborn brother now felt heavier than when we'd parked.

"No," he said. "I'm tired."

"Stross..." I couldn't find more words. I was tired too—of carrying my 45-pound son and the extra 35 pounds of weight I'd already gained during my pregnancy. And I was too tired to try coaxing him anymore. I knew rationalizing or appealing to a 4-year-old's sense of benevolence wouldn't work. He didn't see this as his problem. It was mine. I wanted to yell but knew if I did, I'd risk having him think his refusal was the problem. Instead I started to cry. He looked at me and said nothing.

"Mommy's tired too," I finally said.

But I was more angry than tired—and very familiar with angry tears. Within an instant my anger ignited a burst of energy. I grabbed Stross, grabbed the walker and—still clutching the toy bag—started off for the building's office-side entrance. Walking at a fast pace, I felt the body of my unborn son shift from side to side. The closer I got to the door, the more momentum I felt. I couldn't allow myself to slow down.

Finally outside the unlocked door, I set down the walker, opened the door, stepped halfway through with Stross securely on my hip and then reached back to retrieve the walker before the doors shut behind us. I paused inside to wipe my face, and then took my entire load up eight stairs to the main floor outside the office. I set Stross and his walker in place and—winded—asked him to walk the hallway that led to the sanctuary. He complied, only stopping when he arrived at a set of two steps that descended to the sanctuary door located just off the chancel. I again lifted him and the walker and carried him down those stairs and through the sanctuary door. We had finally arrived at rehearsal, and I set him down with finality.

"There you are," Mark said from where he stood around the piano with the other musicians. "I was beginning to worry."

I briefly thought about not speaking but then decided everyone there needed to know exactly why they *should* have worried. What ensued was nearly a five-minute ranting monologue on disability rights, the injustice of inaccessible worship spaces and the short-sidedness of church members who had the audacity to question the need for renovations. The more I ranted, the guiltier Mark felt about not having been there to help. Soon he—a true peacemaker—began to apologize for all the wrongs I'd suffered, hoping I'd calm. But I couldn't be appeased. When a woman attempted to enter my one-sided conversation, I gathered steam. When another woman tried to blame my emotions on a pregnancy-induced hormonal imbalance, I became more incensed.

"Joy!" Mark broke in with a firm, measured voice of warning. I knew he was reminding me I couldn't solve anything at that moment, and I'd already vented too much.

"No, Mark," I bit back, not wanting to be calmed. "It's not right, and no one understands why."

I wanted the world to change in that instant.

"Please, Joy," he said. His voice pleaded.

"Yes," the director said. " We'd better get started. Some people have other commitments, and we're running out of time."

The accompanist took that as her cue to start playing again—something, anything—to refocus the group. I sat in the pew for a few more minutes with my hand on my belly feeling our baby kick me from the inside. Stross continued to draw pictures on pew cards. He appeared oblivious to how different—how difficult—his everyday life was and would be.

My angry pain had surfaced with the realization I couldn't be his lifetime buffer. In fact there would soon be someone who would, very naturally, illuminate those differences every day: Stross' baby brother. While Mark and I couldn't instantaneously change the world, I hoped we could create an environment within our home where this new son learned to accommodate others as a way of life. Stross' baby brother would have an incredible advantage. He would be born with no stereotypes, no patterns of behavior that automatically excluded others and no definition of normalcy that excluded the abnormal. He could—until his fresh innocence wore off—teach us how to regard a person with a disability in a matter-of-fact way and to look at someone without seeing the differences first. Of course, that would only be true if he were born healthy—normal.

A few weeks after my church hike, Mark spent three weeks in Chicago for software training. His absence required even more physical demands on my seven-months pregnant body. I'd arranged for a female college student to live with me on weekday evenings and nights to help care for Stross, but I still had to expend diminishing energy on him during the day. The most demanding task found me hauling him and his walker up and down a flight of 20-plus steps to attend a summer art program.

A few times other parents volunteered to carry Stross for me, but most days I carried him either up or down the stairway myself. That's why when I learned that I was experiencing pre-term labor, I wasn't very surprised. As a more experienced pregnant woman, I knew the contractions I had every four to six minutes were something to take seriously—not merely dismiss them as just a bunch of Braxton-Hicks as I'd done before. This was July 5th; my due date was August 25th, far enough away for my doctor to prescribe medication and moderate bed rest until August 1 when I'd be 36 weeks along.

"This will give you time to warm up to the possibility of a vaginal birth," she'd told me.

"Or to stress about it," I'd responded.

She knew I liked the idea of a second cesarean and had taken comfort in the familiarity of the procedure. Dr. Emmanuel had confirmed that this child lay in the same transverse breech position that Stross had.

"That means I'll have a cesarean section, right?" I'd asked hopefully.

• • •

"Unless your baby turns," he'd said.

"But how long before a baby gets too big to turn?" I'd asked, looking for a reason to ignore labor preparation again.

"Oh, they can turn up to the point of delivery."

That wasn't what I had wanted to hear.

Then, at our 26-week ultrasound, I learned it was time to take labor breathing seriously. After the wand started transmitting images, the first words out of the technician's mouth were, "Well, your baby's head is in position for delivery already."

"What?" I nearly shouted at her. "That can't be."

"Why can't it be?"

I filled her in on the high points of my earlier ultrasound, believing it would give her reason to reassess. "The baby was transverse last time, and it was supposed to be hard for him to turn and…"

My voice trailed off.

"Well, he managed to get around," she said, "and from the looks of things, he's really tucked in there. You might get lucky, and he'll stay in the birth position for you."

"Well, I want a c-section. I had one the first time, and I want one again."

Mark, sitting with Stross by my head, had been studying the images with a smile on his face. He now started to chuckle at my genuine state of astonishment and my belligerence.

"Mark," I said. "You saw it last time. He was breech."

"But, Joy, he's not now. They think that's good news, so maybe we should, too."

"But I don't want to VBAC, Mark. I don't."

VBAC meant a vaginal birth after cesarean, a now controversial procedure that had gained a degree of popularity during the time I carried our second child. My doctor—Dr. Barbara Coulter-Smith—had presented it as my preferred method of delivery in the absence of a breech presentation. She'd touted fewer complications and a speedier recovery among its benefits. Yet my odds had favored a repeat cesarean—until this appointment.

"That's between you and your doctor," said the technician. "I do know that research shows it's supposed to be better for woman to have a vaginal birth rather than a cesarean, even if they've had a c-section before."

"You sound like my doctor," I said dryly.

"Joy, don't worry about it today," said Mark. "Look at the screen. You can really see the baby now."

He was right. While I'd been agonizing the technician had moved the wand into various positions on my belly and clicked images of our next son's open right hand; his large, right foot; his bent, right forearm; a profile of his face; and a view of his face straight on. Both Mark and I watched intently as she followed the contour of his spine, counting each tiny vertebra as she went. Once again the images of this child showed all bones and internal organs were accounted for and properly formed.

Our child's normal development was a reason to relax even if the method of his upcoming delivery caused anxiety.

In one of my most Joy-being-Joy moments, I crafted a plan to use my persuasive abilities to talk Dr. Coulter-Smith into a c-section anyway. She'd only been delivering babies for a few years, and when I'd shared my fears about VBAC with her—mostly hemorrhaging from a ruptured uterus—she'd readily identified. She was my age with one child who'd also been born by cesarean. Surely I could sway her.

But no.

"Well, Joy," she'd said, maintaining her doctor's perspective, "the times when things go wrong are rare, and you ultimately want to do what's best for you and your baby."

I eventually warmed up to the idea of labor. Now, courtesy of pre-term labor, I even had time to concentrate on my preparation.

Even though Dr. Coulter-Smith was my primary physician, I met the four other doctors in her office, courtesy of a rotating schedule. According to the receptionist, "This way if your primary physician isn't on call, she will know that the doctor who is has had a chance to meet you and is familiar with your case."

I only wanted my doctor. She was the only woman in the

• • •

practice and the only one—I believed—who could identify with the emotions associated with pregnancy and the prospect of a VBAC. Plus having delivered her own child too early, she also identified with my dread over premature labor.

I followed her instructions for fending off contractions and settled into a blue recliner for the last weeks of my pregnancy. With prenatal testing complete, all but the waiting remained. So as I breathed my way through the annoying twinges of pre-term labor, I mentally prepared for the real labor to come and trusted the medication to keep more powerful contractions at bay until our second child could thrive outside my womb.

Mark shifted the furniture in our living room so my chair faced our entertainment center, and he set up my computer and a phone on a side table so I could continue to work on the church's fund-raising campaign. During my very literal down time, I also organized a scrapbook for Son No. 2 and sorted through Stross' baby clothes. Most of the time I read or watched television, spending entire afternoons engrossed in the O.J. Simpson murder trail with coverage of the Waco and Whitewater hearings mixed in.

During these weeks—I began to think of our child as a person—not as Project: Child No. 2. I'd been so focused on a healthy outcome that I'd neglected to think of this baby as a separate human being. But now that I'd become hostage to his best interests, he'd easily achieved full human status. I carried not just a baby but Mark's and my second son—an eager and energetic child who sloshed more than kicked and deserved a name as unique as his older brother.

We decided Mike or John or Bob were too simple. Luke wouldn't work because Luke with Newcom sounded funny, and Levi was dropped from the list because having a brother named Levi would cause Stross unnecessary "Strauss" confusion. As the weeks passed Mark informed me the decision was mine. So after a few attempts at inventing names, I decided to glean the dictionary in search of one-syllable "s" words that could serve as a name. I settled on "Skye," a bright sounding word that conveyed openness and freedom while linking him to his British heritage and the beautiful "Isle of Skye."

• • •

Soon Mark and I would become parents of two sons: the Newcom boys, Stross and Skye.

I spent a portion of my recliner time thinking about the special relationship our boys would share. I instinctively knew that we'd already given Skye something other parents couldn't—a sibling whose life offered incredible insights into lesser-known ways of the world. Aside from instinct I had no way of knowing how Skye would filter and refine those insights before passing them on. As I awaited labor, my anticipation grew: about who Skye would be, about how his life would change our family, and about the fears I must overcome before meeting him face to face.

When August 1 arrived I headed to my doctor's office hoping for the promised all clear and her permission to start walking farther than the distance to our home's bathroom. Instead Dr. Coulter-Smith encouraged me to spend one more week off my feet just to be safe. Unlike her I'd lost respect for my August 25 due date and, even though I honored her instructions, I hoped for unstoppable, full-blown labor. I needed my pregnancy to end. Before Stross' birth I'd hoped for a way to avoid the birth experience at all. This time I courted ways to start it. Restlessness had overcome anxiety. For too many weeks, life existed in suspended animation, and I needed our story to play out regardless of its outcome.

Fortunately Skye arrived early—as I'd hoped—but not too early. Within three days of my release from restricted rest, I felt a pop in my abdomen when I rolled over in bed. Now wiser, I quickly identified the ensuing trickle of fluid as the start of labor—the unstoppable start I'd wanted.

Despite the early morning hour—1:10 a.m.—I began my self-assigned series of phone calls while Mark carried our bags to the car. First, Sandy Damm. She had agreed to stay with Stross while we were at the hospital. Next my parents, then Mark's parents and finally Dr. Coulter-Smith's answering service. She needed to know we were on our way.

"Who's on call tonight?" I asked. The response was as I'd hoped: Dr. Coulter-Smith—but only until 7 a.m.

•••

"Mark, I need to have this baby by 7," I told him after hanging up. "That's when Coulter-Smith's shift is over."

"Joy, I'm pretty sure you'll have it when you have it," he advised.

"I know, but we've got to try by 7, okay?"

"Whatever you say, Joy," he answered. "I'm not sure what we can do about it, but that would be good for Stross' cath schedule. Or at least by 10. Stross could wait until then."

Having Mark available for Stross' cath was a concern. After my pre-term labor began we'd made it a practice to perform Stross' catherization as late as possible. We'd perform one procedure when he went to bed and then one more just before we went to bed. Because it was nighttime—a time when Stross didn't consume liquids—we knew we could safely wait up to 8, maybe even 10 hours to empty his bladder before resuming his regular schedule provided he didn't drink a lot of fluid upon waking.

Unfortunately no one in town other than Mark or me had ever catherized Stross before. One of my labor preparations had been to create detailed instructions for catherizing that Sandy could use (if she felt bold enough) along with advice about taking him to the clinic for nursing assistance if necessary. In truth we'd not fully thought through how to care for Stross while I would be giving birth. Our absolute worst-case scenario involved Sandy driving Stross to the hospital so Mark could leave my bedside long enough to perform the cath himself.

Either we hadn't worried about it because we instinctively knew we didn't need to, or God took care of us. In hindsight, it appears the latter may have been true, for Mark and I were guided through a birthing experience that again reminded us of life's power and beauty. Of course the power wasn't absent of pain, and the beauty existed in spite of it. Labor, I learned, was everything I'd heard it could be and more.

After only a few hours I encountered back labor. But it was the only fear realized in the early morning hours of August 12, 1995. All the rest of it exceeded my expectations starting with Dr. Coulter-

• • •

Smith arriving at my bedside in the middle of the night to reassure me and to listen—like everyone else in the room—as I sang and talked and moaned my way through one contraction after another. I'd refused an epidural based on irrational logic that, "If my uterus ruptures, I want to feel it." And after struggling to find a bed position that accommodated back labor, I settled on burying my face in my pillow while rocking back and forth on my hands and knees.

Then after a few particularly hard contractions, I accepted one dose of "something to take the edge off." While the medication didn't fully relax me, it allowed me to think more about the process of labor and less about its pain. It also fully exposed my personality. I'd always dealt with stress by talking and complaining. Labor only accentuated the technique that now found me moaning and questioning my way through the transition phase.

"You went to seminary," I said to Mark. "Explain the fall of Adam and the curse of Eve to me. Why did she get pain in childbirth? Huh? Tell me."

"I don't know, Joy," he said simply.

Between contractions I simply began a new monologue on the history of labor and the millions of women who'd given birth before me. As Skye worked his way through the birth canal, I intellectually merged with a continuum of women who had brought children into the world under all types of circumstances: slaves in fields, pioneers on wagon trains, immigrants on ships, refugees in deserts and Amish in back bedrooms. Then after a contraction I'd blurt out my most current thought and resume moaning along to the melody of the song playing off my favorite CD.

By 7:15 a.m., I did less talking and more moaning in melodies. My body was ready to push; I'd nearly made my self-imposed deadline. In a grand act of kindness, Dr. Coulter-Smith agreed to stay with me even though her shift was over. She and my labor nurse helped get me into position and gave instructions to attempt two or three good pushes with each contraction.

"Just listen to me," said the labor nurse, "and I'll tell you when."

Mark wanted to help too. So just as he'd done prior to Stross' delivery, he again became my contraction spotter, watching the monitor to announce when my body would experience its greatest amount of force. My first attempts at pushing were awkward and frustrating. I pushed when told and pushed as hard as I believed I could. I'd fit in three attempts as requested but could tell they accomplished little.

"It feels like I'm not doing anything."

"You are doing it, Joy. It's working," said Dr. Coulter-Smith. "Sometimes babies slide back up and have to get pushed down again. Just hang in there."

The image of a tiny human piston moving up and down the birth canal horrified me, so I attempted to bear down harder, bunching my muscles and involuntarily groaning with each effort.

"No, Joy. Try not to make sounds. It's wasted energy. Focus on the pushing only," admonished the nurse.

"I can't help it," I shot back. "I've got to."

Just then a contraction began, and I tried to resist the urge to groan but failed. I had not opened my eyes for a while. Between contractions I only wanted to rest. During contractions I couldn't. Every muscle in my body felt involved in the pushing process, including my face muscles.

"Joy, that's not as productive," said the nurse. "Try not to fight the pain. I know it sounds strange, but try to focus on the pain. Can you feel where the pain is telling you to push?"

"Yes," I said, amazed that I was able to connect to her radical and seemingly contradictory statement. My body, it appeared, was trying to help me understand where to push. Wave after wave of contractions were attempting to force my child out. I simply couldn't get on top of the waves.

After nearly 25 to 30 minutes of pushing, I started to ignore everyone who tried to offer advice. I recognized that my strongest urge to push came after they told me to start pushing. By the time the contraction hit its peak, my energy had already begun to decline. With lingering thoughts of Adam and Eve, I chose to test a theory. If the creator of humans had cursed woman with pain in childbirth,

···

that same creator must have also provided a way to work through the painful condition. My body must have been designed for this moment, I thought. Therefore I needed to trust how my body had been designed.

As labor intensified I became increasingly aware that I'd discovered a new way to collaborate with the creator. Like other collaborations its success depended on my ability to trust divine strength and not assert my own misguided efforts. The ebb and flow of labor could guide me.

"Joy, you're not getting all your pushes in," said the nurse.

"I know," I said. "Just let me do it. You're telling me wrong."

"Okay, but remember to identify where the pain is and then push through it."

Her words struck like lightning. It was exactly what I'd started to attempt. I'd recognized that a contraction's peak carried the greatest moment of intense pain but also the greatest potential for power. Waiting to push had increased my effectiveness. I'd begun to work with the pain instead of fight against it. Rather than three good pushes during a contraction, I produced one forceful and authoritative push. Our baby now moved without retreat. I had, as she'd said, managed to locate the pain and then—literally—push through it.

With each contraction's wave I was lifted to a peak that mixed human agony with divine power. Between contractions I lay still—exhausted, drained, impatient for our son's birth. But my labor euphoria had already begun. Moreover I'd claimed the phrase "pushing through pain" as a metaphor for life. It was how I'd begun to live since Stross' birth. Emotional pain and physical pain, it seemed, shared common traits. Fortunately there was also a common outcome: joy after anguish. The key lay in identifying the source of pain, then becoming weak enough—no, meek enough— to rely on divine guidance. Mastering the method, it seemed, was the best way to overcome the inertia of helplessness no matter the circumstance. It was the best way to move forward.

Within minutes Dr. Coulter-Smith announced that she could see the top of Skye's head. The contractions carried more urgency now and the drive to push had never felt stronger. After the next push she forcefully commanded me to stop.

"But I can't. He's almost out," I said, swept into labor's momentum.

"Joy, you have to stop pushing. I feel fingers. Your baby's arm is in the birth canal, and if you push you may break it."

I began to blow short puffs of air, fighting an overwhelming urge. It felt as if I held back a wall of water and if I spoke or breathed too deeply, it'd gush forth.

"You're doing great," she said. "I just have to deliver his arm first. Don't push."

The energy had to go somewhere so I began to chant: "Hurr-e, hurr-e, hurr-e, hurr-e…"

"I am. You're doing great, Joy," she said sounding too calm. Mark and my nurse offered encouragement as well, but the only words I could hear were my doctor's. I listened to her calling out instructions and requests for instruments to her assistant. I waited, chanting, as she made it possible for Skye to arrive already reaching for life. Her next sentence, I hoped, would give me permission to fully release him into the world. When finally granted, one push is all it took. Skye's birth was accompanied by instant, silent elation. I relaxed into the bed, eyes shut, quietly celebrating what God and I had done.

Yet within seconds God's prominence faded. Instead Mark's cautious jubilation, the sounds of the neonatal nurses clearing Skye's airway, Dr. Coulter-Smith's instructions and then Skye's lusty cry filled my head. The moments seemed vaguely familiar, similar to the moments after Stross' birth and yet incredibly different: different hospital, different birthing method, different doctor, different baby. Even Mark and I were different people than the couple who welcomed Stross into the world.

Eventually exhaustion muted even the outside world; and as they laid Skye on my belly, Mark's voice broke through. He told me he loved me, and he exclaimed how beautiful our son was as he cooed words of wonder into my ear and stroked my hair, damp with perspiration.

Someone told us Skye weighed 8 lbs. and 2 oz. That same

• • •

someone pointed out that his weight matched his time of birth—
8:02 a.m. I'd missed my goal by an hour; but Dr. Coulter-Smith had
stayed with me anyway, helping me conquer my fear of labor.

"I did it, Mark. I went through labor. I did it." Quiet and tired
exclamations attempted to express all that had happened. "I did it."

What I couldn't express is how I'd done it—how I'd been allowed
to participate in an incredible, divine partnership. I'd been granted
the opportunity to deliver this miracle with help from the same God
who'd safeguarded the delivery of our first miracle. And somehow
each child's first breath had made intangible truths tangible. The
wonder, the awe, the elation lingered; and then dimmed too soon as
other truths took over and as my physical pain subsided.

Stross needed to be catherized; Mark needed to drive home
to care for him. There was enough time for him to hold Skye for
a little while, but then he had to leave. He promised to return as
soon as possible and get a hotel room so someone could baby-sit
Stross there. While Skye and I were in the hospital, Stross would
be close enough for Mark to do his caths and close enough to bring
on frequent visits. It was a Saturday, and both sets of grandparents
would soon meet the newest Newcom son. Our life as a family of
four had begun.

• • •

# Chapter 33

# Ready to Fly

• • •

Skye's first year of life flew by, causing little to unnerve us. Newborn jaundice, an ear infection and one bout of something viral were all that broke into our routine of well-baby check ups. Skye—alert, happy and verbal—brought our family a sense of peace and wellbeing, a sense of normalcy.

This time motherhood didn't feel like something I had to figure out. A mother is who I'd become, and because of Stross I'd become the kind of mother Skye needed me to be as well. I'd learned how to adapt my life while accommodating the demands of my children's separate lives. And both Mark and I found the ordinary simplicity of Skye's everyday life enchanting. Through him we'd been allowed a measure of the storybook life we'd always imagined.

Skye loved to laugh at reflections that danced as light on walls. His constant, happy chatter let us know he loved going anywhere and doing anything we did as long as it was action-filled. When I was at the college Skye usually rode on a hip pack that braced his body against mine in a sling. He always faced forward with his chin in the air, the wind floating his fine hair straight up as we walked. Skye always looked as if we'd forgotten to comb his hair or as if he'd just come inside after running a windy mile. If his baby legs could have tolerated it, I believed he'd have run a marathon—as long as there were interesting sights along the way.

I soon learned that my daily life, while fascinating to Stross, was less than interesting to Skye. On days I taught my 8:30 a.m. class Mark entertained Skye—as he'd done with Stross—by taking him along on college errands. Then after class Skye and I headed out for my version of errands. Excursions to the grocery store or trips to deliver or retrieve Stross from preschool were clearly highlights for Skye, as were Stross' therapy sessions. But when Stross was at preschool Skye would quickly grow tired of me. He found little excitement in tasks like washing dishes, vacuuming, folding clothes, grading papers or typing at a computer. Baby toys and apparatuses designed as educational distractions would only go so far.

Skye, it seemed, wanted to roam our house and examine every wall, ceiling or floor surface. Unfortunately he had to rely on me to be his feet the first 10 months of his life. I soon learned to fold clothes or grade papers in a central location in our home so I could move Skye and his blanket to a new room every time boredom struck. I'd stay in the same place but kept a vantage point that let me look into the doorway of the room I'd planted him in. A simple change of scenery kept Skye cooing for 10 to 15 minutes, and I could relocate him up to four or five times before stopping my tasks to give him one-on-one attention for diapering, feeding, rocking, reading books or engaging in conversation.

When Stross was home Skye's house tours were not necessary. Skye adored watching his older brother, and his older brother adored everything about him. I helped Stross assist me when it was time to feed Skye or dress him. Mark and I also made teaching Skye to read, color or learn to walk part of Stross' daily therapies. We also made certain the brothers had opportunities to ride together in the wagon, chase each other in crawling races on our floor, or take turns laughing at each other while swinging under the red maple tree in our front yard.

Each day provided us with opportunities to watch our sons grow and mature, and each day we saw how similar, yet radically different, they were. It certainly didn't mean we loved one son more than the other, or even that we loved each one differently. It meant that our understanding of love had transformed. We now understood how it was possible to fiercely love each child exactly the same, while fighting equally for each child's right to become the person he was intended to be.

We developed a parenthood mission statement for Stross based on what he had taught us: "To help Stross become the best Stross he can be." Therefore, it only made sense that our dream for Skye's future matched; we needed to make it possible for him: "To become the best Skye he can be." Using this principle, each child set his own standard for success. Keeping their separate goals at the forefront of our lives, I believed, was our primary task as their parents. Mark's and my greatest contribution would be to help our sons understand how we measured success in our own lives, hoping it served as a positive, guiding example.

Mark had redefined success when he redefined fatherhood. As a nurturer, he'd managed to incorporate compassion into his career. Caring about students and discovering how each best learned invigorated him. Dozens of new students sat under his teaching each year, and for Mark success was measured in terms of relationships. How he made an impact on someone's life became the way Mark succeeded in the world. His success wouldn't come through building facilities or creating audiovisual productions. Success for Mark would come by supporting my efforts to grow as a person as well as the efforts of Stross and Skye and every other student of life he encountered. Mark, the nurturing teacher and consummate helper, now set his sights on changing the world one student at a time. He'd found his divine calling.

As for me, I now understood success had nothing to do with parking cards, corner offices, awards plaques or making several thousand more dollars than your age each year. Before Stross, even before Forest City, I believed I had defined success without those benchmarks; yet it is not how I lived. An ample supply of accomplishments had boosted my illusions, and I'd had no reason to admit I preferred spending time in life's shallow end. Only after

•••

wading into waters deeper than my ability to feel safe had I learned what it meant to succumb to a force greater than myself. I had to learn that the safety I sought near the shore wasn't really safe. Treading water in life's deepest parts had built inner strength.

The water analogies are endless. I see it most as a child who stands on the edge of a pool's deep end and trustingly responds to her parent's cajoling to leap into the air and jump in. The child finds the act scary and exhilarating, for after her flight she will plunge under the water to await a rescue she is helpless to assist. But for the child, the leap is worth the risk. She is confident of the rescue because she knows she will not drown. She trusts and abides her parent's instruction.

Joy follows her act of obedience.

Joy is the consequence of giving into and overcoming her fear.

Many times during the first years of Stross' life, I'd felt as if I'd drowned; both Mark and I had experienced the overwhelming result of going against the flow. We'd dived into situations and immersed ourselves in circumstances that had threatened to engulf us. But every time we'd been lifted to safety—not as a consequence of our actions—but as the natural outcome.

Just like the child in the pool I found myself turning to my divine parent, after each thrilling rescue to ask for a chance to do it again.

"Only this time catch me sooner," I'd be tempted to ask or "Next time make sure I don't sink as deep."

If it were at all possible, I wanted the joy without the journey—the rescue without the risk. But it is the repeated act of trust that builds faith. It is the jumping in that increases my confidence and affirms my reliance on God. With every leap I come to know God's character more fully. I become aware of how little joy there is in simply resting at the side of the pool.

Until Stross I'd allowed myself to believe I could be one of the people who worked hard enough to have it all: a successful career, a rewarding family life, fulfilling friendships and a deep spiritual desire to better myself while changing the world. It would be irresponsible of me to say that those things aren't possible. Many people profess that they have been blessed with just such a life, and therefore, who am I to say differently?

I simply know that I believed I had it all once and couldn't recognize what had been lacking until I had it. Ironically, because I didn't know differently, simply believing in its truth had been enough. I had believed I had it all, and I could have lived my whole life believing what I had was enough.

It wasn't until after Stross was born, after we moved, after Skye was born, and after Mark and I saw Stross enrolled in a regular education classroom, that I truly felt I had it all—whatever "all" was. In its most simple translation, all to me now means accepting the blessings that come my way. That's how I know joy. Joy comes from acknowledging all I've been given and entrusting it to a greater purpose whenever I encounter life's deeper waters.

Stross' life is, undeniably, the deepest pool I've ever encountered. Each time his life calms to mundane and manageable, our family rests at the pool's edge only momentarily before something plunges us even deeper: a conflict with his teachers at school, a surgery that upsets our family's routine, an even bigger surgery with complications that threaten his life, a financial crisis that finds us signing loan papers for money we aren't sure how to repay or a change in our insurance plan that risks our ability to care for Stross appropriately. The list will be as long as his life, therefore, I ask for the list to be a long one.

Before Stross' birth, even perhaps before his fifth birthday, had I been able to peer into the future, I don't think I'd have been prepared to accept all I would have seen. I'd have fixated on disappointments, anger, helplessness and times of utter despair. I did not have enough character, as the apostle Paul formulates in Romans 5, to persevere through the suffering and reclaim hope. Fortunately I learned how from my oldest son, a child of God who fixates on hope not despair. Even now, 16 years after his birth, he continues to be my example of what I can aspire to be when I grow up.

Eleven years ago he announced that he would "become an astronaut…when I grow up, Mom. I'm gonna fly into space." Then

• • •

a few weeks after his fifth birthday, all he could talk about was space camp. His endless chatter about astronauts and flying, helmets and space suits punctuated all our family conversations. One Sunday he mused through the entire worship service, stopping only to hear either Mark or me provide an answer to his constant questioning, "Is today the day I go to space camp?" He'd asked the question approximately three dozen times in one week. About five of those times happened before or during church.

His fixation that day was partially my fault. A few days before I'd seen an advertisement for space camp on television and, knowing of his interest in space and flying, I'd called the toll-free number to order him a packet of information. I'd hoped some photos and proof of an age requirement would silence him on the topic, at least for a while. In truth I was thrilled he had such a dream, and I wanted to nurture it—to help him believe it was possible to go to space camp someday and even become an astronaut.

I couldn't hold back a smile when, during a prayer, he'd pulled on my sweater and in an anguished whisper said, "But I don't have a helmet."

I cocked my head with a wry look of empathy but offered no verbal answer to his problem, only a slight shake of my head that seemed to say, "Oh, no. What will you do?" To my surprise Stross supplied an answer.

"We can get one after church when we go home," he said.

Our home had always been the place Stross went for the things he needed: food, a hand washing, a story read, a popsicle, his daily catherizations, a good night's sleep. But now, I realized, he was on the verge of having his home become something different.

Stross was about to begin kindergarten—a time when grown-ups other than his parents would help him learn and grow. Other adults would become resources and sources of authority for him, and another location—an elementary school building—would become a safe haven for learning. He'd made it through preschool, an educational kiddie pool. But I wasn't certain it had fully prepared him for all that would come next. Perhaps there was no adequate way to prepare him for the rigors of elementary school: peer pressure, teasing, learning to read, tying shoes, counting to 100. It all seemed so monumental; I could only imagine how Stross would interpret the challenges. For the most part, his grey matter existed as uncharted territory. Every task might present him with a formidable challenge. He was just learning to write his name.

It's not that I feared for Stross' success. We'd set the bar at the height God established: Stross was to become the best he could be—no more, no less. As Stross matured toward that goal, I had no doubt God would rescue him as appropriate, just as he had Mark and me countless times before. My worries lay with how others might perceive him. I feared they would be unable to see the amazing person I knew—that they couldn't get past the walker and would forget he was an impressionable little boy with amazing potential.

Because Stross was still a mystery man of few words, I also feared his educators would grow impatient with his silent responses and stop expecting a verbal response at all. I hoped, instead, the teachers would sign on as partners with us in his education and trust our instincts and belief in his future. Kindergarten, I feared, would require yet another leap of faith.

But this was May. We had an entire summer before Mark and I would drop him off at the elementary door and attempt to not look back. As I gazed down at Stross sitting next to me in the church pew, I offered thanks for my little boy of five who had the courage to hold astronomical dreams. Then I prayed that he'd be blessed with divine perspective. I wanted him to know there was a greater being he could turn to when he needed even more—more than we could offer him at home and more than he could get from his teachers or the friends he'd make at school.

The collective voice of the congregation broke into my thoughts; but instead of joining in prayer, I continued to observe Stross who sat with a distracted look on his face. He appeared lost in thought — still anxious, I believed, about not having a space helmet. I leaned down and whispered in his ear.

"We'll make sure you have a helmet when it's time to go to

•••

space camp."

Stross smiled brightly at me, took a cleansing breath and then directed his attention to the pastor for a few moments before taking a toy airplane from Skye's diaper bag. He was fully at peace, satisfied his dream would be fulfilled.

I took my own cleansing breath, more at peace than I had been in a very long time.

A full five years after Stross' birth, I continue to regard him as my touchstone to the divine. Not just for who he is, but for who I am because of him. And I believe I'm a better person today, not just because I am a mother but because I am *his* mother. He's a constant supply of involuntary joy, offering the emotion in multiple-sized portions whenever I'm ready to drink it in. I struggle to explain how that is so, realizing my ability is limited by the human condition. I also struggle to describe the multidimensional aspects of joy and how joy can be found in the midst of any human circumstance.

I don't know why I couldn't fully connect to the magnitude of life and its inherent joys before. I only know that I can now—that my ability to recognize what matters has improved exponentially. And somehow—for me—Stross is to be given credit.

Perhaps I had other opportunities to gain this divine insight before but missed them.

I think of a smiling woman I met when Mark and I volunteered in one of Des Moines' inner-city shelters and how I regard her life much differently now. What made her memorable before Stross' birth was—of all things—her teeth. Poverty and hard-living had given her teeth that were dirty, broken and askew. As a result she could not close her mouth. In fact her teeth protruded so far that they dug into my shoulder when she hugged me. And I was repulsed.

The woman's hug came from a place of gratitude. I had sung a song for her, and she had enjoyed it. Now I recognize how her hug was both a thank you and an invitation to see life in its fullness—to enter into the joy she knew in spite of life's circumstances. But that day the harder she hugged, the deeper her teeth bit into my clothing, and the more eager I was to pull away. When she finally did release,

I seized an opportunity to move to another part of the room. Then she stopped smiling.

I would react differently today. Today I would stay awhile to talk about things that mattered to her, hoping to connect to her life. Today I would encounter her joy, then receive it for the gift it is in spite of myself.

Involuntary joy.

What made this change possible? I accepted an invitation to live a life full of possibilities rather than dreams unrealized. And because of it, I better understand what I might miss if I don't take invitations to experience joy as they come.

It doesn't mean I've fully conquered my human tendency to pull back in apprehensive reluctance. It means I have a better understanding of how easy it is to overlook invitations for divine communion—the kind that usher in moments of involuntary joy— and what I risk if I choose not to take them.

And I believe others can come to this realization too.

Michele Griswell has said she'll never forget how she felt when she visited Mark and me in the hospital the day after Stross' birth. She said that as soon as she saw us, she "knew that thing God does when unusual events come had happened to you and Mark."

That "thing" God does—I've lived its reality. And I believe those who have received the gift our son is have too.

I continue to believe Stross has an infinitesimal amount of wisdom to offer. And his lessons, it seems, are mine to discover, uncover, and then discern according to God's measure. I once stopped myself from holding an Olympic-sized dream for him, and yet he felt free to dream of flying and orbiting the world. How small must my mind be compared to his?

The irony of his dream was not lost on me. Stross' desire was to fly among the stars in their heavens, if it was at all possible. I praise the Creator God who made both the stars in their heavens and this incredible human being who believes all things are possible. Perhaps by the time he is old enough to become an astronaut, he will also be old enough to understand the wonder of I am—of the

• • •

beginning and the end—of the "whom" through which all things come to pass.

Then again it's entirely possible that Stross already intimately knows the Alpha and the Omega—and that his knowledge of "I am" is vastly more than I can comprehend. The kind of wisdom I've gained because of him only heightens my awareness of how much more there is for me to learn: I have a lifetime of lessons ahead. Therefore I'm prepared to accept them as they come—whether from an aspiring astronaut or a woman offering an embrace and a smile.

So perhaps I really can be like Stross when I grow up, able to take in others' joys and experience them as my own. That kind of living makes it possible to fix my hope on the fulfillment of new dreams—dreams that are born in the waters of tested faith.

And all of this came to be because of a young man who is bold enough to fly.

• • •

# Back to the Future

• • •

I finished what I believed to be the basic manuscript of *Involuntary Joy* in the spring of 2002. During the next week we received a call from a doctor at the Mayo Clinic. She had the results of some additional genetic testing we'd agreed to after one of her colleagues had encouraged us to reopen Stross' case. We had pursued the testing, believing that anything we learned might help us understand why Stross had been born with abnormalities (imperforate anus, close-set facial features and variations in hand structure) that deviated from those more typical for persons with spina bifida such as myelomeningocele (open spine) and hydrocephalus (water on the brain).

Stross' last chromosome study had occurred 10 years previous and only affirmed that he had no obvious chromosomal deletions or duplications—in other words, no Down syndrome and no life-threatening trisomy abnormalities. Since then researchers had diligently mapped the human genome, developing tests that highlighted mutations common to less-known genetic syndromes. Perhaps, a doctor told us, they could now uncover something that might help us better understand Stross' particular genetic makeup. If he did have a variation of some known syndrome, then we could better forecast what might be in store for him medically and even intellectually.

Ascribing to the philosophy that knowledge is power, we

• • •

pursued the testing and hoped that what we learned could help us do a better job of facilitating Stross' unique needs.

It really didn't.

When the doctor called, she reported that a genetic research team had resorted to a molecular study following several rounds of high-powered microscopic evaluations. As a result they found a mutation in Stross' genetic code that had never been documented at the Mayo Clinic before. In fact, she continued, they had been unable to find mention of a similar mutation in any of the research databases with which they share information. She was surprised, she said, that they had found the mutation: an interstital microdeletion on 22q 11.2, telomeric to the TUPLE (DGC/VCFS) critical region probe. In other words something unusual happened in Stross' 22nd chromosome when the cells were dividing and assigning roles. He didn't have any of the usual birth defects associated with the 22nd chromosome. No one had ever seen this particular mutation before.

"So what does that mean for us?" I asked.

"I'm not really sure," she said. "We believe the spina bifida probably occurred separate from this genetic mutation, but this likely accounts for his intellectual deficiencies."

She also reported that their studies of Mark's and my blood showed no indication of a similar mutation. The mutation was Stross' alone.

Basically she was confirming what Mark and I had only suspected before: Stross not only had physical disabilities, he had an intellectual disability too—the kind of disability defined as mildly mentally retarded.

As Stross matured it had become apparent to Mark and me that he was falling behind his chronological peers socially and academically at an accelerated rate. Coursework modifications had made it possible for him to maintain a reading level only one to two grade levels behind his peers by the end of elementary. But as he entered middle school the differences in his academic abilities had become more evident. When discussing accommodations with his teachers I had begun to differentiate between his chronological age and his intellectual age,

• • •

and now I could point to a concrete reason.

The doctor offered more information about how the genetic testing had been conducted and then attempted to place what we had learned in perspective.

"I'm sorry this doesn't give you something specific to work with," she said, acknowledging that there was no web site or support group for a person who is the only one—possibly in the world—with this particular mutation, "but it is an answer. The majority of the time when dealing with abstract cases like this, we end up unable to find something specific. We were quite fortunate to find this."

I could tell she was excited about the discovery of something no one else had known about before the clinic completed its research. I could also sense her appreciation for how impractical the information was to us.

"So basically," I said to her, "we get to be the ones who write the book on Stross, so to speak."

"It's safe to say that you know what his abilities and potential arc the best," she replied.

We both understood that Mark and I had not needed a test to confirm that.

The test, however, verified that Mark and I had not been spared having a son with both physical and intellectual disabilities. I had prayed to be spared this fate on the day Stross was born. Ever since that day I had wondered anyway. Now I knew.

I knew something else: I could not change the core emotion of the story I had finished writing. It told about my first five years as Stross' mother. As such, I believed, *Involuntary Joy* needed to reflect what I'd felt right up to the time my awareness of who I am changed again. I am a different person now than the one who finished writing that story. I am now the mother of a son with both intellectual and physical disabilities.

Actually I always was that kind of mother. I simply had not known.

Sometimes I look at Stross' chronological peers and become nostalgic for their childhood days. I even find myself missing the slide at Happy Time Preschool and the way all of the children played together with little regard to physical differences. I realize that those were incredibly wonderful times: Stross' classmates flinging themselves down the slide while he delighted in their play, and then, when finished with the slide, coming to sit side by side for story time or a snack.

Now because of Stross' genetically stunted intellectual development, he remains in that happy place while his chronological peers follow a trajectory that leads them away from his realities and toward their own self-actualization.

At 16- and 17-years of age they are no different than I was. They are focused on doing whatever it takes to become who they believe they are meant to be.

I retain a vivid memory of riding home from a scholarship competition in the back seat of my parents' car. I was 17 years old, and my report to Mom and Dad of how the essay writing and personal interviews had gone morphed into a conversation about my future. What I remember is sensing strong support for whatever my chosen profession would be. Most profound, however, was my dad's reaction to this statement: "I've decided that I don't want to have children."

He turned to look at my mom who had sharply turned her head to look at him. The ensuing silence made me feel as if I'd just confessed robbery. I'd soon learn that I essentially had.

My dad, our driver, turned his head back in the direction of the highway, and my mom turned forward as well. Neither of them spoke. The weight of the silence told me I shouldn't say anything more.

Finally, "What did you say?" my father asked.

I wasn't sure I wanted to repeat it for I wasn't sure how my statement had been received. I sensed that Mom was awaiting Dad's lead; Dad, I could tell, was formulating his thoughts. I was confused. My dad had always encouraged me to believe I could do anything I wanted with my life—to be anything I wanted to be.

I was fairly certain I didn't want to be a mother.

By my senior year in high school, I'd experienced enough of life to know that I wanted to experience a great deal more. I wanted an exciting career that allowed me to travel. I wanted to go places I'd yet to learn about and try experiences I was only beginning to comprehend as possible. Finding a partner to share life with seemed desirable, but having children to care for while I focused on the things I wanted out of life didn't. I cautiously repeated my earlier statement.

"I don't want to have children." There. I'd said it again.

"Why would you say something like that?" He made it sound like I'd spoken profanity, uttered a racial slur or blasphemed.

Now my voice was more tentative.

"I just don't feel like I need to be a mom. There are other things I want to do in life, and I don't think I could do them and still have time for children."

My dad's tone became disciplinary and firm. He sounded exceedingly disappointed.

"You better think long and hard about that, Young Lady. I find it hard to believe you would actually think that. What a selfish, horrible thing to say. Can you hear how selfish you sound?"

"Honey, be careful," my mom said.

"No. Really," Dad continued. "What are you thinking? Haven't we taught you better than that?"

My dad's clear disgust had me more confused than ever. He had taught me well, I thought. He'd taught me to be confident and to do the best I could at whatever I attempted. Had he been paying attention? Not just at who I'd become but to the prospects a woman my age faced in society. He had been my high school sociology teacher, for heaven's sake. And we'd watched and discussed broadcast news reports together throughout the '70s and the first years of the '80s. Had he not noticed how different things were?

I simply wanted the freedom to see where life could take me.

My dad's lecture shifted into philosophical assertions about legacy and lineage and the priceless assurance that belongs to those whose lives are safeguarded into future generations.

"I believe my best contribution to society—to the world—is you, Joy, and your sister. Should you choose not to have children, all

• • •

of what I've invested in you dies with you. Just think about that."

I *would* spend time thinking about that—lots of time throughout my college years and into married life. And then I would spend even more time thinking about it in the years just after Stross' birth.

I don't think about it much anymore. Sixteen years after the most life-changing event I've ever known, I try to live what I've learned instead. But I'm not always very good at it because there is still so much to figure out.

My dad's speech that day—while passionate—did not lay the best groundwork for an argument in support of having children. No one has the right to make someone else his legacy; no one should raise a child carrying the weight of her genealogical line. And I don't believe that's what my dad meant that day in spite of the words he used. I think he was trying to convey a more universal truth: Children are our future. But more than that, they are the best way to connect to the world—the entire world. They make everyone's future matter.

Until I had Stross I regarded the future in terms of what I did with it. And as my father accurately pointed out, I held a selfish perspective. I wondered: What would I be able to do? Where would I be able to go? What wonderful things would I be able to experience? My questions all focused on me and what I could look forward to because of what I did.

Having a child—having Stross—helped me understand why any of it mattered at all.

Stross became my invitation to interconnectedness. He reminded me of my place in the world and that my place was no better and nothing less than anyone else's. Basically he helped me ask new life questions. One in particular: Who did I think I was anyway? And then he pointed me to the answer: I am a child of God just like he is.

He—and now Skye too—point me to that awareness daily. So does everyone else I encounter. And on days when I haven't reverted to old patterns of behavior, I remember what that means. Life is bigger than I am; my life choices impact others. I'm not just dreaming for myself. I hold dreams for the world. My life only matters because others' lives do too. We're all connected on one wild ride.

Sometimes—when my arrogance becomes unruly—I'm tempted to claim enlightenment. However, just about the time I begin to feel full of myself, I'll get a call from the school nurse saying she needs help with Stross' ostomy or I'll read a note from one of his teachers outlining a concern about an assignment at school. Or I'll see one of Stross' classmates busily working at an after-school job my son can never do. The experiences remind me of how different my life is now. And—depending on the day—grief might resurface, and I might experience a moment of renewed pain. If I don't recognize what's happening soon enough the pain might progress into anger; and I'll leave myself open to the helplessness that comes from circumventing hope. I make my life too much about me.

But when I'm at my best—the best me I can be—I remember all the things that have come before and recognize how they are pointing me toward a future. And not wanting to get in God's way, I jump in. The moment is mine to drink in its fullness.

So really. I'm back where I started. I'm Joy—the 17-year-old turned 42-year-old who wants to experience everything life has to offer. Except I have a life partner—a wonderful man I feel blessed to know every single day. And most amazing of all, I'm a mom. I am Stross' mom. I am Skye's mom. And I wouldn't change one moment of how any of that has come to be. Because of them I have hope for the future…the future we share…all of us.

•　•　•

# Acknowledgements

• • •

During the first years of Stross' life, I would see things happen that I could only make sense of when writing. The process of writing helped me relate images and feelings directly linked to Stross to my understanding of what it meant to be his mother. I began to consider the process an exercise in connecting the dots.

Not long after we moved to Forest City in 1993, I began sorting through these pieces and saw themes emerge. The story of who I was becoming began to unfold even as I was living it. And so I kept writing. It wasn't long before I realized I was writing the type of book I had wanted to read the first weeks after Stross was born. So in 1996, one year after the birth of our second son, Skye, I began to assemble bits and pieces of what I'd written into chapters. My intent was to identify the moments that had defined who I was as a mother of a child with disabilities. But after seven years of writing, I realized the story that unfolded described who I'd become as a person. I just didn't know if the story would be helpful to anyone else the way I'd committed it to paper.

I'm incredibly grateful to friends like Kathy Garfin, Carolyn Frakes, Rita Pray and Michele Griswell who understood my motivation for writing and made time to read my earliest manuscript. Their feedback helped me assemble what I'd written into something that actually resembled a book. Then, once *Involuntary Joy* emerged with a beginning, middle, and end (for now), some of those same individuals read the edited version, contributing valuable insights. So did Julie Jolivette; Dr. Kent and Shud Johnson; Bob Johnson; Rev. Dawn Quame; Michelle Sprout-Murray; and Paula Orth and her friend, Amy. Their questions and affirmations provided direction.

Many friends lived through the experiences described in *Involuntary Joy*, and I could only feel comfortable proceeding to final form after sharing this version of our story with them. I'm deeply grateful for the support these individuals provided by acting as gracious listeners, honest critics and faithful prayer partners: Judy Berry and Leah Boyd (I treasure our monthly breakfasts and plan to take you up on the book tour offer.); Laura and Mike Oanes, Cindy and Ken Korth, Joan and Ray Beebe, and Robin and Brent Aberg (I continue to be amazed by your faithful patience whenever I take the entire group off topic.); Dr. Jill Davidson (I'm grateful to have known you before we both became mothers—before you began the miraculous task of guiding children into the world.); and Dr. Norma McGuire (I knew you were the best doctor for Stross on the day we met.).

I also am grateful for individuals who served a specific role that no one else could have filled: Deb, Steve and Austin Davis, thank you for driving to the hospital that first day; Cindy Canoy and Rita Pray, thank you for welcoming me to motherhood; Charlene Horak and Jenn Horak-Hult, thank you for loving my son as your own; Michele Griswell, thank you for patiently listening while allowing me to be me; Kathy Garfin, thank you for the intelligently reflective way you have helped me stay focused from the very beginning; Shari Sauer, thank you for asking to read my manuscript while beginning to live out your own involuntary journey; Ruth Melby, thank you for setting an example of what it means to have a dream you just have to pursue; Rev. Robert Gremmels, thank you for marking all over my college assignments and helping me learn to love the editing process; Margaret Becker, thank you for music that has provided a soundtrack for some of my life's most holy moments; Dr. Robert Canoy and Rev. Lee Laaveg, thank you for your pastoral care and support during some

...

of our family's most difficult times; Dr. William E. Hamm, thank you for leadership that enabled Mark to live out a divine calling; and Tali, Emilie, Joy, Ben, Teeg, Rujuta, Jackie, and all the other Waldorf College students and alumni who have been relentless about making certain I follow this project through to completion, thank you for your love and diligence.

And to friends who may have grown tired of me talking about this book year after year but loved me enough not to show it: Thank you. Cindy C., Mary A., Dave D., Cathy I., Shirley T., and Carol Z.–I've treasured every conversation, pondering your words in my heart.

Perhaps those who have most grown weary from my plans for this book (and maybe even worried) have been my family. When Mark and I married, we grafted together two incredible family trees.

First, to our siblings and their spouses—Jill and Greg Blank, Iris and Joe Molstead, Jason and Jennifer Newcom, and Dr. David and Kristie Ramey. You each see me for who I am and then love me anyway. Your unconditional love is affirming. (Jill, you've had to do that longer than anyone. Thanks for hanging in there.)

To Mark's parents, David and Carolyn, your son reflects only the best of you, offering it as a gift to others. If you can comprehend how deeply I love him, then you'll know how much I love you as well.

To my parents, Gay and Fran Bowden, I remember many conversations on the topic of "What It's Like to Grow Up." I hope it makes you proud to know that I've learned maturity is not a destination but a process that never ends. Thank you for teaching me about honesty, integrity and honor. And, thank you for two score and two years full of laughter and silliness and fun. I love you.

Stross and Skye, please know that—without you—no page of this book could ever have been written. I love you so much it hurts.

And, Mark, you are my forever soulmate—the only person who can grasp the magnitude of what we've experienced together. Because of you—my true life partner—I'm not alone. Eros, philia, agape.

•   •   •

# Credits

· · ·

Completing this book would not have been possible without committed professionals willing to lend their expertise so that *Involuntary Joy* can reach those most connected to its story. I will forever be grateful to Sonia Solomonson for her accomplished editorial skill; Rachel Riensche for her wise counsel and guidance; Tiffany Olson for her ability to translate images and feelings into beautiful design; and Matt Peake for photographic artistry fueled by a generous heart.

Lyrics to *"All I Ever Wanted"* by Margaret Becker appear courtesy of © His Eye Music. License # 255600. All rights reserved. Used by Permission.

Art Direction/Book Design/Web Design: Tiffany Olson
Cover Photo/Author Photo: Matthew Peake
Web Support: Carrie Cole
Web Hosting: Eric Guth, Epsilon Productions

Additional resources available: www.involuntaryjoy.com

• • •